The Hollywood Book of Extravagance

The Totally Infamous, Mostly Disastrous, and Always Compelling Excesses of America's Film and TV Idols

James Robert Parish

BICENTENNIAL
1807
WILEY
2007
BICENTENNIAL

John Wiley & Sons, Inc.

This book is printed on acid-free paper. ∞

Copyright © 2007 by James Robert Parish. All rights reserved

Published by John Wiley & Sons, Inc., Hoboken, New Jersey
Published simultaneously in Canada

Wiley Bicentennial Logo: Richard J. Pacifico

Design and composition by Navta Associates, Inc.

No part of this publication may be reproduced, stored in a retrieval system, or transmitted in any form or by any means, electronic, mechanical, photocopying, recording, scanning, or otherwise, except as permitted under Section 107 or 108 of the 1976 United States Copyright Act, without either the prior written permission of the Publisher, or authorization through payment of the appropriate per-copy fee to the Copyright Clearance Center, 222 Rosewood Drive, Danvers, MA 01923, (978) 750-8400, fax (978) 646-8600, or on the web at www.copyright.com. Requests to the Publisher for permission should be addressed to the Permissions Department, John Wiley & Sons, Inc., 111 River Street, Hoboken, NJ 07030, (201) 748-6011, fax (201) 748-6008, or online at http://www.wiley.com/go/permissions.

Limit of Liability/Disclaimer of Warranty: While the publisher and the author have used their best efforts in preparing this book, they make no representations or warranties with respect to the accuracy or completeness of the contents of this book and specifically disclaim any implied warranties of merchantability or fitness for a particular purpose. No warranty may be created or extended by sales representatives or written sales materials. The advice and strategies contained herein may not be suitable for your situation. You should consult with a professional where appropriate. Neither the publisher nor the author shall be liable for any loss of profit or any other commercial damages, including but not limited to special, incidental, consequential, or other damages.

For general information about our other products and services, please contact our Customer Care Department within the United States at (800) 762-2974, outside the United States at (317) 572-3993 or fax (317) 572-4002.

Wiley also publishes its books in a variety of electronic formats. Some content that appears in print may not be available in electronic books. For more information about Wiley products, visit our web site at www.wiley.com.

Library of Congress Cataloging-in-Publication Data:
Parish, James Robert.
The Hollywood book of extravagance : the totally infamous, mostly disastrous, and always compelling excesses of America's film and TV idols / James Robert Parish
    p. cm.
   Includes bibliographical references and index.
   ISBN: 978-0-470-05205-1
   1. Motion picture actors and actresses—United States—Biography. 2. Television actors and actresses—United States—Biography. I. Title.
   PN1998.2.P3658 2007
   791.4302'8092273—dc22
                                                                    2006100246

Printed in the United States of America

10 9 8 7 6 5 4 3 2 1

In memory of Purrfect (1990–2006),
an extraordinary cat

Contents

Acknowledgments

I wish to thank the following for their kind cooperation on this project: Academy of Dance on Film (Larry Billman), Patrick Agan, Billy Rose Theater Collection of the New York Public Library at Lincoln Center, Ronald L. Bowers, John Cocchi, Rachel Decoste, Douglas Fairbanks Center for Motion Picture Study, David Ehrenstein, Allan Ellenberger, Filming Today Press (G. D. Hamann), Dave Finkle, Professor James Fisher, Alex Gildzen, Pierre Guinle, Harry Haun, *In* Magazine (Jeremy Kinser), JC Archives, Lynn Kear, Shawn Levy, Alvin H. Marill, Mart Martin, Lee Mattson, Eric Monder, Museum of Television & Radio (Jane Klain), Scott O'Brien, Stephen O'Brien, Jay Ogletree, Jerry Oppenheimer, Kimberly O'Quinn, Photofest (Jill Goodwin, Howard Mandelbaum, and Ron Mandelbaum), Michael R. Pitts, Barry Rivadue, David Rode, Jonathan Rosenthal, John Rossman, Brad Schreiber, Margie Schultz, the late Arleen Schwartz, Nat Segaloff, Stephen M. Silverman, André Soares, Sam Staggs, David Stenn, Allan Taylor (editorial consultant, copy editor, and indexer), Lou Valentino, and Steven Whitney.

With special thanks to my editor, Eric Nelson, and my agent, Stuart Bernstein.

Introduction

During the last century, many entertainers achieved sudden, spectacular success in Hollywood. However, few enjoyed such a swift trajectory to fame as did the iconoclastic James Dean (1931–1955).

In the early 1950s, the Indiana-born actor was just another struggling young performer in New York City, competing with his peers for stage and TV assignments. But by mid-1954, Dean was under contract to Warner Bros. and starring in the big-screen adaptation of John Steinbeck's *East of Eden*. Already, there was industry buzz that he was the successor to such recent trendsetting leading men as Montgomery Clift and Marlon Brando. As Jimmy's star continued to rise, his ego swelled. He became increasingly eccentric, impetuous, self-contained, and distrustful of other people's motives. Because of Dean's incredible box-office potential, Warner Bros. coddled him, overlooking his persistent rebellious ways and self-indulgent, odd behavior. The more leeway the studio and the enthralled Hollywood community gave him, the more (deliberately) unorthodox Jimmy became. He appeared to be greatly amused by his growing celebrity power, which allowed him to overtly disregard the conventions of the Tinseltown establishment—and get away with it.

Then, in late September 1955, Dean died in a car crash near Cholame, California, just as his screen popularity was zooming to enormous heights. He was only 24 years old—in the prime of life. Thereafter, he remained frozen in the public's mind as the maverick icon who had so successfully set old-guard Hollywood on its heels. Dean's star continues to shine brightly to this day, many decades after his death.

Dean's extreme flaunting of social and professional conventions made him all the more appealing to his teenage fans. They thrived vicariously on his antiestablishment approach to most everything and accepted his self-indulgent ways as his due. This attitude was typical in that the public expected, wanted, and often "demanded" that their show business favorites lead supersized lifestyles, gleefully flaunting conventions and thriving on material excess. (In actuality, many show business celebrities' seemingly glamorous, unconventional, and exciting existences became more pivotal to their fame and success than their actual professional accomplishments.)

The Hollywood Book of Extravagance focuses on a selection of colorful Tinseltown celebrities who managed to live larger than their contemporaries in the entertainment world, often thanks to an insatiable appetite for, among other things, power, liaisons, or controlled substances.

Over the years, many Hollywood personalities have succumbed to conspicuous living, overindulging their bad habits, colossal egos, hang-ups, and idiosyncratic behavior. This behavior has not diminished in the new millennium, providing much grist for the rumor mills and celebrity watchers.

PART 1

So Much, So Young

Drew Barrymore

(February 22, 1975–)

Drew Barrymore's self-destructive actress aunt, Diana Barrymore (1921–1960), titled her autobiography *Too Much, Too Soon*. That expression easily could have been applied to Drew, who in 1982, at age seven, became world famous for her role in the blockbuster movie *E.T.: The Extra-Terrestrial*. According to Drew, "Virtually overnight, everybody knew me, and yet nobody knew me. I mean the real me. From early on, I was always this remote, dreamy little girl who loved escaping reality by acting in movies. . . . Without work, I believed I was nothing."

By the time Drew reached her early teens, she had become a serious substance abuser.

Drew Barrymore both starred in and coproduced 2000's Charlie's Angels. Her coleads were Cameron Diaz (center) and Lucy Liu (right).

"Without the ego-boost of work, I got into trouble with liquor and drugs by trying to run from everything. Or to numb it. I was the party girl on the run. If I was high, I thought everything was fine." It seemed the out-of-control Drew had fallen into the same trap as her famous show business forebears, including her legendary grandfather, John Barrymore (and his celebrated siblings Ethel and Lionel), and her own actor father.

• • •

Drew Blyth Barrymore was born in 1975, in Culver City, California, the only child of John Drew Barrymore (also known as John Barrymore Jr.), a former actor turned alcoholic, and Ildiko Jaid Mako Barrymore, a waitress and wannabe actress. The wild and rebellious John Jr. had started making movies in 1950, and, for a brief span, the striking young man seemed destined for fame. However, he got sidetracked by alcohol and bizarre behavior, which sabotaged his future. When he met Jaid in the early 1970s, he was already twice divorced and his life was in tatters. Nevertheless, Jaid was thrilled to be in the company of a member of the acclaimed Barrymore clan. The couple married but were living apart before Drew was born. (Over the years, John Jr. periodically reappeared in his daughter's life, usually drunk and begging for a hand-out. He died in 2004.)

When Drew was a toddler, one of Jaid's friends gave a photo of the cute girl to a casting agent. This led to Drew's being hired for a dog-food commercial. Thereafter, in addition to more commercials, she began winning brief acting roles, as in 1980's *Altered States*. After she appeared in *E.T.*, the young Barrymore was much in demand. Meanwhile, her mother stopped waitressing in order to promote her daughter's career and pursue her own acting opportunities.

The suddenly famous Drew popped up everywhere: she hosted an installment of TV's *Saturday Night Live*, became a regular on the talk show circuit, and attended premieres, nightclubs, and private parties accompanied by her mother. The youngster thrived on the acceptance she received in industry circles—it compensated for her inability to relate to her classmates or deal successfully with her mother (who reveled in her daughter's success but was envious of her achievements).

When Drew was 9, she was secretly smoking cigarettes. Next came drinking, and by the time she was 12 or 13 she'd tried cocaine and other drugs. It reached the point where she did little to conceal her activities from her mother, which led to intense arguments between them. During one of Drew's drug-fueled outbursts, she ordered Jaid to vacate their home. This time, Jaid took constructive action. She escorted her daughter to the ASAP Family Treatment Center, a substance abuse facility in the San Fernando Valley. Barrymore did well there, but, after 12 days, she left to fly to New York to shoot the film *Far from Home*. While Drew was on the East Coast, she started using cocaine again. Later, she and a pal borrowed one of Jaid's credit cards to pay for a flight to Hawaii. When they

stopped over in Los Angeles, they were intercepted by private investigators whom Jaid had retained and Drew was taken back to the rehab facility. She remained there for three months, leaving in late December 1988.

Barrymore trumped the supermarket tabloids set to expose her problems by telling her shocking life story to a national magazine and then collaborating with a reporter to write her candid memoir, 1990's best-selling *Little Girl Lost*. During this intense period she slipped back into smoking marijuana. After she sliced her wrist with a knife in July 1989—an act that she later claimed was a cry for help and not a suicide attempt—she returned to the ASAP Family Treatment Center for another three-month stay.

By her early teens, she had outgrown playing cute youngsters on film. This, in addition to her reputation as a substance abuser, scared off casting directors. In response, Drew broke away from her controlling mother and sought to put her scattered life in order. Patience paid off with her breakthrough role as the sexy young woman in 1992's *Poison Ivy*.

As a young adult, Barrymore still acted impulsively. From 1992 to 1993, she lived with actor/singer Jamie Walters. In March 1994, she married Jeremy Thomas, a 31-year-old Hollywood bartender whom she'd met only a short while earlier. Within weeks they ended their relationship, and they were divorced by February 1995. That same year, the irrepressible actress posed for a nude layout in *Playboy* magazine and flashed her breasts (with her back to the audience/camera) at TV host David Letterman when she guested on his talk show. On a more mature note, she formed her own film production company (Flower Films) and costarred in such movie hits as 1998's *The Wedding Singer* and 2000's *Charlie's Angels* (which she also had coproduced).

Now an established industry force, Drew still had an adventurous side—especially in her choice of significant others. She was linked romantically with rock guitarist Eric Erlandson, then with actor Luke Wilson, and later with comedian Tom Green, whom she married in July 2001. However, within months they split, and by that December they had filed for divorce. Her next major romance was with Fabrizio Moretti, the drummer for the rock group Hole. They were together from 2002 until early 2007.

Meanwhile, Barrymore remained potent at the box office, with such big-screen entries as 2004's *50 First Dates* and 2007's *Music and Lyrics*. Though part of the Hollywood establishment, the once prepubescent substance abuser remains cautious about her success. "I still feel like I have a lot to prove. My biggest burning question is, 'How much more are you capable of?'"

Danny Bonaduce

(August 13, 1959–)

Danny Bonaduce once observed, "Most child actors were lucky enough to get the part in the first place. They cry and complain that now they are no longer little and cute Hollywood has no use for them. What we often fail to appreciate is that being little and cute may have been their only skill. Now that we are not so little anymore, and certainly not cute, some of us may have to face reality, stop whining, and get real jobs."

As a cast regular on TV's *The Partridge Family* from 1970 to 1974, the freckle-faced Bonaduce became quite famous. His enduring image as Danny, the likable con artist son of the Shirley Jones character on this sitcom, proved to be both a blessing and a curse for the ex–child star. Over the decades, it seemed no matter what unfortunate scrape he got into, what dysfunctional lifestyle he was caught up in, or how much the media (or he himself) exploited his miseries, many of his fans were always willing to forgive him. On the other hand, much of the public refused to accept him as an adult who wanted to move on from his confining childhood image.

● ● ●

Dante Daniel Bonaduce was born in Philadelphia, Pennsylvania, in 1959, one of four children of Joseph Bonaduce and Betty Steck. His mother had been the host/writer/producer of a local TV news magazine show, while his father was a photographer who aspired to be a TV scriptwriter. By the early 1960s, the family had moved to the West San Fernando Valley of Los Angeles, and Mr. Bonaduce was writing occasionally for such TV series as *Laredo* and *The Doris Day Show*.

While Danny's father was struggling to find fresh TV assignments, family friends kept suggesting that the impish, outgoing boy should be in show business. When he was 6, Danny did the first of several commercials. In early 1969, Mr. Bonaduce was asked to do a quick rewrite of an episode of TV's *The Ghost and Mrs. Muir*. He agreed on the condition that Danny be allowed to read for a major part in the show. Danny got the job, which led to other acting work, and then to his being hired to costar in *The Partridge Family*, which debuted in the fall of 1970. The warmhearted comedy—filled with musical interludes—quickly became a major hit.

Danny thrived on being a pampered young star, especially enjoying the material perks he received. However, he proved to be a handful on the *Partridge Family* set: he was rebellious, played practical jokes, and had a smart mouth. Shirley Jones tried to instill some discipline in the rough-and-tumble kid. When she and others in the cast and crew noticed that Danny frequently came to work with bruises, they realized he was being physically abused at home (by his father, who was frustrated that his son was working more steadily than he was). The *Partridge* troupe took turns having the boy spend weekends with them, to lessen the time he spent at home. Whenever one of his hosts happened to throw a party, Danny would sneak drinks, and he soon developed a fondness for liquor.

By the spring of 1974, *The Partridge Family* had gone off the air, and suddenly Danny, now in his midteens, found it difficult to get acting assignments. To get away from his troubled father, he moved into his

Danny Bonaduce earned fame in childhood as a regular on TV's The Partridge Family *(which ran from 1970 to 1974). In later years, he made several show business comebacks and many tabloid headlines for his excessive behavior.*

own small house and attended private school. Not caring much about academics, he devoted much of his spare time to partying and experimenting with drugs. Later, he worked as a busboy, then as a restaurant manager, but his drinking and drug use interfered with his job performance. In 1985, he was arrested in West Hollywood for possession of cocaine. The charges were dropped after he completed a drug-counseling program. However, he quickly relapsed into substance abuse, and he sometimes thought of suicide. Also in 1985, he wed Setsuko Hattori, but their unstable marriage ended in divorce in 1988.

By then, Bonaduce had hit a financial bottom. He sold his home, but quickly spent the proceeds on drugs. Thereafter, he was often living on the streets and sleeping in his car—a fact he hid from fans who spotted him and asked for an autograph. When his mother appeared one day at the fleabag motel he was staying at in Hollywood, she found him ravaged by his crack cocaine addiction. Her intervention convinced him to shape up, and he went to live with her in Philadelphia. (By then, she had split from her husband.)

Bonaduce's chance encounter with a programming director at WEGX-FM in Philadelphia led to his being hired as a DJ for the station. The promotion for his new gig traded heavily on his *Partridge Family* pedigree. To Danny's pleasant surprise, he quickly developed a talent for his job. However, while on a business trip to Daytona Beach, Florida, in March 1990, he was arrested and charged with attempting to buy cocaine. He received 15 months' probation. His radio station demanded he enter rehab. He did, but once back at work he fell into his former drug/boozing cycle and was fired from the station. Later, he landed a radio DJ gig in Phoenix, Arizona.

On November 4, 1990, Bonaduce went on a blind date. He was extremely attracted to the blond Gretchen Hillmer, a celebrity booker, and she to him. However, she refused to have sex with him that evening because they were not married. The randy Bonaduce remedied that by immediately locating a minister in the yellow pages, and the two wed that night. (At the time, Danny was engaged to a young woman back in Philadelphia.)

Marriage lessened but did not solve Bonaduce's drug, booze, and sexual addiction problems. In late March 1991, he picked up a hooker, whom he paid $20 to perform a sexual act. Belatedly, Danny realized that she was a he—and a big man at that. There was a rumble between the two as Danny grabbed his money and fled. He was pursued by the police called to the scene. They caught up with him at home, where he was hiding in a closet. Eventually, he pleaded guilty to endangerment and no contest to misdemeanor assault to avoid a trial and any further legal fees. As a result of the notoriety, he lost his radio job, but he was publicly supported by his *Partridge Family* costar David Cassidy.

Bonaduce went on to radio DJ jobs in Chicago, Detroit, and elsewhere, and hosted a TV talk show (*Danny!*) that didn't last a full season. In the late 1990s, he relocated to Los Angeles, where he cohosted a radio show for six years. (He and Gretchen had two children: a daughter, born in 1994, and a son, born in 2001.) In the early 2000s, Danny, who kept falling off the wagon then getting back on, cohosted a TV talk show (*The Other Half*). In the fall of 2005, the VH1 cable network premiered *Breaking Bonaduce*. When the reality series began filming, no one realized the depths of dysfunction to which Danny would sink, or that he would allow his descent to be aired on the show. In one episode, his wife learned that he had had an affair, and she threatened to leave him. He reacted (off camera) by slicing his wrists. While the series went on emergency hiatus, Bonaduce went back into rehab, and then not only taped the remaining segments but agreed to a second season. Meanwhile, in the fall of 2006, he hosted *Starface*, a short-lasting tabloid-themed TV game show. In April 2007, Gretchen Bonaduce filed for divorce from Danny and sought custody of their two children.

Over the years, Bonaduce made the rounds of TV gab programs with other ex–child stars, who sadly recounted their woeful lives after fame had passed them by. In contrast to his peers, the witty Danny—full of self-deprecating humor—never blamed others for the errors of his imprudent life.

Once when Danny was at a show business convention touting his latest media project, he encountered Geraldo Rivera, on whose chat program he had frequently appeared. Rivera smiled and said, "Bonaduce, they just can't kill you, can they?"

Gary Coleman

(February 8, 1968–)

The TV sitcom *Diff'rent Strokes* was a big favorite with home viewers for much of its lengthy run (1978–1986) and made stars of its three young players: Gary Coleman, Todd Bridges, and Dana Plato. But success proved to be a curse for this trio. Bridges suffered years of substance abuse and unpleasant run-ins with law authorities before finally turning his life around. Plato's world fell apart after she left the popular network program. In 1999, at age 34, she committed suicide with a drug overdose. As for Coleman, the mainstay of *Diff'rent Strokes*, he is still coping with the repercussions of childhood fame, which overwhelmed him and those in his inner circle.

• • •

Gary Wayne Coleman was born in 1968 in Lima, Ohio. At four days old, he was adopted by Willie G. and Edmonia Sue Lovelace Coleman, who lived in Zion, Illinois. His father worked for a pharmaceutical firm and his mother was a nurse. When Gary was 22 months old, he was diagnosed with nephritis, a severe inflammation of the kidneys. Before he was five, he had undergone three major operations (including a kidney transplant) for this degenerative disease. As a consequence of his medical conditions, he would always be pint-size. The drugs used to prevent his body's rejection of the kidney transplant were largely responsible for his chubby cheeks.

Because of his shortness, the cute and bright Gary could easily pass for a precocious tyke. One day he modeled in a fashion show at the local mall. This led to modeling assignments for Montgomery Ward and to commercials hawking national products like Betty Crocker and McDonald's. Later, he came to the attention of TV producer Norman Lear, who was so impressed with Coleman that he placed him under contract and used him in guest spots on several of his TV sitcoms.

From 1978 to 1986, Gary Coleman played Arnold Jackson on TV's Diff'rent Strokes. *Others shown in this publicity shot for the sitcom are Danny Cooksey (far left), Mary Jo Catlett (left), Conrad Bain (center right), and Dixie Carter (far right).*

In November 1978, *Diff'rent Strokes* debuted. In this new network offering, Gary Coleman and Todd Bridges played orphaned African American siblings from Harlem who come to live in a fancy Park Avenue apartment with a wealthy Caucasian businessman (played by Conrad Bain) and his teenage daughter (played by Dana Plato). The show quickly became a major hit, with 10-year-old Coleman gaining additional exposure on TV talk shows, where he displayed an engaging presence. Before long, the diminutive star had become the chief asset of a production company formed to showcase him in feature films (like 1981's *On the Right Track*) and telefeatures (such as 1980's *Scout's Honor*). One of his made-for-TV movies led to a spin-off: a Saturday morning animated

children's TV series *The Gary Coleman Show*.

Initially, Gary received $1,600 a week for playing smart-aleck kid Arnold Jackson on *Diff'rent Strokes*. Within a few seasons, his paycheck had increased to $70,000 per episode, and he earned additional income from other acting appearances and merchandizing royalties. When he was not in front of the cameras, he had on-set tutors. As he had with modeling work, Coleman soon tired of his series chores. In particular, he came to hate that the decision makers would not let his character grow up. He also detested giving media interviews. Later, he admitted that during his *Diff'rent Strokes* tenure he would tell his parents, "I either feel like raw meat or a moneybag. You either claw at me or you chase me." He also acknowledged that a few times, when the pressures of the show and life really got to him, he attempted suicide with sleeping pills.

Coleman's health remained precarious. In 1984, he underwent another kidney transplant operation because his system had rejected the first replacement organ. The second surgery did not resolve his medical problems, and dialysis became part of his permanent routine. By the mid-1980s, it was clear that he would never grow taller than four feet eight inches. While this was beneficial to the TV show—he could continue to play the beloved adolescent character for years—it greatly depressed the moody star. According to his costar Conrad Bain, Coleman "was at war with himself. The image of the child that he had to play was repugnant to him. Arnold was the embodiment of everything that he didn't like about himself.

He felt that girls didn't like or pay attention to him because he was small. . . . He became withdrawn and alienated from me and from everyone he had been close to because he associated us all with that character he had come to hate. I tried to persuade him to consider therapy, but he brushed it off." Many on and off the set found the "new" Coleman to be arrogant and temperamental.

When *Diff'rent Strokes* ended its run, Coleman discovered that he was no longer in demand in show business. By 1987, the 19-year-old former star was living on his own. A longtime friend, Dion Mial, was his confidant. In this phase, Coleman fired his parents as his managers and hired Dion and Dion's mother as replacements. This led to a nasty, protracted courtroom battle between Gary and his parents, who were highly paid employees of their son's production firm. Gary received a $1.3 million settlement, which was all that was left in the trust fund of his estimated over $7 million earnings to that time.

By 1988, Coleman had purchased a home near Denver, Colorado, and Dion Mial was his housemate. Gary said of his new life: "For the first time, I was looking to have fun, make friends, do things other guys my age do." The next year, he and his mother were having legal skirmishes because of her efforts to have a conservator appointed to protect her son's interests. She claimed that his medications had made him incapable of making sound business decisions. Over the coming months, he bought other new homes, expended large sums on his elaborate model train collection, and made his pet lizard, Pokey, a top

priority. He also had a penchant for playing video games and kept firearms at home for protection. During the next several years, he worked in a model train shop, financed a video game arcade, toiled as a car salesman, and, later, found employment as a security guard.

In 1998, the onetime celebrity was in the limelight again when he became irate with a female fan seeking an autograph and allegedly physically attacked her. The incident led to a courtroom judgment against Coleman that included his taking anger management classes. In 1999, he filed for bankruptcy in California, listing liabilities of $72,000 and personal assets of about $20,000. In 2003, Coleman was a write-in candidate in the California recall election for a new governor. He lost out to Arnold Schwarzenegger. In recent times, Coleman's TV jobs have included being a product spokesperson and a guest on nostalgia specials about old TV sitcoms and other small-screen fare (such as *The Surreal Life*) exploiting former show business favorites.

Looking back on his once highly lucrative career, Coleman observed: "I took a negative view of Hollywood. That gave me a reputation as a brat." About his parents, he added: "They didn't tell me what to do. Whatever I said went. I suffer now because of it." He noted further, "They made stupid investments. They spent too much on cars, houses, furniture. I did my part, too—I spent thousands of dollars on model trains." Of his fame, he said, "Once you're there, you're there until death. There's no release from the spotlight." As to the impact of his Hollywood stardom years: "It didn't ground me up, but I am well-chewed."

Jackie Coogan

(October 26, 1914–March 1, 1984)

In the early 20th century, when a precocious child with impressive acting abilities and a winning personality became a show business success, the public assumed that the youngster's parents and/or handlers would invest the minor's salary wisely as a nest egg for his or her future. A landmark case of this *not* happening occurred with young Jackie Coogan, who was a tremendous international star of the silent cinema. His brief glory years were from 1921 to 1927, when "the Kid" was a ruling force at the box office and also made a bundle in the lucrative area of merchandizing. Coogan's great fame and fortune was capitalized upon by his advisers and supported their grandiose lifestyle. In 1935, the 21-year-old former star sought control of his hard-earned money, only to discover that his self-centered mother and crafty stepfather had squandered most of their son's massive proceeds.

• • •

John Leslie Coogan Jr. was born in Los Angeles in 1914, the son of John H. and Lillian Dolliver Coogan, vaudeville performers. Initially, the infant was cared for by his grandmother while his parents were on tour. At 18 months, he was reunited with his parents and made his movie debut in a bit in the film *Skinner's Baby*. By age four, Jackie—as he was called—was performing in his parents' act, doing imitations, songs, and dances. In 1919, while playing at the Orpheum Theater in Los Angeles, the talented youngster was noticed by Charlie Chaplin. The famous screen comedian was then preparing a feature-length movie about a tramp adopting an abandoned child who, after several misadventures, is lost. After meeting and being impressed by Coogan, Chaplin tried him out in a two-reel comedy he was then making. Coogan did well in his tryout and was cast in Chaplin's major project, *The Kid*, as the ragamuffin outfitted in oversized trousers and a tattered cap. The highly sentimental movie was an enormous hit, and Coogan—with his pageboy hairstyle and large, expressive eyes—rocketed to global fame.

Immediately, Coogan found himself much in demand by the Hollywood studios and turned out a succession of hits, including 1921's *Peck's Bad Boy* and 1923's *Daddy*. In the mid-1920s, Metro Pictures lured the valuable child star away from the First National lot and signed him to a four-picture deal for $1 million (which translates to nearly $12 million in today's terms). Adding to the boy's income, his parents and managers negotiated several innovative merchandizing deals (for products ranging from peanut butter to lunch boxes to writing pads) that brought in hundreds of thousands of dollars. By now Coogan, who had his own movie production company, was one of the youngest self-made millionaires in history. The family lived stylishly in Hollywood—in a manner befitting a high-priced movie star. (To keep the world-famous young breadwinner "humble," his parents gave him a weekly allowance of only $6.25, although he was earning a fabulous $22,000 per week and was fully aware that everyone on his picture was working for *him*.)

Of course, Coogan began growing up. After making two 1927 releases, the adolescent didn't make another movie until 1930. He returned in the new medium of talkies to play Tom Sawyer in two Paramount pictures. He performed well in these offerings, except now he was no longer a cute child but a gangly teenager. It was the end of his tenure as a major entertainer.

The humbled ex-star was again in the news in May 1935 when he, his beloved father, his actor friend Junior Durkin, and two other passengers were involved in an auto accident. Only Jackie survived the deadly mishap. Subsequently, Mrs. Coogan wed Arthur Bernstein, the family's financial manager. That October, Coogan turned 21 and sought access to the approximately $4 million he had earned in his heyday. His mother and stepfather flatly refused the request, reasoning that the young man had never been promised he would receive the funds from his guardians. Saddened by this greedy response from the high-living Bernsteins, Coogan went on with his life, accepting small acting assignments wherever he could find them.

Two years later, by which time Coogan had wed (in November 1937) screen starlet Betty Grable and needed money to support his bride, he felt obligated to sue his mother and stepfather. The expensive, nasty court case dragged on until 1939. In a final settlement, he was awarded $126,000, half of what was left of all the money he had generated in the 1920s. A bitter coda to the sad outcome was that Grable soon thereafter divorced Coogan. On the plus side—although it gave Coogan no direct benefit—as a result of the much-publicized court case, the California legislature passed the Child Actors Bill (known as the Coogan Act). It decreed that a trust fund must be set up for a child actor to protect his or her income.

After serving in World War II, Coogan returned to show business but was unable to regain a foothold within the industry. In the 1960s, he revived his badly floundering career, to a degree, with costarring roles in the TV series *McKeever & the Colonel* and *The Addams Family* (as Uncle Fester).

One of the all-time most successful child stars was Jackie Coogan, shown here in 1921's Peck's Bad Boy.

Thereafter, the bald, portly actor continued in small supporting roles in films and TV. Over the years, the ex–child star married three more times and had several children. He died of a heart attack in March 1984 in Santa Monica, California.

To Coogan's credit, the many vagaries of his anticlimactic adult life never made him bitter. Not long before he passed away, he said, "I got it all. Four healthy kids and grandchildren and enough work and enough leisure."

Macaulay Culkin

(August 26, 1980–)

Not since the 1930s glory days of the adorable Shirley Temple had Hollywood produced such a successful moppet star as Macaulay Culkin. (Actor Mickey Rooney reached the height of his fame in his late teens.) In 1993, when Culkin was at the height of his popularity, he commanded $8 million a movie, making him filmdom's highest-paid youngster ever. But the *Home Alone* tyke with that captivating mischievous grin was about to see his career come tumbling down.

At age 14, with several recent box-office disappointments to his credit, Culkin withdrew from show business and retreated from the public eye for several years. In Macaulay's case, this was due not just to how the pressures of overwhelming show business acclaim altered him, but to how the boy's tremendous success consumed members of his family.

• • •

Macaulay Carson Culkin was born in 1980 in New York City. He was the third of seven children of Christopher "Kit" Culkin and Patricia Brentrup. His father, a former child actor (and the brother of actress Bonnie Bedelia), grew up in New York City and did odds jobs as an adult. His mother, who hailed from the Midwest, was the daughter of a highway department official. Kit and Patricia, who never married, lived in a small Upper East Side apartment, where they barely scraped together enough funds to raise their large family.

Like most of his siblings (many of whom also became actors), Macaulay took dance classes at the George Balanchine School of American Ballet and at the 92nd Street YMCA. When the boy was about 6, he auditioned for a one-act off-Broadway play and was hired. It led to his being signed by a talent agent. Meanwhile, he and his siblings attended St. Joseph's, a parochial school in the Yorkville neighborhood of Manhattan. (They received free tuition because their father became a sacristan at the church.)

Culkin's feature film debut was in 1988's *Rocket Gibraltar*, starring Burt Lancaster. When Macaulay appeared in 1989's *Uncle Buck*, he received more critical and audience attention than the comedy's star, John

Candy. This prompted John Hughes, who had written and directed *Uncle Buck*, to script 1990's *Home Alone* as a showcase for the precocious youngster. Made for $15 million, the feature earned $534 million in global distribution. Macaulay was now a world-famous celebrity. (Later, he recalled, "It happened really, really fast. I mean, before I was kind of just the local kid around the corner who used to do movies. And then all of a sudden it was just bang, it was all over the place. And it was all these people who used to be my friends are all now trying to . . . peer in through the window or something like that.")

Macaulay's parents, who were his paid managers, now moved their brood into a Manhattan brownstone (and, thereafter, to larger quarters), where they continued to live modestly. Later, Macaulay bitterly recalled that his father—who he claimed was alcoholic and physically abusive toward his wife—micromanaged his children's lives with severity, petulance, and injustice. The boy could not understand why his fame and fortune had not brought the family any happiness, why he personally received so few rewards, and why he felt so desperately alone. He retreated into a protective shell. (One of his few celebrity friends, whom he only saw occasionally, was Michael Jackson. Culkin related to their shared backgrounds: a miserable childhood in the limelight with a calculating father at the helm.)

By the time of 1991's *My Girl*, Macaulay's salary had jumped to $1 million and his father had gained a reputation as an extremely unpleasant negotiator. For 1992's *Home Alone 2: Lost in New York*, the young star received a $5 million fee plus 5 percent of the movie's gross. Already, Macaulay was worn out from his nonstop filmmaking schedule. Not only did Mr. Culkin not consult his son about which new projects to accept, but he continued to make unreasonable demands of film producers.

After 1994's *Ri¢hie Ri¢h*—Macaulay's latest screen vehicle not to do especially well at the box office—no new Culkin projects materialized. The boy had outgrown his once appealing curtness and spontaneity. Moreover, the teenager had finally told his controlling father "No more pictures!"

Escaping into a very private life, with video games being his chief passion, the ex–child star was drawn back into the limelight when he was caught in the middle of the nasty breakup of his parents in 1995 and their battle for custody of the children. When Culkin was 16, he received court approval to control his own savings (about $17 million). He stopped dealing altogether with his father, while remaining close with his mother and siblings. In June 1998, Macaulay wed actress Rachel Miner, whom he had met a few years earlier when they were students at the Professional Children's School in Manhattan. Their impetuous marriage ended in divorce in August 2000.

In the fall of 2000, Culkin decided to practice his craft again. (He reasoned, "Acting found me. I thought maybe I should try to find it again.") He performed on the London stage (and in May 2001 off-Broadway) in *Madame Melville*. He received solid reviews, and went on to make his film comeback with controversial roles in 2003's *Party Monster* and 2004's *Saved!* The still-withdrawn Macaulay (who lived alone in a 5,000-square-foot Greenwich

Cute Macaulay Culkin was already losing his enormous popularity by the time of 1994's Ri¢hie Ri¢h.

charges of possession of marijuana and possession of a controlled substance without a prescription. Later, he received a $1,000 fine and a deferred one-year jail sentence. (Ironically, months earlier, Culkin had admitted of drugs: "I made sure I tried everything once, except when it comes to needles—I don't fuck around. . . . But there is nothing wrong with smoking some dope every once in a while.")

During the many frustrating periods when he could find no acting work, the former child star wrote a book, *Junior*, which was published in 2006. The semiautobiographical novel revealed the author to be still working out years of emotional issues with his father. In 2007, Culkin appeared on screen in the dark comedy *Sex and Breakfast*.

Village apartment with his pets) was much in the news in September 2004, when police detained him in Oklahoma City, Oklahoma, while he was driving cross country with his bulldog. He was arrested on

When a burned-out Macaulay Culkin quit acting at age 14, his mother recalled later, "He thought he could just disappear. . . . He just thought he would outgrow that look, that no one would know who he was when he was older. I said, 'Face it, until the day you die you are always going to be the *Home Alone* kid.'"

Patty Duke

(December 14, 1946–)

By the time Patty Duke was 12 and costarring on Broadway in a huge dramatic hit, she was already a seasoned actress, having appeared in over 50 television productions. By the age of 16, she had won an Academy Award. That same year, the teenager starred in her own TV sitcom

series, and she soon became a recording artist, with a Top Ten hit.

Because Duke received such tremendous acclaim at an early age, it was widely assumed that she would enjoy a terrific professional future. Few individuals knew the brutal truth about her hellish childhood or that she was already suffering from symptoms of manic depression. When she went publicly "wild" and became uncontrollable from the mid-1960s through the early 1980s, most observers assumed that fame and money had overinflated her ego and that she was just another reckless substance abuser.

• • •

Anna Marie Duke was born in 1946 in New York City, the youngest of three children of John Patrick and Frances McMahon Duke. Her father, a taxi driver, was an alcoholic, and abandoned the family when Anna was 6 (he died when Anna was 17). Her mother worked as a restaurant cashier to support the household. However, she suffered from severe depression, which led to outbursts of temper. Periodically she had to be hospitalized.

In the early 1950s, Anna's brother, Raymond, joined a local boys' club, where he participated in dramatics. He was spotted by John and Ethel Ross, who managed child actors, and they fostered his career. When Anna was 8, Raymond introduced her to the Rosses. The couple perceived that the petite youngster had show business potential. They took her on as a client and remolded her life—including changing her first name to Patty. The youngster was bewildered (and, later in life, exceedingly angry) at being so completely reshaped by these strangers who had robbed her of her identity. As part of the Rosses' systematic reorientation, they persuaded the submissive Mrs. Duke to allow Patty to move into their apartment and to only visit with her youngest child when they so approved. The

manipulative couple also insisted that Patty's mother do many of the Rosses' household chores. Patty was so traumatized by being "abandoned" by her real mother that she offered little outward resistance to her keepers' dictates.

Under the Rosses' stringent tutelage, Patty undertook modeling assignments and TV commercials. Next she moved on to TV acting assignments. In 1958, the enterprising managers wangled Duke the opportunity to be a contestant on the TV quiz show *The $64,000 Question*. She won $32,000, which went into the Rosses' bank account and which, like her other earnings, the couple largely used on themselves.

Young Oscar winner Patty Duke took time out from her hit TV sitcom to make 1965's Billie *with Warren Berlinger.*

For all their many faults and misdeeds—which included attempts by both John and Ethel Ross to sexually molest their protégée—the pair provided Duke with training that polished her natural acting abilities. By the time the adolescent auditioned for the role of young Helen Keller, the blind and deaf youngster who grew up to be a remarkable role model for physically challenged people, in *The Miracle Worker*, Duke was well prepared for her stage tryout and easily won the prized part. The 1959 play was a tremendous hit and made the young actress a much sought-after performer.

Not long after Duke re-created her stage part for the 1962 film version of *The Miracle Worker*, she starred on TV in *The Patty Duke Show*. Cast in a dual role, she was buoyant on screen, and the series had a popular three-season run. In the midst of this success, she recorded songs for albums that did well with her fans. However, behind the scenes, all was *not* well with the teenage star. Unable to cope anymore with the invasive Rosses, Duke moved to Los Angeles to live on her own. (John Ross passed away in 1970, Ethel, in 1978.)

As part of her rebellion, the impetuous 18-year-old wed 32-year-old Harry Falk Jr. (an assistant director) in November 1965. The marriage had little chance of succeeding. Already, Duke was suffering from anorexia (at one point the emaciated five-foot-tall performer weighed only 76 pounds), frightening mood swings, and a dependence on Valium, and had attempted suicide several times. With the odious Rosses no longer managing her, Duke's career faltered. She costarred in 1967's *Valley of the Dolls*, hoping her screen role

as a substance-abusing singer/actress would provide her with a mature show business image. Instead, the trashy film caused her to lose esteem within the industry and with fans.

Meanwhile, her marriage and life were falling apart. Her escalating emotional distress led to several hospitalizations. In March 1970, Duke and Falk divorced. She then dated Desi Arnaz Jr., who was six years her junior, and suffered public rebuke from her lover's mother, movie and TV star Lucille Ball, who thought the divorcée was all wrong for her son. The chaos in Duke's life accelerated. Duke did win an Emmy for her sterling performance in a TV movie (1970's *My Sweet Charlie*) and gave an incoherent acceptance speech at the awards ceremony that many onlookers assumed was the result of rampant substance abuse. (Duke was then drinking heavily and using prescription drugs. However, during the telecast she actually was suffering an emotional breakdown.)

A few weeks later, in late June 1970, the unpredictable Duke wed 25-year-old Michael Tell, a rock promoter whom she barely knew. The absurd union ended within three weeks with the marriage being annulled. The next month the actress admitted publicly that she was an expectant mother. Most observers assumed the father was Desi Arnaz Jr. But the pregnancy was actually the result of her secret affair with married actor John Astin. Because Duke was Catholic, she did not consider having an abortion.

Her child Sean was born in February 1971. In August 1972, Duke and Astin (who was now divorced, with primary custody of his three sons) married. She and her 16-years-older husband performed frequently together on TV and in stage tours. The couple became the parents of Mackenzie in 1973. To support their large household, the Astins worked constantly. To outsiders, it seemed Patty had miraculously put her muddled life in order. In reality, she still suffered from extreme mood swings and felt overwhelmed by her struggles to nurture five boys and a spouse while somehow keeping her career alive.

In 1982, Duke was finally diagnosed by a psychiatrist as being manic-depressive and placed on lithium. The medication helped to restore her sanity, but it could not save her floundering marriage. She and Astin divorced in 1985, the same year that she began a three-year term as president of the Screen Actors Guild. In March 1986, she married Michael Pearce, then a U.S. Army staff sergeant. She and her younger spouse (who left the military and became her business partner) later adopted a son (Kevin), and for several years lived on an Idaho farm.

To herald her regained life, Duke authored a memoir (the 1987 bestseller *Call Me Anna*), which she followed up with 1992's *A Brilliant Madness: Living with Manic Depressive Illness*. She continued her career, largely with TV appearances (winning three Emmys in the process), and returned to the New York stage in a 2002 revival of *Oklahoma!* She underwent successful heart bypass surgery in 2004. The next year, Duke, a devoted activist for many causes, started a Web site focused on mental wellness. In 2006, she costarred in the TV movie *Falling in Love with the Girl Next Door*.

The star has said of her roller-coaster life: "I subscribe to the theory that says you're a product of all your experiences. And I am finally, most of the time, happy with the product. I now think it is OK to be Patty Duke."

Lindsay Lohan

(July 2, 1986–)

Every generation provides a fresh array of pretty teenage Hollywood starlets who capture the public's fancy. The new millennium's contingent included Hilary Duff, Mandy Moore, and Lindsay Lohan—all of whom turned out record albums as well as performed in films and on TV. Lohan, in particular, enjoyed a strong career trajectory thanks to her blend of budding sophistication and friendly demeanor. Within eight years of making her big-screen debut, in 1998's *The Parent Trap*, she was commanding a per-movie fee of $7.5 million. She seemed poised for success as an adult performer.

However, more than most of her peers, Lohan underwent a difficult (and very public) adjustment to her growing fame and its attendant perks. She became a media target, with the press chronicling her latest acts of unrestrained behavior on and off the sound stages. (While Lohan's acting abilities placed her in the same league as Scarlett Johansson,

When not frolicking on the nightlife scene, Lindsay Lohan made such films as 2006's Just My Luck.

Lindsay's hyperactivity on the club scene indicated that Tori Spelling and Paris Hilton might actually be her role models.) Nothing was as chastising for the uninhibited Lohan as the public admonishment she received in late July 2006. It came from James G. Robinson, the head of Morgan Creek Productions, for whom she was making *Georgia Rule*, a major movie costarring Jane Fonda and Dermot Mulroney. In a well-circulated reprimand, the CEO chided Lindsay for being tardy on the set and for acting "like a spoiled child," saying that her behavior had alienated many of her coworkers.

• • •

Lindsay Dee Lohan was born in 1986 on Long Island, New York, the first of four children of Michael and Dina Lindsay Lohan. Her father inherited—and sold—a thriving pasta business, and later worked as a Wall Street commodities broker, a restaurateur, and a businessman. As a young man, he had been an actor, which is how he met his wife-to-be, a former Radio City Rockette. Through Mrs. Lohan's contacts in the modeling field, Lindsay got her start in the business when she was 3 years old. (The red-haired girl with freckles went on to make over 60 TV commercials, and her success encouraged her three siblings—Michael, Aliana, and Dakota—to venture into show business as well.)

During elementary school, Lohan appeared on TV soap operas, including *Another World*. When she was in sixth grade, she won the lead (a dual role as twin sisters) in Walt Disney Pictures' *The Parent Trap*. She received solid reviews for being a "natural camera performer with lots of smartness and sparkle." After that, Lohan abandoned acting to resume everyday life as a student. However, following her third year at Cold Spring Harbor High School, on Long Island, she returned to acting—with her mother continuing as her manager. Lindsay was cast in 2000's *Life-Size*, a cable TV movie aimed at youngsters. In 2003, she was the costar of *Freaky Friday*, and was paid $1 million to headline 2004's *Confessions of a Teenage Drama Queen*. (While that entry flopped, she had a hit with the same year's *Mean Girls*.) Lohan had already performed songs on the sound tracks of several movies when she was signed to a recording contract with the Casablanca label. Her debut disc was 2004's *Speak*, followed the next year by *A Little More Personal (Raw)*.

During her teen years, Lohan coped with several family crises, including her father's repeated run-ins with the law, her mother's divorce from her allegedly abusive spouse, and the repercussions of her and her siblings being caught in the middle of the ongoing domestic chaos. (Lindsay publicly vented her feelings on her chaotic home life in a song she wrote.)

During these transitional years, Hollywood's new teen queen dated musician Aaron Carter briefly in 2002, had a relationship with actor Wilmer Valderrama between 2003 and 2004, and was momentarily linked with movie star Christian Slater; Paris Hilton's ex, Stavros Niarchos; and screen hunk Jared Leto. By then, she had her own Los Angeles digs, was an overly enthusiastic partier on the Los Angeles club circuit, and was photographed frequently at trendy hot spots around the country. The supermarket tabloids reported constantly on the junior diva's latest social high jinks, shopping sprees, overindulgent behavior, and reputed lack of discipline on film sets—including 2005's *Herbie: Fully Loaded*. One tabloid labeled the unrestrained Lohan "Hollywood's Biggest Brat." It also came to light that Lohan had suffered previously from an eating disorder and reputedly had experimented with drugs and booze. Meanwhile, the actress was involved in two Los Angeles vehicular accidents in 2005, one caused by a pursuing paparazzo, the other when Lohan's black Mercedes-Benz collided with a van.

Following the ruckus regarding her behavior on the set of *Georgia Rule*, stories surfaced from industry "insiders" claiming she had exhibited similar unprofessional conduct on past movie shoots. (Veteran actor William H. Macy, a coplayer with Lohan in 2006's *Bobby*, slammed Lindsay

by stating that she "should have her a— kicked." Although Macy acknowledged she was a talented performer, he faulted her manners: "You can't show up late. It's very, very disrespectful.")

In more recent times, Lohan turned to Kabbalah and began what for a time seemed to be a serious relationship with the level-headed Harry Morton, the Hard Rock Hotel & Casino heir. However, that romance fell by the wayside, and she turned to other romantic interests, including actor James Franco. Meanwhile, despite months of attending Alcoholics Anonymous meetings, Lindsay's life continued to spin out of control with her heavy drinking. Then, in mid-January 2007, she took time off from acting in the film thriller *I Know Who Killed Me* to check herself into a plush Los Angeles rehab center. The beleaguered young star stated, "I have made a proactive decision to take care of my personal health." (Her mother insisted, "This is a wonderful, giant step she's taking and it's all good. Hollywood's a really, really busy scary place and everything is under control.") Later, while Lohan continued with her substance abuse program on an outpatient basis, she returned to the studio set to complete *I Know Who Killed Me*. Thereafter, she dropped out of an upcoming vehicle (*A Woman of No Importance*), leaving her public relations representative to explain that Lindsay "doesn't want to just yes everyone and compromise herself anymore. If anything has been learned, it's that what she needs comes first—and right now she needs focus."

Despite her colorful tabloid reputation, Lohan has insisted, "People like to think that just because I'm young and like to enjoy my life, I'm some crazy party girl. I hate the term party girl—I hate it. . . . I'm in this career for the longevity of it, not just for doing everything too fast and then running out of steam." Nonetheless, in the *New York Times*, critic Caryn James wondered, "How much does the off-screen image bleed into, and possibly hurt, the reception of the work? . . . The swirling tabloid rumors are dangerous because she is no Paris Hilton, famous for being famous. Her situation is more like that of Colin Farrell, a fine actor who . . . is still best known for drinking and womanizing. . . . Out-of-control behavior can backfire, making the actor seem like some maniac you might stare at on a talk show, but wouldn't want to spend time with in a movie theater."

Tori Spelling

(May 16, 1973–)

A few years ago, actress Tori Spelling was discussing her famous father, mega-millionaire TV producer Aaron Spelling. She enthused, "I'm so lucky—I mean I *am*, to have him as a father, everything he's done for my career. People should be happy for me. They should say: '*You're lucky.*'" However, even Tori, who often seemed to be Miss Semiclueless, appreciated the reality of her situation—to a degree. The truth was that for years, much of the entertainment industry and the public had regarded her as the product of a highly privileged lifestyle who owed her "career" to Daddy's casting her in his TV shows.

Tori said of her detractors who thought she was a show business joke and deserved a comeuppance: "They want to hear bad before they want to hear good. I don't know what it is, but it's something. . . . Well . . . *whatever.*"

• • •

Victoria Davey Spelling was born in 1973 in Los Angeles, to Aaron Spelling and his second wife, Carol Jean "Candy" Marer Spelling, a hand model/interior designer whom he had wed in 1968. Five years after Victoria was born, the couple had a second child, Randy, who also became a performer, largely in his father's TV fluff fare.

Aaron Spelling was born in Dallas, Texas, in 1923, one of five children of poor Jewish immigrants. As a youngster, Aaron was constantly bullied by bigoted classmates. After serving in World War II, he enrolled at Southern Methodist University, where he directed campus stage productions and wrote plays. Later, he worked in regional theater, and then moved to Hollywood, where he became a bit actor. He married actress Carolyn Jones in 1953. (The couple, who had no children, divorced in 1964.)

Aaron became tired of being stereotyped on screen because of his odd looks and turned to writing episodes for and producing TV series. His first hit program was 1963's *Burke's Law*, which led to such major successes as *Starsky and Hutch, Fantasy Island, The Love Boat, Charlie's Angels, Hotel,* and

Dynasty. In the late 1980s, the extremely prolific, hugely wealthy Spelling spent $47 million to build the Manor, a 123-room home in the exclusive Holmby Hills section of Los Angeles. The 56,000-square-foot mansion, which boasted a special room for Candy to wrap gifts in, was thought to be the largest house in Los Angeles.

Aaron Spelling was as protective and pampering of Tori as he was of his wife, which some onlookers say led to a rivalry between mother and daughter. In 1981, 7-year-old Tori made her professional debut in a guest role on TV's *Vega$*. Although awkward and not conventionally cute, she moved on to assignments in other Spelling productions. In private life, Tori and her brother, Randy, had the best that money could offer. One year, when the Christmas holidays were approaching, she complained that she had never seen real snow. In response, Aaron had chipped ice and snow imported to create an impressive white mound in the backyard of the Manor.

Tori attended the fashionable Westlake School in Los Angeles. When Aaron Spelling debuted his newest TV series, *Beverly Hills, 90210*, in the fall of 1990, Tori was cast as Donna Martin, the spoiled, insecure high schooler. The featherweight show became a substantial hit and lasted till 2000. Until the problematic Shannen Doherty left the series cast in 1994, Tori was good pals on and off the set with the unpredictable actress—a situation that led Tori into exploring the wilder side of Beverly Hills nightlife and getting into scrapes.

Although critics gave Tori more attention for changes in her hair color than for her acting, she persisted in the profession. She ventured into TV movies, such as 1996's campy *Mother, May I Sleep with Danger?* She became associated with—and mocked for—these semisleazy telefeatures, which were surprisingly popular. To her credit, she received grudgingly respectful reviews for her work in independent movies such as 1999's *Trick*. However, much of the public still regarded her as a big hoot.

Tori turned to theater work in 2002, appearing on the Los Angeles stage in *Maybe Baby, It's You*. She began dating the show's playwright, Charlie Shanian. Meanwhile, she was living away from her parents, in her own comfortable West Los Angeles digs. When Tori and Charlie announced their engagement, her father insisted that the prospective groom sign a strong prenuptial

Tori Spelling rose to prominence playing Donna Martin on TV's Beverly Hills, 90210 (from 1990 to 2000), one of the many series produced by her industry mogul father, Aaron Spelling.

agreement. Once Aaron was appeased, he spent $1 million on the lavish wedding, which was held at the Manor in July 2004. Tori wore a $50,000 designer gown, Wolfgang Puck catered the reception, and Michael Feinstein entertained the 400 guests.

Soon, Tori life's began to resemble one of her trashy TV films. While shooting the 2006 TV movie *Mind Over Murder*, she became attracted to her costar, Canadian actor Dean McDermott. She and Shanian separated. (They divorced in April 2006.) Meanwhile, McDermott split from his actress wife, with whom he had two children. (The couple divorced in February 2006.) Tori's divorce and new romance caused a serious estrangement from both of her parents. When she and McDermott married in May 2006, none of her family attended the small ceremony in Fiji. The sticky situation was not improved when Tori starred in a 2006 TV series, *So noTORIous*. The comedy lampooned her "tough" real life. Reportedly, Candy Spelling was extremely displeased that the show presented Tori's onscreen mother (played by Loni Anderson) as a shallow shopaholic. After that series faded, Tori and her husband reteamed for the telefeature *Housesitter*. (The couple announced they were expecting a baby boy in spring 2007. The child, Liam, was born on March 13, two weeks earlier than anticipated. Meanwhile, they leased and renovated a bed and breakfast in Temecula, California, a process documented in the 2007 cable TV reality series *Tori & Dean: Inn Love*.)

Aaron Spelling died on June 23, 2006, the result of an earlier stroke. Tori had been out of touch with her father for months but had a brief reunion with him a few weeks before his death. She claimed that she first learned of her father's passing when a friend e-mailed her the news. The tabloid-covered "feud" between Candy and Tori escalated when an Aaron Spelling tribute was scheduled for the September 2006 Emmy Awards. Candy was scheduled to attend, but there were rumors that Tori had not been invited. (Actually, they both came to the event but sat far apart in the auditorium.) Next, a TV special Tori was preparing to celebrate her father's TV work was shelved when Candy purportedly refused to give permission for use of footage from Aaron's many shows. Then came news that the bulk of Spelling's over $400 million estate had been bequeathed to Candy (the sole executor), with Tori allotted only a pittance ($800,000—the same amount left to Randy, who was still living at the Manor).

There was an upside to Tori's latest tribulation. She said her father's death and its aftermath made her more appreciative of everyday folk. "Suddenly, we're on the same page, we're equals, and that's all I want to be. Sometimes you get put on another level as an actor and people aren't able to take you at face value, so it's nice to be put on a more humanized level."

To bolster her spirits, the poor, much-maligned, coddled Tori went on a major shopping spree. Months later, Spelling decided to pen her memoir, explaining, "I've got a million stories to tell. I will definitely talk about all my relationships and how I felt about them." A prime focus of the book would be her complicated ties to her family. Of her much-publicized contretemps with her relatives, Tori insists, "It's important for me to tell people about the struggles."

PART 2

So Much Ego

Richard Burton
(November 10, 1925–August 5, 1984)

Like his good friends and fellow perform- ers Peter O'Toole and Richard Harris, Richard Burton often compromised his remarkable acting talents with his monu- mental consumption of alcohol. Reflecting on his especially heavy period of boozing in the 1970s, Burton acknowledged, "For about five years, I drank hopelessly. I drank and drank. Booze was taking its toll. I was the not-so-innocent victim of the perpetual hangover. . . . You can't drink seriously and hope to remain an actor who receives rave notices. Sadly, very sadly, I discovered that alcohol and acting can never mix." Despite such occasional remorse, for much of his career, Burton continued to squander his gift due to his excessive lifestyle. He had an ego- centric belief that he could burn the candle at both ends and still provide audiences with decent to superior performances— which often proved not to be the case.

Burton had several explanations for why he had allowed himself such heavy, over- board boozing. These included the deadly boredom of the interminable long waits between shooting scenes on a movie, a sit- uation made even more stultifying if the project offered few acting challenges. He added that such work conditions "become very dangerous if you find a congenial actor who likes to drink too." Another of his ratio- nales for excessive drinking was the cyclone of media attention and public fascination prompted by his scandalous affair and then marriage (divorce, remarriage, and second divorce) from the glamorous movie queen Elizabeth Taylor in the 1960s and 1970s. Burton said that because he had such a modest upbringing he was overwhelmed by—aghast at—and yet attracted to Taylor's jet-set lifestyle of constant overindulgence. Such luxuriant, pampered living became his mode during the chaotic Liz years. "Alcohol," said Burton, "cured me from facing the sheer idiocy of a weird world I was forced to live in."

Elizabeth Taylor perceived other causes for Burton's alcoholism. She pointed out that in real life, this world-class actor suf- fered from a "terrible shyness" and that to be the charming person others (and, in turn, he) expected a celebrated entertainer to be, he had to have "a couple of drinks." She also referenced his recurring spells of Welsh gloom, which dragged him into deep melancholy and often triggered intense drinking sprees. (The self-indulgent Burton said of his notorious mood swings, which he did little to check, "I soar from highs to lows. With me, there's very few middles.")

• • •

Richard Walter Jenkins was born in 1925 in Pontrhydyfen, Wales, the 12th of 13 chil- dren of Richard Walter and Edith Maude Thomas Jenkins. When Richard was 2 years old, his mother died and he was sent to live with an older sister.

The youngster hoped to avoid the fate of generations of males in his family who had been coal miners, and he pursued an education. Performing in a class play convinced the teenager that he might have a future on the stage. He was mentored by an instructor, Philip Burton, who later became the young man's legal guardian. Richard adopted his benefactor's surname when he made his professional stage bow in 1943 in Liverpool. The next year, Burton spent six months at Exeter College, Oxford, where he gained a reputation as an enthusiastic drinker who was quick to get into brawls. (Some observers say Richard behaved this way to feel more emotionally allied with his coal miner father and relatives, from whom he felt increasingly alienated because of his rise in social status.) Thereafter, Burton joined the Royal Air Force. A civilian again in late 1947, he pursued stage work.

While making his initial feature film (1949's *The Last Days of Dolwyn*), Burton met South African–born actress Sybil Williams. They married in February 1949 in Kensington, England. That same year he debuted on the London stage and, thereafter, performed on Broadway. Burton's first Hollywood movie was 1952's *My Cousin Rachel*, for which he earned a Best Actor Oscar nomination. (This was the first of his seven Academy Award bids over the year. However, he never won the prize.)

In September 1957, the Burtons became the parents of a daughter, Katharine. The family's home base was in Switzerland, where they resided for tax purposes. The couple's second child, Jessica, was born in the autumn of 1959. (Later on, Jessica was diagnosed as schizophrenic and autistic. Eventually, she was institutionalized.)

The hard-drinking Burton, whose iron constitution allowed him to outdrink most anyone, starred on Broadway in the musical *Camelot* in late 1960. Six months later, Twentieth Century-Fox paid a large sum to gain Richard's release from the show so he could appear opposite Elizabeth Taylor in the upcoming screen epic *Cleopatra*. During months of lazing about the Eternal City waiting to be needed on the sound stages, Burton became better acquainted with Taylor (then married to her fourth husband, singer Eddie Fisher). By the time the costars shot their scenes together in January 1962, they were in love. This situation made Burton and Taylor the focus of global press attention. In the wake of the resultant scandal, the lovers cast aside their respective mates.

Burton and Taylor reteamed for 1963's *The V.I.P.s* and, by the next year, both of them had finalized their divorces. They wed in March 1964. Over the next several years, the globe-trotting, high-salaried couple paired in such pictures as 1966's *Who's Afraid of Virginia Woolf?* and 1972's *Hammersmith Is Out*. During this enormously indulgent period for the celebrated twosome, Richard became progressively more insecure about his identity apart from his cinema diva wife. He wondered if the plush life (and his dissipated ways) had forever ruined his dream of becoming the world's greatest actor. He and Taylor fought constantly and made up publicly, and he increasingly indulged in affairs and carousing. The (in)famous couple divorced in

June 1974, splitting up $12 million in community property. Much to their almost immediate regret, the duo remarried in October 1975, but by the following August had divorced again. Taylor said of Burton, "We were just too explosive to get along with each other."

By August 1976, Richard had wed for the fourth time. His latest bride was 27-year-old Susan Hunt, a onetime London model. After he sleepwalked through such paltry screen ventures as 1974's *The Klansman*, he sought to redeem himself professionally. He curtailed his wild life and was able to give a sterling performance in the 1977 film *Equus* (re-creating a part he had played with distinction on the Broadway stage in 1976). However, by then, decades of alcoholic abuse and chain-smoking, as well as the ill effects of bad nutrition in childhood, were catching up with the fiftysomething star. Assorted health issues caused Burton to abandon a tour of his 1980 New York revival of *Camelot*. A few years later, he struggled through a Broadway rehash of Noël Coward's *Private Lives* costarring his ex-wife Taylor.

Meanwhile, Burton's union with Susan Hunt ended in February 1983. That July, he married Sally Anne Hay, a film continuity supervisor several years younger than the groom. By now, Burton was semiretired. In August 1984, he was stricken with a cerebral hemorrhage and died in Geneva, Switzerland. His last film, *1984*, was posthumously released that October.

In reviewing his years of conspicuous consumption of alcohol, the hedonistic Burton noted offhandedly, "I am just not civilized with drink. It is all or nothing with me." In his peak drinking years, he said he had no problems "knocking off three bottles a day of vodka or whiskey," adding, "I had to keep away from the rum because I then fancied I could take on [boxers] Muhammad Ali or George Foreman. Or, on a heavy day, both."

Bette Davis

(April 5, 1908–October 6, 1989)

Bette Davis acknowledged, "I was a legendary terror. I was insufferably rude and ill-mannered in the cultivation of my career. I had no time for pleasantries. I said what was on my mind and it wasn't always printable. I have been uncompromising, peppery, intractable, monomaniacal, tactless, volatile, and ofttimes disagreeable. I suppose I'm larger than life."

The highly competitive Davis explained, "I always had the will to win. I felt it baking cookies. They had to be the best cookies anyone baked." That she had the stamina for being ruthless was undisputed. Even early in her film career, Bette was a budding prima donna. Barbara Stanwyck, the star of 1932's *So Big!*, said of Davis, who had only a featured role in that drama,

"She's an egotistical little bitch." Humphrey Bogart, also a screen novice like Davis in the early 1930s, had a remedy for Bette's aggressive, uptight behavior: "What she needs is a good screw from a man who knows how to do it."

In actuality, Davis had a strong sex drive and often indulged in quick flings to work off excess energy. Other times, she pursued affairs, as with billionaire Howard Hughes, her frequent costar George Brent, or directors William Wyler, Vincent Sherman, and Anatole Litvak. The star married four times but claimed her matrimonial choices had been ill-considered because her mates were unable to stand up to her or, as an alternative, congenially sank into the background as Mr. Davis. (A theory prevalent in the film colony held that Davis despised being a woman in a man's world and, as revenge, sought to castrate the men in her life. She disagreed. "I never wished I'd been a man. I always felt like a woman and wanted to be a woman. I wanted to be fulfilled professionally and personally, as a woman. There are some who might say I had penis envy, but I only had penis admiration.")

Davis, who often rewrote troublesome situations in her life to appease her ego, romanticism, and conscience, observed self-righteously in her final years, "They said I was a monster, but if I became a monster, it was because I was in a monstrous business. I couldn't ever afford to have my armor penetrated, because underneath, I was unprotected. Or so I thought. Now, as I approach the winter of my life . . . I realize that I've nothing to be ashamed of as a person."

•   •   •

Ruth Elizabeth Davis was born in 1908 in Lowell, Massachusetts, the first of two daughters of Harlow Morrell Davis, a future patent attorney, and Ruth (Ruthie) Favor Davis, a portrait photographer. (The younger sister, Barbara—known as Bobby—suffered increasingly from emotional problems in adulthood, a situation aggravated by existing in the shadow of her demanding, famous sibling.) Her parents separated when Ruth Elizabeth was 7; three years later the couple divorced. By her freshman year in high school, the ambitious teenager had chosen to go on the stage. She studied theater arts in New York City at the Robert Milton–John Murray Anderson School. In 1928, Bette Davis, as she was now known

Bette Davis and then husband Gary Merrill costarring in 1951's Another Man's Poison.

professionally, worked with a stock company in Rochester, New York. The abrasive newcomer quickly annoyed Miriam Hopkins, the group's experienced leading lady. Hopkins screamed to the director: "The bitch doesn't know her place!" Subsequently, an unsettled Bette withdrew from the troupe.

Bette made her Broadway bow in 1929's *Broken Dishes*. The next year, she was hired by Universal Pictures. The studio was perplexed as to how to showcase this unorthodox-looking newcomer with her boyish figure and pop eyes, and she stagnated in unmemorable assignments. Davis moved over to Warner Bros. for 1932's *The Man Who Played God*. That film lot placed her under contract and threw her into one picture after another with little concern for her career growth. (In reaction to being so poorly treated, Davis lashed out at her leading men by being aggressive on the set and often stepping on their lines. She quickly learned the tricks of keeping the camera's focus on her.)

Davis's strong performance in 1934's *Of Human Bondage*, made while she was on loan to RKO, earned her an Academy Award nomination, the first of 11 over her career. She won her first Oscar the next year for *Dangerous*. When the studio still failed to give her better projects, she fled to England to make movies there. However, Warner Bros. sued her and won its case. She returned to the Burbank, California, lot for 1937's *Marked Woman*.

With Davis vehicles like 1938's *Jezebel* (for which she earned her second Oscar), Bette became Warner Bros.' top actress. Her success made her even more demand-ing, temperamental, and self-indulgent. When her old enemy Miriam Hopkins was cast as Davis's costar in 1939's *The Old Maid*, the two divas battled both on and off camera.

Back in August 1932, Davis had wed bandleader Oscar Harmon Nelson Jr. He became extremely sensitive about her earning far more than he did. It was he who went along with Ruthie Davis and the studio in convincing Bette to have (at least) two abortions in the mid-1930s so as not to interrupt her career. Since Bette was increasingly powerful at the studio, she felt the usual rules did not apply to her marriage. She had flings, including a grand passion—at least in her mind—with her *Jezebel* director, William Wyler. (In 1938, he married another actress, the far more congenial Margaret Tallichet.) Davis and Nelson divorced in December 1938.

By the early 1940s, Davis had become the First Lady of the Screen. In December 1941, she wed New England innkeeper Arthur Farnsworth. He, too, got caught in her large shadow. Soon after she made 1943's *Old Acquaintance*, Farnsworth died of an aneurysm. The coroner said it resulted from a prior blow to the head. Because of Bette's star power and the studio's clout, her spouse's mysterious death was soon put to rest. However, the actress later told friends that she believed Farnsworth's fatal wound had happened when Arthur attempted to prevent her from embarking on a train bound for Mexico, where she intended to rendezvous with married director Vincent Sherman (who, as events developed, decided not to meet her there). During the argument, the hot-tempered Davis pushed her husband away. As the train gathered speed, he fell off the train car's steps and smacked his head on the station platform.

In 1943, Warner Bros. added former MGM star Joan Crawford—a longtime adversary of Davis's—to its roster of stars. Interestingly, Crawford won an Oscar for 1945's *Mildred Pierce*, a role that Davis had rejected. Davis left Warner Bros. in 1949. Now that she was middle-aged, her stardom days seemed behind her. However, she grabbed the lead role in 1950's *All About Eve* and won another Oscar nomination.

Davis had married artist William Grant Sherry in November 1945, and their daughter, Barbara Davis (B.D.), was born in May 1947. By July 1950, the fickle Bette had discarded husband number three. Less than a month later, she wed Gary Merrill, her leading man in *All About Eve*. The newlyweds adopted two children, Margot (who proved to be retarded and was ultimately institutionalized in 1951) and Michael, in 1952. It was not long before the two heavy drinkers were battling each other. In July 1960, the vicious relationship ended in divorce.

By the early 1960s, Davis's career was at an impasse. Ironically, her comeback was the result of Joan Crawford's suggesting they team for 1962's *What Ever Happened to Baby Jane?* Two years later, while making another joint vehicle (*Hush . . . Hush, Sweet Charlotte*), Crawford bowed out, unable to cope with making another picture with Davis.

The 1980s proved Davis's thesis that "growing old is not for sissies." She

endured a mastectomy in 1983, and, thereafter, suffered several strokes. However, Bette refused to stop acting—or acting up. While making the 1985 telefeature *Murder with Mirrors*, she badly upset her costar, Helen Hayes. Davis also terrorized another coplayer, John Mills. (The veteran actor remarked, "I was never so scared in my life. And I was in the war!") But all this was a mere warm-up for the nastiness that Davis dished out to esteemed screen and stage star Lillian Gish on 1987's *The Whales of August*. In one of her moments of high pique, Davis snapped of her genteel, aged coplayer, "[She] ought to know about close-ups. Jesus, she was around when they invented them!"

One fight the pugnacious Davis had not anticipated was with her daughter B.D. In 1985, B.D. published *My Mother's Keeper*, a horrifying portrait of the selfish star and her alleged acts of cruelty toward those trapped in her orbit. Davis was astounded by such a public betrayal. The living legend wailed, "She lived off me, and I lent her husband money to start his own business, and they have both conspired against me. . . . I, who was not the best mother in the world, but in *no* way abusive . . . and I always tried my best!" Mother and daughter never spoke again, and Davis cut B.D. out of her will.

In October 1989, at age 81, Davis succumbed to her lengthy battle with cancer. She died at the American Hospital in Neuilly, France, having just attended a film festival tribute. She was buried at Forest Lawn Memorial Park in Hollywood Hills, California. Her tombstone legend read, "She did it her way."

Rex Harrison

(March 5, 1908–June 2, 1990)

In a bygone era when drawing room comedies were exceeding popular stage fare, the urbane Rex Harrison was master of that delicate theater genre. He was droll, had immaculate timing, and always looked to the manner born in his natty attire. On screen, he was equally adept at providing a polished, highly dimensional portrayal. His Julius Caesar was one of the few memorable aspects of that colossal bore of a screen epic, 1963's *Cleopatra*.

As an actor, this Brit regarded his limitations (e.g., an inability to play successfully a blue-collar man) a virtue, because he could focus on the type of parts he did best. On

Dapper Rex Harrison and Lilli Palmer, the second of his six wives, team for a cameo appearance in 1953's Main Street to Broadway.

the other hand, he felt himself far too versatile to be so completely associated with his most famous role: Professor Henry Higgins in the long-running 1950s Broadway musical *My Fair Lady* and its Oscar-winning 1964 screen adaptation.

Being a top-ranking star for so many decades provided him with the income to enjoy an elegant lifestyle, particularly at his villa on the Italian Riviera. In Harrison's gilt-edged world, everything revolved totally around him, and damn the fool (or "shit" as he often said) who presumed to steal his limelight. He was a conceited snob who blithely ignored others' opinions. (He was convinced he knew everything on the subject of wine and, in bullheaded fashion, got into heated arguments with sommeliers at the best restaurants, even though he was often dead wrong about the qualities of a particular vintage.) Interacting with the self-absorbed, demanding Harrison could be an overwhelming chore, whether the victim be a lover, a friend, a business associate, or a tradesperson. Even he admitted, "I don't have heart attacks. I give them to other people."

This supreme egotist could downplay his arrogance and emphasize his charm when it suited him—particularly when flirting with the opposite sex. He despised the media for labeling him "Sexy Rexy." But it was an apt title for the lithe star, who was six times married and had many affairs over the decades. As with all other matters, the chauvinistic Harrison remained self-focused in his love affairs. "I vowed," he said once, "never to fit into the life of some woman. She has to fit into mine." In typical fashion, all his amorous unions proved highly stressful to his mate of the moment. One old friend of Harrison's observed of Rex's then current spouse: "I've never met a more unhappy woman in all my life." To which the cavalier star rejoined, "Oh, haven't you? . . . I have. All my other wives."

• • •

He was born Reginald Carey Harrison in 1908 in Huyton, Lancashire, England, the third child (he had two sisters) of William Reginald and Edith Carey Harrison. The family's forebears had once been wealthy, but that rich legacy had been dissipated over the years. As a youngster, Reginald was sickly. (A severe case of measles left him nearly blind in one eye.) By age 8, he had become enthralled with the theater and was staging performances at home. The youngster adopted a new first name when he discovered that Rex meant king in Latin. At 16, he quit academics to apprentice at the Liverpool Repertory Theatre. Within a few years he had gained confidence in his stage work and in his social life. For a time he affected carrying a long cigarette-holder and wearing a monocle in his bad eye. This proved irresistible to many impressionable young women.

In 1930, Harrison made his film debut (in *School for Scandal*) and his West End bow (in *Getting George Married*). Four years later, he wed Noel Marjorie Collette Thomas, the daughter of a retired British Army major. Their son, Noel, was born in January 1934. Rex had a substantial hit on the London stage with 1936's *French Without Tears*. He continued to alternate between stage and movie work. Harrison was so career-focused and had such an affinity for pretty ladies that his marriage fell apart. Collette took Noel and left him in 1938. (The couple divorced in 1942.) From 1941 to 1945, Harrison did World War II military duty in the radar division of the Royal Air Force. While on leave in January 1943, he wed Lilli Palmer, a charming Austrian-born actress he had met some months earlier. Their son, Carey, was born in February 1944.

After World War II, Harrison went to the United States to fulfill a contract he had negotiated with Twentieth Century-Fox. He made his Hollywood movie bow in 1946's *Anna and the King of Siam*, while Palmer found her own work in the American cinema. Much of Tinseltown treated the snobbish, rude Harrison as an outsider. He ignored the snubs and found diversion in romantic trysts, including a longish affair with screen actress Carole Landis. When she committed suicide in January 1949, Hollywood turned its back on Rex, who, they concluded, had driven her over the brink. He and Lilli (who stood by him through the scandal) fled to New York City, where he won plaudits on stage in *Anne of the Thousand Days*. His greatest triumph of the 1950s was headlining the Broadway musical *My Fair Lady*.

By the mid-1950s, Harrison was in love with the twentysomething Kay Kendall, a vivacious redhead in the cast of Rex's recent film, *The Constant Husband*. Meanwhile, Palmer had become involved romantically with actor Carlos Thompson and asked Harrison for a divorce in 1956. The next year, Harrison wed Kendall, who, unbeknownst to her, was dying of leukemia. (Harrison already had in mind that by the time Kay passed away, Palmer would have tired of Thompson and would obligingly divorce him and remarry Rex.) Kendall died in 1959, but Palmer remained with Thompson till her own death in 1986. As for Rex, he settled for marrying British actress Rachel Roberts in 1962. Eventually, she had enough of his overbearing manner. (It was Roberts who observed, "Rex is one of those who thinks living well is the best revenge. It may be, but the revenge is taken out on his nearest and dearest.") The couple divorced in 1971; in 1980, she committed suicide. In 1972, the dapper Harrison married Elizabeth Rees-Williams, the ex-wife of actor Richard Harris. This tumultuous union terminated in 1976. (She said of him: "I was very fond of Rex before we were married, and even more fond of him

after we were divorced, it was the bit in between which got so difficult.") Two years later, Rex Harrison was wed for the sixth and final time, to Mercia Mildred Tinker.

After his Oscar win for 1964's *My Fair Lady*, Harrison's screen career began its descent as his age and changing tastes limited his film options. He remained active on the stage (and occasionally on TV). In 1989, he was knighted by Queen Elizabeth II. Later that year, he appeared on Broadway in a revival of the drawing-room comedy *The Circle*. A few weeks after he left the production in May 1990, 82-year-old Rex died of pancreatic cancer. Shortly before he passed away at his New York apartment, the irascible Harrison—who had *not* mellowed with old age—beckoned his older son to his bedside and murmured, "And by the way, Noel, there was something I always wanted to tell you. I could never stand the sound of your fucking guitar."

To paraphrase *Hamlet*: We shall not see the likes of Rex Harrison again.

Al Jolson

(May 26, 1886–October 23, 1950)

Al Jolson immodestly billed himself as the "World's Greatest Entertainer." In fairness, most everyone who saw the magnetic star perform on stage agreed that he had amazing talent and verve. They also cited the showman's unquenchable desire to please audiences and, in turn, have them shower him with endless adoration.

On the other hand, the egocentric, highly

competitive, hypochondriac Jolson—who lived for being in the spotlight—was *not* well liked by his show business peers. Song-and-dance notable Harry Richman said of the braggart, "Words can't describe the meanness of this man." He also noted, "Jolson made a habit of discovering talent and then, when an individual became successful, dropping him." Alice Faye, the star of *Rose* of *Washington Square*, the 1939 film in which Jolson played himself, remembered Al as an "obnoxious boor." According to veteran entertainer Milton Berle, "Jolson used to steal gags from vaudeville actors and then have his lawyer write them letters saying they had stolen the jokes from *him*, and that they had better cut the material from their acts."

When Jolie (as he was nicknamed) was starring in Broadway productions in the 1910s and 1920s, it was not uncommon for him to stop the show in midstream and ask the audience if they would prefer him to serenade them with a one-man concert rather than continue with the scripted musical. Unfailingly, they agreed, and the rest of the cast found themselves pushed aside into the wings. Now, having the crowd all to himself, Al would launch into his signature boast ("Folks, you ain't heard nothin' yet") and start the *real* show. Fellow trouper George Burns observed wryly of the insecure Jolson, who suffered recurrent bouts of depression, "When he came down to breakfast, he made an entrance. When he went to the bathroom, he made an exit. And when he came out of the bathroom, he wanted applause."

Off stage, the swaggering Jolson, who had a knack for making life miserable for those around him, had a favorite gambit when a subordinate dared to question one of his dictates. The star pulled a fat wad of money from his pocket and waved it in his opponent's face to demonstrate that his terrific income proved he was right in all matters. Jolson could also be tight-fisted with associates. In 1913, he was about to sign a lucrative multiyear stage pact with the Shuberts. Wanting to get even with his own

Al Jolson in a reflective mood while playing cards with entertainer Jack Pearl (right) in the late 1940s.

talent agent, who he felt had not done right by him in a past deal, Jolson pushed the representative into ending their long-term business arrangement for $700. The next week, Jolson's Shubert deal was announced, and the agent discovered he had lost out on a $10,000 commission. However, the mercurial Al later made up with his former agent. "That was Jolson," said Eddie Cantor, Al's show business rival and longtime acquaintance. "[He ran] hot and cold."

Ironically, while beloved by millions of fans, Jolson was so mean-spirited and self-involved that he had few friends. He relied on an entourage of cronies and yes-men to fill the void. He kept himself constantly busy because it gave him less time to think about how lonely he actually was.

Jolson was married four times, and the first three unions were especially problematic. (The short-tempered Al sometimes lashed out physically at his spouses.) One of his ex-wives was stage and film star Ruby Keeler. When Al was to be the subject of 1946's *The Jolson Story*, Columbia Pictures approached Keeler for approval to use her name in the screen biography. She refused, insisting she did not intend her children "to grow up someday and maybe see the picture and know I was married to a man like that." Eventually, the studio paid Keeler $25,000 not to have her name mentioned in the screenplay but to allow her backstory to be incorporated into the amalgam wife created for plot purposes.

• • •

He was born Asa Yoelson in 1886 (or 1885) in the Russian village of Seredzius—later part of Lithuania. He was the fifth and last living child of Rabbi Moshe Reuben and Naomi Cantor Yoelson. In 1890, his father immigrated to the United States to establish himself and then send for his loved ones. Four years later, the rest of the family joined the rabbi, who had settled in Washington, D.C. In 1895, Mrs. Yoelson died during childbirth. The tragic loss marked the future singer for life: thereafter, he judged all women by the standard of his beloved mother. The trauma also stunted his emotional growth, leaving him a perpetual man-boy.

By 1899, the teenager—who soon adopted the stage name of Al Jolson—had appeared on stage and then toured in vaudeville with his older brother Harry. Later, Al became a solo act. He found that he gained confidence in front of an audience when he appeared in blackface (a convention used by many performers of the time). In the follow-

ing years, he divided his time between starring in vehicles on the New York stage (and on tour) and making recordings.

In September 1907, Jolson wed showgirl Henrietta Keller. As became customary, once he had married, he quickly lost interest in his bride. (She could never compete successfully with his passion for entertaining a big audience.) They divorced in June 1919, and in August 1922, he wed another showgirl, Ethel Delmar. She felt so ignored by her career-driven, philandering spouse that she turned to heavy drinking. The couple split up in April 1926. Next, Jolson took a shine to 19-year-old Broadway tap dancer Ruby Keeler. She was then involved romantically with a gangster, who might have killed his rival but instead graciously bowed out of the picture. Al and bride number three wed in September 1928. Famously, when she was starring on Broadway in the 1929 musical *Show Girl*, Jolson stole her thunder by rising from the audience to serenade her with "Liza" as she performed a tap dance solo. This went on for a week before Jolson reluctantly left town to fulfill other commitments.

Jolson's career received a big boost when he starred in 1927's *The Jazz Singer*, a movie noted for its innovative sound (both dialogue and singing) sequences. Overnight, Al became the biggest draw on the silver screen. However, within a few years, his overly sentimental film musicals (such as 1929's *Sonny Boy*) wore out his welcome with moviegoers, who now demanded more sophisticated film fare. Jolson returned to Broadway and starred on radio. When he came back to movies, one of his ventures was 1935's *Go Into Your Dance*. It costarred

Keeler, then much in vogue thanks to her own popular screen musicals. Throughout the late 1930s, the arrogant Jolson's star dimmed and he spent much time at the racetrack and sitting at home bemoaning other entertainers' career successes. In December 1939, he and Keeler—who had adopted a baby boy—divorced.

During World War II, Jolson found a new venue in which to shine: he entertained the troops at home and abroad. His activity was cut short in 1944 when he contracted malaria and pneumonia. (While he was recuperating in the hospital, the star's fever shot up to 103 degrees. When Jolson was told this, he jumped up in bed and asked, "What's the record?") The next year, in March, he wed 22-year-old Erle Chennault Galbraith, an X-ray technician. The couple adopted two children.

The vain Al had to settle for dubbing the songs for young actor Larry Parks (who played Jolson) in *The Jolson Story* and its 1949 sequel, *Jolson Sings Again*. However, the two pictures revived the veteran showman's sagging career, and he had fresh successes as a recording artist and radio star. In October 1950, a few weeks after he returned from a USO tour to Korea, he died in San Francisco of a heart attack.

Jolson left an estate of over $4 million, much of which went to charities (and bypassed several long-standing acquaintances and staff). It required nearly three years to complete his imposing burial site at Hillside Memorial Park in Culver City, California. His impressive shrine consisted of a large circular canopy supported by six massive white stone columns and a series of terraced, cascading waterfalls. Nearby this extravaganza was a three-foot bronze statue of Jolson shown in his famous kneeling "Mammy" pose. Even in death, Al Jolson demanded center stage.

Jerry Lewis

(March 16, 1926–)

In his encyclopedia of film stars, cinema historian David Quinlan aptly described Jerry Lewis as the "long-faced, crop-haired, harassed-looking American star comedian whose goofy, child-like, disaster-prone comic creation was a tremendous hit in the late forties and fifties, in partnership with Dean Martin."

Another aspect of Lewis, the clowning actor who developed into a talented moviemaker, was his growing megalomania. During his successful show business partnership with Dean Martin (which lasted from 1946 to 1956), Jerry became increasingly concerned with controlling every aspect of their films. Lewis's rising ambitions overrode his great admiration for Martin. Jerry later acknowledged of this difficult period: "Was my ego growing? Was I enthralled, enamored, enraptured by all that I was learning about film? Was I knocked out by the unlimited comic possibilities for the Jerry

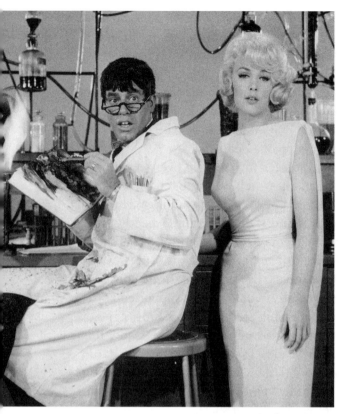

Jerry Lewis, at the height of his fame and power, in a scene with Stella Stevens from 1963's The Nutty Professor.

dictatorial Jerry Lewis was king of the hill and *everyone* got out of his way . . . or else!

When Lewis's studio joyride ended in 1965, it was the start of his career descent. Increasingly, critics took Jerry to task for the disappointing caliber of his new offerings (but not in France, where he was still idolized). He claimed not to be bothered by such negative responses. He reasoned, "The answer to all my critics is simple. I like me. I like what I've become. I'm proud of what I've achieved. And I don't really believe I've scratched the surface yet. I'm an egomaniac. I may have an ego that's bigger than others, but thank God if that's brought me to where I am. And that's my answer."

If that rebuttal was not sufficient, Lewis took further aim at his attackers. "I'm a multi-faceted, talented, wealthy, internationally famous genius. I have an IQ of 190, that's supposed to be genius. People don't like that. People really don't want waves made. . . . [They ask] Why does he have to write, direct, produce, et cetera? Why? That's no one's fucking business."

• • •

He was born Jerome (not Joseph as often stated) Levitch in Newark, New Jersey, in 1926, the only child of Danny and Rae Rothberg Levitch. His parents, under the stage names of Danny Lewis and Mona Lewis, were in show business. His father was a struggling nightclub singer and his mother was a pianist at a Manhattan radio station who sometimes accompanied her husband's singing act. His parents were so preoccupied with their careers on the road that they left their son with relatives—or on his own. The sorely neglected boy developed

character onscreen? . . . Yes, yes, and yes." Jerry's increasingly abrasive take-charge, know-it-all attitude led Dean to break up their act.

Thereafter, Lewis became an innovative movie director/producer/scripter/star who turned Paramount Pictures, his home lot, into his personal playground. As long as the profits on his pictures remained healthy, no one at the studio opposed him. Whether being tyrannical on the sound stage, running roughshod over executives at a studio conference, or madly charging across the film lot in his personal golf cart, the increasingly his own fantasy world and dreamed of becoming a movie entertainer. In the summertime, when his parents performed at Catskills resorts, the youngster joined them. At age 5, he made his debut doing a song number at the borscht-belt hotel where his father was emceeing.

Jerry found little pleasure in the schoolroom and diverted himself by becoming the class clown. His disruptive behavior got him into trouble with the faculty, and he left high school after the 10th grade. Already he had developed his own comedy act (pantomiming to records) and gained some small bookings. He supported himself with odd jobs, such as movie theater usher and factory shipping clerk. During one of his occasional performing stints, he met Patti Palmer, a big-band singer, and they wed in October 1944. (They had six sons, including one who was adopted.)

During July 1946, Lewis was performing solo in Atlantic City when an entertainer on the bill took ill. Jerry suggested that the owner hire the young singer Dean Martin, whom Lewis had met previously when they both worked at a Manhattan venue. After a few nights of performing separately on the club bill, Martin and Lewis joined together in an impromptu act. Their zany shenanigans, which mixed physical shtick with trading insults and witticisms, along with some crooning by Martin, proved to be a big crowd-pleaser. Within months, they were booked at major clubs throughout the United States and were earning $5,000 a week. Later, the duo was signed by producer Hal B. Wallis at Paramount Pictures. The comedy team debuted on screen with 1949's *My Friend Irma*, and it was a hit. The pair continued to make films as well as perform on radio and television and in clubs.

As the years passed, the Martin and Lewis movie romps became increasingly formulaic and Jerry began hogging more of the on-screen antics and making more of the team's creative decisions. For a spell, Dean, who much preferred to play golf and relax, allowed this takeover to happen. Then, as in a bad marriage, each man became upset with everything and anything the other did. *Hollywood or Bust*, released in late 1956, was the pair's final joint release. Martin went on to an extremely successful solo career as a film star, a TV host, and a recording artist. He died in December 1995. As for Jerry, after starring in several features (such as 1958's *The Geisha Boy*) for which he was often the producer as well, he added the duties of director and scripter for 1960's *The Bellboy*. He reached his professional peak with 1964's *The Disorderly Orderly*.

After Lewis left Paramount, the quality of his movies declined, reaching a creative nadir with 1970's *Which Way to the Front?* His long-in-the-works—and costly—*The Day the Clown Cried*, a 1972 film drama, was never distributed. Over these years, Lewis headlined TV series (including a talk show and a variety program), but could not sustain viewership ratings. In the 1950s, he had recorded albums in which he crooned nostalgic songs, but this forum dried up for him as well. In October 1982, Patti Lewis divorced Jerry. Later in the decade, media stories and book biographies alleged that the comic star had been a philanderer for years, had been a martinet with his sons, and had sustained a lengthy addiction to pain medication.

In February 1983, Lewis married dancer SanDee Pitnick, who had performed a small part in Jerry's 1980 movie, *Hardly Working*. They adopted a baby girl, Danielle, in March 1992. In recent decades, Lewis has made forays into feature films (including 1983's *The King of Comedy* and 1995's *Funny Bones*), had a Broadway success (taking over a key role in the revival of *Damn Yankees* in 1994), and made occasional TV guest appearances (including on a 1993 episode of *Mad About You* and a 2006 segment of *Law & Order: Special Victims Unit*).

When Lewis's career was on the downswing in the mid-1960s, he began hosting an annual Labor Day weekend telethon, a fund-raiser for the Muscular Dystrophy Association. Over the years, he raised an enormous amount for the charity, and the event became a tremendous forum for Jerry to reassert his forceful presence as a show business personality.

During the past decades, the star coped with, among other ailments, heart disease, prostate cancer, a severe ulcer condition, horrendous back pain, and an addiction to steroids given to him to combat one of his health problems. Not only did Lewis bounce back from each calamity, but he retained his total belief in himself. He claimed that his travails and age had helped him to mellow and be more tolerant of others. "A lady that comes over, and you're trying to have dinner, and she's not going to go away? Twenty years ago, I'd have taken her by the back of her hair and helped her to a cab. But now I give her the three or four minutes to get it done gentlemanly and diplomatically."

Madonna

(August 16, 1958–)

It's one thing to disparage an everyday person who is extremely brash, temperamental, and egocentric. However, it is quite another matter to effectively put down an in-your-face, highly strung, and self-concerned individual who has become world famous *and* a huge money-earner. After all, how can one criticize successfully a major celebrity's aggressive nature and acute self-focus when such negative character traits have not impeded her march to fame and fortune?

During her decades of superstardom, Madonna made an indelible imprint on the music scene—both in recordings and on the concert tour stage. Being calculating, selfish, and full of attitude has not prevented the "Material Girl" from achieving her musical career ambitions and remaining a favorite with the public.

The shrewd Madonna has said, "I know I'm not the greatest singer or dancer, but that doesn't interest me. I'm interested in being provocative and pushing people's buttons." Certainly she has lived up to these goals; the lyrics of several of her songs (such as "Like a Virgin") and the visual impact of her music videos and concert performances (including the controversial crucifix tableau in her 2006 world tour show) have made the confrontational performer notorious. In the process, she has garnered tremendous media coverage, all of which has increased her commercial viability in the musical field.

Madonna has noted about her megasuccess, "I am my own experiment. I am my own work of art." This broad statement ignored all those creative trends she followed and expanded upon in her career and those mentors who helped to shape her performance style. But this musician's I-did-it-all-myself attitude was, and is, part and parcel of her ego-driven nature.

In a blend of apology, rationalization, and haughtiness, Madonna also said of her diva-like reputation: "I can be arrogant sometimes, but I never mean it intentionally. I can be really snotty to people but that's not anything new really. I always acted like a star long before I was one. If people don't see my sense of humor then I come off as being expensive, but I always endear myself to people when I find their weaknesses and they acknowledge it. It's the people who try to hide everything and try to make you think they're so cool that I can't stand."

•   •   •

Madonna Louise Veronica Ciccone was born in 1958 in Bay City, Michigan, to Silvio (Tony) Ciccone and Madonna Louise Fortin Ciccone. She was the third of the couple's six children. Her father was a design engineer for Chrysler/General Motors. When the future performer was 6, her mother died of breast cancer. Thereafter, Mr. Ciccone moved with his children to Pontiac, Michigan, where, three years later, he was remarried—to the family's housekeeper. Madonna, the oldest of the three Ciccone girls, was deeply offended by the changes in the household. As a youngster she wanted to become a nun, but by junior high school, she was participating in class plays and enjoying such experiences. However, her greatest pleasure was dance and it became her new obsession. When Madonna was 14, she met the much-older Christopher Flynn, who became her guru. This gay man helped her to hone her proficiency on the dance floor. Following high school she won a dance scholarship to the University of Michigan, where she took classes in jazz dancing. Within a year or so, she quit college to focus on becoming a professional dancer.

By 1978, she was in Manhattan, living in sparse surroundings in the East Village.

Madonna and director Uli Eden on the set of 1993's Body of Evidence.

She did figure modeling and labored in a doughnut shop, among other jobs. In 1979, she made *A Certain Sacrifice*, a soft-core porn movie. (The film resurfaced in the mid-1980s, after the singer had become well known.) Then, Madonna joined the third company of the Alvin Ailey Dance Troupe, but left after a few months. Later, she encountered rock musician Dan Gilroy at the apartment of an ex-boyfriend (graffiti artist Norris Burroughs). With Dan, who became her new lover, and his brother Ed she formed the Breakfast Club, her first band. Thereafter, she quit this group to organize a new-wave rock group.

Madonna was already focused on having a solo career. In this pursuit, she became a regular at the hip rock discos, where her fascination with rap-dance music developed. She became pals with—and then the lover of—deejay Mark Kamins. It was Kamins who brought Madonna to Sire Records, which signed her to a recording contract. Her first album, *Madonna*, appeared in mid-1983. The music video to one cut ("Lucky Star") became popular on MTV. Such cable TV exposure did much to advance the savvy newcomer's career. Madonna's follow-up album, 1984's *Like a Virgin*—with its notoriously controversial title song—established the singer as a major international star.

Madonna's costarring role in the 1985 film *Desperately Seeking Susan* expanded her fan base. Also that year, she crisscrossed the United States with her highly successful concert tour. By now, the me-girl was noted for her hot temper, arrogance, and undiplomatic micromanaging. That August, she wed the volatile actor Sean Penn in Malibu, California. Their explosive union was filled

with public skirmishing with each other and Penn's scuffles with the paparazzi. She and the bad-tempered Sean ended their grueling union in September 1989. During her turbulent Penn years, Madonna continued to record, do concert tours, and build up her bank balance, which allowed her to pamper her every whim.

She was still anxious to be a big-screen notable and costarred in 1990s *Dick Tracy*. During its production, she began a much-ballyhooed affair with its director/star, Warren Beatty, who was much older than she. By the time the feature was distributed, Madonna had split from Beatty. Meanwhile, she returned to the concert stage for her lucrative *Blonde Ambition* tour. In a self-aggrandizing move, she had the trek chronicled for 1991's *Truth or Dare*. The documentary provided audiences with intriguing insights into the many dimensions of the controlling, edgy, and manipulative Madonna.

Madonna increased her notorious standing when she concocted 1992's *Sex*, a lavishly produced book filled with soft-core erotic photography (including provocative shots of herself and other female notables, as well as striking poses of her with past men friends). In spite of the blistering reviews it generated, the expensive tome made a bundle of money for Madonna.

One of Madonna's unfulfilled goals was to become a world-class film star. Having failed so often in that medium, she relentlessly pursued the lead assignment in 1996's *Evita*. She turned in an adequate performance in the screen musical but lacked the necessary acting chops to sustain a full-length characterization.

The star diverted attention from her *Evita* failings when she became a mother in October 1996. With her customary disregard for social conventions, she did not bother to marry her child's father (Carlos Leon, her personal fitness trainer). The baby girl was named Lourdes Maria Ciccone Leon, and the singer capitalized on her latest public image: aggressive single parent.

Over the years, the unbridled, unconventional Madonna had many lovers, including rap musician Vanilla Ice, eccentric basketball star Dennis Rodman, porn performer Tony Ward, and actor/writer Andy Bird. Then, in the late 1990s, she met the talented British filmmaker Guy Ritchie, who was 10 years her junior. He became the father of their son Rocco, born in August 2000. That December, the couple married in a fancy, high-society ceremony held at a medieval castle in Skibo, Scotland. The couple and their children lived in England. (Madonna had already developed a very affected British accent.)

While Madonna's ill-conceived film comedy, 2000's *The Next Best Thing*, was a flop, she did well on her latest world concert tour, which concluded in September 2001. Her next movie was 2002's *Swept Away*, directed by Ritchie. It tanked, but the humiliation did *not* make her noticeably more humble. In late 2005, she released the successful album *Confessions on a Dance Floor* and supported it with a global tour that showcased her in the "Hung Up" number in which she posed on a glittery cross. The stunt generated tons of media coverage as church authorities in various countries denounced this apparent act of irreverence.

Like many divas who have reached a certain age and acquired a fortune along the way, in recent times, Madonna has proclaimed that she wanted to be more "earth mother" and less prima donna. (It led her, in October 2006, to arrange to adopt a 13-month-old boy from the African country of Malawi.) The singing star insisted, "I'd like to be more involved in making the world a better place. I'd like to be more concerned about humanity. . . . Because people look up to me, it's my responsibility to think more about that." It's a noble ambition for the artist still known as the Material Girl.

Jayne Mansfield

(April 19, 1933–June 29, 1967)

Actors are often self-absorbed and narcissistic. Few were more self-focused than Jayne Mansfield. She was frequently dismissed as a poor man's Marilyn Monroe. However, Mansfield had as much, or more, determination to succeed in show business as her more famous rival. According to the shapely Jayne, "I didn't come to Hollywood to be the girl next door. I came to be a movie star." The sex symbol also allowed, "I will never be satisfied. Life is one constant search for betterment for me." One of Mansfield's greatest obstacles to achieving her professional goals was her ultimate inability to convince the entertainment industry to take her seriously. (Oscar winner Bette Davis sneered of this busty would-be movie queen: "Dramatic art in her opinion is knowing how to fill a sweater.") Mansfield's unyielding mania for self-promotion of any sort—no matter if it was only making a command appearance at the opening of a supermarket—quickly made her a Tinseltown joke. But the spectacularly curvaceous performer refused to acknowledge defeat. Even when her fame evaporated, she remained convinced that if she found the right new publicity gimmick, she could be back on "top" again. Unfortunately, in her tunnel-vision drive to become a major movie star, many of those in her orbit—including her husbands and children—were frequently shunted aside, sacrificed to her grand ambition.

Jayne Mansfield glowing for the cameras in 1957's Kiss Them for Me, *with Ray Walston (left) and Harry Carey Jr. (right).*

• • •

Vera Jayne Palmer was born in 1933 in Bryn Mawr, Pennsylvania, the only child of Harry Palmer, an attorney, and Vera Jeffrey Palmer, an elementary school teacher. (The family's home was in Phillipsburg, New Jersey.) When the youngster was 3, her father died of a heart attack. In 1939, mother and daughter relocated to Dallas, Texas, where Mrs. Palmer wed sales engineer Harry "Tex" Peers. During high school, Jayne, who dreamed of becoming a cinema star, fell in love with another student. She and Paul Mansfield were married secretly in January 1950. When Jayne became pregnant, her parents threw a second, public wedding. That November the Mansfields' daughter, Jayne Marie, was born. By now, Paul was enrolled at the University of Texas in Austin, while Jayne worked as a dance studio receptionist and was active at the Austin Civic Theater.

During the Korean War, Paul was called to active duty. Now on her own, Jayne went to Los Angeles. (She left Jayne Marie with the child's maternal grandmother.) Jayne studied at UCLA and entered the Miss California competition (not mentioning her marital/parental status). She was a local winner in the contest, but when her conservative husband learned of this, he made her quit the pageant. Before grudgingly returning to Texas, the ambitious young lady had a bit part in the 1950 film *Prehistoric Women.*

Back in Texas—and with her spouse still in military service—Jayne enrolled in college in Dallas, took acting classes, and appeared on a local TV show. When Paul completed his army duties in 1954, he honored his prior agreement to accompany his wife to Hollywood so she could pursue anew a screen career. Her brunette hair was now colored platinum blond. She quickly found an agent. Using the screen name Jayne Mansfield, she was cast in *Female Jungle*. (The film was not released until 1956.) Paul despised the Hollywood lifestyle and finally accepted that he and his starstruck wife had too little in common. He returned alone to Texas. Their divorce became final in January 1958.

Mansfield's press representative, James Byron, helped to turn his eager client into a recognized personality. Her statuesque figure (she claimed dimensions of 40-21-35), her unique sashaying walk, and her breathy baby talk made his task far easier with the media. On a press junket to Florida, Jayne posed in a skintight red bathing suit and arranged one of the shoulder straps to fall away on cue. The "mishap" got tremendous news coverage. Her memorable *Playboy* magazine nude spread in February 1956 confirmed Jayne's remarkable physical assets. Soon, she negotiated a modest contract at Warner Bros. studio, where she was frequently cast as a gangster's moll, as in 1955's *Hell on Frisco Bay*.

When her film deal was not renewed, Jayne accepted the lead in a 1955 Broadway sex farce called *Will Success Spoil Rock Hunter?* The risqué entry became a hit, and Mansfield vigorously maximized her promotional opportunities as "Broadway's Smartest Dumb Blonde." (She also developed into a diva at the Belasco Theater: not showing up for the performance until almost curtain time, strutting about backstage in the buff,

demanding full attention from the stagehands, and, in general, being egotistical.) During Jayne's Manhattan stay, she met Hungarian muscleman Mickey Hargitay, Mr. Universe, who was then a member of Mae West's nightclub act. Although Hargitay was known as that veteran vamp's private property, the lusty Jayne easily won him away from the far older West.

Twentieth Century-Fox hired Jayne to be one of the film lot's new threats to their troublesome blond star, Marilyn Monroe. Mansfield's studio debut was in 1956's *The Girl Can't Help It*. The satirical comedy proved amusing and led to her re-creating her *Will Success Spoil Rock Hunter?* role on screen. In 1957's *The Wayward Bus*, she turned in an effective dramatic performance, but the picture was not a success.

In January 1958, days after her split from Paul Mansfield became official, Jayne and Hargitay married. Most of those who attended the gaudy ceremony were members of the press. The couple would have three children: Miklos Jr. (born in 1958), Zoltan (born in 1960), and Mariska (born in 1964). The Hargitays' residence was a 15-room, 7-bathroom mansion on Sunset Boulevard. Jayne insisted that the white-stucco house be repainted her favorite color—pink. Because Hargitay had been a building contractor, she demanded that he personally (to save money) create a heart-shaped pool for their backyard and a heart-shaped bathtub inside. Since she had paid for the "Pink Palace," she thought it fitting that the grillwork of the property's front gate contain an entwined "J" and "M," her initials.

Obsessed with achieving greater fame in any way possible, Jayne starred in Las Vegas club shows—with Mickey included in the proceedings. By now, Twentieth Century-Fox was losing interest in Mansfield and sent her abroad to do films, often on loan to other studios. In Italy, she and Hargitay costarred in 1960's *The Loves of Hercules*. By the early 1960s, the public had become satiated with the onslaught of titillating photos of Mansfield's famous curves. In 1962, Fox, discomfited by her blatant self-promotion ploys and her increasingly wild personal life, dropped her option. Two years later, in August, the Hargitays divorced.

With no studio to guide her career, Mansfield drifted professionally. She made the tawdry sexploitation movie *Promises! Promises!* (1963) and posed nude a second time for *Playboy*. She made several minor pictures abroad, then wed 28-year-old film director Matt Cimber in September 1964. Their son, Anthony, was born in October 1965. As Jayne grew more depressed about her career future, she depended increasingly on alcohol to ease the stress. The excessive drinking gave her a bloated look. Meanwhile, she and ex-husband Hargitay battled over custody of their children.

Mansfield continued to make mediocre movies, appeared in stock productions, and wondered how to regain her fame. In July 1966, Matt Cimber and Mansfield parted company. Thereafter, Jayne become enamored with San Francisco lawyer Samuel S. Brody. The married man sacrificed his career and family to be at her beck and call as she embarked on a round of sleazy club engagements abroad. She soon was making headlines for her drunken scuffles with Brody and for being named in a divorce suit by Brody's wife. Back in California, Jayne earned more unfavorable press when Jayne Marie, her 16-year-old daughter, was placed into protective custody because Jayne and Brody purportedly were mistreating her.

In 1967, Mansfield accepted a club engagement in Biloxi, Mississippi. On the trip, Jayne was accompanied by Brody and three of her children. In the early morning of June 29, 1967, she was going by car from Biloxi to New Orleans for an interview. Her vehicle smashed into the back of a stopped tractor trailer. Jayne's driver, Brody, and Mansfield died instantly. Her children, asleep in the backseat, escaped any serious injury. Following a memorial service in Beverly Hills, Jayne's remains were shipped to Pen Argyl, Pennsylvania, for burial in the family plot.

Burt Reynolds

(February 11, 1936–)

Good ol' boy Burt Reynolds recalled, "I once went to group therapy. Everyone there blamed someone else—their mother, their father, their agent. When it got to me, I said, 'You're all full of shit. You're gonna be here forever. Look in the mirror. You are responsible for every mistake you made.'"

In his lifetime, veteran star Reynolds made more than his fair share of missteps. When Sean Connery bowed out of the lucrative James Bond film franchise in the early 1970s, the producers asked Burt to take over the coveted part. "And I said in my infinite wisdom, 'An American can't play James Bond. It just can't be done.'" The know-it-all Reynolds also turned down costarring in *Terms of Endearment*, which won the Best Picture Oscar for 1983, to do the sloppy action comedy *Cannonball Run II*. In retrospect, Reynolds said, "[Filmmaker] Jim Brooks wrote the part of the astronaut for me. Taking that role would have been a way to get all the things I wanted."

In the personal arena, Reynolds's standing as a ladies' man led him into several ego-driven stumbles over the decades. After a bad first marriage and years of being a lothario, he found great chemistry (and public endorsement) when he dated singer/talk show host Dinah Shore, who was several years older than he. However, their relationship came unglued when he persisted in seeing other women. Thereafter, he and Oscar-winner Sally Field, Burt's *Smokey and the Bandit* costar, had a long-term romance, which splintered for much the same reason. (When Reynolds belatedly tried to make amends with Field, she refused to take him back.) Then, in April 1988, the self-focused actor wed actress Loni Anderson, who had nursed him through a long health crisis. (During this marriage, the couple adopted a son, Quinton.) Later, he tossed Anderson aside when he found a new playmate (Pam Seals). In the course of the couple's high-profile, ugly divorce in March 1995, Reynolds severely

Burt Reynolds in the 1970s, when he was on the fast track to becoming a box-office magnet.

damaged his public image with his nasty, media-driven attacks on Loni.

Ironically, and in typical Reynolds fashion, Burt's vindictive tactics with Loni came back to bite him. First, Anderson won a large financial settlement in their breakup. (When Reynolds tallied up what his inappropriate actions had cost him, he conceded how "stupid" he'd been.) Years later, in 2004, by which time his relationship with Seals had ended badly, Burt got embroiled in a vicious courtroom tug-of-war with Pam. The fierce battle of wills ended in mid-2005 with an out-of-court settlement, but the bitter fracas further diminished Reynolds's once-lofty standing.

• • •

Burt Leon Reynolds Jr. was born in Lansing, Michigan, the second child (following

Nancy) of Fern and Burt Leon Reynolds Sr. His mother had been a nurse and his father was a policeman. In 1946, the family moved to Riviera, Florida, where his disciplinarian father became the town sheriff and his mother ran a small restaurant. A few years later, Mr. Reynolds moved up to becoming the sheriff of West Palm Beach. Buddy—as Burt was then called—entered the local high school. There, to surmount bigotry because he was part Native American, he became a roughhousing jock who shone on the football field. By age 14, the studly student had lost his virginity. While in high school, he got a local prom queen pregnant. (She had an abortion.)

Thanks to his athletic prowess, Reynolds was offered sports scholarships to several colleges. He chose Florida State University in Tallahassee. When he damaged his knee cartilage during a football game in the fall of 1955, his gridiron career ended. That Christmas, the wild Buddy wrecked his father's car and nearly died in the accident. After switching to Palm Beach Junior College in 1956, he became involved in theater, which led to stage work in New York City. Thereafter, Reynolds relocated to Los Angeles, where he often worked as a TV stunt man.

Universal Studios put Reynolds under contract and costarred him in the 1959 TV series *Riverboat*. Because Burt refused to toe the company line, he was dropped from the show and, later, from his studio pact. He had a recurring role on *Gunsmoke* from 1962 to 1965 but groused about his one-dimensional part. In June 1963, he married British actress Judy Carne, but their relationship was contentious, accentuated by her show business success and his career stagnation. By October 1966, the two had divorced, with her claiming he had physically abused her.

Reynolds appeared in two additional TV series and was featured in forgettable "B" films. In the early 1970s, Burt's career suddenly took off. His appearances on TV talk shows demonstrated that beneath his smug, uptight macho posturing, he had a witty, wicked sense of humor. Then, too, his budding relationship with Dinah Shore helped to counter his past chauvinistic image. His celebrity status zoomed higher in 1972, when he did a nude centerfold for *Cosmopolitan* magazine, while filmgoers were impressed by his dramatic flair in *Deliverance*.

With the release of 1977's *Smokey and the Bandit*, Burt became a top box-office attraction and remained so for several years. However, for every solid picture he made (such as 1979's *Starting Over*), he chose to star in lowbrow junk like 1981's *The Cannonball Run*. (The glib star jested, "I've become the No. 1 box-office star in the world not because of my movies—but in *spite* of them.") He found creative solace in his dinner theater and acting school based in Jupiter, Florida, and continued to divert himself with a parade of women. While making 1984's *City Heat*, he suffered a fractured jaw, which mushroomed into other health problems. The ailments sidelined him for many months. In the process, he became addicted to painkillers and had to deal with rumors that his extreme weight loss (a result of his difficulty eating) was due to AIDS. He returned to moviemaking, but the public had found new favorites.

Reynolds had a career resurgence in the

early 1990s with his hit TV sitcom, *Evening Shade*. Yet again, he proved to be difficult on the set. In the mid-1990s, besides his media circus divorce from Loni, he coped with scaling back his lifestyle after he filed for bankruptcy. Then he made yet another career comeback—this time as a character lead in 1997's *Boogie Nights*. (While making this film, the prickly Burt had differences with the film's young director, Paul Thomas Anderson, which reputedly cost Reynolds the chance to appear in the moviemaker's next film, *Magnolia*. In recent years, the still highly opinionated Reynolds remained active in films, often appearing in low-caliber entries such as 2001's *Hotel* or such direct-to-DVD entries as 2006's *Grilled*.

Over the decades, whether his career was flying high or not, Burt Reynolds remained (in)famous as a world-class womanizer. Such a status confounded several of his movie leading ladies. Dolly Parton quipped, "Burt and I are too much alike to be involved. We both wear wigs and high heels and we both have a roll around the middle." Sarah Miles snapped, "A toupee and lifts—the man's an impostor." Even the vain Reynolds, who went to great lengths to retain a "youthful" look, wryly cracked of his inflated image, "I'm not a superstud, though I'm labeled as one. The reason I get myself into these kinds of [complicated romantic] situations is because I talk too much."

Arnold Schwarzenegger

(July 30, 1947–)

Long before Arnold Schwarzenegger became a world-class bodybuilder, a giant action-movie star, and a powerful politician, he had the drive and ego to succeed in a big way. According to Schwarzenegger, "Ever since I was a child, I would say to myself, 'There must be more to life than this,' and I found that I didn't want to be like everybody else. I wanted to be different. I wanted to be part of the small percentage of people who were leaders, not the large mass of followers. I think it was because I saw that leaders use 100 percent of their potential. . . . I was always fascinated by people in control of other people." To achieve his goals over the years, Schwarzenegger put into practice his

belief that "a man can get anything he wants, provided he's willing to pay the price for it."

• • •

Arnold Alois Schwarzenegger was born in 1947 in Thal, Austria, a tiny town adjacent to Graz, the Styrian capital. Arnold was the younger of two sons of Gustav Schwarzenegger and Aurelia Jadrny Schwarzenegger (who had been married previously). His hard-drinking father was the local police commandant. In the family's very modest household, Gustav was a strong disciplinarian, often violent (especially when he was inebriated), and openly favored his older son, Meinhard (who died in 1971

Arnold Schwarzenegger, the brooding action super-star, in the late 1980s.

while driving drunk). As a boy, Arnold became fascinated with the Hercules movies (especially those starring Reg Park) and the Tarzan films (with Johnny Weissmuller) that he saw at the local cinema. The adolescent vowed that one day he would be stronger and more famous than his new-found hero, Reg Park. In high school, Arnold's soccer coach made the team do weight training to improve their prowess on the field. In short order, Arnold became obsessed with bodybuilding and pushed himself hard at the gym he attended in Graz. As time passed, he overcame some of his shyness to persuade professionals in the field to coach him.

When Schwarzenegger was 18, he entered the Austrian Army to fulfill his one-year military obligation. While in the service, he sneaked off the base to go to Stuttgart, Germany, to enter his first body-building event, the junior division of the Mr. Europe competition. He won the contest, but as punishment for going AWOL, he spent a week in the brig. After completing his army duty, he moved to Munich, Germany, where he managed a gym and continued his obsessive bodybuilding regimen, in which "pain and suffering were not obstacles you even think about." In 1966, he flew to London to enter the NABBA (National Amateur Bodybuilders Association) Mr. Universe competition. He came in second, but the next year, 20-year-old Arnold won the title. In subsequent years, he won three Mr. Universe contests, plus seven Mr. Olympia contests.

With his superb physique (22-inch arms, 28½-inch thighs, 20-inch calves, a 57-inch chest, and a 34-inch waist), the six foot two-inch Schwarzenegger was known as the "Austrian Oak." During these years, Arnold delighted in psyching out his opponents through psychological and verbal intimidation and, reportedly, sometimes cruel pranks. (He later changed this tactic of daunting his rivals to a more humorous approach.) Arnold also discovered that women flocked to him because of his looks, his reputation, and his huge self-confidence. These sexual conquests boosted his ego tremendously but made him extremely cavalier about using/discarding his dates.

Since childhood, Arnold had dreamed of coming to the United States. "I did not want anything about my life to be little. What I wanted was to be part of the big cause, the big dreamers, the big skyscrapers, the big money, the big action. Everything in the United States was so big." He arrived in the United States in 1968 to participate in a bodybuilding competition. He soon established a working relationship with Joe Weider, who published several bodybuilding magazines and had many ties to industry merchandizing and contests. Schwarzenegger settled in Los Angeles, where he collaborated on physical training articles for Weider's publications.

With another bodybuilder (Franco Columbu), Schwarzenegger started a bricklaying business; then he began a mail-order firm that sold fitness books and cassettes. He also bought an apartment building, which launched him into the real estate field. Meanwhile, largely through correspondence courses, he earned a degree in business and international economics from the University of Wisconsin in Superior.

Arnold had already begun to fulfill his dream of becoming a movie star when he appeared in 1970's *Hercules in New York* (in which his heavily accented voice was dubbed). After several supporting movie roles, he scored a big success in 1982 with the expensively mounted *Conan the Barbarian*. This led to such further hits as 1984's *The Terminator* and 1987's *Predator*. During his rise to film stardom, Schwarzenegger dated Barbara Outland, a waitress, and had a romance with Brigitte Nielsen, his costar in 1985's *Red Sonja*. However, it was TV news reporter Maria Shriver, a niece of President John F. Kennedy, whom he wed in April 1986. (The couple would have four children, born in 1989, 1991, 1993, and 1997.) Many observers were surprised that Arnold, who had regarded Republican

president Richard Nixon as a role model for achieving political success, and had campaigned for Republican president Ronald Reagan in the 1980s, should marry into such a prominent Democratic dynasty. It was another example of Schwarzenegger's adapting and taking advantage of situations.

In 1991, Schwarzenegger was at the top of his box-office form with the hugely successful *Terminator 2: Judgment Day*. He was now earning $15 million per movie, had an elaborate compound in Pacific Palisades for him and his family, owned a trendy Santa Monica restaurant, was a celebrity principal in the Planet Hollywood eatery chain, and had many other business enterprises. Said the ego-driven Arnold, "Everything I have ever done in my life has . . . stayed. I've just added to it. . . . I will add to the type of roles I will play. I will add to the kind of responsibilities I take on with my movies. But I will not change. Because when you are successful and you change, you are an idiot."

Feeling invincible, he starred in 1993's *Last Action Hero*, an enormously expensive action picture created with the conceit that any Schwarzenegger vehicle would go over big with the public, no matter how mechanical and derivative. The picture was a critical and commercial disappointment and the beginning of Arnold's descent from box-office champ to the point where his vehicles, such as 2002's *Collateral Damage*, became major flops. Briefly, he turned the tide with 2003's popular *Terminator 3: Rise of the Machines*, for which he received $25 million. However, Arnold, now in his mid-50s, knew that his action-starring days were numbered, and he changed direction.

He entered politics, a career that had interested him long before he became a naturalized American citizen in 1983 (and especially after his 1990 appointment as chairman of the President's Council on Physical Fitness and Sports under chief executive George H. W. Bush).

Thanks to Schwarzenegger's movie fame, his own impressive resources, wealthy donors, and political allies, Arnold successfully campaigned for the governorship of California during the October 2003 recall election of Governor Gray Davis (Democrat) and was sworn into office on November 17, 2003. During the next several years, the "Governator," as he was nicknamed, had a roller-coaster ride in public office, especially when his four highly promoted reform measures were defeated in a special November 2005 election. (Another 2005 setback occurred when he was forced to relinquish purported conflict-of-interest ties to Weider Publications, which was contracted to pay Schwarzenegger's company, Oak Productions, at least $1 million a year for consulting fees.) Undaunted by his political setbacks, Schwarzenegger ran for reelection in November 2006 and won.

With his tremendous self-focus, Arnold Schwarzenegger rose from humble beginnings to become a world-renowned movie star, a best-selling author, an entrepreneur, and a politician, with an estimated personal fortune of $800 million. These accomplishments make one wonder at Schwarzenegger's statement back in 1986: "People wonder how I've changed, but I haven't. I have never sold out. I am always the same, no matter where I am or who I'm with. . . . Sometimes I'm too driven, and I lose patience with people around me. I expect everyone out there to be hungry, I expect too much from people, but there is really nothing about myself I would change. I have had no big disappointments in my life. I would not want to live anyone else's life. I don't get depressed. I'm not a person who sits down and analyzes things too much. That's one of the worst things people can do."

Barbra Streisand

(April 24, 1942–)

Over her long career, Barbra Streisand has demonstrated her talent in clubs and recordings, on the Broadway stage, and in concert venues, as well as on television and in film. In the process, she won many industry awards but also acquired a number of detractors. Many of these critics have faulted her for being far too controlling, too often a penny-pincher, and much too frequently an egotistical diva.

Streisand's strong self-focus was already evident in the early years of her stardom. In 1966, she informed *Life* magazine in a mixture of chutzpah and tongue-in-cheek, "I am a bit coarse, a bit low, a bit vulgar, and a bit ignorant. I am also part princess, sophisticated, elegant, and controlled. I appeal to everyone." Over the years, others would dispute this supposed universal esteem. Omar Sharif, her costar in two films and with whom she had an affair, noted, "She's a monster. But she's a fascinating monster. I think her biggest problem is that she wants to be a woman and she wants to be beautiful and she is neither." Peter Bogdanovich, who directed the actress in 1972's *What's Up, Doc?*, described his high-maintenance star with: "She a real kvetch . . . always moaning about something or other, a really hard-to-please lady." Filmmaker Martin Ritt, who helmed Streisand's 1987 film, *Nuts*, came away from that traumatic experience believing that "she's got the balls of a Russian infantryman." He did allow, "She is not as selfish as she's made out to be. Except as a performer; then it's me-me-me-me . . . the demon diva." Actor Elliott Gould, who was Streisand's husband from 1963 to 1971, acknowledged, "My toughest job was being married to Barbra Streisand."

On the other hand, the songstress had her theory on why so many in show business have had it in for her. She told *Playboy* magazine in 1977, "It's a very male-chauvinist world. I resent it deeply." She explained, "A person who's a bitch would seem to be mean for no reason. I'm not a mean person. Maybe I'm rude without being aware of it—that's possible." She also rejected the notion that she was overly conceited: "To have ego means to believe in your own strength. And to also be open to other people's views. . . . So, yes, my ego is big, but it's also very small in some areas. My ego is responsible for my doing what I do—bad or

On her road to fame, Barbra Streisand smiled more often for her public, as in this shot from her 1966 TV special, Color Me Barbra.

good. I just don't want to be hampered by my own limitations."

• • •

Barbara Joan Streisand was born in Brooklyn, New York, in 1942. Her father, Emanuel "Manny" Streisand, was a schoolteacher (with a PhD degree from Columbia University) and also taught at a local yeshiva. Her mother, Diana (actually born Ida) Rosen Streisand, was a bookkeeper turned housewife. The couple's first child, Sheldon, was born in 1935. When Barbara was 15 months old, Mr. Streisand died. Mrs. Streisand returned to bookkeeping, but she had difficulties making ends meet. In 1950, she married real estate dealer Louis Kind. The next year the Kinds had a daughter, Rosalind (later known as Roslyn). The nonconformist, attention-seeking Barbara was constantly at odds with her family, especially her stepfather. (Her mother said later, "Barbara was a very complex child. She always saw everything depending on how it affected her. She bottled up everything inside her.")

As an adolescent, Barbara fantasized about becoming a movie star, despite her unusual features. By the time she graduated from Erasmus High School in 1959, she was determined to become a stage actress. To that end, she moved to Manhattan, but the fledgling talent had many obstacles to overcome. With her prominent nose, she lacked the conventional look demanded by most casting agents. She also possessed a heavy Brooklyn accent and had developed into a kooky free spirit who schlepped about in an odd mixture of retro clothing. In addition, she had become highly self-centered. One acquaintance from that period recalled, "She could be thoughtless toward innocent people. She could be inconsiderate. . . . But when she wanted something, it was 'Pack it, do it, move it, *now!*'"

Despite such roadblocks, by 1961 Streisand was singing at Greenwich Village bistros and appearing on Manhattan-based TV talk shows. (Already she had altered her first name to Barbra.) She made her professional stage bow that October in the off-Broadway show *Another Evening with Harry Stoones*. That revue closed after one night, but her next project, 1962's *I Can Get It for You Wholesale*, had a decent Broadway run, and she was nominated for a Tony Award. Meanwhile, she signed with

Columbia Records after a long haggle about creative control. She was now sharing a small New York apartment with *Wholesale's* leading man, Elliott Gould.

In 1963, Streisand won her first Grammy, performed at major club venues, and was singing on television variety shows. That September, Streisand and Gould married. The next year, she starred in the Broadway musical *Funny Girl*, and her special look and mannerisms captured the public's fancy. Next, she starred in TV specials, in which she was given great creative control. In December 1966, she gave birth to son Jason.

Barbra received $200,000 to play the title role in the film version of *Funny Girl*. On the sound stage she made it clear she wanted to run the show and didn't hesitate to tell veteran director William Wyler how "their" film should be shaped. Despite the flare-ups on the set, the movie was a major hit, and Streisand won an Academy Award. During the making of 1969's *Hello, Dolly!* her brazen behavior (which she excused as a desire for artistic perfection) alienated director Gene Kelly and aggravated costar Walter Matthau. (Matthau insisted, "I had no disagreements with Barbra Streisand. I was merely exasperated at her tendency to become a complete megalomaniac.") Later, ego battles between Streisand and leading man Yves Montand contributed to their lack of chemistry in 1970's *On a Clear Day You Can See Forever*. On that film, Jack Nicholson, cast as Barbra's brother, was more than unhappy when Streisand had his screen footage severely trimmed, as she did with Montand's.

Streisand had extracurricular romantic interests during her marriage to Elliott

Gould. He hated being Mr. Streisand and sought refuge in gambling and substance abuse. The battling couple divorced in July 1971. During the making of 1972's *What's Up, Doc?* she found distraction with her leading man, Ryan O'Neal. However, she struck out when she pursued Robert Redford, her costar in 1973's *The Way We Were*, which was a huge hit. In 1974, Barbra began a long-term relationship with the aggressive Jon Peters, a hairstylist/entrepreneur. Peters produced—and Streisand executive produced—1976's *A Star Is Born*. Her colead was Kris Kristofferson, who said that working with Streisand was "like sitting down to a picnic in the middle of a freeway."

Hollywood's old boys' club never reacted well to women who dared to grab power within the industry. Thus, Barbra almost met her match when she badgered and wheedled to get the 1983 musical *Yentl* made. She wore several hats on this long-brewing project: producer, director, coscenarist, and star. Her leading man was actor/singer Mandy Patinkin, who found that he had no songs in the film. By the time Streisand finished *Yentl*, she and Jon Peters were no longer together.

It was four years before Streisand returned to the screen, in 1987's *Nuts*. Off camera the star garnered many tabloid headlines with her relationship with studly actor Don Johnson. To her great mortification, he ditched her to remarry his ex-wife, actress Melanie Griffith. Barbra's ex-boyfriend Jon Peters, now in charge of a film studio, agreed to Streisand's making 1991's *The Prince of Tides*, which she directed, as well as costarred in with Nick Nolte. During that year, Barbara, nearing 50, began dating tennis champ Andre Agassi (he was three years younger than her son, Jason). When that strange bond evaporated, Streisand, a fervent Democrat, exhibited keen support for Bill Clinton in his 1992 bid for the United States presidency.

Streisand had a hit with her 1993 *Back to Broadway* album, and at the end of the year returned to the concert stage after a 22-year hiatus. She also starred in and directed 1996's *The Mirror Has Two Faces*, a mediocre film more famous for Streisand's on-set contretemps with several members of her cast and crew than its success at the box office. In July 1998, she and actor James Brolin, a year her senior, married in a lavish ceremony at her Malibu, California, compound that gave the bride ample opportunities to be temperamental.

Barbra embarked on a "farewell" tour in 2000, which added an estimated $30 million to her impressive net worth. She made 2004's *Meet the Fockers*, and the rather lame comedy was a major commercial hit. Her 2005 album, *Guilty Pleasures*, was also a substantial success. Despite protestations that she wanted to retire, Streisand dieted off much of her excess weight to embark on a second "farewell" tour in the fall of 2006.

Back in 1963, rising songbird Barbra Streisand was a guest on the TV variety series hosted by Judy Garland, the veteran singing star. During their on-camera chit-chat, Streisand said "jokingly" to Garland (who had a major reputation for being difficult both in and out of the limelight), "You're so great I've been hating you for years. In fact, it's my ambition to be great enough to be hated by as many singers as you." In the coming years, and in many ways, Streisand's wish came true.

Mae West

(August 17, 1892–November 22, 1980)

In 1970, Mae West made *Myra Breckinridge*. It was her first feature film since 1943. The icon—then in her 70s—explained in her trademark languorous, nasal drawl, "It's a return, not a comeback. I've never really been away, just busy." And she had been, with books, plays, club acts, recordings, and occasional radio and TV appearances.

What made West, the empress of innuendo, so unique in the annals of popular culture was her delicious and daring approach to the subject of sex. Of key importance to Mae's success was the element of burlesque lurking behind her racy witticisms on the topic, such as "It's not the man in your life that counts. It's the life in your man" and "Good girls go to heaven. Bad girls go everywhere else."

West had a captivating way of delivering her saucy material. She explained, "It isn't what I do, but how I do it. It isn't what I say, but how I say it, and how I look when I do it and say it." The roll of her saucer-size eyes, her inimitable sashaying walk (which sprang from the five-foot-one-inch talent walking on 10-inch-high wedgie shoes to give her stature), the conceited manner in which she patted her blond curls (often wigs), all contributed to the illusion of an unusual sex goddess (not young, not thin, not conventionally pretty). What made West's performances so beguiling was the intensity with which she wholeheartedly believed in her public persona.

The offstage West was a bright and pleasant person and a shrewd businesswoman (who owned a great deal of Los Angeles real estate). But the primary focus of her lengthy life was the on-stage Mae, her all-consuming alter ego (whom she always referred to in the third person). To maintain the Mae West illusion over so many decades, the narcissistic entertainer had a strict regimen of eating healthfully, avoiding alcohol and tobacco, taking high colonic enemas, and doing special exercises. ("I massage my breasts . . . 'cos the muscle under the arm doin' the massagin' holds the bust up an' keeps the breasts firm.") Such sacrifices hardly fazed her. After all, she was doing what she knew her fans expected of her—coddling one of the great wonders of the world.

• • •

Mary Jane West was born in 1892 (some sources list 1893) in Brooklyn, New York, the first of three children (later there would be Mildred [Beverly] and John Patrick II) of John Patrick West, a prizefighter, and German immigrant Matilda Delker Doelger West, a corset designer. From an early age, Mae—as she was known—was far more intrigued with show business than with classroom lessons. At 6, she made her stage bow in a Brooklyn theater, offering a song and dance on amateur night. Later, she performed with a local stock troupe and then became a strong woman in a Coney Island acrobatic act. By age 15, she was touring in vaudeville.

When West was around 13, she lost her virginity to her 21-year-old music teacher. Thereafter, she bragged, she was never "without a man for more than a week." (Over the years, her lovers included men from many professions, but she had a weakness for boxers, musclemen, and well-built hoodlums.) In April 1911, she married jazz singer Frank Wallace in Milwaukee, Wisconsin. Months later, West thought better about matrimony (she really had no interest in the distractions of domesticity or motherhood) and left him. However, the couple did not officially file for divorce until July 1942. She never remarried.

Mae made her Broadway debut in 1911, and quickly made her mark as a forward-thinking, risqué entertainer. In 1920, she tested for the lead opposite boxer Jack Dempsey in a silent serial (*Daredevil Jack*). Although she did not win the part, she and the pugilist had a brief fling. West shocked Broadway when she headlined 1926's *Sex*, a titillating play she had written with the help of others. Morality groups persuaded law enforcers to close down the production and to arrest its "lascivious" star. Mae was sentenced to 10 days in jail and a $500 fine. Less infamous but more commercial was her *Diamond Lil*, a 1928 Broadway play dealing with a highly charged gold digger.

Onetime underworld thug George Raft had become a movie notable in the early 1930s. He suggested Mae, with whom he'd had a sizzling romance, for 1932's *Night After Night*. Although she only had a featured role in this Paramount film, her zesty

wisecracking was the picture's best attraction. Audiences were intrigued by this middle-aged blonde (she was nearly 40 at the time) with the hourglass figure as she wiggled through the story line, halting long enough to punctuate her double entendres with attention-grabbing "aahs." Thrilled studio big shots offered West over $100,000, top billing, and other perks to star in a vehicle for them. The entry, 1933's *She Done Him Wrong*, was based on her play *Diamond Lil* and was a box-office bonanza.

West starred in and collaborated on much of the tangy screenplay for 1933's *I'm No Angel*. She received a whopping $200,000 for her contributions. However, by 1934's *Belle of the Nineties*, the controversial star was the target of powerful morality groups, including the Catholic Legion of Decency. As a result, Mae was forced to dilute her movie characterizations and plot lines.

When the tame *Every Day's a Holiday* was released in 1938, it seemed that West had exhausted her box-office welcome. However, two years later, she returned to moviemaking, teamed at Universal Pictures with another iconoclastic talent, W. C. Fields. The result was the enjoyable *My Little Chickadee*. She had far less success with 1943's *The Heat's On*, a Columbia Pictures offering.

If Hollywood didn't require Mae's services, Broadway did. She starred in 1944's *Catherine Was Great*, her take on the randy Russian empress. She revived *Diamond Lil* on the New York stage in 1949. During its popular run, she generated much media coverage from her off-stage liaison with the much younger Steve Cochran, one of the production's leading men. In 1954, the

The one-of-a-kind Mae West, promoting her night-club act in the mid-1950s.

veteran trouper debuted her club act in Las Vegas; her chorus line consisted of nine chiseled musclemen. Among the beefcake was 28-year-old Mickey Hargitay, whom West considered her private property. When the show played Manhattan, Mickey came under the spell of shapely film actress Jayne Mansfield, who was 40 years Mae's junior. The two women, both experts at self-promotion, publicly feuded over the hunky Hargitay. The clash concluded with the Hungarian abandoning West's act to be with Mansfield. Although the tiff had generated terrific hype, the vain West was not one to quickly pardon an adversary— especially a young blond one.

West toured with her play *Sextette* in mid-1961. Her leading man was Jack LaRue, a former lover who had been in Mae's 1928 production of *Diamond Lil*. LaRue was not the only admirer to orbit around West's limelight for decades. Paul Novak, a muscleman member of her club act in the 1950s, became her loyal companion for the last 27 years of her life. He was about half her age but totally devoted to the myth of Mae.

West received many film offers over the decades before she agreed to make 1970's *Myra Breckinridge*. Initially, the aged celebrity was convinced that the studio wanted her to play the young female lead. However, for a fee of $350,000 and only 10 days of work, she agreed to strut her stuff as a man-hungry Hollywood talent agent.

Thereafter, it was eight years before Mae made another picture. This time it was a screen version of *Sextette*, and it proved to be her cinema finale. In July 1980, West suffered a severe stroke. She died that November, survived by her sister, with whom Mae had long quarreled.

In reviewing her extraordinarily successful career, West noted, "I freely chose the kind of life I led because I was convinced that a woman has as much right as a man to live the way she does if she does no actual harm to society." The frank lady also admitted, "I never loved another person the way I loved myself."

PART 3

So Much Neurosis

Woody Allen

(December 1, 1935–)

As a stand-up comedian, actor, and film-maker, major fussbudget Woody Allen craftily blurred the lines between his professional and private personas. It was often hard to distinguish where the real-life neurotic Allen left off and the phobic, nerdy public Woody took over.

Many of Allen's memorable witticisms reflected his deepest concerns in life. Even in childhood, the bespectacled worrywart was overly concerned with his mortality. In adulthood, Woody quipped, "I'm not afraid of dying. I just don't want to be there when it happens." His extreme dread of death turned him into a major hypochondriac. Over the years, he established doctor-patient relationships with an array of medical specialists to cover almost every part of his anatomy. The comedian was noted for carrying a silver pillbox in his pocket that contained emergency fix-its (including Donnazyme, Librium, Zantac, and Excedrin). It reassured him that he was prepared for most any physical or emotional crisis that arose, until he could scurry to his favorite specialist.

For a hypochondriac and a neatnik, Allen had strange habits regarding personal hygiene. "Bathing is snobbish," he said. "Bathing isn't good for you. It washes off the natural juices that keep you young. . . . I douse myself with talcum and liberal helpings of spice. I break down about every third day and have a shower." When the eccentric Woody did shower, he had partic-

ular rules. The shower's floor drain must *not* be in the center, but to one side, because when he set down his special shower mat before commencing his cleansing, he didn't want soiled water washing back over his feet. He also refused to use communal showers at gyms because he was sensitive about his slight physique.

Allen made a specialty of portraying middle-class Jewish intellectual schlemiels and insisted, "My one regret in life is that I am not someone else." Yet when interviewed by the media, he did his best to promote himself as the living counterpart to his show business alter ego. In reality, he was not anyone's version of a disorganized New York everyman. He actually lived in great luxury on Manhattan's East Side, consumed fine cuisine and wines, rode in a chauffeur-driven limousine, and was extremely methodical about charting his daily activities in order to be highly productive.

The celluloid Allen was a man grappling with life's bigger issues and trying to score with the ladies. He might not succeed in these goals, but he found some delight in merely staying in the game. The off-camera Woody was a victim of anhedonia (a condition in which one suffers the absence of pleasure from the performance of acts that would normally be pleasurable). He reasoned, "I think there is too much wrong with the world to ever get too relaxed and happy." Eventually, his overriding pessimism (and neuroticism) led him to seek counseling.

Over the decades, the celebrated director spent thousands of hours—and dollars—in psychoanalysis. While it assisted him in better understanding his emotional problems, it did *not* help him (as therapy might have) to deal with and/or overcome any of his many stumbling blocks to living a "normal" life.

Allen claimed he knew a woman was right for him when she rejected him. Long before it became public knowledge, he was drawn to young females. They had the vitality he found missing in his own life, and also, being more adoring than sophisticated, they likely would not challenge his set lifestyle. Yet even these relationships usually ended with Woody becoming bored with his untutored companion or her awakening to what a mature adult man should be and, upon finding Woody wanting in these characteristics, leaving him.

• • •

Allen Stewart Konigsberg was born in the Bronx, New York, in 1935, the first child of Martin and Nettie Cherry Konigsberg, both second-generation Jewish immigrants. (Another child, Letty, was born in 1944.) Based in Brooklyn, the family scraped to survive the Great Depression. Martin switched from one bleak job to another, while Nettie, the disciplinarian, toiled as a bookkeeper. The family moved frequently, and sometimes the boy lived with his grandparents. This nomadic existence, plus his volatile mother's inability to show him much love, made the child withdrawn, insecure, and morose. As a youngster, the puny Allen's major interests were comic books, the cinema, and the streets of Manhattan.

The intelligent but naive youngster was

Woody Allen poses with China Lee to promote his feature film, 1966's What's Up, Tiger Lily?

not fond of school. Away from the classroom he amused himself by learning magic tricks, going to movies, and watching (but not participating in), sports. As a teenager, he learned to play the clarinet and did feats of magic for audiences. He also aspired to become a comedian. By age 17, he had come up with his show business name of Woody Allen and was providing his own jokes to New York newspaper columnists. That same year he had his first gig as a stand-up comic. Following high school, he attended—then quit—first New York

University (in its cinema studies program) and then City College of New York.

In 1955, Woody moved to Los Angeles to write for TV's *The Colgate Variety Hour.* The next year, in March, he married his Brooklyn-born girlfriend, Harlene Rosen. Allen soon gained recognition as both a TV comedy writer and a stand-up comic. Later, he both scripted and appeared in the 1965 film *What's New, Pussycat?* Meanwhile, Woody and Harlene divorced in 1961. By then he was already dating actress Louise Lasser, whom he wed in February 1966.

In 1969, the multitalented Woody enjoyed a Broadway success (*Play It Again, Sam*) and wrote, directed, and starred in the film comedy *Take the Money and Run.* It was also in that year that he divorced Lasser. (Subsequently, she suffered a nervous breakdown, and to make amends, he cast her in his 1971 film, *Bananas.*) Both Allen and Diane Keaton—with whom he was engaged in a long-term affair—reprised their stage roles in the 1972 movie adaptation of *Play It Again, Sam.* By the time they costarred in 1979's *Manhattan,* the duo had parted ways but remained friends.

In November 1979, 46-year-old Woody met Mia Farrow. He was fascinated with the 34-year-old star, even though they were opposites in many ways: she was Catholic, he was Jewish; she adored country life, he thrived on the bustle of the city; she loved children (and had several, born or adopted during her second marriage, to composer/pianist André Previn), Woody had little patience for kids; she did not mind living in chaos or being impetuous; he required order and was not spontaneous. What they shared in common was that both were *not*

what they seemed. Just as Allen differed from his public image, so Farrow was not the perpetual, vulnerable flower child that the world envisioned her to be. In reality, she was motivated to grab all that life had to offer.

The two mismatched individuals emerged in 1980 as a celebrated kooky pair and soon became a film team, with her appearing in 13 of Allen's features (including 1992's *Husbands and Wives*). Then, in January 1992, everything changed. Farrow discovered that Allen—who still had not married her—was having an affair with one of her adopted children: Soon-Yi Previn, a South Korean teenager. A very public war developed between Woody and Mia. Allen sued for custody of their biological son, Satchel, and the two children who had been adopted by the couple. Meanwhile, Farrow charged her ex-lover with having sexually molested Dylan, their young adopted daughter. Eventually, it was concluded that Dylan had not been abused. As for Allen's cause of action, he lost his custody case and was allowed only brief, supervised visits with Satchel (which soon stopped happening).

As a result of all the nasty publicity over the breakup, Woody lost favor with many moviegoers, although he continued to turn out his annual movies. (His most commercially successful film in recent years was 2005's *Match Point.*) In December 1997, he married 27-year-old Soon-Yi, with whom he later adopted two infant Asian girls. To accommodate his expanding family, Allen sold his East Side penthouse and relocated to a five-story townhouse on East 92nd Street.

One might have thought that, at least, the filmmaking process had provided Allen with some contentment throughout the years. However, not so for the famous neurotic. The always anxious Woody observed that it remained difficult for him to mingle with an assemblage of people he often scarcely knew. He noted, "That's the worst problem of movie direction for me, the fact that I loathe group activity."

Jean Arthur

(October 17, 1900–June 19, 1991)

When *Los Angeles Times* film critic Charles Champlin wrote a tribute to the late Jean Arthur, he enthused about her curious way of talking. "That voice . . . was an enrapturing, split-level croak that somehow made funny lines sound wittier, love lines more deeply romantic and hard lines more urgent and meaningful." He also cited her distinctive cinema image: "She was nothing so banal as the girl next door, which always hints of a placid demureness, golden and empty. This was a woman of spirit, smart, free, loyal, resilient, loving, not quite tomboyish."

Veteran actor Roddy McDowall, one of Arthur's friends, said of this unique actress with a piquant charm: "She was an original—I keep coming back to that word—and the emotions that she exhibited made one feel, even when she was functioning at her best, that she wouldn't be able to function the next day because she was this strange individual. . . . And I'm sure that as a young girl she was made enormous fun of and was made to feel like a freak."

Once Arthur gained movie stardom in the mid-1930s, she proved to be a major handful for her studio bosses, directors, and coplayers, and especially for the publicity department. She abhorred being interviewed by reporters ("My personal life is my own business," she said repeatedly) and did anything possible to avoid dealing with the press. She panicked when fans sought her autograph and did her best to avoid them. Making an appearance at any social function was highly stressful for her. (She allowed, "I can't seem to be able to do the things grown-up people do.")

In an age where most film performers accepted being harnessed to long-term moviemaking contracts, Arthur remained rebellious of the studio system. She so despised Harry Cohn, her Columbia Pictures studio boss for over a decade, that she fantasized about ways to have him murdered. Arthur was extremely picky about her acting roles. The fact that she finally said yes to doing a picture did not preclude her vetoing the assignment at the last minute. On the sound stage she was often frosty to coplayers. Actually, it was torture for the actress to even walk onto the set most days. Her conflicting emotions about a project and/or her performance usually caused her to rush to her dressing room immediately after a sequence was filmed. There, she often threw up.

Despite Arthur's persistent oddball behavior, she was a wonderfully gifted performer who excelled in a variety of movie genres. But why, many industry workers wondered over the decades, did she have to be so damn difficult?

• • •

She was born Gladys Georgianna Greene in Plattsburgh, New York, in 1900, the fourth and last child of Hubert Greene, a photographer and painter, and Hannah Nelson Greene. Her three brothers were several years older than Gladys, and she

Jean Arthur, romantically frisky on camera with William Powell in 1936's The Ex-Mrs. Bradford, *was notoriously press shy and eccentric in real life.*

developed an inferiority complex from being bossed by the four men in the strait-laced household. The family moved often, and it was difficult for her to build friendships. As a result, she withdrew into herself. She also developed a superiority complex as a defense mechanism. Frequently during her childhood, her father vanished, only to return home months later. Her mother supported the family by operating a boarding-house in Portland, Maine.

By the mid-1910s, Gladys and her parents were living in New York City. When her dad disappeared yet again, Gladys quit high school and became a stenographer. Next, she began a side career as a model. In mid-1923, she signed to a contract with Fox Films. She and her mother moved to Los Angeles. (It was at this time that she became known as Jean Arthur.)

Arthur was cast as the lead in her first picture (1923's *The Temple of Venus*) but was fired for being too amateurish. This humiliating start to her movie career marked her for life. A few months later, the studio dropped Arthur from its roster. She then made several pictures (mostly Westerns) for independent companies. This grueling apprenticeship period left its marks. "Oh, I'm hard-boiled now. I don't expect anything."

Arthur joined Paramount Pictures in 1928. During that same year, she wed photographer Julian Ancker. However, the marriage was annulled after only one day and the bride returned to filmmaking.

Jean's talking picture debut was in 1929's *The Canary Murder Case.* Already the fan publications were labeling Arthur peculiar, citing that she called herself "a negative personality" who hated the Hollywood social scene. She found a mentor in studio executive David O. Selznick, but when she refused to commit to their romance, he left her to marry someone else. In 1931, Arthur was let go by Paramount. She went to New York and did stage work. There, in June 1932, she married Frank Ross Jr. He was a vocalist turned actor whom she knew from her Paramount days and was four years her junior. By 1934, she was back in California working under a five-year contract with Columbia Pictures.

Now spunkier on camera, Arthur did well in 1935's *The Whole Town's Talking*. Next, Frank Capra, Columbia's top-ranking director, matched her with Gary Cooper in 1936's *Mr. Deeds Goes to Town*. The hit picture made her a genuine star, and led to such successful vehicles as 1938's *You Can't Take It With You*, 1939's *Mr. Smith Goes to Washington*, and 1943's *The More the Merrier* (for which she was Oscar-nominated). By now, Jean was well known in Hollywood for her antisocial ways, and many thought her somewhat "cuckoo." The press had given up on her being cooperative for interviews, and this meant that moviegoers rarely got to read about the off-camera Jean Arthur. None of this bothered the quirky star, whose rule of thumb was "You have one life, you do what you want to do."

Arthur's tumultuous tenure at Columbia —full of suspensions—ended with 1944's *The Impatient Years*. Reputedly, on the final day of shooting that picture, she ran about the studio lot gleefully shouting, "I'm free! I'm free!" Next, she contracted to star in the Broadway-bound comedy *Born Yesterday*. However, during tryouts she went into an emotional panic (supposedly heightened by anxiety over an affair she was having with a married Chicago doctor) and quit the show. Subsequently, she turned down several film offers. Instead, she enrolled at Stephens College in Columbia, Missouri. Her educational career lasted for several weeks, then she quit to make the 1948 movie *A Foreign Affair*.

By 1949, Arthur was in psychoanalysis, and that March she divorced Frank Ross. Their marriage had been largely in name only for some time. (Over the years, there was gossip that Arthur was a lesbian, rumors sparked by her long-lasting friendship with singer/actress Mary Martin.) In 1950, Jean had a big success on Broadway playing Peter Pan. In 1953, she was lured back to the screen for *Shane*. The Western proved to be her big-screen finale. In 1966, she starred in a short-lasting TV sitcom, *The Jean Arthur Show*.

Her last decades were spent largely in seclusion in upstate California, where her favorite companions were her pets. Occasionally, she attempted to return to stage acting. However, as with 1975's *First Monday in October*, she would quit the project during its pre-Broadway tryout. Arthur died of a heart attack in 1991. In her last years, whenever the media sought to interview Jean, her retort was consistently, "Quite frankly, I'd rather have my throat slit."

Why did this most private of persons venture into a career of public performance? Her answer: "I guess I became an actress because I didn't want to be myself."

Kim Basinger

(December 8, 1953–)

Even in Kim Basinger's early screen work (such as 1981's *Hard Country* and 1984's *The Natural*), there was something vaguely unsettling about this five-foot-seven-and-a-half beauty with the large blue-gray eyes and long blond hair. She exhibited a perpetual wariness that seemed more the result of far-reaching timidity than streetwise cautiousness. By 1997's *L.A. Confidential*, for which she won a Best Supporting Actress Oscar, she was entering middle age, and a tense quality now overlay her still striking countenance. Put into the context of her complex personal life, this tenseness indicated that her show business success really had not allayed the phobias and quirks that had developed in her youth.

• • •

She was born Kimila Ann Basinger in 1953 in Athens, Georgia, the third of five children of Donald Basinger, a loan company manager, and Ann Cordell Basinger, a one-time model. Her father had been a big-band musician in Chicago before being side-tracked by World War II military service, while her mother had performed in aquatic ballets with cinema star Esther Williams. As a child, Kim was so unusually shy that it was feared she might be autistic, but she wasn't. Part of her plight was a strong emotional reaction to her parents' continuous squabbling and the damaging effects of her dad's constant criticism. ("I just couldn't please him enough. He never complimented me.

Ever. And I saw a lot of silence. Children always read into silence something terrible.") She recalled being an extreme loner: "I kept to myself and observed. I was very, very shy, painfully so, and I had a lot of trouble in school."

By high school, she had somewhat outgrown her extreme reserve. She made herself audition for the cheerleading squad and was accepted. At age 16, the stunning girl was competing in local beauty contests. Eventually, she was spotted by Eileen Ford, who ran a top modeling agency in New York City.

Initially, Kim declined Ford's offer of a contract. Instead, she enrolled at the University of Georgia. However, months later she quit college and moved to New York to be a fashion model. From the start, she loathed the work ("It was very hard to go from one booking to another and always have to deal with the way I looked. I couldn't stand it. I felt myself choking"). Nevertheless, it was a means of making a name for herself, and, she hoped, it would pave the way to a film career. Even receiving $1,000 a day did not make Basinger like modeling any better. She had little regard for her income or how she used it. She argued continuously with Ford about the modeling gigs offered her. To relieve her frustration, she took acting workshops and sang at open mike night at Greenwich Village cafés.

In 1976, Basinger finally quit modeling and relocated to Los Angeles, joined by her current boyfriend, model/actor Dale Robinette. Her good looks won her small acting assignments on TV series. By early 1977, she had the colead of a short-lasting cop show, and in 1978 she played the title role in the TV movie *Katie: Portrait of a Centerfold.*

While making her feature film debut in *Hard Country*, she met makeup artist Ron Britton. He was nearly 15 years her senior. The status-conscious Kim convinced her new lover to change his name (which he did briefly) to presumably sound less ethnic and quit his career (which he did frequently) so Basinger would not be viewed as being tied to someone beneath her rising status. They married in October 1980 and he became, in effect, her business manager. Her career leaped forward when she played a Bond girl in 1983's *Never Say Never Again.* Basinger received laudatory reviews for her "flash-dance physicality and golden-eagle elegance." She earned more attention that year from her nude layout in *Playboy* magazine.

Basinger loathed portraying a sexual slave in the tawdry *9½ Weeks.* (While making this 1986 picture, she wondered if the cast "weren't all sick to do this," adding, "but in the end I faced my own fear and came through it.") Although reviewers roasted the soft-core movie, it was a moneymaker and generated substantial industry attention for her. Basinger now commanded $1 million per film.

Previously, Kim had been linked off the set with several of her leading men. However, during the making of 1989's *Batman* she became caught up with its producer, Jon Peters. This ended her long-disintegrating marriage to Ron Britton, and they divorced in December 1988. In the set-

Bruce Willis and Kim Basinger share an uncomfortable moment in 1987's Blind Date.

tlement, she provided him with over $8,000 monthly alimony and made mortgage payments on their San Fernando Valley home, where he still lived.

There was talk that once Kim was single again, she might marry Phil Walsh, her Aussie personal fitness trainer. However, that relationship sputtered out. Thereafter, she dated singer/musician Prince (who had created songs for *Batman*). He was five years her junior and five inches shorter than she. Kim relocated with Prince to Minneapolis (his hometown). During her Midwestern stay she recorded an album but later shelved the results as being unworthy of release. After she and Prince split up, she was replaced as his colead in the 1990 film *Graffiti Bridge.*

Back in Hollywood, she negotiated a $2.5 million fee for doing 1991's *The Marrying Man.* During the screen comedy's bumpy shoot, she had a passionate romance with costar Alec Baldwin. The two appeared to bring out the worst in each other. Their lateness on the set, temper tantrums, unreasonable demands, and heated disputes with the film's producers and studio bosses made them the focus of negative industry talk. To make matters worse, *The Marrying Man* was an embarrassing misfire.

In the next few years, much of Basinger's time was devoted to litigation concerning her refusal to honor an alleged oral agreement to star in the movie *Boxing Helena*. The lawsuit ended with a $9 million judgment against her, which was later reduced. She was forced to declare bankruptcy and to end her participation in an investment group that planned to renovate and commercialize Braselton, Georgia. Alec Baldwin stuck loyally by her through these ordeals—even assisting her financially—and the pair married in August 1993. The newlyweds teamed for 1994's *The Getaway*, which failed to take off at the box office. In October 1995, Basinger gave birth to their daughter, Ireland. When Baldwin escorted his wife and child home from the hospital, he got into an explosive tussle with a member of the paparazzi stationed in front of their home, leading to another courtroom episode for the Baldwins.

After earning her Academy Award for *L.A. Confidential*, Kim was away from pictures until 2000's *I Dreamed of Africa*, a less than stellar offering. This was followed by such movies as 2002's *8 Mile*. In the interim, Basinger's turbulent union to Baldwin had crumpled. He wanted to reside on the East Coast and enter the political field, while she wished to remain in Los Angeles. Because of her ongoing agoraphobia (which sometimes kept her secluded at home for months at a stretch), she quaked at the thought of becoming a politician's spouse. Basinger filed for divorce in January 2001, with the split becoming final in February 2002. Kim and Alec continued to be tabloid fodder as they fought continuously (she passive-aggressively; he with oversized outbursts) for control over their daughter.

Kim devoted so much effort to her nasty tug-of-war with Baldwin that her career took a backseat, with only occasional acting roles, such as in 2004's *Cellular* and the 2006 TV movie *The Mermaid Chair*. One of her remaining unfulfilled professional goals is to perform on Broadway: "I have to tackle that because it's a fear of mine. . . . I have a tendency to go toward anything I fear."

Marlon Brando

(April 3, 1924–July 1, 2004)

Between costarring in 1951's *A Streetcar Named Desire* and playing the lead in 1957's *Sayonara*, Marlon Brando was nominated five times for a Best Actor Academy Award, and won an Oscar for 1954's *On the Waterfront*. However, the mighty

Brando—who along with Montgomery Clift and James Dean modernized the style of Hollywood film acting—quickly grew disenchanted with his craft. This prompted Brando, who had also helped to revolutionize Broadway stage acting in the late 1940s, to complain, "Acting is an empty and useless profession" and "Acting is the expression of a neurotic impulse. It's a bum's life. Quitting acting is a sign of maturity."

By the time Brando began filmmaking in 1950, he had already earned a reputation for being unorthodox, rebellious, pigheaded, and exasperating. Because of his perplexing mix of audacity, modesty, and exhibitionism, few people knew when Marlon was being serious and just how much of his "pose" was calculated to gain attention. One time he asked rhetorically, "Would people applaud me if I were a good plumber?" On another occasion he scoffed, "I don't want to spread the peanut butter of my personality on the moldy bread of the commercial press."

The moody Brando seemed to find great personal amusement in shocking the world, but professed with apparent seriousness, "I don't know what people expect when they meet me. They seem to be afraid that I'm going to piss in the potted palm and slap them on the ass." He thrived on pushing the entertainment industry establishment to its limits with his demands and antics, but he couldn't easily accept that studio executives had had enough of his costly excesses and aberrant behavior. The quirky talent also rebelled against the usual demands that a show business celebrity be accessible to the media and to his public. Throughout his stardom years, Brando insisted on his privacy—even going to the length of escaping the limelight by building a retreat on a Tahitian atoll. He proclaimed, "I'm not going to place myself at the feet of the American public and invite them into my soul. My soul is a private place."

Over the years, the virile Marlon jumped into intense but brief romantic encounters (with both women and, occasionally, men) but never found lasting love in any of his relationships. As for close companions in his adult life, two of his stronger rapports were with his pet raccoon and with his longtime pal, actor Wally Cox. When Brando wanted to let off steam in his younger adult years, he used to bang away on bongo drums, which also served the purpose of making him the center of attention. Marlon often made pronouncements and insisted upon particular likes and dislikes, only to change his mind and say or do the opposite. As one assistant said of Brando, "The only thing he's consistent about is his inconsistencies."

In retrospect, it did not seem so out of character that the supremely idiosyncratic, self-destructive Marlon Brando, once a hunk of a man, should end up a grotesque caricature of himself, weighing 400 pounds.

• • •

Marlon Brando Jr. was born in Omaha, Nebraska, in 1924, the third and last child (sister Jocelyn became a professional actress) and only son of Marlon Brando Sr. and Dorothy Pennebaker Brando. His father manufactured chemical feeds and

Jack Nicholson (left) and Marlon Brando costar in 1976's The Missouri Breaks. *By now the increasingly oddball Brando had outgrown his earlier image as a Hollywood hunk.*

insecticides, while his mother was an actress who, for a time, worked with the Omaha Community Playhouse and was a member of its board of directors. The callous Mr. Brando was a philanderer with a penchant for drinking, and Mrs. Brando was an alcoholic, which overshadowed her artistic talents, good intentions, and decorum. Although the boy loathed his cold-hearted father and pitied/despised his pathetic mother, he hated being ignored by them. Their neglect produced a raging anger within Marlon and caused him to shield himself against life and people. The headstrong youth (known to many as Bud) was a difficult, mischievous child who favored athletics over academics. He was later shipped to a military academy, where he quickly gained a reputation as an oddball (he protested that bathing would

destroy the body's natural oils) and an exhibitionist (for nonchalantly parading nude along the dorm corridors). He was expelled only weeks before graduation because of his annoying pranks.

After deciding against becoming a Protestant minister, Brando, who had been bypassed for World War II military service because of a bad knee (or, according to some sources, by playacting at being psychotic), moved to New York City. There he took acting classes at the New School. Marlon made his Broadway bow in 1944's *I Remember Mama*. However, it was as the slovenly, complex Stanley Kowalski in 1947's *A Streetcar Named Desire* that the "Method" performer was applauded as the new giant of the American theater. He made his film debut in 1950's *The Men*, and reached a career peak with his iconic performance in 1954's *On the Waterfront*. Then, after his run of superior screen assignments, he trapped himself into many ill-advised projects, such as 1959's *The Fugitive Kind*. By the early 1960s, the unpredictable Brando was becoming increasingly unapproachable, problematic, and overweight. The icon often fled to his Tahitian island retreat of Tetiaroa, returning to moviemaking only when he needed to refill his bank accounts.

Brando had been a womanizer during his 1940s years in Manhattan, and he continued this practice in 1950s Hollywood. He went out with Marilyn Monroe briefly, but he was far more attracted to Puerto Rican actress Rita Moreno. They had a powerful but difficult 12-year relationship that included her teaming with him on the 1968 film *The Night of the Following Day*. (His unfaithfulness drove her to attempt suicide in 1961.) While still seeing Moreno, Brando also dated Mexican actress Katy Jurado. Their affair was relatively brief.

The fiery Anna Kashfi was 30 when she met Brando. The exotic actress, who made her first movie in 1956, claimed she was from India. In reality, she was Joan O'Callaghan from Cardiff, Wales. She and Marlon wed in October 1957. The next June, their son, Christian, was born. They divorced in April 1959 but battled for years over custody of their child.

Marlon had first encountered Mexican actress Movita Castenada in 1951, and she turned up the next year as an extra in his film *Viva Zapata!* She was about eight years older than the star and far more worldly than most of Brando's other girlfriends. Their romance was rocked by his promiscuity. Nevertheless, in June 1960, they wed. Their son, Miko, was born in February 1961 and their daughter, Rebecca, arrived in September 1967. That same year the couple's marriage was annulled because her prior marriage had not been legally ended before she wed Marlon. Meanwhile, there was Tarita Teriipaia, a former waitress turned actress whom Brando had cast in his 1962 epic, *Mutiny on the Bounty*. He and his Tahitian mistress had two children together, daughter Tarita Cheyenne (who committed suicide in 1995) and son Tehotu. The bond between Marlon and Tarita endured. Late in life, Brando had several children by his housekeeper Cristina Ruiz, as well as from other liaisons.

Throughout the 1960s, while Brando became increasingly involved in the causes of African Americans and Native Americans, his movie standing sank with such duds as 1966's *The Chase*. His career was salvaged by 1972's *The Godfather* (for which he won an Oscar but created a maelstrom by refusing to accept his award). He proved intriguingly obscure in 1979's *Apocalypse Now*. After 1980, Brando did not make another movie until 1989. By then, he was accepting cameo assignments at big fees and causing tremendous on-set difficulties. Many think Brando gave his best performance off camera—as a sobbing courtroom witness in 1991 when his son Christian was on trial for having killed his half-sister's boyfriend. Marlon's final screen performance was in 2001's *The Score*; during filming, the star decided he would not perform his scenes unless the director, Frank Oz, vacated the set.

In his final years, Brando remained the confirmed eccentric and seemed increasingly befuddled by life. He resided like a giant Buddha at his Los Angeles compound, often having his refrigerator padlocked to prevent his food binges. His neighbor Jack Nicholson was a friend, as was the peculiar singing star Michael Jackson. It was rumored that the once distinguished Brando was in constant financial straits, but when he died of pulmonary fibrosis in July 2004, he left an estate valued at $20 million. His cremated ashes were scattered in two places: Tahiti and Death Valley.

Joan Crawford

(March 23, 1904–May 10, 1977)

Like the character Madame Defarge in Charles Dickens's novel *A Tale of Two Cities*, Joan Crawford was a world-class knitter. Crawford was obsessed with the craft. Wherever she was—including on the sound stage waiting to film a scene—she was busy knitting. (A few of her many lovers insisted Crawford also practiced her hobby while engaged in sexual intercourse in her boudoir.) Joan found the click-clacking sound of the fast-moving needles to be very relaxing.

Knitting was but one of Crawford's many manias. Another was clothing. (She was obsessed with the quality and quantity of her wardrobe. She frequently switched outfits 10 times a day and traveled with as many as 35 suitcases.) Yet another was cleanliness. She had a strict regimen about keeping her surroundings (at home, at work, on the road) spotless, with everything in its decreed proper order. Her obsession with hygiene extended to her even scrubbing down the bathroom in her studio dressing suite. Joan also had a fetish for frequently cleansing her hands. This compulsive practice led some wags to suggest that the celebrated movie star had a good deal in common with Shakespeare's Lady Macbeth.

Crawford's compulsions about organizing life to suit her dictates included her dealings with her public over many decades. She was so extremely grateful for the luxurious perks that being a great movie luminary had brought her that she felt an overwhelming obligation to her fans. No week was complete without her personally supervising replies to every individual who had written to her. (Joan even had special outfits and gloves that she wore to handle such tasks.)

Most infamously, the icon's warped psyche pushed her into bizarre behavior with her several adopted children. Initially, they were brought into her sphere as a publicity gimmick to soften her public image. Joan quickly decreed that these youngsters must demonstrate total obedience to her every command and *never* interfere with the flow of her rigidly self-controlled lifestyle. The more she believed her career and personal life were floundering as she aged, the more she demanded that her brood measure up to her imperial dictates. And when, in the mid-1940s, she became increasingly alcoholic and embarked on nocturnal rampages at home, her terrified kids became her primary victims.

• • •

Lucille Fay LeSueur was born in San Antonio, Texas, in 1904 (some sources list 1905, 1906, or even 1908) to Thomas LeSueur, a French Canadian laborer, and Anna Bell Johnson LeSueur, a Scandinavian Irish woman. (Previously, the couple had had a daughter, Daisy, who died in infancy, and they had a son named Hal.) Early in Lucille's life, Thomas disappeared, and her mother—a promiscuous woman—later wed

Henry Cassin. The household was reestablished in Lawton, Oklahoma, and Lucille (nicknamed Billie) became Billie Cassin. Henry got into difficulty with the law, and the Cassins moved to Kansas City. Soon afterward, Anna left him. During her haphazard childhood, Billie switched from one school to another and stayed in one seedy hotel room after another. By age 11, she was at Rockingham Academy, laboring as a kitchen helper in exchange for board and tuition at the private school. Humiliating as that was, it was better than being with her bossy mother and cruel brother.

By 1922, Billie was at Stephens College in Columbia, Missouri, where she toiled on campus to earn her keep. After a few months she quit, feeling too socially and intellectually inferior to remain at Stephens. Back in Kansas City, she became a shopgirl and then got herself hired as a chorine for a traveling stage show. When the tour fell apart, she went to Detroit. Later, she turned up in Chicago, and was a hoofer in underworld-controlled speakeasies. (Gossip suggested that during these struggling years the teenager also might have been a prostitute and that she might have made pornographic films.) Eventually, she made the necessary connections that led to her becoming a chorus girl on Broadway in *The Passing Show of 1924*. Between 1923 and 1924, she was married to, then divorced from, musician James Welton.

The highly ambitious performer maneuvered a screen test, which led to a contract with Metro-Goldwyn-Mayer. By 1925, the aggressive movie fledgling had been in several silent films and had acquired a new professional name: Joan Crawford. In the late 1920s, she turned herself into Hollywood's most spirited flapper and did her best to forget her sordid past.

Crawford appreciated the benefits of marrying well. She permitted herself to fall in love with the good-looking Douglas Fairbanks Jr., an actor who was a few years her junior. He was the son of Hollywood's unofficial king, Douglas Fairbanks Sr., and the stepson of its queen, Mary Pickford. Joan and Doug Jr. wed in June 1929. He was far less career oriented than his obsessed wife and each took refuge in extramarital flings. She became involved romantically with Clark Gable, her married colead from 1931's *Dance, Fools, Dance*. (Their relationship persisted for several years, even as each partner went in and out of new marriages.) Two years after Joan divorced Fairbanks Jr., in May 1933, she wed the sophisticated

In the 1940s, the increasingly neurotic superstar Joan Crawford still maintained a glamorous allure.

Broadway actor Franchot Tone, then under MGM contract. It was not too long before the sophisticated groom hated being Mr. Crawford and distracted himself with liquor and affairs. The couple split up in April 1939. As was traditional with Joan, each time she got rid of a mate, she completely redecorated her expensive home, which required replacing every toilet seat in the house.

Crawford suffered a career backslide in the late 1930s, but she rebounded with such strong fare as 1941's A Woman's Face. In the meantime, in 1940, the grand star at last became a mother. (Earlier in life she had suffered botched abortions, which may have caused the several miscarriages she had while wed to Fairbanks Jr. and to Tone.) Because it was then difficult for a single woman—especially a divorcée—to adopt a child, Joan went through underworld associates and the black market to obtain a three-month-old infant, first called Joan Jr. and then renamed Christina.

In 1942, Joan's 18-year reign at MGM ended. That July, to divert herself, she wed a young actor named Phillip Terry. The badly mismatched couple officially ended their union in April 1946. Thereafter, she quickly changed the name of their adopted boy from Phillip Jr. to Christopher.

Crawford was far too determined a survivor to retire from moviemaking. She moved over to Warner Bros., where she served as a potent threat to that studio's temperamental queen bee, Bette Davis. Joan proved her worth when she starred in 1945's Mildred Pierce and won an Oscar for her gritty performance. She was now commanding $200,000 per picture. Soon she

adopted two other children, Cynthia and Cathy, who were fraternal twins. Crawford remained at Warner Bros. through 1952's This Woman Is Dangerous. That same year, Joan earned her third and last Oscar nomination, for Sudden Fear, a film noir thriller produced at RKO.

In May 1955, Crawford tied the knot with Alfred N. Steele, the dynamic CEO of Pepsi-Cola. She inaugurated a new career for herself as a glamorous (and demanding) corporate goodwill ambassador. She believed Steele would be her companion for life, but he succumbed to a heart attack in April 1959. (Some Crawford biographers reference the financial/emotional stress he had endured coping with his willful and big-spending spouse.) With scant meaningful movie parts available for a veteran screen legend, Joan sublimated all her energies into being a high-profile Pepsi executive.

Crawford enjoyed an amazing career rejuvenation when she and Bette Davis reluctantly teamed for 1962's What Ever Happened to Baby Jane? The horror tale led to Crawford's starring in such further genre entries as 1967's Berserk! The heavy-drinking screen veteran now resided in Manhattan and was alienated from her two oldest children. In the mid-1970s, she was let go by Pepsi-Cola. She became a Christian Scientist and gave up drinking and smoking. Joan also become reclusive, not wishing her public to see how she had aged. The indefatigable legend passed away in May 1977. The next year, Crawford's daughter Christina published Mommie Dearest, which forever thereafter branded Joan as the neurotic mother from hell.

Greta Garbo

(September 18, 1905–April 15, 1990)

In the early 1930s, MGM promoted Greta Garbo, its extremely aloof star, as the "Swedish Sphinx." The intriguing nickname referred to the Scandinavian import's avoidance of the media and their interview requests. (Some sources suggested that this policy was a decision of her Hollywood employers, who feared that the blunt Garbo—still ill at ease conversing in English—might reveal to the public how little she really thought of most of her film vehicles, the studio system, and most of the Tinseltown colony. There were also studio concerns that she might let slip references to her bisexual lifestyle. Others noted that by minimizing Garbo's contacts with the press, the studio could build her into a lady of great mystery and this would draw more filmgoers to her pictures.)

After Garbo stopped making films, in 1942, she became progressively more moody, self-focused, inflexible, and reclusive—all well beyond normal behavior, even for a temperamental celebrity. Some attributed the legend's recurrent bleak gloom to her Swedish heritage; others suggested that she suffered from serious manic-depressive traits. Then, too, years in front of the camera had made the star increasingly egocentric and vain. Thus, she found it extremely difficult to deal with the diminishing of her beauty as she aged. Her response to growing older was to become even more introverted and detached from the world that seemed to be passing her by.

During Garbo's New York "exile" after Hollywood, she became less and less interested in many topics and in most other people's problems. The strenuous guarding of her privacy and the details of her past became an even greater obsession for the wealthy ex–movie star. (Interestingly, while she went to tremendous lengths to maintain a low profile in Manhattan and on her world travels, the narcissistic part of her nature delighted when she noticed out of the corner of her eye that a passerby had recognized her.)

Over the decades, several in Garbo's small circle of acquaintances commented on her childlike, occasionally jubilant nature. Some people saw this quality as a refreshing insight into the inner child that lurked behind Garbo's usually self-contained, dour persona. Others attributed her infrequent bursts of childish enthusiasm to the fact that this mystifying woman who seemed so cosmopolitan, cynical, and pragmatic, was actually a girl-woman who had never matured emotionally.

Several individuals who knew the actress marveled at her great business acumen and her sophisticated taste in art. But others pointed to the fact that this poorly educated woman who grew up in poverty and without culture was actually a product of mentors such as director Mauritz Stiller, conductor Leopold Stokowski, health guru Gayelord Hauser, shipping magnate Aristotle Onassis, and social figure George Schlee (who was wed to couturiere Valentina).

The elusive Greta Garbo in a scene from 1929's The Single Standard *with costar Nils Asther.*

Certainly, too, the complexities and contradictions of Garbo's puzzling nature were influenced by her ambiguous sexual lifestyle. She may have had heterosexual relationships with actors John Gilbert and George Brent, director Rouben Mamoulian, and other men later in life, such as Leopold Stokowski. However, the majority of the star's emotional/sexual encounters were with other women (including actresses Fifi D'Orsay and Dorothy Sebastian, actress/writer Salka Viertel, and writer Mercedes de Acosta) or such bisexual men as aristocratic British photographer/set

designer Cecil Beaton. In many people's estimation, Garbo had become asexual by the time she was in late middle age.

In short, to have worked with, hobnobbed with, or dealt with the divine Garbo may have been exciting at that moment. However, many people—on and off the film set—found coping with the self-contained, detached, and often demanding lady to be exceedingly frustrating, disappointing, and draining.

• • •

Greta Lovisa Gustafsson was born in Stockholm, Sweden, in 1905, the third of five children of Karl Alfred Gustafsson, an unskilled laborer in the city's sanitation department who cleaned latrines, and Anna Lovisa Karlsson Gustafsson. When Greta was 13, her father—who was often out of work—became seriously ill. She left school to care for him. Within a year, he died. Her first paying job was a menial one in a barbershop, where she soaped men's faces. Later, she worked at the PUB department store. There, in 1921, the still plump, five-foot-seven-and-a-half-inch teenager made her movie debut, appearing in an advertising short subject. This led to her trying out for, and winning, a scholarship to the Royal Stockholm Theater School.

Later, director Mauritz Stiller, a Russian Jewish émigré important in Swedish cinema, cast Greta Garbo (her new screen moniker) in his 1924 silent photoplay, *The Atonement of Gosta Berling*. The following year, she played in G. W. Pabst's film *The Street of Sorrow*. At this juncture, Hollywood film executive Louis B. Mayer was hunting for new talent for the recently formed MGM. He asked Mauritz Stiller to come to Hollywood to direct features. The latter agreed, but only if Greta was made part of the deal. Mayer, who thought the chubby Greta had dubious movie potential, halfheartedly hired the 24-year-old at a relatively modest salary ($400 a week). Stiller and Garbo sailed for the United States.

Once Garbo was on the studio payroll, she was ordered to diet and to submit to dentists to fix her crooked teeth. She was assigned to 1926's *Torrent*. Moviegoers responded well to her luminous screen presence. Soon she was cast with matinee idol John Gilbert in 1927's *Flesh and the Devil*. The love team impressed audiences, and the studio boosted the illusion with a publicity blitz about the costars' passionate off-screen romance. Sources differ as to whether the bisexual Garbo really cared for Gilbert or whether her attraction to him was calculated to promote her career and/or disguise her sexual attraction to women. In any event, Gilbert frequently begged the elusive Garbo to become his third wife. When she continued to make excuses about marrying him, he wed another woman. Meanwhile, she busied herself with her lucrative career, which now earned her $5,000 a week plus many perks.

Garbo successfully made her sound film bow in 1930's *Anna Christie*. For 1933's *Queen Christina*, her leading man was her ex-lover John Gilbert, who was in the midst of a great career slump. (He was then wed to young actress Virginia Bruce.) The film classic ended with a huge close-up of Garbo silently pondering her future. Her blank face, which said so much and so little, was an instance of art imitating life.

During Greta's Hollywood years, she never was attracted to the city's glittery nightlife. She preferred to mingle quietly with a sophisticated group of lesbians and/or members of Tinseltown's Continental crowd who accepted her alternative lifestyle. Always restive and unimpressed with most material possessions, the free-spirited actress lived in 11 different residences during her 16-year stay in Tinseltown.

By 1935, the star had grown weary of the filmmaking process. She disliked revealing her emotions in front of a film crew and was bored playing a string of tragic screen figures. But her $250,000-per-movie fee kept her tied to MGM. For 1936's *Camille* she earned her second Academy Award nomination (her first was for 1930's *Romance*). MGM created a new (lighter and more contemporary) alter ego for Garbo in 1939's *Ninotchka*. Its success (and her Oscar nomination) prompted the studio to concoct 1941's *Two-Faced Woman* for her. Sadly, the picture was an embarrassingly inept showcase that failed at the box office. Garbo and MGM parted company.

By the early 1950s, Garbo concluded that she had aged too much to make any further attempts to return to the screen. Now retired, the naturalized American citizen divided her time between Switzerland, the French Riviera, and a seven-room apartment on New York's East 52nd Street. Living in the same building as the actress was her good friend/counselor George Schlee, a Russian-born financier, and his increasingly jealous wife, fashion designer Valentina. (Schlee died in 1964.) When abroad, Greta traveled with such jet-setters as the Rothschild family. When asked where her life was now heading, the celebrated recluse said, "I don't know. I'm just drifting."

In her last years, a glum Greta could infrequently be spotted stomping about Manhattan, disguised by her sunglasses, large hat, and trench coat. By the late 1980s, her kidneys were failing and she had to give up her walks. In this period, she became closer to a few of her surviving relatives, in particular her niece Gray Reisfield, who lived in New Jersey. The icon died in April 1990 of pneumonia and end-stage renal disease. The location of her ashes was kept secret because her family dreaded unwanted publicity. Her estate—worth many millions—was bequeathed to her niece.

In death, as in her life and career, the divine Greta Garbo remained, according to *Newsweek* magazine, "an enigma in the form of a goddess."

Betty Hutton

(February 26, 1921–March 11, 2007)

In her heyday of the 1940s and early 1950s, the hyperactive Betty Hutton—known as the "Blonde Bombshell," "America's #1 Jitterbug," and the "Blitzkrieg Blonde"—was a top singer/actress who made her mark in Broadway shows and Hollywood features, and on recordings and the radio. She was ranked just below Judy Garland as America's most popular female entertainer of that era. The highly emotional Hutton was only 31 when her spectacular career began to disintegrate—the result of bad career and marital decisions and changing public tastes. Matters weren't helped by her enormous ego and extreme outbursts, which eventually antagonized relatives, friends, and business associates.

As Hutton's once tremendous career sank in the mid-1950s, she embarked on a series of show business retirements/comebacks and personal crises that, over the years, prompted suicide attempts. Just like Betty's bombastic performance style, her attempts to end her life were dramatic bids to feed her enormous hunger for love and adulation.

• • •

Elizabeth June Thornburg was born in 1921 in Battle Creek, Michigan. Her unwed mother, Mabel Lum Thornburg, was already the parent of nearly 2-year-old Marion. (From the beginning, the two sisters competed for their mother's attention—the often bitter sibling rivalry continued until Marion's passing in 1987.) Elizabeth June never knew her father, who had vanished before her birth. To support her family, the uneducated Mabel ran an illegal beer/gin club out of her seedy apartment. The Thornburgs moved often, frequently one step ahead of lawmen out to enforce Prohibition. The precocious 3-year-old Elizabeth performed at her mother's tawdry bar, understanding that if she sang, the drunks would calm down and her mother might be spared their physical abuse. The trio later relocated to Detroit. By then, Mabel was a full-blown alcoholic, and young Elizabeth often made the rounds of local backroom saloons seeking her errant mom. At these stops she sang to earn a few coins from her audience. By age 15, she had quit school and gone to New York City. Her efforts to break into show business failed and she returned home.

In 1937, the ambitious teenager and her sister were singing in small Detroit clubs. One evening famed bandleader Vincent Lopez heard Elizabeth perform and signed her to be his new band vocalist. On opening night she had severe stage fright. To save the situation she tossed down a few drinks. She went back on stage, belted out her songs recklessly, and danced a fractured jitterbug with band members and the audience. She was a sensation and made this attention-grabbing performance style her trademark. It was Lopez who renamed her Betty Hutton. (The more decorous Marion, who also sang with Lopez's group before joining Glenn Miller's orchestra, took the Hutton surname as well.)

Betty headlined with Lopez's band in New York and elsewhere, and made her movie debut in the 1938 short subject *Queens of the Air*. She quit Lopez to appear in the 1940 Broadway musical revue *Two for the Show*. That same year, songwriter and stage/film producer Buddy DeSylva contracted Hutton to support Ethel Merman in *Panama Hattie*. On opening night, Merman demanded that Betty's key musical number be cut. A stunned Betty pleaded with DeSylva to intercede. He made Hutton an offer she could not refuse: remain with *Panama Hattie* for its run and then go to Hollywood. He disclosed that he was soon to become a top executive producer at Paramount Pictures and he would make her a movie star. She agreed to his deal. When Hutton arrived on the Paramount lot in late 1941, gossips claimed she was DeSylva's mistress, to which Betty retorted that they were merely pals. Whatever the actuality, her privileged position annoyed many coworkers and set the pattern of "persecuted" Hutton against the world.

Betty was handed a lead part in her debut feature, 1942's *The Fleet's In*. Her madcap singing and noisy performance wowed moviegoers. She mugged with Bob Hope in 1943's *Let's Face It* and he labeled her "a vitamin pill with legs." In Preston Sturges's satirical classic, 1944's *The Miracle of Morgan's Creek*, she proved she could be entertaining without singing. By 1945's *The Stork Club*, her studio protector was phasing out of his Paramount chores because of failing health. In the meantime, the temperamental Hutton was adding to her negative status on the film lot. If a cast member did not suit her, the diva had the person fired. She was now frequently late to the set—inexcusable behavior even for *the* star of the picture. Like Judy Garland, her MGM-based rival, Betty was taking prescription medications to calm down at night and other tablets in the morning to counteract the nighttime pills.

In September 1945, Betty wed Chicago camera manufacturer Theodore Briskin. He foolishly hoped she would abandon her movie career for domesticity. Their union (during which they had two daughters) was punctuated by emotionally draining separations and reconciliations. By January 1951, they had divorced. While Hutton had a hit with 1947's *The Perils of Pauline*, the high-priced star kept vetoing suggested new projects. She demanded to star in 1948's *Dream Girl*, a nonmusical. During its making, she meddled far too much in creative decisions and was supported on the set by a growing staff of yes-people. That movie failed, and her next, 1949's *Red, Hot and Blue*, was not a sufficiently major hit to compensate for the star's bothersome antics.

Earlier, Hutton had pestered Paramount to acquire the screen rights to Irving Berlin's Broadway hit *Annie Get Your Gun*. However, MGM outbid Paramount, and Judy Garland was given the plum assignment. After Garland had a nervous breakdown and left the production, Hutton campaigned relentlessly to take over the part. She prevailed, but nearly everyone on the MGM shoot was icy to her throughout filming—they were all Garland boosters. The experience so unnerved the emotionally fragile Betty that she lost enthusiasm for moviemaking, despite the fact that her income that year was a mighty $260,000. (Her disillusionment with Hollywood led her to say one time: "I was a commodity, like a hot dog. It was like hot dogs and Betty Hutton.")

While making 1952's *Somebody Loves Me*, she behaved extremely badly on the set, her excuse being that she was livid that Frank Sinatra had not been hired as her costar rather than the miscast Ralph Meeker. On the plus side, the neurotic

Betty met husband number two (choreographer Charles O'Curran) on this production. However, the new marriage did not calm down the hyperactive diva. When Paramount refused to allow O'Curran to helm *Topsy and Eva* later that year, Betty walked off the costly project. The irate studio pushed Hutton into letting them buy out her contract.

Thereafter, a distraught Betty—who momentarily threatened to retire from show business—leaped from moviemaking to concertizing in the United States and abroad. She did club work in Las Vegas and elsewhere, made more highly publicized retirement bids, and took two major stabs at TV: a lavish spectacular (*Satins and Spurs*, in 1954) and the sitcom *Goldie* (aka *The Betty Hutton Show*, which ran from 1959 to 1960). On each of these expensive flops she was tyrannical, unpredictable, and frantic. Divorced again in February 1955, she went through two more marriages (to Alan Livingston, from March 1955 to October 1960, and Pete Candoli, from December 1960 to June 1967) and had a third daughter. She turned down playing Ado Annie in 1955's *Oklahoma!*, insisting the screen role was insufficient for a star of her magnitude. Yet, two years thereafter, the mercurial Hutton replaced Judy Garland in a low-budget drama, *Spring Reunion*, her last feature.

Later, she made brief forays on Broadway as cast replacement in long-running shows. Her greatest visibility occurred in the mid-1970s, when she was discovered working as a domestic in a rectory in Portsmouth, Rhode Island. She revealed that she had frittered away an estimated $11 million, suffered years of drug/alcohol dependency, lost her mother in an apartment fire, was often alienated from her children, and had repeatedly tried suicide. She announced that she had found herself by participating in the Catholic church. In 2000, Hutton appeared in a cable TV interview, recounting the many highs and lows of her extremely self-destructive career.

The exuberant talent died of complications from colon cancer in March 2007 at her Palm Springs, California, apartment. Official news of her passing was not released until after her funeral, as, according to her close friend and executor, Carol Bruno, "She wanted to have everything totally private."

Jennifer Jones
(March 2, 1919–)

In *The Song of Bernadette*, a big-budget Hollywood release of 1943, Jennifer Jones portrayed a simple 19th-century French farm girl who experienced miraculous religious visions. Her wholesome good looks struck a positive chord with filmgoers, and her intense performance earned the relative screen newcomer an Academy Award. Unbeknownst to most people then, Jones was not only married (to actor Robert Walker) and had two children, but she also had fallen under the romantic sway of the married David O. Selznick, a top independent film producer. The strain of her complicated domestic life pushed the shy and fragile Jones to her emotional limits. Her biggest comfort was to focus on her lifelong ambition to become an acclaimed actress.

Thirteen years later, Jones was married to Selznick (with whom she had a young daughter) and had been a major screen figure for well over a decade. However, now—in such films as 1956's *The Man in the Gray Flannel Suit*—her once vibrant performances were marred by facial mannerisms and body posture reflecting high stress. It was an indication of the high price of fame for this retiring Midwesterner who had sacrificed everything for her career.

• • •

Phylis Lee Isley was born on March 2, 1919, in Tulsa, Oklahoma. She was the only child of Philip and Flora Mae Suber

The high-strung Jennifer Jones in 1952's The Wild Heart *(aka* Gone to Earth*).*

Isley, who operated and starred in a traveling summer tent show. During the winter months, the Isleys resided in Oklahoma City, where Philip operated movie theaters.

When Phylis was not in the classroom, she helped out in her family's touring stock company, serving as ticket taker or candy seller. Because the beautiful youngster was so painfully introverted, her parents encouraged her to perform in the troupe's plays, hoping the experience would encourage her to become more outgoing. Later, Phylis used this acting experience to win roles in high school productions and then at Tulsa's Monte Cassino Junior College. By now, the well-mannered, reticent Phylis had resolved to become a great actress. Dating and other typical teenage interests meant little to her.

For a year, Phylis studied drama at Northwestern University. Then, in September 1937, she enrolled at the American Academy of Dramatic Arts in New York City. Months later, the nervous brunette encountered a gawky young classmate. His name was Robert Walker and he was from Salt Lake City. Within weeks, the two were constant companions. Shortly thereafter, they left the academy and found work together in Oklahoma at a local radio station. In January 1939, they married and drove to California. Phylis gained a few small roles at Republic Pictures, and Robert had walk-ons in other studios' product. When nothing else materialized, they returned to New York. Phylis modeled hats, while Robert labored on multiple radio series. Over the next few years they became the parents of two boys (Robert Jr. and Michael).

In mid-1941, Phylis auditioned for the touring company of *Claudia*, a hit Broad-

way play. She lost the role to another but caught the eye of David O. Selznick, who owned the film rights to the romantic comedy. She tested in Manhattan for the screen lead but gave a highly agitated performance. She then burst into tears and dashed from the building. Phylis did not realize that she had made a terrific impact on Selznick. She was amazed when he soon put her under screen contract. Phylis devoted much of the next months to studying with New York acting coaches. By year's end, the mercurial Selznick had sold off many of his screen properties (including *Claudia*), hoping in some way to help the Allies win World War II. However, he kept in force his organization's contracts with various actors and directors. (He made a tidy profit loaning them out to other filmmakers.)

By 1942, Phylis had a new screen name (Jennifer Jones) and had tested successfully for *The Song of Bernadette*. Meanwhile, to keep Robert Walker preoccupied, Selznick arranged an audition for him at MGM, where he was put under contract. Hollywood insiders, as well as Walker and Selznick's wife, Irene, soon suspected there was a personal relationship developing between Jones and Selznick. However, David was a man of great industry power and did largely as he pleased. This included teaming Jones and Walker in his new movie project, 1944's *Since You Went Away*. Early into filming, Jones informed her husband she wanted a separation. He quietly complied but soon began to drink heavily. On March 2, 1944—her 25th birthday—Jones won her Academy Award. The following day, she filed for divorce, which became final on June 20, 1945. She won custody of the two boys.

Although Jones's relationship with the still-married Selznick was the talk of Hollywood, much of the public was naively unaware of the true situation. The stress of the clandestine romance was almost more than Jennifer could bear. With her strong Catholic background, she was increasingly unable to deal with the Hollywood social scene as Selznick's mistress. She retreated into seclusion and nearly had an emotional breakdown. She might have found a beneficial outlet to the messy situation in her acting career. However, at every turn she was under the thumb of the micromanaging Selznick. (Gossip columnist Louella Parsons observed later of the Jones-Selznick tandem, "I think Jennifer would rather be miserable with David than happy with any other man.") On one occasion, years later, during the filming of 1953's *Indiscretion of an American Wife* in Rome, even the repressed Jones had had more than enough of Selznick the eternal puppet master. She flew into a rage and ran into the street. When he caught up with her, she turned around and, in a fit of hysteria, slapped him.

By early 1949, Irene Selznick had finally divorced her spouse, and that July, Jennifer and David at last wed. In 1950, she suffered a miscarriage, which left her distraught for months. Her despair was exacerbated when Robert Walker died in August 1951, following his latest drinking rampage. As with past crises, Jones sought relief in yoga and psychoanalysis and survived her rash of disasters thanks to high-priced psychiatrists.

In August 1954, Jennifer gave birth to Mary Jennifer, the couple's only child. Jones continued making movies, including 1955's *Love Is a Many-Splendored Thing.*

Ironically, when she received accolades for her effective performance in this entry—including an Oscar nomination—the praise only made her more introspective, insecure, and withdrawn. At times, the complex actress revealed her deep emotions in public. She was at a Beverly Hills party when she learned that a coveted role in 1956's *Tea and Sympathy* had gone not to her but to Deborah Kerr. Jones expressed her extreme frustration by jumping into her hostess's swimming pool—fully clothed! On another occasion, when asked why she avoided interviews to promote her career, she replied nervously, "I'm a difficult subject and always have been. There's not much to be said by me or about me one way or the other. My work should speak for itself." (Jones also was indifferent about receiving professional accolades. According to Selznick, "She has no interest in fame or money. All her awards, including the Oscar, have mysteriously disappeared from our house. She acts because she must. It's a compulsion.")

Selznick showcased his wife in 1957's *A Farewell to Arms* and 1962's *Tender Is the Night*, but both pictures flopped. In June 1965, Selznick, 63, died of a heart attack. Two years later, on November 9, Jennifer, who lived an isolated life in Los Angeles and who acted increasingly peculiar when forced to interact with others, attempted suicide. Fortunately, she was discovered in time in the surf at Malibu Beach. (Previously, the star had sought to end her life in 1945—with an overdose of sleeping pills—when the pressure of being Selznick's mistress grew too heavy a burden.)

In 1971, Jennifer met multimillionaire industrialist/art collector Norton Simon.

A few weeks later, in late May, the couple married. In 1974, Jennifer accepted a character lead in *The Towering Inferno*. In May 1975, 21-year-old Mary Jennifer Selznick killed herself by jumping from the roof of a Los Angeles office building. In the mid-1980s, Norton Simon became increasingly infirm and, in June 1993, he died at age 86. Thereafter, the highly reclusive Jones made very few public appearances. She had become a prisoner to her lost past and unfulfilling present.

Oscar Levant

(December 27, 1906–August 14, 1972)

At the height of his acclaim in the 1940s and 1950s, concert pianist, film actor, radio and television personality, and author Oscar Levant was, perhaps, the world's most famous neurotic. Full of devastating wit, the chain-smoking, self-deprecating raconteur observed, "There is a thin line between genius and insanity. I have erased that line." His pessimistic outlook on life prompted his tart, almost savage approach to everything and everyone, including his idol/friend, George Gershwin, the musical great. Enfant terrible Levant was manic-depressive, obsessive-compulsive, and a hypochondriac. He was a troubled soul perpetually crying out for attention. One of his friends observed, "There's nothing the matter with Oscar that a good miracle couldn't cure," while a psychiatrist suggested to Levant, "Maybe life isn't for everyone."

There were many topics that the superstitious and often self-contradictory Levant strictly forbade being discussed in his presence, including death, Sara Lee cakes, and the number 13. His substance abuse encompassed prescription medicines (particularly pills to combat insomnia) and booze. He admitted, "I tried to become an alcoholic. I drank steadily for one year but it didn't take." He was a brilliant pianist, a talented composer, and a voracious reader. (His eclectic knowledge ranged from minutia about classical music to obscure baseball statistics.) He was devoted to analysis and, in later years, was often a patient at mental facilities. He bragged, "I was thrown out of one mental hospital because I depressed the patients."

Bing Crosby (left) and the usually frenetic Oscar Levant in 1940's Rhythm on the River.

Unlike most of his celebrated contemporaries, who hid their quirks and failings from the public, Levant eagerly shared his real and imagined ailments with anyone who would listen—and that was many during his prime as a Broadway/Hollywood wit; a film, radio, and TV celebrity; and the author of three autobiographical volumes: 1940's *A Smattering of Ignorance*, 1965's *The Memoirs of an Amnesiac*, and 1968's *The Unimportance of Being Oscar*.

Summing up his self-destructive life, Levant concluded, "In some situations, I was difficult, in odd moments impossible, in rare moments loathsome, at my best, unapproachably great."

●   ●   ●

He was born in 1906 in Pittsburgh, Pennsylvania, the fourth and last child (he had three older brothers) of Max and Annie Radin Levant, who were Orthodox Jews. His father owned a jewelry store. After Oscar became famous, he quipped, "I paid thousands of dollars to psychiatrists to forget my childhood." However, his unhappy formative years triggered phobias that lasted a lifetime. His father was overly stern and his mother (who had hoped her fourth child would be a girl) never felt that anything her last-born son did was good enough. Early on, the rebellious boy displayed far more talent for the piano than for classroom academics. When Mr. Levant died in 1921, Oscar quit school and moved to New York.

In Manhattan, the keyboard prodigy studied classical music, then gravitated toward playing piano in nightclubs, working with Ben Bernie's band and performing in theater-pit orchestras for stage shows. He made his acting debut in the 1927 Broadway drama *Burlesque*. By then, Levant had met George Gershwin and was on the path to becoming his greatest devotee. (After Gershwin's death in 1937, Levant devoted himself to concerts and recordings featuring his hero's music.) When Paramount filmed *Burlesque* as 1929's *The Dance of Life*, Levant was hired to re-create his stage role. He remained in Hollywood to write music for several RKO films. By the mid-1930s, he was creating music at Fox Films (including a mini opera for 1936's *Charlie Chan at the Opera*). He returned to Broadway later in the decade to conduct orchestras for two Broadway shows.

In January 1932, Levant wed Broadway dancer Barbara Woodell. Neither honored their wedding vows but what ended the union was her aborting a pregnancy without consulting Levant. The couple divorced in September 1933. In December 1939, he married June Gale, a Broadway musical comedy performer, whom he had met while she was under contract at Twentieth Century-Fox. The couple had three daughters. Being married to Levant was a heavy strain on Gale and led to many fights and separations over the years. However, she always returned to his side. Oscar quipped about his seesawing domestic life: "Marriage is a triumph of habit over hate."

Levant gained widespread popularity when he joined the radio talk show *Information Please* in 1938, and he remained on its panel for six seasons. He returned to movie acting with 1940's *Rhythm on the River* in the type of role that became his trademark: the caustic sidekick. He began giving concerts in 1942 and was an enormous success.

He played himself in 1945's *Rhapsody in Blue*, a film "biography" of George Gershwin, and became a regular on Al Jolson's radio show, *Kraft Music Hall*, in 1947. Two years later, he moved over to television as both a guest performer on panel and talk entries and the host of his own programs (including *Guest House*). However, on camera, the acid-tongued, fascinating Oscar was so unpredictable in his comments that he repeatedly short-circuited his own bright future in the medium. In 1952, a few weeks after suffering a coronary occlusion, he was at MGM to make one of his best movies, *The Band Wagon*. In 1955, Levant had a featured part in the movie *The Cobweb*. His role was definitely a case of strong typecasting—he portrayed an intense neurotic, one of several patients at an exclusive sanitarium. This picture proved to be his final film assignment.

By 1958, the master neurotic (who now suffered from several facial ticks) had abandoned his concert career and only occasionally made a TV appearance. Much of his last decade was spent as a recluse at his Beverly Hills home. He died of a heart attack in August 1972. Sometime earlier, the malcontented genius summed up the results of his failing to live up to everyone's tremendously high expectations for him. "Instant unconsciousness has been my greatest passion. . . . My life is a morbid rondo. . . . Every moment is an earthquake to me." As one of his screen characters said, "It's not what you are, but what you don't become that hurts."

Marilyn Monroe

(June 1, 1926–August 4, 1962)

Few performers have generated as much idolization and discussion as has Marilyn Monroe, Hollywood's most legendary blonde. Over the years, many statements were attributed to the tragic movie queen. Among them was "No one ever told me I was pretty when I was a little girl. All little girls should be told they are pretty, even if they aren't." She also said, "Being a sex symbol is a heavy load to carry, especially when one is tired, hurt, and bewildered" and "I want to grow old and without face-lifts. I want to have the courage to be loyal to the face I have made."

What emerges from the many biographies and documentaries on the enigmatic Monroe is that at the height of her movie fame she was far more sensitive to life than her naive and vulnerable screen alter ego, that she had a native intellect and was not merely a "dumb blonde," that she appreciated the differences between her image and her private self, and that such professional steps as her studying at New York's Actors Studio were not a publicity gimmick but a genuine desire to improve her craft.

Other facets of the complex icon were her propensity for emotional unbalance (including her suicidal urges), her overreliance on prescription drugs (including uppers and downers), her confusion from years of seeking self-understanding through psychoanalysis, and the cumulative impact of romantic partners, studio executives, acting coaches, analysts, and "friends" who imposed their agendas on this too impressionable talent.

•   •   •

Norma Jeane Mortensen (listed as Norma Jeane Mortenson on her birth certificate) was born in Los Angeles in 1926. Her mother, Gladys Pearl Monroe Mortensen, was a film lab technician, and her father, Martin Edward Mortensen, was a baker who deserted Gladys during her pregnancy and filed for divorce, although it had not yet become official at the time of Norma Jeane's birth. (Martin, who was killed in a motorcycle accident in 1929, is thought by many sources *not* to have been Norma Jeane's real father. Her biological father was believed to have been C. Stanley Gifford, who worked with young Gladys at Consolidated Film Industries in Hollywood and who had a fling with her.)

During much of Norma Jeane's childhood, her emotionally frail mother was institutionalized. As a result, Norma Jeane ended up in a succession of foster homes and orphanages. (The movie star claimed to have been a victim of sexual abuse both in her childhood and adolescence. Some sources regard her accusations as total or partial fabrications by the actress to generate sympathy for herself.)

In June 1942, when Norma Jeane was 16, she avoided being sent to yet another foster home by marrying. The groom was 21-year-old James Dougherty, her neighbor and an aircraft factory worker. While he was away serving in the merchant marine during World War II, Norma Jeane worked for a spell at a San Fernando Valley defense plant. She began modeling (typically in formfitting sweaters) for local photographers, which led to her doing photo layouts used in major girlie publications. In July 1946, she signed a $75 weekly contract with Twentieth Century-Fox. The studio gave her a new name: Marilyn Monroe. Two months later the ambitious starlet and Dougherty divorced.

Monroe had occasional bit roles at Fox (such as in 1948's *Scudda Hoo! Scudda Hay!*) before her studio option was dropped. Through her industry connections she was hired on a short-term basis at Columbia Pictures and had a lead in their economy musical, 1948's *Ladies of the Chorus*. She began dating vocal coach/composer Fred Karger. He did not think she was marriage material, and his rejection caused Marilyn to attempt suicide.

The high-powered Hollywood talent agent Johnny Hyde met Monroe at the end of 1948. He became so smitten with her that he left his wife and children. (While she loved the short, middle-aged man, she was not *in* love with him.) Hyde engineered small roles for her in major films, including 1950's *All About Eve*. Also that year, Hyde finalized a new Twentieth Century-Fox pact for her. When he died of a heart attack in December 1950, Marilyn was guilt-ridden for not having reciprocated his great passion for her.

Monroe used casting-couch strategy and clever self-publicity to make Fox executives notice her. As a result, the studio promoted

Marilyn as their new blond bombshell. By 1953's *How to Marry a Millionaire*, she was the company's key female box-office attraction. However, her growing emotional insecurities were causing her to be repeatedly late on the set and to have temper tantrums that seemed to come out of nowhere. On the sound stage, she only heeded the advice of her acting coach, Natasha Lytess. The studio put up with Monroe's diva behavior because of her popularity with moviegoers.

Once Monroe realized her value to the studio, she began vetoing suggested projects. Sometimes she was suspended; other times the frustrated executives replaced her with another actress under contract. Meanwhile, Marilyn was planning Marilyn Monroe Productions with photographer Milton Greene and dreamed of one day controlling her own screen destiny.

In January 1954, the sex siren married Joe DiMaggio, the renowned baseball player. The 39-year-old sports hero hoped his wife would abandon films to become a housewife and mother. Instead, he was mortified to find himself becoming "Mr. Monroe." He became increasingly jealous and abusive. The couple divorced that September. By the beginning of 1955, Monroe was AWOL from Fox. She was in New York promoting her newly formed production firm and studying at the Actors Studio. That institution's Lee Strasberg and his wife, Paula, became Marilyn's new acting coaches/controllers.

Eventually, Marilyn returned to Fox and garnered good reviews for 1956's *Bus Stop*. Despite this success, she continued to clash with the studio management. As her anxieties increased, so did her consumption of

pills and booze. In June 1956, she married celebrated playwright Arthur Miller. Months later, she had a miscarriage, as she did again in 1957 and 1958. These tragedies made her suicidal and, along with her growing paranoia about Miller, helped to undermine their marriage. Her 1957 picture, *The Prince and the Showgirl*, flopped. However, she had a tremendous success with 1959's *Some Like It Hot*. On each project, she was enormously difficult to deal with, for both cast and crew.

Marilyn became distraught when her fling with France's Yves Montand, her costar in 1960's *Let's Make Love*, fizzled and he reconciled with his wife. Monroe was wildly out of control while shooting 1961's *The Misfits*, with a screenplay written for her by Miller. The two of them were now bitterly disillusioned with each other, and they divorced in January 1961. Because of Monroe's suicidal behavior, her analyst (Marianne Kris) persuaded the movie star to enter Manhattan's Payne Whitney Psychiatric Clinic in February 1961. After three terribly upsetting days there, Monroe convinced Joe DiMaggio to get her released.

In 1962, Monroe allegedly was involved briefly with both President John F. Kennedy and his brother Bobby. She purchased a simple bungalow-style home in Brentwood, California, and was in constant psychiatric therapy. Marilyn finally returned to the studio in April 1962 to begin *Something's Got to Give*. Although she looked fine, she was falling to pieces emotionally. On the few days she appeared on the set, she was frequently unable to remember her dialogue. In the past, Fox would have pampered her through this latest crisis. However, the studio was having tremendous financial problems and therefore had little patience when Monroe was repeatedly absent from the set due to alleged illness. (When she flew to New York in mid-May 1962 to sing "Happy Birthday" to President Kennedy at Madison Square Garden, studio bigwigs were furious.) Then Monroe returned to the West Coast and was more compliant than usual at work. Fox hoped for the best.

On June 1, Monroe celebrated her 36th birthday with a party on the set. Six days later, she was dismissed from the movie because of new "unprofessional antics." The studio filed a $750,000 lawsuit against her. Thereafter, the studio executives changed their minds and said filming would resume with Monroe remaining aboard. On August 1, 1962, Fox signed her to a new contract at $250,000 per picture. However, it was all for nothing. In the early morning hours of August 5, Marilyn was found dead in her bedroom. (Her death, which occurred several hours earlier, was ascribed

to a fatal overdose of Nembutal and chloral hydrate.) Then and later, many conspiracy theories arose: some insisted Monroe's alleged suicide was a homicide; others claimed she had taken an accidental overdose of pills and that it was not a suicide.

A decade after Monroe's passing, Joseph L. Mankiewicz, who had directed Marilyn Monroe in *All About Eve*, observed in 1972, "More mawkish horseshit has been intoned and written about how 'Hollywood destroyed Marilyn Monroe.' Her particular pattern of self-destruction had been completed long before she ever heard of Schwab's Drugstore. But the movies—and her sudden, staggering, inexplicable movie stardom—did shape the finish for her, and hurry it. And cushioned it, in my opinion—in a strange way made the end easier for her. With the fantastic miracle of her 'career' already a shambles ten years ago, can you imagine Marilyn Monroe today alive—existing as what? Where? How? Think about it."

Sean Penn

(August 17, 1960–)

Just as Academy Award winner Sean Penn has long been noted for powerful, committed performances on screen, so too has he has gained a reputation off screen for his combustible personality. In the 1980s—at the height of Penn's off-camera antics, which often got him into legal scrapes—James Walcott profiled the rising star for *Vanity Fair* magazine. In that piece, Walcott

suggested the possibility that Penn, who grew up with a comfortable southern California lifestyle, was compensating for his privileged background through belligerent behavior. According to the writer: "Penn seems to want to bleed any suggestion of frivolity of normality from his surfer-boy past in order to sheathe himself in a rugged weave of rattlesnake skin."

Veteran actor Dennis Hopper, a longtime friend of Penn's who directed him in 1988's *Colors*, theorized about the notorious scrape that Sean got into with an extra on that shoot. Hopper, who had gone through decades of his own bad-boy behavior, said, "Somewhere in there, there's got to be something that tells you what round it is, you know? And if it's the last round, you're better to take the dive. But Sean's a very sensitive guy, and if things are ticking him, you can't stop it."

• • •

Sean Justin Penn was born in Santa Monica, California, in 1960, the second of three sons of actor/director Leo Penn and former actress Eileen Ryan. Sean was not a big fan of formal education, and repeatedly he got into minor incidents with authorities. After he graduated from Santa Monica High School in 1978, he spent two years with a Los Angeles theater troupe. Meanwhile, he appeared on TV in such shows as a 1978 episode of *Barnaby Jones*. His New York stage bow was in 1981's *Heartland*. That same year, he was effectively intense as a military academy cadet in the film *Taps*. However, it was his performance as the surfer dude in the 1982 comedy *Fast Times at Ridgemont High* that made Penn popular with moviegoers. Subsequently, he was impressive in pictures that did not match his skills (such as 1984's *Racing with the Moon*). As Penn climbed to stardom, his antagonism toward the media grew stronger. He reached the point where he insisted that if any reporters were permitted on his movie sets, they were *never* to be allowed in his direct line of vision. He posted a notice on his dressing room door: "Never Enter Without Knocking. Never Knock Without Need."

By 1985, the wiry Penn, a member of Hollywood's Brat Pack, had already had romances with actresses Elizabeth McGovern and Mary Stuart Masterson. That January, he met Madonna, whose singing career was taking off. Sean was fascinated with her, but the Material Girl did not have, at first, the same strong feelings for him. (At the time, she was dating Prince and had no intention of not seeing the singer just to accommodate the highly jealous Penn.) This situation led to a battle of words at Madonna's Manhattan apartment, where the extremely annoyed Sean reportedly smashed his hand through her front door.

In June 1985, Madonna flew to Tennessee, where Penn was making *At Close Range*. The unlikely couple became engaged. One day in Nashville, a paparazzo attempted to photograph the famous duo. Sean grew furious, hurled a few stones in the man's direction, and then chased after him. The actor was charged with misdemeanor assault and battery. Ultimately, he was fined $100 and given a 90-day suspended sentence. Penn's disgust with the media intensified weeks later when nude photos of Madonna (shot in the late 1970s) were published in *Penthouse* magazine.

In August 1985—on her 27th birthday and the day before his 25th—they wed at a friend's plush estate in Malibu, California. Reports of the top-secret event leaked out, and press helicopters hovered overhead throughout the service. A livid Sean not only screamed at the aerial party-crashers; he also reputedly fired two warning pistol shots at the craft. (Earlier, the groom-to-be had run down to the beach and written "Fuck Off" in the sand, hoping the press in the helicopters would heed his warning.)

By early 1986, the newlyweds were in Hong Kong to make *Shanghai Surprise*. The shoot was a near disaster. Dissatisfied with the project and angered by the intrusive media, Penn found it difficult to deal with being married to one of the world's most prominent women. To diffuse his misery, Sean drank a good deal over the course of the shoot. His conduct made him and Madonna (no longer herself very cooperative with journalists) media targets. When the two went to England to complete the picture, the British press labeled them the "Poisoned Penns."

In April 1986, the Penns were back in Los Angeles. At a club in Silver Lake, songwriter David Wolinski came over to his friend Madonna and kissed her in greeting. An incensed Sean hit and kicked Wolinski and then struck him with a chair. The victim pursued legal recourse, and the actor was fined $1,000 and placed on a year's probation.

By that August, the controversial duo were in New York, keeping a low profile after the negative response to *Shanghai Surprise*. One evening, a photographer followed the Penns as they returned home from a nearby restaurant. Sean spat at the intruder, and, reportedly, the man reacted by shoving the actor. In the resulting scuffle, Penn hit both this individual and another photographer. While the two men did not press charges against the actor, the episode did nothing to improve Sean's reputation with the world at large.

Filmmaker Sean Penn at work on 1991's The Indian Runner.

On the set of *Colors*, in the spring of 1987, an extra tried to shoot photographs of the star. Penn spat on the man, who then returned the gesture. Sean went ballistic and beat him. The victim filed an assault charge. Penn, already on probation from earlier fracases, turned himself in to the authorities. He was released on his own recognizance pending the hearing. Later, Penn was detained by the police for running a red light and for speeding. He was charged with reckless and drunken driving. In June 1987, he was sentenced to 60 days in jail and two years of probation, and ordered to undergo counseling.

A few days after Penn began serving his sentence, he was permitted to leave jail to fulfill an acting assignment in *Judgment in Berlin*, which was being directed by his father. Following the shoot he returned to jail. After serving 33 days, he was released (with time off for good behavior). He reunited briefly with Madonna, but their continual disagreements throughout 1988 led to her filing for divorce that December. Two weeks later she withdrew her action. But in January 1989, the singer filed again for divorce, and this time followed through. (Years later Penn said, "It was a miserable marriage, but I [now] like her a lot. [At the time] I still had a lot of demon doors to go through. . . . I've talked to her a couple of time since, and there's a whole person there. I just didn't know it.")

Once Penn and Madonna split, the media spectacle that enveloped him (thanks to her huge fame) largely ended. Nevertheless, Sean still had a bumpy road ahead as he moved into middle age. There were snags in his long relationship with actress

Robin Wright (with whom he had two children) both before and after their April 1996 marriage, and contretemps between him and filmmaker Woody Allen on 1999's *Sweet and Lowdown*. Penn won an Oscar for his starring role in 2003's *Mystic River*, but the award apparently did not mellow him. He continued to battle those who did not agree with him.

Describing life with Sean, Robin Wright Penn has said, "It's always been drama in my life with Sean, always. It's pronounced: that's the word I would use for him, in every way—presence, emotional life— 'pronounced.' I think it's in his blood. He's always at the heart of something. Never a dull moment."

Peter Sellers

(September 8, 1925–July 24, 1980)

Today, the masterful actor Peter Sellers is best remembered for his bumbling Inspector Jacques Clouseau in the slapstick Pink Panther film series, as well as for playing multiple roles (a specialty of his) in 1964's *Dr. Strangelove or: How I Learned to Stop Worrying and Love the Bomb* and a childlike man in 1979's *Being There* (for which he earned his second Best Actor Oscar nomination). However, for those who knew the comedic genius on the sound stage or in private life, he was frequently a most maddening individual. Sellers's mean quirks, impetuous self-indulgences, and frequent nastiness to those (including wives

and children) in his orbit—whether or not he was using drugs at the time—were legendary.

When Sellers was riding high on a career upswing, he grew suspicious that his luck would desert him, and he rushed into a frenzy of show business projects that were often beneath his talents. During down periods in his professional life, he became even more morose than usual as he envisioned a bleak finale to his life's work. In the best or worst of his times, he was so internalized that he came across to others, even those closest to him, as largely a blank page. He said on more than one occasion, "If you ask me to play myself, I will not know what to do. I do not know who or what I am." He also claimed, "There used to be a me behind the [public] mask, but I had it surgically removed" and "To see me as a person on screen would be one of the dullest experiences you could ever wish to experience." (One film director noted of working with Sellers, "He was a receptacle rather than a person. And whatever parts he played completely filled the receptacle, and then they were drained out. And the receptacle was left empty and featureless.")

• • •

Richard Henry Sellers was born in 1925 at Southsea, Hampshire, England, to William and Agnes (Peg) Marks Sellers. (His nickname "Peter" was in memory of his stillborn older brother, Peter.) He came from a family of show business performers, including his withdrawn father (a pianist and a musical director) and his highly aggressive mother (an actress). His parents were on the vaudeville circuit, and Sellers made his stage debut at age 5 when he appeared in a revue with them. Peter spent a good deal of time with his mother, who was as obsessive about controlling her son as she was about advancing her minor career. He was spoiled by her and developed the habit of throwing temper tantrums when he did not get his own way. Because of his mother's suffocating ways, he had little opportunity to make friends his own age, and thus never developed the skills necessary to interact on any meaningful level with others. (The love-hate relationship Sellers had with his dominating mother twisted his approach to everyone in his life, especially women.)

The young Sellers was an undistinguished student in school except in the area of drawing. He developed a strong interest in drumming and, later, won jobs with local dance bands. In 1943, when he was just 18, he enlisted in the Royal Air Force. Poor eyesight prevented him from becoming a pilot, and he settled for more mundane duties. While stationed in India, he performed comedy skits and impersonations at camp shows. Later, he toured the Middle East with the RAF Gang Show. By now he had developed an impressive knack for mimicry.

After his discharge from military service in 1946, he spent the next few years working largely in London vaudeville houses. After a stint on BBC Radio on the series *Show Time*, he moved, in January 1952, to the *Goon Show*, a new comedy radio show that also featured Spike Milligan and Harry Secombe. Over his eight-year run on the popular program, Sellers polished his talents for clowning in dozens of voices. Meanwhile, he developed his reputation as a film comedian in such British-made entries as 1955's *The Ladykillers* and 1957's *Your Past Is Showing*.

Sellers married Australian actress Anne Hayes in September 1951. From the start, he was jealously possessive of her and was angered when her work separated them (although he had no such qualms when he was busy with his own projects). They had two children: Michael (born in 1954) and Sarah Jane (born in 1957). As in his dealings with his wife, the erratic Peter was frequently dismissive with his children—too preoccupied with his career to consider them anything more than a nuisance, and often becoming either extremely remote or

Peter Sellers in 1962's Only Two Can Play.

angry with them. At times, he also could be exceedingly cruel and thoughtless with his family, just as he often was with coworkers or the director on a film shoot.

While making 1960's *The Millionairess*, Peter became obsessed with his costar, Sophia Loren. Although she was already married and rebuffed all of Sellers's romantic overtures, Peter persisted in his one-sided courtship. The romance was a delusional fantasy in Sellers's mind, but he insisted upon advising his wife that their marriage was over. They parted in 1961 and were divorced in March 1963. The next year, in February, he wed the striking Swedish actress Britt Ekland, who was 17 years his junior. (They made a few films together, including 1966's *After the Fox*, and became the parents of a daughter, Victoria, born in 1965.)

On April 8, 1964, while working on *Kiss Me, Stupid* in Hollywood, Sellers went into cardiac arrest. Before he was finally stabilized his heart had stopped beating eight times. If he had lived life to excess (often fueled by substance abuse) before this incident, he became extreme in his approach thereafter. Even more so than before, he indulged himself in expensive whims (cars, electric trains, whatever gadget of the moment appealed to him). Like his attachment to people, these purchases were usually quickly forgotten, and he moved almost maniacally onto his next interests, which prompted more outrageous purchases (including homes) that he quickly ignored. He became addicted to following the advice of psychics, which did not improve his choice of screen projects or acquaintances. He had many superstitions, including a dread of the color purple (which symbolized death to him). He also continued to enter into brief love affairs and remained highly disruptive, frequently tardy, and infuriatingly bizarre on movie sets. (He was not above having the cast or staff fired off a picture for no good reason, and he often undermined the authority of the director. Seemingly, he was amused by his own inexcusable bad behavior.)

In December 1968, he and Ekland divorced. (She commented later of her ex-husband, who, in contrast to his humane image on camera, was full of dark moods and violent outbursts in real life: "There were interludes when he was truly a loving, gentle, and generous human being, but these moments were like flashes of sunshine.") In August 1970, Sellers wed Australian model Miranda Quarry. She divorced him in September 1974.

A decade earlier, Sellers had been highly successful with his film role of the inept Inspector Clouseau in 1964's *The Pink Panther* and its sequel, *A Shot in the Dark*. He revisited the popular characterization in 1975's *The Return of the Pink Panther*. It was a huge hit, as were the next installments (in 1976 and 1978). Meanwhile, in February 1977, he wed British actress Lynne Frederick, who was 29 years younger than he. As with his previous wives, he had a vacillating relationship with her that was filled with marital discord.

After completing *The Fiendish Plot of Dr. Fu Manchu* in 1980, Sellers planned to fly to the United States to undergo heart surgery. He stopped over in England, where he suffered a massive heart attack and died that October. This was the finale of a talented but unfathomable man who once wrote in a magazine article, "If I can't really find a way to live with myself, I can't expect anyone else to live with me."

PART 4

So Much Partying

John Barrymore

(February 14, 1882–May 29, 1942)

The impressive actor John Barrymore was called "The Great Profile." More important, he was a superior talent—descended from a long line of performers—who could be particularly compelling on stage. His dazzling Hamlet was a triumph on Broadway in 1922 and the engagement might have extended indefinitely. However, the theater's great matinee idol was then preoccupied by this jealousy of his spouse, poet Michael Strange. She was then abroad and he (rightly) feared her infidelity. Walking

The dissipated John Barrymore, once known as "The Great Profile," cavorting on radio in the late 1930s.

away from *Hamlet* was but one of the impulsive, self-destructive choices Barrymore made during his lengthy career.

In particular, Barrymore devoted much of his hectic life to struggling with his alcoholism. Of more import to John was his dread that he would end up like his stage star father: a debauched individual who went insane from, and died of, syphilis.

• • •

John Sidney Blyth was born in Philadelphia in 1882, the third and last child of prominent stage troupers Georgiana Drew and Maurice Blyth (who both adopted the professional surname of Barrymore). John's older siblings—Lionel (1878–1954) and Ethel (1879–1956)—would also have impressive acting careers. When John was 11, his mother succumbed to tuberculosis. A few months later, his father wed Mamie Floyd. Unlike the first Mrs. Barrymore, she was not celebrated, but she was young, attractive, and lusty. When John was 15, his stepmother seduced him. Remorseful at having cuckolded his father, the teenager developed a lifelong mistrust of attractive females and an addiction to liquor.

The hedonistic Barrymore studied art abroad, planning to bypass the family's tradition in the theater. Later, he worked in Manhattan as a cartoonist and then as a newspaper illustrator. After being discharged from both jobs, he turned to acting, making his professional debut in 1903. Within six years, the naturally talented actor established himself on Broadway with the comedy *The Fortune Hunter*. In 1910, he impetuously married socialite Katharine Harris; he was 27, she was 17. It was a stormy union, with both partners guilty of infidelity. By 1917, they had divorced.

In the meantime, Barrymore—known to friends as Jack—pursued his flourishing stage career and performed occasionally in films, such as 1920's *Dr. Jekyll and Mr. Hyde*. (He attributed his professional success to "fervor and champagne.") That same year, the dissipated playboy wed his pregnant lover, Blanche Oelrichs (the poet who employed the pen name Michael Strange). Their daughter, Diana, was born in 1921. The marriage was tumultuous, and the couple had many long separations. During these breaks, Barrymore enjoyed several romantic capers. (Among others, he seduced Mary Astor, his young costar in 1924's *Beau Brummel* and 1926's *Don Juan*.) In the mid-1920s, the eminent actor was at the height of his cinema fame (where careful makeup and lighting still could camouflage the effects of his dissolute lifestyle.)

Six days after terminating his marriage to Strange, in November 1928, Barrymore wed 19-year-old blond actress Dolores Costello. (He had first met Costello at Warner Bros. where they both were under studio contract. The two furthered their personal relationship while costarring in 1927's *When a Man Loves*.) Barrymore promised his bride that he would give up drinking but was unable to keep that vow for long. The couple would have two children: Dolores Ethel Mae and John Jr.

When talkies arrived, the almost-50-year-old Barrymore was still in demand for his rich voice and what remained of his great profile. He performed with Greta Garbo in 1932's *Grand Hotel* and portrayed comical characters in 1933's *Topaze* and 1934's *Twentieth Century*. In 1935, he and Dolores (who could no longer abide his adultery or his alcoholic binges) divorced. She won custody of their children.

By the mid-1930s, age and Barrymore's excessive indulgences had taken their toll: his once handsome face had become flaccid, he had great problems recalling dialogue on camera, and he endured chronic spells of near insanity. His last solid film performances were in supporting roles in such features as 1936's *Romeo and Juliet* and 1938's *Marie Antoinette*. The declining star sought fresh diversion in youth. He became involved with 19-year-old New York City college student Elaine Jacobs (who later used the stage surname of Barrie), but his impulsive interest in Elaine quickly evolved into feelings of boredom mingled with jealousy. She chased him to Hollywood, with the press reporting on the mismatched couple's latest public shenanigans. On November 9, 1936, she and 54-year-old Barrymore, now a remnant of his once glorious self, married. Within eight weeks, she sought a divorce, then changed her mind.

In films, the once distinguished Barrymore was reduced to portraying sad caricatures of himself, such as in 1938's *Hold That Co-ed*. Now he drank even more to forget how much his career and life had declined. He had not performed on stage since the mid-1920s, but his ambitious wife convinced him to costar with her in *My Dear Children*.

The weak comedy exploited the coleads' chaotic personal life. Following an East Coast tour, John became ill. When the show reopened in St. Louis, the couple were no longer speaking and she had to be replaced in the cast. The couple divorced in November 1940. The self-indulgent Barrymore had not learned his lesson and prowled for new young women to amuse him.

By this time, the ailing and bankrupt Barrymore took on any type of buffoon screen parts. Many of his remaining friends had deserted him. As one acquaintance said, "I sometimes went down an alley to avoid him. With Jack it was going to be a hard night. You had to drown with him. He could pull you down faster than you could pull him up one inch. When he got hold of you, he would be so terribly lonely that he didn't want to go home. He would do anything to keep you with him all night—talk about what you were interested in, *give* himself. He was an expert at that. After all, it was his trade."

By the spring of 1942, Barrymore was coping with several physical ailments, including cirrhosis of the liver, which had bloated his once trim body. On May 29, 1942, he died. Having earned about $1 million over the years as an actor, he left an estate of only $10,000—which was divided among his three children.

John was only one of a number of Barrymores who suffered from substance abuse. His sister, Ethel, was an alcoholic, while his brother, Lionel, had a drug addiction. His daughter, Diana, squandered her acting potential on booze and partying. She passed away in 1960 of a likely accidental mix of liquor and sedatives. As to Barrymore's handsome son, John Jr., he ruined his film career with substance abuse and bizarre antisocial behavior. Years of near-derelict existence ended with his death in 2004. John Jr.'s daughter, Drew, who also became an actor, broke the Barrymore curse by overcoming the addictions of her youth and turning her life around.

John Belushi

(January 24, 1949–March 5, 1982)

In 1970s and 1980s Hollywood, many of the industry's movers and shakers (both in front of and behind the cameras) were caught up in the crazy, expensive world of drugs. Seemingly, they gave little thought to the potential perils of excessive substance abuse and how such reckless living might drastically impinge on their future—both professionally and personally.

One of that era's most enthusiastic drug users was the popular actor/comedian John Belushi, who proudly admitted, "You know what I love to do? Get fucked up." The off-the-wall talent, who had a meteoric rise to fame, adored marijuana, relied on amphetamines and barbiturates, and experimented with LSD and peyote. Gradually, Belushi progressed to harder stuff: heroin and cocaine. In March 1982, the 33-year-old star overdosed on drugs and died. In the long history of Hollywood, Belushi's far-too-short life became a yardstick of how excessive drug use could eradicate a high-octane show business career.

• • •

John Adam Belushi was born in Wheaton, Illinois, in 1949 to Adrian and Agnes Belushi. His father, an Albanian immigrant, was in the restaurant business. John had an older sister and two younger brothers (one of them, Jim, also became an actor). During John's high school years, he was on the football squad, was the drummer for a rock 'n' roll band, and became enthralled with acting. After being turned down for a football scholarship at one college, he enrolled at the University of Wisconsin (at Whitewater), which had a superior drama department. Later, Belushi transferred to the College of DuPage in Glen Ellyn. During summer vacations, he acted with stock companies.

In 1971, the chunky Belushi joined the Second City Troupe, the famed Chicago-based revue group known for its improvisational skits. The newcomer relished being part of this world of comedy, where he had the opportunity to combine slapstick with heavy satire and moments of dramatic reality. Even at this juncture, the hyperactive performer was relying on alcohol and a widening assortment of drugs (including sunshine acid) to give him extra force for his work, and then to take him off his performance highs. Bursting with high energy and inventiveness, John earned solid critiques for his madcap stage work. His rapid rise in

show business led to his being featured in the cast of the 1973 off-Broadway production *National Lampoon's Lemmings*—for which he was both an actor and a writer.

The defining moment in Belushi's career came when he was hired to be a cast member of a bold new TV comedy/variety series, *Saturday Night Live*. The innovative network program debuted in October 1975, and it quickly evolved into a major hit. Among the show's talented cast members (which included Dan Aykroyd, Chevy Chase, Jane Curtin, and Gilda Radner), the

John Belushi in 1981's Continental Divide, *released just months before his death from a massive drug overdose.*

volatile and unique Belushi became a favorite with home viewers. His repertoire of way-out characters included the bizarre Samurai Warrior and one of (along with Aykroyd) the vocalizing, problem-prone Blues Brothers.

Off camera, the antiestablishment Belushi gave new meaning to the term "party animal." His craving for booze and hard drugs was enormous, and he was soon spending a good portion of his over $100,000 annual income on illegal substances. This ongoing drug habit made him less disciplined and more difficult at work. It led to his being fired and then rehired repeatedly during his *SNL* tenure. Doctors again and again cautioned Belushi that his heavy-duty use of cocaine and other drugs would likely kill him. He ignored such admonitions, preferring his usually wired state. In the meantime, in December 1976, John married his high school girlfriend, Judith Jacklin (a book illustrator and designer), who had been his lover since Belushi's Second City times.

As *SNL* alumnus Chevy Chase had done before him, Belushi turned to moviemaking. In the role of John "Bluto" Blutarsky, John was the focal point of 1978's *National Lampoon's Animal House*. Moviegoers reveled in the film's coarse humor and the crude antics of John's outrageous frat brother character. The picture's potent box-office profits prompted Belushi to leave *SNL* and focus on the better-paying and less-pressured arena of films.

Belushi soon discovered that with his protruding eyes, bulging belly, and raspy voice, he scarcely resembled the typical Hollywood leading man. This made casting him as a movie's hero very difficult. This obstacle to a successful film career made John increasingly anxious about his professional future. He indulged in frequent food binges, which caused his weight to fluctuate greatly. The more self-doubting he became, the more he also turned to drugs to "cope" with his emotional problems. This destructive cycle caused him to keep away from his pals. (Belushi was insistent that he did not wish his friends to see him while he was seriously under the influence.)

Belushi tried to skirt around the casting limitations imposed by his girth and unusual looks. However, he did not have much good fortune in selecting screen vehicles. (His misfires included 1979's *1941* and 1981's *Continental Divide*. A number of these movies—such as the misguided *Neighbors*, in 1981—teamed him with his good friend Dan Aykroyd.) It also did not help Belushi's career trajectory that often he was so under the influence of drugs and/or booze during the shoot that he could scarcely get through the day's scenes. (Ironically, Belushi was sufficiently organized to establish drug contacts/suppliers in almost any city he might be in, but in all other areas of his life he was becoming progressively scattered.)

Belushi decided to create a fresh screen image for himself as a dramatic actor, one who could indeed undertake romantic leads. He coscripted his own starring vehicle, *Noble Rot*. However, he had no luck in selling the property to a Hollywood studio. Enraged over this latest career setback, John flew to Los Angeles, having left his wife back in Manhattan. He registered at the

Chateau Marmont hotel in West Hollywood and moved into bungalow number 3.

John was in a gloomier mood than usual when he began partying heavily on the evening of March 4, 1982. His smorgasbord of drugs (including a speedball injection of heroin and cocaine) proved too much for his constitution, and he died on March 5.

He had been living on borrowed time for a long while.

Once, when a concerned physician ordered Belushi to quit his lethal cocaine habit, John answered, "I give so much pleasure to so many people. Why can I not get some pleasure for myself? Why do I have to stop?"

Montgomery Clift

(October 17, 1920–July 23, 1966)

Deborah Kerr, who costarred with Montgomery Clift in 1953's *From Here to Eternity*, observed of the handsome actor, "He wanted to love women, but he was attracted to men, and he crucified himself for it." That was merely one of Clift's numerous emotional conflicts. His angst-filled relationship with his parents made him a longtime prisoner of his anger at them and a victim of his guilt about having such "abnormal" feelings about them. Another internal clash within the cerebral Clift concerned his acting craft. Performing was his chief reason for being. As a young man he had been a highly promising Broadway stage actor, but he could not resist the temptations of fame and fortune offered by Hollywood. Once he became a movie star he caved under the pressure of being a celebrity and came to loathe himself for having sold out. His career disillusionment made him increasingly insecure about his talents and cynical about his professional future.

To cope with his internal pain, the hypersensitive Clift sought relief through years of psychiatric therapy. However, his spirit was so bruised that he was unable—or unwilling—to combat his inner demons satisfactorily. By the late 1940s, the soft-spoken actor had turned to liquor and then, increasingly, to an assortment of pills. (His regimen came to include a near daily bottle of scotch, barbiturates, tranquilizers, and other medications to sedate the furies within him.) Fred Zimmermann, who directed Clift in two of his best movies, said of the self-destructive star: "His drinking was more deadly than Spencer Tracy's. Drunk or sober, Spencer knew who he was, but when Monty drank he seemed to lose his identity and almost melt before your eyes."

After Clift's near-fatal car accident in 1956, his chaotic life spun further out of control. The mishap had disfigured his face so badly that not even extensive plastic surgery could restore his once striking looks. He retreated deeper into substance abuse, which heightened his manic behavior and further destroyed his health. Because he was now considered so unreliable within the

The handsome Montgomery Clift in an early 1950s publicity pose, before his substance abuse began to ravage his looks and life.

industry, he had great difficulty in finding screen work. His ruination was near complete, and not even loyal friends like movie queen Elizabeth Taylor could save him.

• • •

Edward Montgomery Clift was born just after his twin sister, Roberta, in Omaha, Nebraska, in 1920. They had an older brother, Brooks. His father was a thriving banker who would fall on difficult times during the Depression. His mother, Ethel "Sunny" Fogg Clift, had her own life's mission. As a youngster she had been adopted, and only years later did she discover that she was actually descended from Southern aristocracy. In her determination to reclaim the heritage of her lineage, she expended a good deal of her husband's income. When the Clifts settled in Chicago in 1924 and then moved to New York in 1930, Sunny continued to pursue her dreams of living a refined life. She frequently took her children abroad, with her husband remaining behind.

Clift's handsome looks prompted several family acquaintances to suggest that he become a model. However, Monty had already decided to become an actor. He made his Broadway bow in the 1935 comedy *Fly Away Home*. By the point of 1940's *There Shall Be No Night* and 1942's *The Skin of Our Teeth* he was secretly involved in gay affairs in which even the participants never discussed with each other their alternative lifestyle. Then there was the actor's link to Libby Holman, a former actress/torch singer whose first marriage had ended with her wealthy husband's mysterious death. She was 16 years older than Clift and, like him, bisexual. Over the years, there was much conjecture about their reportedly odd sex life. Meanwhile, Clift was rejected for World War II military service due to the aftermath of the amoebic dysentery he had contracted during a vacation in Mexico with one of his mentors/special pals (conductor Lehman Engel).

Filmmaker Howard Hawks hired Clift to act opposite the rugged John Wayne in *Red River*. The Western was made in 1946 but not released until a few months after 1948's *The Search*. (The latter picture won Monty the first of his four Academy Award nominations.) When Clift costarred with Olivia de Havilland in 1949's *The Heiress*, he was paid $100,000 for the assignment and was now regarded as Hollywood's major new talent. Clift was already overwhelmed by leading a double life (in this closeted era before gay liberation): as a romantic idol of the screen and, secretly, as a homosexual. The more well known he became, the more deeply troubled he was about the increasing media scrutiny of his personal life. His substance abuse worsened and brought on recurrent blackouts. (He also had an underactive thyroid, which contributed to his disoriented demeanor.)

When not filmmaking, he would return to New York City, where he could enjoy more privacy. Much of Monty's free time in Manhattan was spent in the company of actor Kevin McCarthy and his actress wife, Augusta Dabney. The trio was such a familiar sight around town that onlookers wondered about the full nature of the friendship. When forced to be in southern California, Monty socialized with Elizabeth Taylor, his costar in 1951's *A Place in the Sun*. When the often married movie queen was wed to British actor Michael Wilding in the 1950s, Clift was a constant figure in their lives.

The turning point in Clift's troubled life took place on May 12, 1956. He had been working for over a month on *Raintree County*, a movie epic of the old South that reteamed him with Taylor. That evening he had attended a dinner party at the Wildings' in Los Angeles. After leaving their home and while driving down the winding road in the fog, an inebriated Clift slammed his car into a power pole. The near-fatal mishap left the actor's face a shattered mess, necessitating painful reconstructive surgery. He had always been prideful about his looks (which he believed were the primary basis for his fame), and now his fragile self-confidence unraveled further. He completed *Raintree County*, but he looked odd and disturbed on the big screen.

The devoted Elizabeth Taylor demanded of the producers that Clift be her costar in 1959's *Suddenly, Last Summer*. However, his performance was dragged down by his substance abuse and his emotional pain. When Clift made 1962's *Freud*, he was continually harassed by director John Huston. The latter, a swaggering male chauvinist, was aghast to discover that Clift was homosexual. This, in addition to the actor's great difficulty in performing his scenes, led to a battle of wills on the shoot between director and star. Thereafter, the emotionally worn-out Clift did not work for another four years, and then it was in the lackluster *The Defector*, a 1966 misfire. The 45-year-old actor looked haggard and old. By the time the spy drama was released, Montgomery Clift was dead.

The cause of the star's passing, in July 1966, was a heart attack, exacerbated by decades of excessive booze and medications and his personal torments.

Sandra Dee

(April 23, 1944–February 20, 2005)

"For the first time in my life I don't want to die," the 56-year-old Sandra Dee revealed in 1998. To anyone familiar with mid-twentieth-century American culture, it was an astounding statement. After all, the speaker was *the* movie star who had once defined the ideal of the beautiful young blonde: innocent and vulnerable but capable of being pouty, perky, and sassy. For moviegoers of that era, Dee created an indelible impression as the original screen Gidget, the appealing lead figure in two Tammy movies, and the good-girl-in-trouble in 1959's *Imitation of Life* and *A Summer Place*. Seemingly, she led a charmed life — a successful child model turned popular movie actress who had wed her first love, the dynamic singer/actor Bobby Darin.

In reality, however, Sandra Dee was far from a bubbly teen queen and contented young wife/mother. The emotional scars from her tormented childhood led Dee into years of anorexia and alcoholism. She had a consuming fear that her problems and flaws would be revealed to the world and destroy the grand illusion of Little Miss Perfect that her controlling mother, the studio, and Dee had concocted years before.

• • •

She was born Alexandra Cymboliak Zuck in 1944 in Bayonne, New Jersey. Her father, John, a bus driver, was an alcoholic. Her mother, Mary, who was 18 when she had Alexandra, was a secretary. Before the girl was 5, the Zucks divorced. In the third grade, the youngster became self-conscious when she began developing a bust. (Later, when Alexandra grew to a size 34D, she was "mortified.") Mrs. Zuck's remedy for Alexandra's plight was to clothe her "in little velvet dresses" with her chest "taped underneath."

In 1950, Mary remarried, this time to a successful Manhattan commercial property owner who was 40 years her senior. Even before Eugene Douvan wed Mary, he was fondling her daughter. Later, he began a routine of expanded sexual abuse. Alexandra was too ashamed to tell her mother. Instead, she became highly introspective and overly concerned with being ultrathin and "perfect" — to please her tormentor and her demanding mother. Alexandra developed into a classic eating-disorder victim.

In 1952, when the dysfunctional family moved from Long Island to New York City, Alexandra was enrolled at the Professional Children's School. She began modeling, and within four years, she was earning over $70,000 annually. In 1956, her stepfather died, and a few days thereafter, she was screen-tested by movie producer Ross Hunter and signed to a seven-year contract with Universal Studios. Her debut movie was 1957's *Until They Sail*. By the late 1950s, Dee was a certified screen star, if not yet an accomplished actress. In 1960, she flew to Italy to make *Come September*. Her colead in that romantic comedy was the nearly eight-years-older Bobby Darin, a talented pop vocalist.

Hardly had Dee stepped onto the *Come September* set in Rome than the cocky Darin announced, "I'm going to marry you someday." Initially, the ultrashy girl thought he was obnoxious and wondered how she was ever going to work with him on camera. Her domineering mother/chaperone insisted that the teenager date him to break the ice and to salvage the professional situation.

When Dee returned to the States, Darin gave her a seven-carat diamond engagement ring. Mary Douvan's reaction to the situation was to grab her daughter's two dogs ("my only friends") and disappear for two months. When the actress and Darin married in December 1960 in a quiet ceremony, her still furious mother was not present.

Dee's wedding night proved traumatic. The occasion triggered all her bad memories of sexual abuse. "I sat on the couch for 12 hours in my coat. Bobby finally went to bed." (Dee never told him about her stepfather till after their divorce. "I didn't want him to look at me as if I were dirty. He didn't. When I told him, he cried.")

The Darins honeymooned in Palm Springs in a home he had purchased to be near his pal, actor Jackie Cooper. Three days later, Dee was back on the sound stages. When she returned on weekends, the singer was usually preoccupied, playing poker with pals. She soon discovered, "There was no lover anymore, just a husband." Their house was always overflowing with his band members and hangers-on, and she, not having any friends of her own, felt increasingly isolated.

A studio-enhanced photo of Sandra Dee to publicize 1959's Gidget. *At the time, Dee was already suffering from anorexia, and would soon develop a reliance on alcohol and prescription drugs.*

After the birth of their child, Dodd, in December 1961, Dee hoped to retire from the screen. However, the studio, her mother (now back on the scene), and her husband pressured her to return to filmmaking. This time it was to costar with Darin in 1962's *If a Man Answers*. Dee was so unhappy that she began a cycle of pill (uppers/downers) and alcohol dependency.

Meanwhile, Darin had shifted focus from his recording career to moviemaking, He also became deeply involved in politics and with his music publishing firm. During this period, the couple's relationship seemed to improve, and Dee continued to make movies. But then Darin began losing interest in her. Dee claimed the finale occurred on her 24th birthday, when he saw her talking to playboy actor Warren Beatty at a party about possibly making a film together. The next day, without explanation, Darin moved out of the house. The couple's divorce was final in March 1967. On several occasions the couple sought to reconcile, but they had too much bad history together. Nevertheless, when he died, in December 1973, of congestive heart failure, Dee was devastated, and never found the courage to seriously date again.

By the time of Darin's death, Dee's movie career—the only rock of security in her sheltered world—had fizzled. Increasingly, the depressed woman turned to her young son for support, and even allowed her mother to resume full control of her life. Eventually, Dee suffocated once again under Mary's unrelenting dictatorship. For relief, the unemployed actress turned to heavy drinking (often a quart or more of vodka or scotch daily) and scarcely ate anything (the five-foot-four-inch actress weighed only 80 pounds). Later, in an explosive moment, she confessed to Mary about having been abused by her stepfather. Her mother refused to deal with this shocking revelation and the matter was never discussed again. Mary died in 1988.

After years of hiding her debilitating problems, which often kept her a prisoner at home, Sandra Dee went public with her troubled past in 1991. Before she did so, she confided in her mother's sister, Olga, and her uncle Peter. Her aunt told the ex–movie star, "Sandy, you haven't done anything wrong. You have nothing to be ashamed of. Hold your head up high."

Sadly, the middle-aged Dee, who had become a grandmother, was never able to fully deal with her unpleasant past—despite years of therapy. Because of the physical damage caused by decades of anorexia and alcoholism, she remained in tentative health. Her emotional frailty often pushed her back into substance abuse.

In 1994, Dodd Darin wrote *Dream Lovers: The Magnificent Shattered Lives of Bobby Darin and Sandra Dee*. A decade later, Kevin Spacey starred in *Beyond the Sea*, a movie biography of Darin, in which Kate Bosworth portrayed Dee. Both projects brought Dee back into the limelight. However, by the time the biopic was released she was in the final throes of kidney disease, and she died of pneumonia in February 2005.

Robert Downey Jr.

(April 4, 1965–)

When Robert Downey Jr. was at the height of his substance abuse during the 1990s—and making ugly headlines as a result of it—he said of his drug addiction, "It's like I have a loaded gun in my mouth, and I like the taste of metal."

Few actors of Downey's generation are as talented as this engaging Oscar nominee. Ironically, Robert's great charisma was nearly his fatal undoing. Because he was in such demand for acting gigs and because he was so charming, many show business decision makers chose to overlook Robert's serious drug habit and the chaos his self-destructive lifestyle brought to the workplace. Even when the hapless star was forced by court order to enter rehab, he was often yanked out of the treatment process too soon because he was needed for a movie project. In short, many within the film community enabled the troubled celebrity, as did many of his well-meaning friends. For a long spell, it appeared that Robert, who also suffered from a belatedly diagnosed bipolar disorder, was headed for oblivion.

• • •

Robert John Downey Jr. was born in New York City's Greenwich Village in 1965. He was the younger of two children (following sister Allison) of underground moviemaker Robert Downey Sr. and his actress wife, Elsie Ford. During his childhood, he and his family moved frequently. At age 5,

Robert made his film debut (playing a puppy) in his dad's offbeat movie *Pound*. The nonconformist Robert Sr. was a member of the hippie generation and smoked marijuana. He and his wife agreed that there was nothing wrong with allowing their children to do so also. (Robert Jr. recalled, "When my dad and I would do drugs together, it was like him trying to express his love for me in the only way he knew how.")

By 1977, his parents' marriage had disintegrated. Robert lived with his mother for a while, then went to southern California to be with his dad. He attended Santa Monica High School. Already, Robert had little regard for conventional values, and he wasn't challenged by his academic curriculum except for music and drama classes. Eventually, with his father's approval, he dropped out of school in the eleventh grade and moved back to Manhattan.

To support himself while auditioning for roles in regional theater, he worked as a busboy and a shoe salesman. In the spring of 1983, he appeared in an off-Broadway play, and then turned to making films, such as 1984's *Firstborn*. One of his coplayers in that screen drama was Sarah Jessica Parker, and they began a romance. (His escalating drug problems killed the seven-year relationship.) Downey joined the cast of TV's *Saturday Night Live* for its 1985–1986 season. By now, he was not only hooked on alcohol and pot, but also had tried cocaine.

In 1987's *Less Than Zero*, Robert was more than credible portraying a nihilistic Los Angeles drug addict. In 1988, his talent agent confronted him about his addictions and Downey tried rehab. However, within a few years, he returned to his old bad ways.

By the point of 1990's *Air America* with Mel Gibson, Downey realized he was too often accepting inferior projects just for the high pay. His search for quality work led him to invest a great deal of effort into portraying "The Little Tramp" in 1992's *Chaplin*—for which he won an Academy Award nomination.

Robert Downey Jr. in 1991's Soapdish. *By then, he was already overusing drugs and alcohol.*

Meanwhile, Robert's substance abuse continued. While in one of his rehab programs he met actress Deborah Falconer and, 42 days later, in May 1992, they married. Their son, Indio, was born in September 1993. Downey's new family stabilized him to an extent, but his highly addictive behavior still controlled him. When he had severe cocaine seizures in the spring of 1995, he tried rehab treatment yet again.

In June 1996, Downey was charged with driving under the influence in Malibu. Los Angeles County sheriffs found heroin, cocaine, and an unloaded .357 Magnum gun (with bullets) in the car's glove compartment. In mid-July, while the actor was out on bail awaiting trial, he wandered into the unlocked home of Malibu neighbors, where he fell into a drugged sleep on the empty bed belonging to the owners' 11-year-old son. (The family chose not to press charges against Downey.) On July 18, a Los Angeles County Municipal Court judge remanded the actor (now reduced to 138 pounds from his usual weight of 170) into a full-time, supervised drug treatment program. Two days later, Downey fled the facility through a window, but was recaptured and placed in county jail for nine days. Then he was shipped to a lockdown rehab center. In September, he pleaded no contest to both the felony drug possession charges and the misdemeanor charges of driving under the influence and possessing a concealed weapon. That November, he was sentenced to six additional months at a live-in treatment center, along with three years' probation and periodic drug tests.

During the next months he was furloughed long enough to do a TV interview and to host *Saturday Night Live*.

In 1997, Robert made, among other features, *Hugo Pool* with his father. Also that year, Robert and his wife separated, with her being given custody of their son. When the actor missed his mandatory drug testing appointment, the judge ordered that he serve 180 days in jail. Five weeks later, Robert was let out to make the film *U.S. Marshals*. Once back in Los Angeles County Jail, in February 1998, the actor got into an argument with three other inmates and was bashed on the nose during the melee. Thereafter, as a protective measure, he was put into solitary confinement. After a few days of furlough to finish *In Dreams*, he was released from jail on March 31, 1998, and placed into a four-month treatment program.

During 1999—in which year he had three films in release—Downey was back in court for failing to do his required drug testing. He was sent to a closely monitored rehab program. In August, at his sentencing, the judge ordered the defendant to spend three years in a state prison. Thanks to his attorneys' appeal, he was released early (on August 2, 2000).

The freed actor was hired for several episodes of the TV series *Ally McBeal* and turned in good performances. Then, on Thanksgiving weekend 2000, he went on an alleged drug binge in Palm Springs and was arrested on suspicion of possessing cocaine and methamphetamine, for being under the influence, and for committing a felony while on probation. The celebrity was released on bail, with a court date set for January 2001. At the hearing he pleaded not guilty. (While awaiting the trial, Downey returned to *Ally McBeal*.) He was back in the news again when he was arrested in April 2001, this time in Culver City on suspicion of being under the influence of a controlled substance. Meanwhile, the actor and the TV series had parted company. The court concluded that the Culver City brush with the law did *not* demand further jail time, especially since the actor was already in a detox center, where he was to spend six months.

By July 2001, Downey changed his pleas in the Palm Springs incident to no contest. This allowed him to take advantage of a new state law that mandated treatment, *not* prison, for many types of drug offenders. Downey was sentenced to a year of live-in drug rehab and three years' probation. As part of his healing process, he was permitted to work in his profession but under supervision. By 2002, he was back making films. On the set of one of them (2003's *Gothika*) he fell in love with producer Susan Levin, and they wed in August 2005. By then, he was in the midst of a very busy moviemaking schedule and had even found time to record an album (2004's *The Futurist*).

Downey said of his new marriage and his return to Hollywood's A-list, "Now that I'm clean, the answer for me is to commit on as many levels as I can." He also noted, "I've been really humbled by my inability to live life on life's terms and I've made a tremendous discovery: there's no benevolent God out there keeping an eye on my career."

Chris Farley

(February 15, 1964–December 18, 1997)

Like his idol John Belushi, Chris Farley became a major comic force in the entertainment world after having been a popular cast member of TV's *Saturday Night Live*. To an even greater extent than the pudgy Belushi, the hugely overweight Farley found that his career was defined by his girth. His size (the five-foot-eight-inch performer sometimes weighed well over 290 pounds) prevented the agile entertainer from obtaining conventional leading man assignments in Hollywood and from feeling at ease in normal dating situations. In reaction, Farley developed a compensatory manic comedic style that, eventually, pervaded his entire personality and existence. In 1996, Chris admitted to feeling terribly fenced in "by always having to be the most outrageous guy in the room." Also, the sensitive Farley claimed that he was still "working on trying not to be that guy in my private life."

Like Belushi, Farley had a highly addictive personality, which drew him into binges of food, booze, drugs, and sex. Paralleling his hero, Belushi, Chris died as a direct result of substance abuse. Like the highly talented John Belushi, Chris Farley was only 33 years old when he died.

• • •

Christopher Crosby Farley was born in 1964 in Madison, Wisconsin, the son of Thomas (a successful businessman) and Mary Anne Farley. The boy was the third of five children in this Catholic family.

(Farley's younger brother Kevin also became a comic, costarring in the 2000 TV series *2Gether* and being featured in such movies as 2005's *Callback*.) As a youngster, Chris already suffered from an obesity problem (as did his father). Because Chris was often taunted by classmates, he learned quickly to make his peers laugh before they could insult him.

In contrast, Farley's energetic clowning did not earn a good response from the nuns at the grade school he attended. When he moved on to high school in 1978, he used his bulk to become a linesman on the football squad. As an upperclassman he was a full-fledged party animal who craved being the center of attention. Despite Farley's seemingly frivolous approach to life, his grades were sufficiently high for him to be accepted by Marquette University in Milwaukee. There, he majored in theater and communications.

Soon after graduating from college in 1986, he moved to Chicago, where he joined the ImprovOlympic, the training ground for the celebrated Second City Troupe. Many of Farley's show business heroes (including John Belushi and Bill Murray) had labored there, and Chris hoped to follow in their successful career path. By late 1988, Chris was part of the Second City team. However, not only was he impatient for rapid recognition, but his compulsive need always to party to the max had become a major priority for him.

In the fall of 1990, Chris was added to the cast of *Saturday Night Live*, along with Adam Sandler and David Spade. Farley quickly made his presence known by creating a repertoire of crude, perspiring characters that appeared in various outrageous skits that season. Now that he was earning a six-figure salary, he began hiring prostitutes as well as increasing his substance abuse. His unbridled lifestyle became so detrimental to his performances on air that the producer/creator of *SNL*, Lorne Michaels, insisted that the unmanageable comic enter drug rehab—or suffer the professional consequences. After Farley spent three months in recovery, he returned to the TV show. Meanwhile, the troubled talent explored another aspect of himself by attending mass faithfully and working in his church's volunteer program for senior citizens.

It was not too long before Farley's excessive behavior reemerged, a signal that he had relapsed into extreme substance abuse. Eventually, friends staged an intervention and Chris entered the Exodus Recovery Center in Los Angeles. By the time he completed his stay there, the comedian seemed to have a better grip on his drug abuse. On the other hand, he was still compulsively indulging in food and hookers. (He blamed his addictions on the strain of trying to be continuously funny on live TV.)

Farley made his feature film debut in 1992's *Wayne's World*. This led to his being cast in such movies as 1993's *Coneheads* and 1994's *Airheads*. While Chris was now focusing much of his excess energy and urges into his career, he was not succeeding in building a healthy social life.

At the conclusion of the 1994–1995 TV season, the 31-year-old left *SNL*. In 1995's *Tommy Boy*, the oversized Chris was paired with the wispy David Spade. Farley was paid $2 million for the lowbrow project, which grossed $32 million at the box office. Farley was now headquartered in Los Angeles and felt adrift there. To compensate for the gaping holes in his life, he turned again to drugs and alcohol, as well as to his usual food and sex sprees. (Sometimes, his weight rose to 350 pounds.) Warned by pals and coworkers to somehow get a better grip on life, he seemingly refused to take their advice seriously. Actually, he was privately seeking religious counseling at his church, hoping that prayers would bolster him during this extremely difficult period.

While Farley's life and health were going to pieces, he reteamed with Spade for 1996's *Black Sheep*, then headlined—on his own—1997's *Beverly Hills Ninja*. As everything in Chris's life whirled further out of control, he checked into a rehab facility in Atlanta, Georgia. In the fall of 1997, after wrapping 1998's *Almost Heroes*, Farley went to Manhattan to host an episode of *SNL*. The star was so high on drink and other substances that an emergency oxygen tank was kept just off camera.

Subsequently, Farley entered a drug treatment center in Chicago. However, within weeks, he had left the facility and was back to indulging his old addictions: food, alcohol, drugs, and prostitutes. Between making his usual rounds of Windy City hot spots, he would return to his high-rise apartment and snort cocaine. When out on the town, the renowned comic compensated for his loneliness with strippers, party groupies, and an exotic dancer. The latter was with Chris during his final hours in December 1997. When she left him on his last morning, he was zonked out on the floor of his apartment. She presumed he was sleeping off the effects of hard partying. Sadly, when Farley's brother John visited the apartment that afternoon, he found Chris dead. Reportedly, there was a white, foamy liquid coming from his mouth and blood-saturated fluid dribbling from his nose. Like his beloved John Belushi, Chris had died of a drug overdose.

In the spring of 2006, with the permission of Chris Farley's family, the comedian's image was used in a billboard campaign in Los Angeles to promote a new program for treating drug and alcohol addiction.

W. C. Fields

(January 29, 1880–December 25, 1946)

W. C. Fields became an enduring icon playing a character who was an unyielding old grouch, a man who constantly railed against the law, animals, children—in fact, most of humanity (with the exception of attractive young women). Many fans assumed that Fields's indelible portrayal of a man who talked grandiosely but did a minimum of constructive activity was a reflection of the star's actual personality. However, it was pretty much invention on his part. On the other hand, like his show business alter ego, who was a sharp-tongued tippler, the real-life Fields had a great thirst for liquor.

The raspy-voiced, bulbous-nosed comedian so relied on having his daily libation that he maintained a large private hoard of his preferred alcoholic beverages, ever fearful that Prohibition might be reinstated and leave him in the lurch. His fondness for booze was so entrenched that he never seriously dealt with his long-term, chronic alcoholism. Eventually, the disease was a primary factor in ending his lengthy show business career and, ultimately, his life.

•   •   •

William Claude Dukenfield was born in 1880 in Philadelphia, the first of five children of James Lynden and Kate Felton Dukenfield. The future celebrity, always a very private individual, kept many details about his life to himself. To cover over the truth, he was prone to exaggeration and/or lies when recounting any facet of his supposedly grim childhood. (Fields's occasional recollection of his childhood years always sounded like a chapter out of a Charles Dickens novel, but that was no surprise since Dickens was the entertainer's favorite novelist.)

Fields's purportedly foul-tempered, liquor-gulping father was a Brit who ran a small pub in the City of Brotherly Love and, later, became a fruit peddler. Early on, the boy became determined to avoid having a conformist childhood and ached to be on his own. He began his wanderings (with occasional returns home) when he was 11 years old. He made his stage debut at age 14 as "Whitey, the Boy Wonder." Within four years, he was successfully working in vaudeville in New York City.

In 1900, he went to England to perform his juggling act. Also that year, in August, he married Harriet Hughes, a chorine. Their son, William Claude Jr., was born in September 1904. Since the couple held opposing views on most every subject in life, it was little wonder that the incompatible duo separated months later. Despite his later repute as a major skinflint, the show business figure regularly sent his family money. (The Catholic Hattie refused to divorce her unreligious spouse. However, this did not stop the entertainer from having several romantic liaisons over the years, the last being with minor film actress Carlotta Monti.)

W. C. Fields (as he had become known professionally) appeared on Broadway in the prestigious *Ziegfeld Follies of 1915* and that year made his film bow in the one-reel silent comedy *Pool Sharks*. After appearing in several editions of the *Follies*, he starred in the 1923 stage musical *Poppy*. In that show he played Professor Eustace McGargle, a role he repeated on camera in 1925's *Sally of the Sawdust*.

At age 51, Fields made his talkie movie debut in 1930's *The Golf Specialist*, the first of several comedy shorts he turned out. Next, he signed with Paramount Pictures, where he was repeatedly cast as the shifty curmudgeon who did daily battle with inanimate objects, little children, and a parade of authority figures. His films for the studio

included 1932's *If I Had a Million*, 1933's *International House*, and 1936's *Poppy*, many of which he scripted, employing various aliases (such as Charles Bogle). Soon the unique comedian became a major hit with the moviegoing public.

In 1936, a combination of tuberculosis and pneumonia and his ensuing long recuperation forced Fields to refrain from filmmaking. Once again, his concerned doctors warned him that he must stop drinking. However, as always, W. C. refused such sensible but inconvenient advice. By the late 1930s, the new management at Paramount Pictures had decided that Fields's worth at the box office did not compensate sufficiently for the expense and bother resulting from his habitual drinking on the sound stage, his extreme ad-libbing on camera, and his progressively unpredictable behavior on the movie lot. The studio ended his contract.

The 58-year-old alcoholic oddball found a new outlet—radio—for his personae, often as the foil of ventriloquist Edgar Bergen and his beloved dummy, Charlie McCarthy. This success led Fields to a new contract, this time with Universal Pictures. At a $150,000 per film fee, Fields made his bow for the studio in 1939's *You Can't Cheat an Honest Man*, as the grumpy owner of a circus. The next year, Fields was paired on screen with another former Paramount star, Mae West, in *My Little Chickadee*, a comedic Western. Teetotaler West was deeply perturbed by Fields's on-set imbibing, as well as by his scene-stealing antics. The entry was a hit, so the studio forgave W. C. for his frequent drunkenness and misanthropic actions during the shoot.

Due to increasingly poor health (the result of decades of heavy drinking), Fields had to reject an offer to return to Broadway in the early 1940s. His last movies (including 1944's *Song of the Open Road*) were fluff, and he was too ill to give a full-fledged performance. During the last year of his life, W. C. was a patient at the fashionable Las Encinas Sanitarium in Pasadena, California. Because of his longtime substance abuse, there was little that could be done for the dying movie great. (To ease his confinement, Fields had

an assistant deliver to him there a weekly shipment of a case of gin, half a case of vermouth, and a case of beer.) One day when someone inquired why the terminally ill patient was suddenly reading the Bible, the star retorted, "Looking for loopholes."

In death, the frugal Fields (who left an $800,000 estate) was extolled by his friends as a great artist. However, W. C. always understood that he had sacrificed much in life to his passionate love of alcoholic beverages.

Judy Garland
(June 10, 1922–June 22, 1969)

According to Judy Garland, "[MGM] had us working days and nights on end. They'd give us pep-up pills to keep us on our feet long after we were exhausted. Then they'd take us to the studio hospital and knock us cold with sleeping pills. Then after four hours they'd wake us up and give us the pep-up pills again so we could work another seventy-two hours in a row." While this was an overexaggerated recollection typical of Garland, the teenage performer certainly did become reliant on prescription drugs during the late 1930s. Thereafter, the great songbird, who suffered from a highly addictive personality, constantly relied on medications (as she did booze and food) to help her cope with, or better yet, escape from, life's realities.

Gerold Frank suggested in *Judy*, his 1975 biography of Garland: "Pills were the answers to everything, to what she thought

she had missed in a childhood she felt had been stolen from her, to the cruelty and thoughtlessness she felt had victimized her. They made this frightened little girl ten feet tall. With Benzedrine, she could say, 'Fuck you, I don't give a shit!' And with Seconol she could blot them all out, and all the memories of her own guilt, her own responsibility for what had happened to her."

Just as there were tremendous highs and lows in Garland's legendary career—which included a remarkable number of comebacks—her chaotic private life was full of dramatic mood swings as she fought real and imaginary demons. Some observers have said this was the tragic price the self-destructive artist was forced to pay for her enormous talent. But for many individuals caught in the maelstrom of Garland's frenetic life in and out of the spotlight, the cost was almost unbearable.

•   •   •

Frances Ethel Gumm was born in 1922, in Grand Rapids, Minnesota, the third daughter of struggling Irish tenor Frank Avent Gumm and Ethel Marion Milne Gumm, a vaudeville house pianist. The couple ran the local New Grand Theater. When Frances was just 2 and a half years old, she made her show business debut by coming onstage to join her parents and performing "Jingle Bells." (The "unplanned" event was devised by her domineering mother.)

By the late 1920s, the Gumms had moved to southern California, initially settling in Lancaster, 70 miles north of Los Angeles. There Mr. Gumm managed a movie theater. Meanwhile, his ambitious wife engineered her daughters' careers. Between 1929 and 1931, the trio appeared in movie shorts and toured with their singing act. By mid-decade it was clear that the youngest girl—now known as Judy Garland—was the star of the act. While the Garland siblings auditioned for several movie executives, it was Judy alone who was contracted by MGM in 1935. That same year Mr. Gumm died. Judy's $150 a week income largely supported her family. MGM was uncertain of how to present their chubby young singer, so they loaned her to Twentieth Century-Fox for 1936's *Pigskin Parade*. Her vocal abilities registered well on camera and she was quickly put to work in MGM features.

Metro had intended to borrow Shirley Temple from Twentieth Century-Fox to star in 1939's *The Wizard of Oz*, but that deal fell through and Garland was substituted as Dorothy; "Over the Rainbow" became her signature number. (She also earned a special Oscar for her endearing performance.) Her screen success continued with 1939's *Babes in Arms*, one of many films to team her with the equally diminutive Mickey Rooney.

In her early MGM years, the naive Garland was somewhat compliant with her employers' dictates—except regarding dieting. (Eating placed Judy into a temporary comfort zone.) To curb Judy's intake, she was given diet pills. Thus began her lifelong addiction to drugs, which soon included medication to sleep at night and other tablets to allow her to function in the morning.

The pill regimen aggravated Garland's recurrent bouts of paranoia and self-loathing. She fixated on Lana Turner (MGM's luscious young leading lady) as being everything she was *not*: curvaceous, sexy, and seemingly carefree. The "competition" heightened when playboy bandleader Artie Shaw, whom Judy had dated, eloped to Las Vegas with Lana in February 1940. This rebuff prompted Garland, always anxious to be considered an adult on and off the screen, to rush into a hasty marriage (in July 1941) with composer David Rose, 12 years her senior. It was a poor love match from the start. The crucial event that killed their relationship was Judy's pregnancy. She was ecstatic, but MGM and her controlling mother begged her to have an abortion so her career would not be interrupted. Rose went along with their reasoning, which devastated Judy. The couple separated, and Judy filed for divorce in June 1944.

Judy increasingly felt betrayed by the pivotal figures around her and she became

Jerry Van Dyke shares the spotlight with Judy Garland on her ill-fated 1963 TV series, The Judy Garland Show.

moodier and more defiant of the studio. Matters escalated when she became involved with the older, married Joseph L. Mankiewicz, the MGM writer/producer. It was this erudite man who urged Garland to try psychiatry. But the sessions seemed just to deepen her syndrome of Judy-against-the-world.

Initially, Garland clashed with director Vincente Minnelli while making 1944's *Meet Me in St. Louis.* However, she came to depend on him both professionally and personally. The film was a huge hit, which cemented their growing relationship. They

wed in June 1945 and, for a time, Garland even abandoned her drug crutch.

The Minnellis became the parents of daughter Liza in March 1946. Garland experienced postpartum depression and was further distressed at being coaxed into signing a new MGM pact. (She had hoped to retire into motherhood with only occasional freelance movie appearances.) When she made 1948's *The Pirate,* she was again heavily reliant on diet and other pills. She became very thin, constantly agitated, and excessively paranoid. She was sure Minnelli (long known in Hollywood circles for his interest in men) was favoring colead Gene Kelly (a former unrequited love of hers) over her. The troubled and expensive picture was not a box-office winner, and studio executives assigned a lot of the blame to Garland's sound-stage shenanigans.

By the time of 1950's *Annie Get Your Gun,* Garland was a total emotional wreck. She was sent to Boston for a rest cure while Paramount's Betty Hutton took over the lead in *Annie,* which became a gigantic hit. In June 1950, Garland attempted suicide. In the coming months, the new MGM regime terminated her contract. In March 1951, she and Minnelli divorced, leaving Garland adrift in life.

She was rescued by Sidney Luft, who helped her make an amazing comeback on the concert stage. A grateful Judy wed Luft in June 1952. Their daughter, Lorna, was born that November, and their son, Joseph, in March 1955. It was also Sid who engineered his wife's return to movies in 1954's *A Star Is Born.* Judy caved under the pressure of carrying this big-budgeted extravaganza and fell back on drugs, booze, and undisciplined behavior. The lavish musical earned Judy an Academy Award nomination but also reminded the film industry that she was a costly diva.

In subsequent years, Garland bounded back and forth between triumphant and sloppy concert engagements, depending on the level of her substance abuse and the status of her emotional/physical exhaustion. She survived a near fatal bout of acute hepatitis in the late 1950s. In April 1961, she gave a hugely successful concert at Carnegie Hall. She was Oscar-nominated for a Best Supporting Actress for 1961's *Judgment at Nuremberg*, and made her final film, *A Child Is Waiting*, in 1963. Her much-heralded TV variety series lasted but one season (1963–1964). Thereafter, the star's life and career fell into an abysmal slump.

Garland and Luft ended their acrimonious relationship in May 1965. (He claimed that Judy had attempted suicide 20 times in the 13 years of their marriage.) That November she wed the younger actor Mark Herron. They divorced in April 1967. Her fifth groom was discothèque manager Mickey Dean, also several years younger than Garland. They married in London, where, three months later, in June 1969, Judy was found dead in her apartment, a victim of an (accidental) pill overdose.

Roy Bolger (the Scarecrow in *The Wizard of Oz*) observed after Garland's untimely end: "Judy didn't die. She just wore out."

David Hasselhoff

(July 17, 1952–)

In 1977, a few years into his successful six-year gig on the TV soap opera *The Young and the Restless*, the hunky David Hasselhoff projected optimistically, "I'm an adventurer who wants to do everything, go everywhere. I want to get to the point . . . where I can have an apartment in three or four cities around the world." His career ambitions included branching out as a professional singer. "I don't want people to say, 'Oh, there's another soap-opera actor singing.' I want them to say, 'This guy's a singer!'" While Hasselhoff achieved these goals to some degree, he did not count on succumbing to substance abuse, a growing problem that haunted him in later years and generated myriad tabloid headlines.

• • •

David Michael Hasselhoff was born in 1952 in Baltimore, Maryland, the fifth child (following four girls) of Joseph and Dolores Hasselhoff. The family moved frequently because of the demands of his father's employment as an executive with the Brink's security firm. The boy was never an enthusiastic student, preferring to devote his energy to playing Little League baseball. When that sport was out of season, his mother encouraged the restless youngster to try acting, dance, and voice lessons to keep busy. By the time Hasselhoff was in junior high school he was regularly portraying men on stage because he was almost six feet tall. The shy adolescent found theater work to be one of the few constants in his life as the family continually relocated around the country. In high school—near Chicago—the six-foot-four-inch student remained devoted to theater work, while ignoring academics. As a result, he found it difficult getting accepted into college.

Eventually, Hasselhoff enrolled at the California Institute of the Arts (in Valencia). However, his stay there was short-lived and he was soon waiting tables while making the rounds of casting calls. (He earned extra money singing with local bands.) He caught a career break when he was hired to play the studly Dr. Snapper Foster on the daytime TV drama *The Young and the Restless*, which he did from 1975 to 1982. Meanwhile, his efforts to branch out into feature films or a nighttime television series met with little success.

An NBC network executive spotted Hasselhoff on a plane and suggested that the handsome actor audition for a new series, *Knight Rider*. By the fall of 1982, Hasselhoff was starring on prime-time TV as a crime fighter partnered with a super high-tech car. With its lighthearted approach, the program became an international hit, especially with young viewers. During the show's four-year reign, Hasselhoff wed

actress Catherine Hickland, in March 1984.

The mid-1986 fadeout of *Knight Rider* left Hasselhoff in limbo. He was so identified with the role of the series' glib hero that casting directors could not visualize him in any other part. With Hasselhoff's career and income suddenly in question, his personal life fell apart. He sought distraction in other women, travel, and alcohol. His marriage disintegrated—he and Hickland divorced in March 1989.

Meanwhile, the thirtysomething performer had already recorded such albums as 1984's *Night Rocker*. Like Hasselhoff's TV series, his pop/rock music was far more popular abroad. As a result, he began touring Europe, Scandinavia, and South Africa, and turned out more albums. Later, Hasselhoff admitted that his offstage life in this period was out of control: "I played to crowds of thousands, then I'd go back to the hotel alone and drink. . . . Actually, I was a spoiled guy, feeling sorry for myself."

The year 1989 was a turning point for Hasselhoff. He met and fell in love with actress Pamela Bach, and they wed that December. He was also hired by NBC-TV to headline a new series, *Baywatch*, in which his character was in charge of lifeguards stationed at Malibu Beach. Critics scoffed at the program's overemphasis on scantily clad beautiful people, and the entry was canceled at the end of its first season. However, the vehicle, with Hasselhoff now as both star and executive producer, was resurrected in 1991 as a syndicated series (both in the United States and abroad). During the next decade, *Baywatch* became a tremendous international hit, airing in well over a 100 countries, and Hasselhoff's Mitch Buchannon became a positive role model for millions of TV watchers.

By the early 1990s, the Hasselhoffs were the parents of two daughters. Despite his *Baywatch* triumph, the star was sorely frustrated that he couldn't jump-start his recording career in the United States or make inroads as a movie leading man. He returned to the stage occasionally (as in *The Rocky Horror Show*), but it was *Baywatch* that gave him professional currency. In the mid-1990s, he executive produced and starred in *Baywatch Nights*, but the spin-off show sank after two seasons.

In 2000, Hasselhoff, now in his late forties, ended his lengthy *Baywatch* run. Again, his life went noticeably askew. That March he was hospitalized with what was passed off as dehydration due to flu. The tabloids, however, suggested that the cause might have been an overdose of pain pills.

In late June 2002, Hasselhoff entered the Betty Ford Center in Palm Desert, California, to deal with his escalating drinking problem. A day later he bolted from the facility and checked into a nearby hotel, where he spent the evening consuming the liquor supply in his mini-bar. The next morning he was found unconscious in his room and rushed to the local hospital. Once stabilized from this rock-bottom bender, he returned to the center for substance abuse treatment.

The veteran star was back in the head-lines in June 2004 when he was arrested in Los Angeles on a DUI charge. He entered a rehab facility in Utah but left after a week to accept a lead role in a London production of the stage musical *Chicago*. That October, at his Los Angeles court hearing, he was ordered to attend AA meetings, perform community service, and pay a fine.

By early 2006, David Hasselhoff and his wife sought to legally end their union. The divorce proceedings dragged on acrimoniously for many months before being finalized. Among Pamela Bach's allegations were that her spouse had fallen off the wagon yet again (leading to claimed domestic violence) and had refused her pleas that he reenter rehab treatment. Hasselhoff continued to generate headlines in July 2006, when he was denied boarding on a flight from London to the United States. It was alleged by some British papers that he had been inebriated. The actor countercharged that his disorientation was due to pain medication taken for a recent injury to his hand.

With the golden years of his popularity seemingly behind him, Hasselhoff has more recently settled for such TV exposure as being a judge on the reality show *America's Got Talent*, and occasional supporting roles in feature films such as 2006's *Click*. In February 2007, Hasselhoff costarred in a Las Vegas production of the musical *The Producers*. In the condensed stage presentation, he played cross-dressing Roger DeBris, the flamboyant theater director. His dishy autobiography, *Don't Hassel the Hoff*, was published in May 2007.

Dick Haymes

(September 13, 1916–March 28, 1980)

Frank Sinatra gained his greatest popularity as a big-band singer during the late 1930s and early 1940s. Dick Haymes—with his rich baritone voice—was a close second to his more famous rival. Like Sinatra during the forties, the good-looking Haymes also found success as a solo recording artist, as well as a star on radio variety series and in Hollywood musicals. Both talents had a great fondness for women and a penchant for alcohol that often intruded on their professional and personal lives. In the case of Haymes, his drinking frequently inflated his ego, colored his decisions, and contributed to the slowdown of his once stellar career. The most publicized (and damaging) of his missteps occurred during his high-profile marriage (from 1951 to 1953) to thirtysomething screen goddess Rita Hayworth. The volatile, often hard-drinking couple brought out the worst in each other. Their combustible personalities led them into unpleasant situations and generated nasty headlines. This barrage of bad press haunted them—especially Haymes—for the rest of their lives.

• • •

Richard Benjamin Haymes was born in 1916 in Buenos Aires, Argentina, to Benjamin and Marguerite Haymes. His father, who was of English-Scottish descent, was a local cattleman; his mother, who had an Irish background, was a talented vocalist. In 1921, a recession ruined the Haymes cattle business. By the next year, the couple had split up, with Marguerite and her son going to New York. (As revenge for her desertion, Benjamin refused to divorce her. He died in 1933.) In 1923, she gave birth to Robert, the result of an adulterous relationship with a married banker. Marguerite agreed to put her husband's surname on the child's birth certificate if her wealthy paramour subsidized her and her children.

For a time, she and her sons stayed with her parents in Santa Barbara, California; then they relocated to Rio de Janeiro, where she opened a dress shop and found a new lover. That business thrived, and she took her children to Paris. Later in the decade, after the Great Depression had hit, the trio returned to the United States, settling in New York City in modest digs. In the coming years, Marguerite moved back and forth between America and the Continent, often leaving her sons in odious boarding schools while she maneuvered the family's next financial steps. This constant uprooting negatively impacted her boys.

In 1935, Richard visited Los Angeles to try his luck in movies. Thanks to his athletic prowess he got occasional stunt jobs or bits in pictures. When no further screen roles materialized, he sang at a Los Angeles club with a quintet he had organized. Later, Haymes moved to New York City, where Marguerite earned some income as a vocal coach.

Now calling himself Dick Haymes, the

fledgling crooner made professional head-
way in 1939 by performing with Bunny
Berigan's band. The next year, he joined
Harry James's prestigious musical group. In
late 1940, Haymes wed band vocalist Edythe
Harper, initially believing her lie that she
was pregnant. The couple divorced in the
summer of 1941. By year's end Haymes had
joined Benny Goodman's band. Thereafter,
his recording career took off and he soon
had several hit songs to his credit. He also
headlined his own radio show.

Meanwhile, the singer had wed again, in
September 1941. His new bride was Joanne
Marshall, a model turned showgirl. (Later
in the decade, she would become a Hollywood film star using the name Joanne
Dru.) When the United States entered
World War II, Haymes, a resident alien,
gained a draft deferment by signing an affidavit of non-belligerency (as a citizen of
Argentina). His decision was swayed by the
fact that his wife was pregnant (they would
have three children) and that he feared
interrupting his show business career. Later
in the war, he took two Army physicals but
was rejected both times from military duty
due to hypertension.

Twentieth Century-Fox placed Haymes
under contract in the mid-1940s. His best
assignment was the 1945 musical *State Fair*.
When that studio dropped his contract in
1947, he went over to Universal Pictures,
but found himself cast in subordinate
parts. As his once wildly successful career
tapered off, his marital problems flared
up—aggravated by his womanizing and
drinking and his wife's increasingly successful screen career. The couple divorced
in July 1949. Almost immediately, he wed

*Mickey Rooney, Jody Lawrence, and Dick Haymes
in 1953's* All Ashore.

Nora Eddington, the ex-wife of swashbuckling movie star Errol Flynn (a friend of
Haymes's). Haymes hoped the new union
would distract him from his woes. The mis-
match ended in divorce in September 1953.

In the early 1950s, Haymes toiled at
Columbia Pictures in two low-budget musical comedies. Also on the studio lot at the
time was Rita Hayworth, then making *Miss
Sadie Thompson*. Earlier in 1953, Hayworth
had divorced her third husband, playboy
Prince Aly Khan. Aly and Rita had a child,
3-year-old Yasmin, of whom each parent was
fighting for custody.

When Hayworth went to Hawaii for location work on her current movie, Haymes
chased after her. Because he had lost his
alien registration card and could not enter
Hawaii (which was not yet a state) without

one, he applied for a replacement at the Immigration Office. Later, when he returned to Los Angeles, he found himself suddenly confronted by bureaucratic red tape that insisted he was not entitled (under recent laws), because of his affidavit of non-belligerency during World War II, to become a naturalized citizen. Therefore, he was subject to deportation because of having reentered the United States "illegally." The messy situation became worldwide news. (Many in Hollywood suspected that Harry Cohn, the Columbia Pictures mogul, had instigated the government investigation of Haymes to separate the crooner from the lot's valuable leading lady.)

For her part, Hayworth, always dependent on strong men to make decisions for her, was looking to Haymes to separate her from her odious studio contract, to join her in a united front against pressures from Aly Khan, and to provide her with domestic contentment. In late September 1953, Haymes and Hayworth wed in Las Vegas.

Whatever hope the codependent celebrity couple had of finding happiness was short-lived, as they increasingly were affected by the media maelstrom that followed their every move. Because of Hayworth's studio battles, she was not earning a salary. Also, she was emotionally drained by her war against Aly Khan. Haymes was in equally bad financial and emotional shape: he incurred huge legal fees fighting the government's court case against him (which, eventually, he won) and was desperate for work. What singing gigs he found often didn't match the cost of supporting Rita and himself, let alone help in dealing with back alimony payments or his creditors.

The sorely frazzled Haymeses soon were engulfed in heavy drinking bouts and domestic spats. The end came in the summer of 1955, when, during one of their drunken arguments, he hit her. She left him, and they were divorced in December 1955.

Having never lost his vocal talents, Haymes continued performing in any venue possible. In 1958, he met the young singer Fran Jeffries. They wed that November and became the parents of a daughter the following July. The couple performed together in nightclubs and on TV, but their life together was marred by his alcoholism. By 1963, the couple had separated and she went to Los Angeles for an acting role in a film directed by Haymes's pal Richard Quine. Jeffries and Quine fell in love and married in 1965, soon after her January 1965 divorce from the singer became final.

In 1963, Haymes relocated to England to refocus his life and career. There he met Wendy Smith, a young British model. They married in January 1965. Encouraged by her, he pushed ahead with singing engagements. By the mid-1970s, he and Wendy were back in the United States, where he performed in clubs, appeared on TV, and did occasional recording sessions. His voice was sterling as ever. Sadly, he developed lung cancer and died in March 1980.

Looking back on his tempestuous life, Haymes once assessed: "My swinging days got so involved with my own ego that I blew it. I certainly don't blame circumstances or anyone else. I'm the instrument on which the tune is played. I called the shots and I played them the way I saw things at the time. There is no good or bad in my life for which I'm not directly responsible."

Whitney Houston

(August 9, 1963–)

Over 21.3 million home viewers tuned in to *Primetime Live* on December 4, 2002, when Diane Sawyer, the TV show's anchor, grilled singer/actress Whitney Houston about her turbulent lifestyle. When asked about the tabloid gossip of her anorexia, the diva shot back, "I am not sick. Okay? I've always been a thin girl. I am not going to be fat ever. Whitney is not going to be fat, ever." However, this was just a warm-up for the on-air discussion concerning Houston's long-rumored drug dependency. Whitney danced around the topic. "I like to think . . . I had a bad habit . . . I don't like to think of myself as addicted." When Sawyer inquired if, besides marijuana and pills, Houston had ever used cocaine, the celebrity had an on-camera meltdown. She spat out, "Crack is whack!" Given what the public already suspected or knew about the temperamental diva, the statement made Whitney the butt of cruel jokes for years to come.

On a more compassionate level, Houston's legion of fans wondered what had brought this high-voltage talent to such a sad state.

• • •

Whitney Elizabeth Houston was born in 1963 in Newark, New Jersey, the second child (and first daughter) of John and Emily "Cissy" Drinkard Houston. (Cissy already had a son from a prior relationship.) Whitney's father was a municipal worker. Her mother had a distinguished musical background. As a youngster, Cissy was part of her family's gospel singing group, the Drinkard sisters. Later, Cissy and her cousins—Dionne and Dee Dee Warwick—formed a trio, the Gospelaires. When the group broke up, Cissy organized the Sweet Inspirations, a quartet that harmonized backup vocals for the likes of Elvis Presley and Aretha Franklin. Eventually, Cissy became minister of music at the New Hope Baptist Church in Newark.

A few years after Whitney's birth, the Houstons moved to nearby East Orange, New Jersey. As a child, Nippy (as Whitney was nicknamed) was a tomboy who trailed after her energetic older brothers, especially when her mother was away for recording gigs and concert tours. Church activities (particularly singing in the choir) were an important part of Whitney's youth. Because Cissy knew the many downsides of show business, she tried to discourage her daughter from a singing career. But the strong-minded Whitney already knew she wanted to be an entertainer.

By 1978, her parents had separated; they would later divorce. The next year, 16-year-old Whitney became a backup singer for a number of Cissy's club and recording sessions. In 1980, Houston's newly acquired managers determined that if she worked as a model it would give her experience working in front of an audience. The highly attractive Whitney became a successful

A vibrant Whitney Houston in the early years of her recording career in the late 1980s.

model—not an easy accomplishment for an African American in an era still filled with racial prejudice. After completing high school in 1981, she began appearing on TV with guest parts on sitcoms such as *Silver Spoons*.

Arista Records producer Clive Davis signed Whitney to his label in 1983. He carefully crafted her image as she fine-tuned her performance skills on the concert circuit. Her debut album, 1985's *Whitney Houston*, sold a whopping 13 million copies. Her follow-up LP, 1987's *Whitney*, included a Grammy Award–

winning track, "I Wanna Dance." Before the end of that year, the newcomer's first two albums already had sold 21 million copies. In 1988, the singing star received a multitude of industry awards and grossed $45 million.

Now a world-famous star, Houston purchased a $2.7 million estate in Mendham, New Jersey. She dated such celebrities as movie stars Eddie Murphy and Robert De Niro and TV personality Arsenio Hall. One bond that especially fascinated the media was that of Whitney and her longtime pal Robyn Crawford. She was the talent's personal assistant and lived at the singer's New Jersey mansion. Houston snapped to *Time* magazine: "People see her with me, and they draw their own conclusions. . . . Let people talk. It doesn't bother me, because I know I'm not gay. I don't care."

Houston's third album, 1990's *I'm Your Baby Tonight*, did not sell as well as her prior ones. But Whitney was preoccupied elsewhere. She had met Bobby Brown, the sexy R&B vocalist. The Massachusetts-born singer was over five years younger than Houston. Many onlookers were astounded that the seemingly wholesome Whitney had the chosen street-smart Bobby as her boyfriend, but she loved his bad-boy reputation. She was pregnant with his baby during the shoot of *The Bodyguard*—her debut feature film—but suffered a miscarriage in the spring of 1992. In July of that year, the two singers married. Robyn Crawford moved to her own place miles away and, by 2000, was no longer part of Houston's business empire. In March 1993, Whitney gave birth to daughter Bobbi Kristina Houston

Brown. (Bobby Brown already had four children by other women.)

As the new mother returned to her career, there was negative buzz about her increasingly self-absorbed, indulgent ways, as well as rumors that she had been hospitalized for taking a deliberate overdose of diet pills. She returned to filmmaking with 1995's *Waiting to Exhale* and 1996's *The Preacher's Wife*. Meanwhile, she and her spouse split and then reconciled. (She said of her chaotic relationship with Brown, "Contrary to belief, I do the hitting, he doesn't. . . . When we're fighting, it's like that's love for us. We're fighting for our love.") She suffered another miscarriage during 1996. In 1998, her new album (*My Love Is Your Love*) continued the downward trajectory of her recording career.

In the late 1990s, Houston sought to dispel the growing gossip about her substance abuse. She informed *Newsweek* magazine, "No, I'm not a drug addict, and neither is my husband. If that were so, you'd get a lot less work out of me. It would show in the performance and then in the work." In January 2000, airport security workers on the island of Hawaii discovered a reported half ounce of marijuana in Houston's handbag as she prepared to board her flight. She and Brown left for the mainland before police arrived. (Ultimately, the misdemeanor charge was dropped when a New Jersey drug counselor informed the court in Hawaii that the singer did not need substance abuse treatment.) Some weeks later, Houston was "unable" to sing at the Academy Awards, and then she failed to appear

at her Rock 'n' Roll Hall of Fame induction. Such situations further damaged her industry reputation and gave more credence to long-circulating stories about her addictions. Meanwhile, her relationship with Brown continued to be tumultuous. (In mid-2000, Bobby was placed in a Florida jail for violating his probation relating to earlier drunk driving charges.)

In 2001, Whitney signed a new recording contract worth $75 million. However, by September 2001, when she was a guest on *Michael Jackson's 30th Anniversary Celebration* (a live special televised in November), she looked emaciated and her voice was tremulous. Her 2003 album (*One Wish: The Holiday Album*)—her most recent to date—was a flop. By 2004, Houston's life had became a crazy circus as she checked in and out of drug rehab, only to repeat the cycle again and again. Meanwhile, her spouse continued to have scrapes with the law. In the summer of 2005, Whitney joined with her husband for the cable TV reality series *Being Bobby Brown*. The couple's wacky, indulgent shenanigans on the show did nothing to enhance their reputations. By the next year, the dysfunctional couple were often living apart. In September 2006, Houston filed for legal separation from Brown, announcing that she intended to divorce him. (Later, she began dating 26-year-old singer Ray J.) As for Houston's once-lustrous recording career, she was again working under the aegis of Clive Davis and hoping to record a new album.

Buster Keaton

(October 4, 1895–February 1, 1966)

In the pantheon of Hollywood's great silent screen comedians, the stoic Buster Keaton ranks at the top along with such funsters as Charlie Chaplin and Harold Lloyd. Although Keaton was known for his deadpan expression on and off camera, his sharp look suggested that he did not miss much that was going on. His sad eyes also mirrored a troubled soul that had endured too many of life's hardships. In later times, Keaton's weathered countenance reflected years of hard drinking and decades of coping with bad luck (both professionally and personally).

• • •

He was born in 1895 in Piqua, Kansas, where his vaudevillian parents (Joseph and Myra Cutler Keaton) were performing with a traveling medicine show. (Later, the Keatons had two more children.) Legend has it that Harry Houdini, later the world-famous magician and then a trouper pal of the Keatons, witnessed the hyperactive 6-month-old tot tumble down a flight of stairs backstage and emerge unscathed. He commented to Mr. Keaton, "What a buster your kid took!" The nickname Buster stuck.

At age 9 months, Buster crawled out on stage one night, intrigued by the sound of applause greeting the finale of his parents' act. He liked the sound, and within a few years, he joined the family's acrobatic act. The boy displayed great agility and a wonderful sense of timing and was soon featured

in "The Three Keatons." Offstage there were problems because his father had become a heavy drinker and was physically abusive toward his family. (His mother also liked to drink.) On stage, Mr. Keaton's alcoholism began to affect the intricate act. In 1917, Buster went out on his own.

In New York, Keaton signed to appear in *The Passing Show of 1917*, but quit the stage venture to try motion pictures. He had just met Roscoe "Fatty" Arbuckle and the rotund comedian offered him a small role in his new short subject, *The Butcher Boy*. Buster quickly became an integral part of Arbuckle's team. Later that year, Fatty's filmmaking operation—financed by producer Joseph M. Schenck—moved to Los Angeles, and Fatty's stock company went along. Buster's family came to live with Keaton on the West Coast. A young lady named Natalie Talmadge, who helped out at the studio, boarded with the Keatons. (Natalie was the sister of screen stars Norma and Constance Talmadge. Norma was then wed to Joseph Schenck.)

By 1918, Keaton was earning $250 a week. His film career, however, was interrupted when he was drafted into the army and shipped to the war in France. He was back in southern California by the spring of 1919. In the coming year, Schenck established Buster in his own studio to star in two-reel comedies. Meanwhile, Keaton decided to marry. (By then he had enjoyed sexual encounters with various young women whom he met in vaudeville and on movie sets.) His bride-to-be was Natalie Talmadge, who had played bits in movies but was considered too unassuming to achieve stardom on a parallel with her famous sisters. Some sources say Schenck and Mrs. Talmadge pushed Buster into marrying the 22-year-old; others suggest that Keaton, who felt insecure in Hollywood society because of his helter-skelter background, thought marrying into the Talmadge clan would give him status within the film colony and would further his working relationship with Schenck. The couple wed in May 1921.

By 1924, Keaton has starred in such silent features as *Sherlock Jr.* While his hugely inventive movies pleased the critics, they were so costly that they were not huge moneymakers. By now, the poorly educated Buster, who had no aptitude for finances, headed a filmmaking corporation of which he had no stock shares and earned a lucrative salary, which was turned over to his wife to manage. The couple were now the parents of two sons: Joseph (born in 1922) and Robert (born in 1924).

Natalie demanded that Keaton build her an "Italian Villa" in Beverly Hills to rival Pickfair. He complied. The sprawling mansion cost over $250,000 to construct (plus $100,000 for furnishings). In their huge manse, Natalie insisted on separate living arrangements: she had her large private suite, while Buster was relegated to far smaller quarters. Locked out of his wife's bedroom, Keaton turned to liaisons with film starlets (including Viola Dana and Mae Busch). By now, Buster's social drinking had turned into a serious attraction to liquor.

Despite the advice of friends, Keaton agreed to Schenck's plan to sell Buster's contract to Metro-Goldwyn-Mayer. Although the comedian now received $3,000 a week—which he needed to maintain his plush lifestyle—he soon found that he had lost his artistic freedom, especially after he started making talkie films. He drank more heavily and was involved in a long affair with actress Dorothy Sebastian. His frequent inebriation made him troublesome on the sound stage. Then, in February 1931, he got into a scuffle with Kathleen Key, a 25-year-old MGM contract player, whom he had once dated. The embarrassed studio heads forced him to pay her $10,000 (out of his own pocket) to hush up the potential scandal.

In April 1932, Keaton's wife accused him of attempting to kidnap their sons when he sought merely to take the boys on a trip to Mexico. That July, Natalie and her detective surprised Buster aboard his $120,000 yacht while he was in bed with another woman. The Keatons filed for divorce that same month, with Natalie gaining custody of their sons (whose surnames were changed to Talmadge). Devastated, Buster sank further into alcoholism (consuming a daily bottle of whiskey), and went in and out of sanitariums to treat his addiction. In February 1933, MGM terminated Keaton's contract due to his continuously undisciplined behavior. His reputation for being unreliable prevented him from getting work at the other major studios.

Meanwhile, one day in January 1933, while in the midst of an alcoholic daze, Keaton wed Mae Scriven, a registered nurse whom he had met during one of his drying-out attempts. The couple remarried that

October because his divorce from Natalie had not been final when he and Mae first tied the knot. By now, Buster was slaving in low-budget short subjects to earn a paltry income. In 1934, he declared bankruptcy.

During the fall of 1935, Keaton swore off drinking (a vow he kept for five years). A year later, in October, Scriven divorced him, taking half of his remaining few assets. By the late 1930s, Buster was allowed back on the MGM lot but now as a lowly gag writer earning but a fraction of his past studio income.

In May 1940, Keaton wed 21-year-old dancer Eleanor Norris. The felicitous union was the start of his rebirth: he was reunited with his two sons, he found increasing public interest in his old silents, and he succeeded in getting some work in films, summer stock, and television. Throughout this comeback period, however, he suffered recurring bouts of heavy drinking, one of which almost killed him in 1955. The next year, *The Buster Keaton Story* was released. It starred Donald O'Connor in a highly fictionalized biography of the comic giant.

Keaton worked right up to the end, including appearances in several Beach Party movies and his last release, 1966's *A Funny Thing Happened on the Way to the Forum*. He died of lung cancer at his southern California home in the San Fernando Valley in February 1966. A year before he passed away, he told a newsperson, "I can't feel sorry for myself. It all goes to show that if you stay on the merry-go-round long enough you'll get another chance at the brass ring. Luckily, I stayed on."

Veronica Lake
(November 14, 1922–July 7, 1973)

She was scarcely five feet two inches tall and, in her early Hollywood years, was often timid off-screen—which led her first husband to nickname her "Mousie." However, in front of the camera, Veronica Lake packed a sizable wallop. Director Preston Sturges observed, "The screen transforms her, electrifies her, and brings her to life."

Lake's rise to movie fame in the World War II era was based largely on a gimmick: a thick lock of her silver blond hair that cascaded over her right eye. The actress became world-renowned for her unique "peekaboo" hairdo. However, there was far more to her than that attention-grabber. She had an erotic, smoldering quality that belied her petite frame and innocently beautiful face.

Lake famously said, "I wasn't a sex symbol. I was a sex zombie." This mockery of her mannequinlike cinema image was part of her cynical overview of Hollywood moviemaking and its flashy, status-conscious lifestyle. As her movie popularity soared to great heights in the early 1940s, she increasingly felt used by the studio system and indifferent to the array of men (including multimillionaire businessmen Aristotle Onassis and Howard Hughes and screen star Errol Flynn) who pursued her before, during, and after her marriages. She took refuge in the self-destructive chip on her shoulder, her mocking approach to lascivious suitors, and, especially, booze.

• • •

Constance Frances Marie Ockleman was born in 1922 (some sources suggest 1921 or 1919) in Brooklyn, New York, the only child of Harry and Constance Trimble Ockleman. Her father was a seaman and frequently away from home on long work assignments. In 1932, Ockleman was killed as he and his crew were launching a vessel from dry dock in Philadelphia. A year later, his widow wed Anthony Keane, a staff artist with the *New York Herald*. By 1937, the family was residing in Florida and the teenaged Constance was attending Miami High School. She had long rebelled against the classroom regimen and now found release from academic tedium by entering local beauty pageants. Her ambitious mother envisioned that her attractive daughter might well have a career in films.

In June 1938, the Keanes drove to Los Angeles, where the determined mother kept angling for her daughter to be screen-tested. Meanwhile, Constance took acting classes and made the rounds of studio casting calls. (The underage novice actress also began visiting nightclubs, where she developed a taste for alcoholic beverages.) She found extra work in such films as 1939's *Sorority House* at RKO. By the time of 1940's *Forty*

The reluctant film star Veronica Lake shares the microphone with her frequent costar Alan Ladd for a 1946 episode of Lux Radio Theatre.

Little Mothers at MGM, she had adopted her distinctive hairdo. When not on the sound stage, she walked about the Metro-Goldwyn-Mayer studio lot, where her provocative look and shapely body attracted the attention of several male staff workers. One of these admirers was associate art director John S. Detlie, who began courting Constance. Because he was several years older than she, she nicknamed him "Pops."

Meanwhile, a Paramount Pictures producer saw screen footage of the newcomer, and she was hired to play the nightclub siren in 1941's *I Wanted Wings*, a big-budget production. Veronica Lake, as she was now known professionally, easily stole the picture. She was placed under studio contract at $350 a week. (Her weekly wage later soared to $4,500.)

By now, Lake and Detlie had married (in September 1940), and she soon became pregnant. Impending motherhood frightened and annoyed her, especially the demands of becoming a responsible parent. Later, when Detlie was drafted into World War II service, Lake became increasingly addicted to drinking as an escape from dealing with the adult world. (During this period, she had an affair with a married producer at the studio and grew increasingly indifferent to her rising fame.) On one of Detlie's military leaves home, she became pregnant again. Her second child was born in July 1943 but died a week later. (Lake had tumbled on a film set when she was six months pregnant, and many felt that the "accident" had led to the infant's death.) By that December, the incompatible Detlies divorced.

A year later (in December 1944), Lake wed Hungarian-born director Andre De Toth, recklessly ignoring warnings from her acquaintances that the dapper filmmaker had a reputation for being abusive and a user. During their stormy marriage the couple had two children, and Lake learned the hard way just how much De Toth lived up to his negative reputation. As the forties came to an end, so did the actress's screen vogue. Her decline was accelerated by her temperamental on-set behavior, her escalating drinking, and her refusal to take any part of her career seriously. Her Paramount tenure ended with the weak 1948 comedy *Isn't It Romantic?*

When Lake and De Toth divorced in June 1952, he left her broke, and she was jobless. She abandoned Hollywood and moved to New York City. Her sad downward spiral continued, exasperated by her penchant for self-destruction. She found occasional work in stage tours and infrequent TV performances. In August 1955, she wed songwriter Joseph A. McCarthy. He was also a heavy drinker. They fought frequently, and the drunken relationship ended in 1959. By the early 1960s, Lake was staying in low-rent hotels, working as a barmaid, and recurrently being arrested for drunken disorderly conduct. A revealing newspaper article catapulted the life-worn ex-star back into the public eye briefly. The whatever-happened-to publicity generated a few stage and TV jobs for Lake, and even led to a few new film assignments (albeit grade-Z horror entries).

Her last great love was Andy Erickson, a merchant seaman who died in 1965. Lake made one final stab at marriage in June 1972 when she wed Robert Carleton-Munro, a retired English naval officer. She was in the process of divorcing him—and once again nearly penniless—when she became extremely ill from hepatitis. Long estranged from her children, she died in a Vermont hospital in July 1973.

Once when she was asked about her initially promising career and life that took so many bad turns, Veronica Lake said, "I wouldn't live it any differently than it was. How would I learn to be a person otherwise?"

Bela Lugosi

(October 20, 1882–August 16, 1956)

In 1994, Martin Landau gave a telling performance as a drug-addicted Bela Lugosi in the movie *Ed Wood*. The picture effectively traced the pathetic end of the once great horror film star and how Edward D. Wood Jr., a schlock movie director (played by Johnny Depp), sought to befriend him. The film, as well as Landau's Best Supporting Actor Oscar for this role, brought renewed interest to the life and hard times of thespian Lugosi—the man whose Hollywood screen career was both made and destroyed by his starring in 1931's *Dracula*.

Once Lugosi was typecast as the screen's most memorable vampire, he was stuck in a Hollywood career rut that rose and fell as the horror film genre went in and out of popularity. (Bela's choice of film roles was also limited by his heavy middle European accent, which he refused to abandon, and by his overinflated ego after his *Dracula* triumph.) Because of Lugosi's long association with Dracula-type screen assignments, people forgot—if they ever knew—that decades earlier, back in his homeland of Hungary, he had been a stage matinee idol, and that he had made several silent features in Germany.

In Lugosi's sad final decades he sought solace from his physical and emotional pains through alcohol and drugs.

• • •

Béla Ferenc Dezsö Blaskó was born in Lugos, a little Hungarian town in Transylvania, in 1882. He was the fourth child of Itstvan Blaskó (a baker who later became a bank executive) and Paula Vojnits Blaskó. As an adolescent, Bela was ambitious and full of wanderlust. He left home at the age of 12, working in mines and factories to pay for his daily needs. In his late teens, he became interested in the theater and enrolled in Budapest's Academy of Theatrical Art. By 1900, he had made his stage bow, and two years later he became a member of the National Actors' Company. During this period, he acquired his professional surname of Lugosi. From 1913 to 1919, he performed with the National Theatre of Hungary in Budapest, where he became a popular performer who enjoyed the esteem and favors of several female admirers. To supplement his income, he made movies. (In 1914, he enlisted in his country's army to serve in World War I. When he was released from duty in 1916 after receiving several injuries on the battlefield, he returned to theater work.) In June 1917, Bela married Ilona Szmik, a banker's daughter. Because of the rising wave of Communism in his native country, he moved to Germany, where he worked both on stage and in movies (including 1920's *Der Januskopf*). While he was there, his wife— who was still in Hungary—divorced him.

In March 1921, Lugosi came to New York, where he headlined and produced several Hungarian-language plays. That September, he wed Austrian actress Ilona

Montagh de Nagybanyhegyes (their relationship lasted until February 1924). In 1922, he made his Broadway bow, in *The Red Poppy*, and in 1923 he made his U.S. film debut, in *The Silent Command*. It was a comparatively easy step for the Hungarian actor to star on Broadway in 1927's *Dracula*—he had already appeared in a theater production of *The Werewolf*. The production was a success both in New York and on the road. While performing as the urbane vampire in Los Angeles, he was hired by

MGM to play in *The Thirteenth Chair*. During this time, he enjoyed a romantic fling with Hollywood's "It" Girl, Clara Bow. In September 1929, Bela wed for a third time. His latest bride was Beatrice Woodruff, a San Francisco widow. The union lasted a mere four days.

Lugosi was Universal's last-minute choice to star in their filming of *Dracula*, and he received a paltry salary for doing the picture. Once the movie was released, the middle-aged actor found himself (briefly) much in demand with Hollywood producers. He had no idea that he had reached his career zenith and loftily rejected starring in *Frankenstein* for Universal because his on-camera dialogue would be grunts and his face would be hidden behind monster makeup. (Boris Karloff was substituted in *Frankenstein*, and the picture made him a star.)

Throughout the 1930s, Lugosi found himself cast in starring parts in low-budget features or supporting assignments in major productions. He returned to Broadway in 1933 for *Murder at the Vanities*. That same year, in March, he wed his secretary, Lillian Arch. Their son, Bela Jr., was born in 1938. During the many lulls in his career, the actor turned to alcohol to drown his professional disappointments and his recurrent financial pressures. (Bela often lived well beyond his means.)

Lugosi's career and bank account had reached a low point when Universal hired him to be the deformed Ygor in 1939's *Son of Frankenstein*, with Karloff again as the crazed monster. By the 1940s, Bela had become a fixture in poverty-row movies and

The dashing Bela Lugosi in the 1930s, before life and his sagging film career got the best of him.

he was no longer considered for major releases. In a career irony, 12 years after he had rejected the lead as Frankenstein's monster, he played the monster in *Frankenstein Meets the Wolfman*. In this period, he and Lillian separated, but they later reunited. This ongoing domestic tension, along with money worries and pain from an ulcer and sciatica (the results of leg injuries he sustained in World War I), led him into heavy drinking and to drug use. By the time of 1948's *Abbott and Costello Meet Frankenstein*, the ravages of time and substance abuse had taken a severe toll on the once handsome talent.

The new decade was a difficult time for the aged and progressively unwell performer. He was spending much of the scant income he earned from acting to pay for his drugs (which included methadone, Demerol, and barbiturates). By now, most Hollywood filmmakers had either forgotten Lugosi or thought of the eccentric old man as a mere camp joke. He toured the United Kingdom in a *Dracula* stage revival, which helped to restore a bit of his self-confidence. While abroad, he made the 1952 British feature *Old Mother Riley Meets the Vampire*. Back in the United States, his fourth wife divorced him in July 1953, charging that he was extremely jealous and excessively possessive. The breakup separated Bela from his son. Lugosi's movie career was at a nadir and he was a lonely senior citizen.

Eventually, he decided to conquer his long-standing drug addiction—and possibly win back his ex-wife, Lillian. Because he could not afford private treatment, Lugosi had himself committed to the Metropolitan State Hospital in Norwalk, California. Later, he wrote of the torments he endured during his "cold turkey" withdrawal from liquor and drugs. ("My body grew hot, then cold. I tried to eat the bedsheets, my pajamas. My heart beat madly. Then it seemed to stop. Every joint in my body ached.") When the actor was released after the grueling 90-day regimen, there were many newspaper and tabloid articles about the "recovered" veteran performer. One of the fans who had written to Lugosi during his hospital stay was Hope Lininger. On August 25, 1955, 20 days after he left the facility, he and the 30-years-younger Lininger married. The relationship proved to be an unhappy one.

Bela joined with several other genre relics (including John Carradine) for 1956's *The Black Sleep*. In June of that year he was on stage in Los Angeles for three performances in *The Devil's Paradise*, an antidrug exploitation drama. Lugosi had just started production on Ed Wood's appallingly awful *Plan Nine from Outer Space* when his fragile health deteriorated even further due to age, ailments, and recurrent heavy drinking. One day in August 1956, while his wife was out doing errands, Bela succumbed to a heart attack. Lugosi was buried in his trademark Dracula black cape and tuxedo. During his long acting career, he had earned over $500,000, but his only asset at death was a building lot worth less than $2,000. Drugs, poor career choices in his post-peak years, and bad luck had robbed him of any tangible legacy for his beloved son.

Liza Minnelli

(March 12, 1946–)

Show business superstar Liza Minnelli has been the subject of countless lurid tabloid headlines over the years due to her recurring battles with substance abuse, her several health crises, her many romantic entanglements (and marriages), and her assorted comeback efforts. Buried in the decades-long media blitz is the fact that this giant of the entertainment world has won Oscar, Tony, Emmy, and Grammy awards.

Like her legendary mother, Judy Garland, Liza rarely found a proper balance between her professional life and her private life. Like her vulnerable parent, Liza often sought love in all the wrong places, made bad career decisions, and found temporary escape through liquor and drugs. Paralleling Garland's roller-coaster existence, Minnelli coped with a rash of calamities both in and out of the limelight.

Liza's frightening number of misfortunes, missteps, and miseries would have long ago destroyed a weaker soul. Luckily, the five-foot-four-inch luminary possessed a remarkable resiliency that allowed her to survive the constant chaos in her high-profile life. Surprisingly, given the tribulations of her often self-destructive lifestyle, she retained a magical sense of childlike optimism in the face of adversity. According to her, "Reality is something you rise above." She also could say (and seemed to *really* believe) in the new millennium—even after her latest batch of career and personal setbacks—"I feel like I haven't done my best work yet. I feel like there's a world of possibilities out there."

•   •   •

Liza May Minnelli was born in Los Angeles in 1946, the only child of Judy Garland, the Metro-Goldwyn-Mayer singing star, and Vincente Minnelli, the acclaimed movie director. When Liza was 2, she made her film bow in 1949's *In the Good Old Summertime*, seen briefly as Garland's daughter. By 1951, the self-destructive Judy had been discharged by her studio, attempted suicide (yet again), and divorced Minnelli. The following year, Garland wed promoter Sid Luft, who guided her to fresh success on the concert stage and engineered her powerful film comeback. Garland and Luft had two children (Lorna and Joey). They ended their often contentious marriage in 1965. To survive being in the wake of her mother's tumultuous life, Liza had to mature emotionally far too fast. It left her ill-equipped to deal with her own troubles in the future.

In 1962, Liza starred in a school production of *The Diary of Anne Frank*. The next year, Minnelli made her off-Broadway debut in a revival of *Best Foot Forward*. She debuted on Broadway in 1965 in the musical *Flora, the Red Menace*. By then, she had already recorded several albums (including 1964's *Liza! Liza!* and 1965's *It Amazes Me*).

Through family connections, Minnelli

won her first adult film role: a supporting part in the 1967, British-made *Charlie Bubbles*. (During the shoot, she became romantically involved with the movie's star, Albert Finney.) Later, matchmaker Garland introduced Liza to Australian-born entertainer/composer Peter Allen. (Previously, he had been part of Judy's club act.) Minnelli debated about wedding Allen—who was gay—but, in March 1967, she and Peter married. Over the next years, Liza earned an Academy Award nomination for 1969's *The Sterile Cuckoo*, arranged Garland's funeral (in June 1969), toured the nightclub circuit, and appeared on TV.

By the early 1970s, the high-energy, chain-smoking Liza was leading a frantic lifestyle. When not performing, she was partying hard—and constantly. (Minnelli later claimed that she had first used drugs when a physician prescribed Valium to calm her after her mother's funeral.) She and Peter Allen were still married but in name only. (They divorced in June 1974.) Minnelli made news with her romance with Desi Arnaz Jr., the son of Lucille Ball and Desi Arnaz. She was 7 years older than he. The two became engaged, but their intense relationship quickly burned out. Meanwhile, she starred in the 1972 movie *Cabaret* (for which she won an Oscar) and had her own TV special, *Liza with a "Z"* (for which she won an Emmy). In the romantic arena, she generated much media attention for her impulsive and often short-lived affairs with the likes of Peter Sellers, Edward Albert, Ben Vereen, and Assaf Dayan.

The impetuous Liza, who was gaining a reputation for substance abuse, jumped off the social merry-go-round (at least briefly) when she married movie/TV producer Jack Haley Jr. in September 1974. He was 12 years her senior and the son of one of Garland's costars from 1939's *The Wizard of Oz*. Minnelli found it difficult to settle into domesticity, and instead busied herself with show business projects and a hectic night-life. The Haleys divorced in April 1979. (As she had with her first husband, she remained friendly with her ex.)

During the making of the 1977 film musical *New York, New York*, Minnelli fell in love

Liza Minnelli, the plucky show business survivor, with veteran entertainers Sammy Davis Jr. (left) and Frank Sinatra (right), promoting their 1989 television concert.

with her director, Martin Scorsese. In this period, her affinity for drugs and booze grew. She had become friendly with the clothing designer Halston, and they and their hedonistic crowd became a fixture at the notorious Manhattan club Studio 54. In December 1979, Liza, whose movie career had faded, took husband number three. He was Mark Gero, a stage manager turned sculptor who was 7 years younger than his bride. During the next years, Minnelli suffered several miscarriages. (Her marriage to Gero ended in January 1992.)

Liza finally appeared in a new film hit, 1981's *Arthur*, but much of the credit went to her leading man (Dudley Moore). Minnelli had starred on Broadway in 1977's *The Act*, and returned with another stage musical (*The Rink*) in 1984. During the show's run, the troubled Minnelli left the cast due to her escalating drug problems. That July, she entered the Betty Ford Center near Palm Springs, California, to deal with her addictions to alcohol and drugs. She spent seven weeks there, but by that November she was suggesting to the media that she'd had a setback. It was the start of a long, expensive, and exhausting cycle of relapses and recoveries.

Liza's father passed away in mid-1986, and he bequeathed her $1 million. The following year, she headlined a TV tribute to him (*Minnelli on Minnelli*). In May 1987, she had a hugely successful three-week engagement at Carnegie Hall. In movies, however, she floundered in such weak fare as 1988's *Rent-a-Cop*. In 1992, it was rumored that Minnelli might wed Billy Stritch, a much younger pianist who had been part of a cabaret trio, but it never happened.

In the early 1990s, Liza was most often in the news due to her health problems (including hip and knee replacement surgeries). The supermarket newspapers continued to speculate about her life as a party animal, her boy toys, and her drug and alcohol dependencies. In January 1997, she replaced Julie Andrews for a month in the Broadway musical *Victor/Victoria*.

Now into her 50s, Minnelli underwent new substance abuse treatment and insisted, "I'm taking care of myself." She was touring with a stage production in 2000 when, in May, she was hospitalized for a severe hip condition. That October she nearly died from viral encephalitis. Her medical ordeal prompted a reconciliation between her and her sister, Lorna, after years of noncommunication. The spring of 2001 found Liza undergoing additional hip and back surgery.

In 2001, Liza met event planner/TV producer David Gest, who was seven years her junior. The oddly matched couple soon announced they would wed. Meanwhile, Minnelli was once again treated for substance abuse, and through dieting, she lost 90 pounds. Their flamboyant nuptials were held in New York City in March 2002. Gest's prodding prompted Minnelli to return to the concert stage both abroad and in the United States. (At one venue she bounded on stage and announced, "Liza's back from AA and she's doing okay!") The Minnelli-Gest union soon fell apart and, in October 2003, she filed for divorce. (The day before, Gest had initiated a $10 million suit against his wife, declaring that her repeated violence against him had gravely damaged his health.) Their nasty divorce war—with its increasingly bizarre counter-claims—decelerated in January 2007 when the couple reached an undisclosed financial settlement and agreed to pursue a no-fault divorce in Tennessee where Gest resided.

As to Minnelli having any regrets over the many pitfalls of her life to date, she insisted, "They're not enough to slow me down. There's too much to look forward to."

River Phoenix

(August 23, 1970–October 31, 1993)

Over the years, numerous Hollywood notables (including Wallace Reid, Barbara LaMarr, Jeanne Eagels, Montgomery Clift, John Belushi, and Chris Farley) died from drug overdoses. After a time, such untimely exits were no longer considered so shocking by much of the public. However, in the instance of talented actor River Phoenix, that was *not* the case.

Several individuals close to the young celebrity in his final years knew of the dramatic transformation that pessimism and substance abuse had made in the once gentle, insightful Phoenix. Yet, his tragic finale—played out so publicly—was difficult for the public at large to comprehend. Before his life spiraled out of control, the blond, blue-eyed River was a sensitive actor who had the potential to be one of the Hollywood greats. Even now, years after his death, his absence is keenly felt. Many of his fans regard him as an iconic cult figure—a martyr to the crass commercialism of Hollywood.

• • •

He was born River Jude Bottom in 1970 in a log cabin communal house on a mint farm in Madras, Oregon. His father, John Lee Bottom, had once been a carpenter, and his mother, Arlyn Sharon Dunetz Bottom, was a secretary from the Bronx. The hippie couple had first met in California in 1968 when they were itinerant fruit pickers. By the time River was 2, his parents were members of the Children of God, a radical counterculture sect. Later on, the family (which included River's siblings Joaquin, Summer, Rain, and Liberty) relocated to South America, where John was the sect's Archbishop of Venezuela. In 1977, the Bottoms abandoned the Children of God cult and settled in central Florida. There they changed their surname to Phoenix. During this difficult transitional period, the family suffered financially, and River and Rain often performed songs on street corners to earn handouts.

The young River had long been drawn to the world of music. By 1978, he and sister Rain were performing at local gatherings and winning talent contests. The following year, the family moved to Los Angeles. Mr. and Mrs. Phoenix hoped all their children might break into show business and, should they became famous, spread the family's beliefs to the general public. In the coming months, River and Rain were hired as pre-show entertainers for a children's TV show. Next, Phoenix played his guitar on a TV game program. Then the 11-year-old was cast on a 1982 TV series, *Seven Brides for Seven Brothers*, a show that lasted one season. For a spell, River did commercials, but he hated it.

River made his feature film debut in 1985's *Explorers*. However, it was the popular 1986 film *Stand by Me* that brought him to national notice. Unlike many rising young performers, River was shy about doing publicity; he detested being drawn into media hype. His first starring role was in 1988's *A Night in the Life of Jimmy Reardon*, which miscast him as a girl-chasing teen. Another misfire was *Little Nikita*. Far better was *Running on Empty*, for which River was Oscar nominated in the Best Supporting Actor category. The film featured Martha Plimpton as River's love interest, and they became involved off camera.

River's star continued to rise with 1991's *My Own Private Idaho*, in which he portrayed a narcoleptic gay street hustler. Phoenix now had his pick of parts and chose to be in the next year's *Sneakers*, a heist thriller. By this juncture, many people in Phoenix's sphere had noticed significant personality changes in this young adult, once so admired for his innocent whole-someness. He was still the firm vegetarian who wore no leather and who worried so much about the diminished South American rainforests that he purchased many acres of them in Costa Rica. He was also the person who remarked once, "I don't see

any point or any good in drugs that are as disruptive as cocaine. I never tried heroin. I tried alcohol and most of the others when I was 15, and got it out of the way—finished with the stuff." Unfortunately, the new Phoenix seemed a cynical soul who had gone far astray into the world of substance abuse.

Some decided that the movie actor's radical turnaround was an overreaction to competing in the cutthroat world of show business and being his family's primary breadwinner for so many years. Others concluded the changes in his personality were the result of his revolt from his emotionally painful childhood and that he was now bent on testing every limit, including taking hard drugs. Then there were those onlookers who pegged him as a lost soul who had succumbed to his demons and to drugs but who would not deal with recovery.

Whatever the case, in the early 1990s, Phoenix deserted acting for periods of time to return to Florida to live in Gainesville with his family, and then on his own. For a while, he called himself Rio. He formed a band, Aleka's Attic, which also included sister Rain. He remained a firm environmentalist, a devoted animal rights activist, and a strict vegetarian, and had a new love interest, Suzanne Solgot.

For all of Phoenix's growing power within the film business, he made odd professional decisions. He appeared in 1994's *Silent Tongue*, a strange, uncommercial Western. Phoenix's incentive for starring in the unremarkable *The Thing Called Love* may have been that his part called for him to play guitar on camera. (His leading lady, Samantha Mathis, became his new real-life girlfriend.)

Reports surfaced that Phoenix was drugged out through much of the making of this film and that it explained why his performance looked so unfocused on camera. Once back in Los Angeles from the location shoot in Nashville, Tennessee, River finally attended a few 12-step meetings, but generally remained in denial to himself and others about his mounting difficulties.

In mid-1993, River started filming *Dark Blood*. The picture was largely lensed in a remote part of the Utah desert. By late October, cast and crew were back in Los Angeles to do interior shots. One of the last scenes Phoenix filmed was his character's death.

On October 30, after working on *Dark Blood*, River returned to his accommodations at the Hotel Nikko in Los Angeles. There he met his sister Rain, his brother Joaquin (by now a rising talent himself), and his girlfriend, actress Samantha Mathis. Later, the group went to a party in the Hollywood Hills and then moved on to the Viper Room, a hip rock club on West Hollywood's Sunset Boulevard. By now, River was noticeably intoxicated and drug-dazed. Some on the scene recalled later that the actor looked pale, thin, and enervated and that he was slurring his words.

In the men's room of the club, River was offered an exotic type of heroin and had a bad reaction to it. He was given Valium to reduce his agitated high. Subsequently, he began throwing up, and passed out briefly. When he revived, he said he was having difficulty breathing and wanted some fresh air. With the assistance of Joaquin and others, he went outside the club. Very soon thereafter, River collapsed on the sidewalk and went into convulsions. Paramedics were

1994's Silent Tongue *was River Phoenix's last completed film, released after his October 1993 death from a drug overdose.*

summoned. Soon after River arrived by ambulance at the emergency room of Cedars-Sinai Medical Center, he was pronounced dead. Phoenix's autopsy revealed that he died of acute multiple drug intoxication, including marijuana, Valium, cocaine, and heroin.

Memorial tributes were held both in Los Angeles and at the family's Florida ranch (where River's ashes were scattered). As for the uncompleted *Dark Blood*, it was shelved. It was a sad finale to the troubled life of the talented 23-year-old movie star. How ironic that a few years earlier, Phoenix had said, "I'd rather quit while ahead. There's no need to overstay your welcome."

Elvis Presley

(January 8, 1935–August 16, 1977)

Elvis Presley was an icon among icons. He was a 1950s phenomenon who not only altered the world's musical tastes through his (in)famous bump-and-grind rock 'n' roll, but he had a significant impact on pop culture. Among many other things, he forever changed how the public viewed a major (musical) celebrity. So tremendous was Presley's acclaim around the world that when he died, a good number of his many fans insisted that the "King" still lived.

Over the years, many books and documentaries explored the life of this Southern country boy who became an enormous celebrity and was overwhelmed by his huge fame. What came to light in several of these chronicles was just how deeply self-destructive Elvis had been regarding his talents and his relationships.

It has been well documented that Presley had terrific appetites for both food and drugs. (He also binged on material acquisitions, including jet planes, fancy cars, a flashy wardrobe, the Graceland mansion, and a gun collection. In addition, to prove his status and to salve his loneliness, he supported a large retinue of relatives, bodyguards, and girlfriends.) In particular, it was Elvis's substance abuse that led to his professional and personal downfall—and to his untimely death at age 42.

With so many individuals involved in his life—including his longtime manager, Colonel Tom Parker—the major question is, why didn't anyone care enough to make him confront his drug addiction and push him into substance abuse treatment? In 2005, Priscilla Presley, Elvis's ex-wife, elaborated on this very subject. "People have asked, 'Why didn't you initiate an intervention?' People who ask that don't know Elvis. Elvis would no more have responded to an intervention than a demand to give up singing. It's important to realize that, for two different reasons, he never considered himself a drug addict. First, his drugs were all prescribed. That made a big difference in his mind. And secondly, he hated street drugs and campaigned for their elimination. So how could he be an addict himself? He refused to believe he had a problem. He would have undoubtedly laughed away any attempt at an intervention. There's no one, including his father, who could have pulled that off."

●   ●   ●

Elvis Aron Presley was born in Tupelo, Mississippi, in 1935, to Vernon Elvis Presley, who did odd jobs, and Gladys Love Smith Presley, a former garment factory worker. (Elvis was born at home, 35 minutes after his stillborn identical twin brother, Jesse Garon.) When Elvis was 13, the financially strapped family moved to Memphis, Tennessee, where Elvis graduated from Humes High School in 1953. At one time, he was a movie theater usher, then later, a truck driver. He began singing as "The Hillbilly Cat," and did recordings for a regional label before being signed by RCA in 1955. (By then, Elvis had come under the control of his greedy manager, Colonel Tom Parker.) The pelvis-gyrating Presley quickly became a show business phenomenon, leading to his screen debut in 1956's *Love Me Tender*, the first of his more than 30 feature films. The raw country boy began dating a bevy of Tinseltown starlets, Las Vegas chorines, and Memphis beauties.

It was major news around the globe when 23-year-old Presley was drafted into the army in March 1958. He spent much of his nearly two-year hitch stationed in Germany. What went unpublicized at the time was that his prescription drug habit was accelerating. In the past, he had used diet pills to keep his weight down, but now—thanks to a fellow serviceman's advice—he was using amphetamines to boost his energy. He became such a strong advocate of the little tablets that he briefly considered opening a drugstore (when his military service was over) so he would have an unlimited supply of the magic pills. In 1960, he returned to civilian life and to moviemaking (in *G.I. Blues*). He and most of his good ol' boy staff

were enjoying a fast-paced existence that included much partying, many women, and a lot of Dexedrine, Valium, and other drugs. With Presley's fame and connections, he had little difficulty in having a massive number of prescriptions filled to supply his needs and those of his coterie.

While in Germany, Presley had become infatuated with 14-year-old Priscilla Beaulieu, the stepdaughter of an American Air Force captain. When she turned 16 and Presley was back in the United States, he invited his "teen angel" to visit him. Priscilla spent the next four years with Elvis before the singer agreed to marry her. By then, she was well acquainted with his pill habit— which he tried to convert her to—his promiscuous ways, and the fact that he spent far more time with his musicians, pals, and handlers than he did with her. Despite all these problems, their kitschy wedding took place in Las Vegas in May 1967. Nine months and a few days thereafter, the couple's daughter, Lisa Marie, was born. (Once Priscilla became a mother, Elvis lost all interest in her sexually, somehow equating his wife with his idealized, deceased mother, whom he revered above all other women.)

Presley's crew observed the marked personality changes coming over Elvis in the mid-1960s as he continued to churn out movies and recordings. One staffer noted "slight touches of the Colonel that were negative. [There was a] sense of danger that was never there before." The staffer added about Elvis: "He loved to sit there high and wiggle in the chair, just wiggle his legs with a big pitcher of ice water in front of him [as he watched TV]. . . . He didn't give a damn whether you did anything. He was going to do what he wanted to do anyway." (During one of his drug-induced stupors, Presley stumbled into the bathroom, fell, and smacked his head on the bathtub.)

By the end of 1960s—with the release of *Change of Habit*—Presley's film career was essentially over. He returned to the concert stage, made TV appearances, and was still recording. His weight and the quality of his performances fluctuated greatly, depending on the number of pills he consumed and how much partying he had done. Even with his diminished popularity in the face of changing music styles and the onslaught of new rival singers, he still was able to fulfill his most every whim. However, one thing that he craved badly he couldn't seem to obtain, and this led to one of the more ironic moments in American history.

The drug-addicted Presley decided he needed a Federal Narcotics Bureau badge, so he would have some authority to wage his personal war on street drugs. He traveled to Washington, D.C., in December 1970, where his badge request was denied by John Finator, the deputy director of the U.S. Narcotics Bureau. Undaunted, Elvis then made a personal call on President Richard Nixon to help him obtain the desired credential. Nixon used the bizarre occasion for a great photo opportunity, and then arranged for Presley to receive the coveted badge.

In succeeding years, Presley's life and career spun further out of control, and he battled increasingly with his chief keeper, the Colonel. (However, Parker had so many gambling debts he didn't dare break with his increasingly unmanageable client.) By now, Priscilla had grown weary of Elvis's volatile mood swings and his bouts of restlessness during which not even food, drugs, or reading seemed to calm the star's agitated mind. She was also fed up with being pushed to the sidelines, knowing that her husband was off partying with girlfriends and staffers. In retaliation, she became close with Mike Stone, a karate instructor from Hawaii. In 1972, her anger with her spouse's extracurricular activities led her to tell Elvis that she planned to leave him for Stone. The Presleys divorced in October 1973.

For companionship, Presley turned to Linda Thompson, Miss Tennessee. He remained somewhat faithful to her for the next year but then resumed his womanizing ways. On more than a few occasions Linda saved the singer's life when he was zoned out on drugs (now including cocaine). One time, he dozed off at dinner, slumping headfirst into a full soup bowl. She pulled his head back and saved him from drowning. The duo finally split in 1976. Next, he took up with Ginger Alden, 20, of Memphis. In contrast to many others in the legend's life, she did not easily give in to his caprices. This just intrigued Presley more.

At the end of January 1977, while Elvis was in his favorite spot (his Graceland bathroom), he proposed marriage to Ginger. She agreed to become the new Mrs. Presley. However, months later, in mid-August, she awoke one day at Graceland to discover the singing star dead in the adjoining bathroom. The final autopsy report revealed that there were 14 drugs in Presley's body, at least 10 of them in significant amounts. The major cause of death was polypharmacy—too many powerful drugs in his system. Even the King had a mortal threshold to his lengthy and reckless drug habit.

Richard Pryor

(December 1, 1940–December 10, 2005)

In its obituary of the trailblazing, profane comedian Richard Pryor, the *New York Times* assessed, "Mr. Pryor's comic imagination and creative use of the blunt cadences of street language were revelations to most Americans. He did not simply tell stories, he brought them to vivid life, revealing the entire range of black America's humor, from its folksy and rural origins to its raunchier urban expressions." The *Times* also noted, "Episodes of self-destructive, chaotic and violent behavior, often triggered by drug use, repeatedly threatened his career and jeopardized his life."

Pryor once said of his devastating drug habit: "I couldn't escape the darkness." At his most excessive level of usage, the stand-up comic/film star was spending about $250,000 annually to feed his dependency. Once a psychiatrist asked the performer what he liked so much about his drug of choice (cocaine). He answered, "It fucks me up good. I like that ping it puts in my head." Pryor claimed that one of the reasons he had first used drugs (as a young teenager trying to survive in the tough ghetto of Peoria, Illinois) was that he wanted "to experiment, to find out who I was," adding, "Mostly I did it to accept the fact that I was no street-fighter." Later in life, when the incisive talent had broken through the barrier of racial prejudice and had become famous as an edgy stand-up comic, he said that his substance abuse stemmed from the fact that he had "a lot of guilt about being

successful." He elaborated, "I'm not able to deal with the success that I have. And I have a lot of pressure. It's not about the big head or nuthin' like that, it's about my life."

• • •

Richard Franklin Lennox Thomas Pryor III was born in Peoria, Illinois, in 1940, the only child of LeRoy Pryor (aka Buck Carter) and Gertrude Thomas. His mother, a prostitute, often disappeared on drinking binges for months at a time. He was 4 years old before he first saw his father, a sometime bartender, boxer, and pimp, who had been away in World War II military service. Pryor was raised by his paternal grandmother, Marie, who operated several saloons and brothels in town. As a result, the boy learned far too much about the tawdry side of life at an early age. As school, the hyperactive Richard was the class clown. When not in the classroom, Pryor often hung out at the local community center, where he became involved in the drama group and found he enjoyed performing in front of an audience. By age 15, after the latest of his disputes (which centered around his rebellious nature and dislike for authority) at school, he was expelled. In 1957, the hard-living Pryor, who was working odd jobs, fathered his first child, a girl. The next year he enlisted in the army and served for two years, part of it stationed in West Germany (where he experienced racial discrimination and got into additional scrapes).

The young Scott Schwartz with Richard Pryor in 1982's The Toy.

By his early twenties, Pryor was performing on the black club circuit developing his comic characters—several of them drawn from the whores, pimps, and winos he had lived among when he was growing up. Already he was spending much of his $50-a-week income on drugs; initially, marijuana and uppers (later, he turned to harder stuff). While on the road touring, this black outsider often clashed with white police, who frequently arrested the foul-mouthed, agitated stand-up comedian.

When Richard got his girlfriend Patricia Price pregnant, he married her, shortly before she gave birth to their son, Richard Jr.,

in 1960. Not long afterward, Pryor left them. (The couple divorced around 1961.) He went to New York City, where he gained a foothold entertaining in Greenwich Village venues and, thereafter, on TV variety shows. By the end of the decade, he was playing Las Vegas clubs and had released his debut comedy album (*Richard Pryor*). By 1967, he had divorced his second wife, Shelley Bonus, whom he married in 1967 and with whom he had a daughter. By now, the wild, unpredictable, and usually angry Pryor was seriously addicted to cocaine.

In 1970, Pryor, furious with himself for becoming too "white" a comic, walked off the stage at the Aladdin Hotel in Las Vegas. He moved to Berkeley, California, where he thrived on the local hippie culture. When he reemerged many months later, he had discovered his true comic voice: crude, brutally honest, and raunchy. Having already made his movie bow in 1967's *The Busy Body*, he devoted much of the early 1970s to appearing in blaxploitation pictures such as 1973's *The Mack*. On a more mainstream level, he appeared in 1972's *Lady Sings the Blues* and collaborated on the script to Mel Brooks's 1974 Western spoof, *Blazing Saddles*. Pryor continued to score with his electrifying comedy albums (such as 1975's *Is It Something I Said?*), his movies (including 1976's *Silver Streak*, which first paired him with Gene Wilder), and his dynamic one-man concerts. In 1976, Pryor negotiated a long-term, multimillion-dollar contract with Universal Pictures—the most lucrative such pact yet for an African American.

In September 1977, Richard wed model

Deborah McGuire, and they had a daughter; the pair ended their abusive marriage in August 1978. Meanwhile, the drugs, the booze, his anger with life's injustices, and his sorrow over the late 1970s death of his grandmother all combined to lead Pryor into unwise career and life choices.

Pryor came extremely close to dying in June 1980. Initially, he insisted he accidentally set himself on fire when he lit his pipe while freebasing. Actually, the profoundly depressed and cocaine-dazed Pryor had doused himself with cognac and then flicked on his pocket lighter. The resultant blaze left him with third-degree burns over most of his upper body. That he survived such a horrendous nightmare was miraculous. Following his recovery, he professed to be cleaning up his act, but he found he could not (or would not) kick his drug habit.

Richard's drug abuse also led him into wild antisocial behavior toward others. For example, after yet another major clash with his new woman (Jennifer Lee, whom he would marry in August 1981 and divorce in October 1982), the highly paranoid star wanted to shoot her with his .357 revolver. A few minutes later, his violent mood swung back the other way. For the profoundly addicted man (he often used an entire kilo of drugs over a weekend), no bad situation he created was really his fault. He told himself he was just an innocent victim.

In 1983, Pryor signed a five-year deal with Columbia Pictures for a reported $40 million. (One of his pictures for the studio was 1986's *Jo Jo Dancer, Your Life Is Calling,* which he not only starred in but also produced, directed, and scripted. In this semi-autobiographical drama, he dealt frankly with his addictions and the notorious free-basing incident.) Even with such professional validation, Pryor could not bring himself to break his cocaine addiction. He tried therapy to little avail. It took a shocking discovery to wake him up at last and calm him down—medical tests revealed that he was suffering from multiple sclerosis. In the late 1980s, his health continued to decline and he grew increasingly thinner and slower of movement. After he survived quadruple heart bypass surgery in 1991, he announced publicly that he was suffering from multiple sclerosis. By then, he had remarried (in April 1990) and was soon to redivorce Flynn Belaine, to whom he had previously been wed from October 1986 to January 1987.

In the 1990s, increasingly crippled by his illness and now wheelchair-bound, Pryor abandoned drug use and much of his earlier self-destructive behavior. He performed his act occasionally and authored his autobiography (1995's *Pryor Convictions: And Other Life Sentences*), and was the subject of many show business testimonials. In his fragile times, he turned to ex-wife Jennifer Lee for emotional support. (They remarried in June 2001.) He died in December 2005.

Having *never* made it easy on himself or his audiences, the groundbreaking comedian once summed up his crazy-quilt existence with, "I had some great things and I had some bad things. The best and the worst. In other words, I had a life."

Zachary Scott

(February 21, 1914–October 3, 1965)

Playing a screen cad can be a meaty acting challenge. However, if an actor does so too convincingly, he can get stereotyped in such confining roles. In his third Hollywood movie, 1945's *Mildred Pierce*, Zachary Scott appeared as Monte Beregon, a sophisticated, sneering scoundrel. His polished performance as a gilt-edged heel proved to be the peak of Zachary's film career. Thereafter stuck in an artistic rut, and coping badly with his sexual ambivalence, the sensitive actor turned to heavy drinking. It was a vice that plagued him for years.

• • •

Zachary Thomson Scott Jr. was born in Austin, Texas, in 1914, the second of three children (he had two sisters) of Dr. Zachary T. Scott, a prominent physician/surgeon, and Sallie Lee Masterson Scott, whose family were wealthy ranchers. One of Dr. Scott's ancestors had wed George Washington's sister and had manufactured the first American firearms employed by the Continental Army.

To ensure that Zachary did not become too spoiled growing up, his parents sent him to public school and required that he earn spending money through such jobs as clerking at the local drugstore. He attended the University of Texas at Austin, where he was active in the campus drama group. Scott dropped out of school at 19 to study acting in England. To earn his transatlantic passage, he labored on a freighter bound for

England. Once there, the well-bred American quickly made contacts among people in the theater. He joined the English Repertory Company and, later, performed with the Theatre Royal in Bath. Over the next year and a half he was in several productions, traveled about the continent, and enjoyed an active social life. (Many of his newfound acquaintances were successful older gentlemen involved in show business. Several of them were homosexuals.)

He was 21 when he returned to the United States. When no acting assignments materialized, he resumed his studies at the University of Texas. In February 1935, Scott wed Elaine Anderson, whom he had met on campus. They had a daughter, Waverly. Their mutual friends advised Scott to go east and work in summer stock to gain an acting foothold. This led to parts on Broadway, including in the successful 1943 romantic comedy *Those Endearing Young Charms*. Warner Bros. studio mogul Jack L. Warner saw the play and signed Scott to a studio contract.

Zachary (now sporting a mustache to compensate for his too sensitive look and sometimes precious manner) debuted in the title role of 1944's *The Mask of Dimitrios*. Cast as the suave villain, he acquitted himself well. The next year, he was loaned to United Artists for the key part of the sharecropper farmer in *The Southerner*. He was now earning $1,500 a week, but could never curtail his extravagant lifestyle and had to constantly borrow money from his parents.

For a while, the genteel Scott abided by the studio's decision to pigeonhole him as a debonair heel. However, as he gained more confidence in his acting abilities, he began to reject roles and register his annoyance by arriving late to work or not coming on the lot at all. Such rebellious behavior put him in continuous conflict with Warner Bros. (In 1945, the increasingly malcontented actor suffered an "accident" in which both his wrists were somehow slashed. This was likely a suicide attempt.) During his Warner Bros. tenure, there were rumors concerning Scott's alleged homosexuality. Years later, studio contract director Vincent Sherman noted, "He may have been double-gaited. But there was no great scandal. Zach was always beautifully behaved."

Scott bridled at his mostly unchallenging film parts and hoped MGM would borrow him for their 1949 drama *That Forsyte Woman*. Unfortunately, the role in question went to Warner Bros.' swashbuckling star, Errol Flynn. Adding to Scott's dissatisfaction with life was his unfulfilling marriage. At one juncture, his wife suggested that he go off alone and "try to find understanding and a true evaluation of things." He did so but came to no practical decisions. Mrs. Scott resolved their marital discord when she met and fell in love with famed novelist John Steinbeck. She divorced Scott in December 1949, charging he had a violent temper. The decree became final a year later. Elaine then wed Steinbeck, and Zachary continued his heavy drinking, which led him into a few skirmishes with the law.

Scott's Warner Bros. contract concluded with 1951's *Lightning Strikes Twice*. There-after, he freelanced at other studios and appeared on TV. In July 1952, he wed actress Ruth Ford and adopted her daughter, Shelley, from a prior marriage. (The new union had its problems, none of them helped by the actor's drinking and reckless spending.)

His screen assignments continued to diminish in quality and quantity. The fortysomething actor, who now wore a gold earring in one ear, returned to the theater—largely in summer stock tours. He and Ruth costarred on the London stage in 1957's *Requiem for a Nun*, written for them by William Faulkner. About two years later, the Scotts brought the show to Broadway, but it closed after a short run. His last film was Jerry Lewis's *It's Only Money*, which easily could have summed up Scott's feeling about working in Hollywood. In 1965, he was diagnosed with brain tumors. Despite radiation treatments and surgery, he died in October 1965 at Sweetbrush, his family residence in Austin, Texas.

Zachary Scott and Carole Matthews in 1955's Treasure of Ruby Hills.

Charlie Sheen

(September 3, 1965–)

Charlie Sheen emerged on the show business scene in the mid-1980s, boasting an intriguing industry pedigree. He was the son of distinguished actor Martin Sheen and the younger brother of Hollywood Brat Packer/movie leading man Emilio Estevez. The newcomer's acting résumé soon contained solid performances in such quality features as 1986's *Platoon* and 1987's *Wall Street.* (Later, he descended artistically to such pap as 1993's *Hot Shots! Part Deux.*) More recently, Sheen gained fresh popularity as the Emmy-nominated star of the long-running TV sitcom *Two and a Half Men,* which began in 2003. However, it was as a Hollywood bad boy that Charlie Sheen earned his greatest notoriety, an image he playfully teased on camera, as in the 1999 film *Being John Malkovich.*

• • •

He was born Carlos Irwin Estevez in New York City in 1965, the third of four children (each of whom became a performer) of actor Martin Sheen and his artist wife, Janet Templeton. Within a few years, the family was living in Malibu, California, because of Sheen's mushrooming movie career. When the future actor was 10, he had an uncredited bit in Martin's telefeature *The Execution of Private Slovik.* That experience prompted the boy to consider becoming an actor. However, while on location in the Philippines with his father for 1979's *Apocalypse Now,* he witnessed his father suffer a near-fatal heart attack and decided instead to become a professional baseball player.

Meanwhile, Emilio had begun his acting career and was gaining recognition for his work, and his highly competitive younger brother often was finding himself on the wrong side of the law. At 16, with a new BMW to zoom around in, Charlie was arrested for allegedly using marijuana, but his family rescued him from that

The hard-partying Charlie Sheen faces the camera with Kristy Swanson in 1994's The Chase.

predicament. Next, the teenager engaged in a mini-spree of using other people's credit card numbers to purchase merchandise. When the police apprehended him (in a classroom at Santa Monica High School), the Sheens saved the day by making restitution.

On the romantic front, when Charlie was 16, he dated actress Robin Wright (who years later married actor Sean Penn). Then he and his high school girlfriend Paula Profitt had a child (Cassandra) out of wedlock. Soon, the couple went their separate ways. Back on the academic front, the confirmed truant was caught purchasing exam answers and assaulting an instructor and was expelled from school. He now concluded that becoming an actor might be easier than trying to become a major-league ball player.

He billed himself as Charlie Sheen, and his first major role was in 1986's *The Wraith*. He experienced his professional sports dream when he was cast as a baseball player in two late 1980s pictures: *Eight Men Out* and *Major League*. Along the way, Sheen became a dedicated party animal. (He said later, "There was a time when I couldn't leave the house until I'd smoked three joints, taken tranquilizers, and drunk a bottle of bourbon.")

Sheen's career momentum was derailed with drivel like 1990's *Navy SEALs*. His use of drugs and booze increased, hampering his work in front of the camera. Charlie became so caught up in his addictions that in August 1990, after a family intervention, he went to a rehab clinic for a month. Once back in circulation, he soon returned to his bad habits. For a bit, he was linked with comedian Eddie Murphy's ex-girlfriend Charlotte Lewis. Sheen's relationship with actress Kelly Preston ended, allegedly, when he "accidentally" shot her in the arm.

Charlie had a career uplift with the successful 1991 movie comedy *Hot Shots!* Now back in the money, Sheen was spending big on partying. He was well known for his list—annotated with his ratings—of Tinseltown's sexiest women. He boasted about his relationship with porn star Ginger Lynn Allen. During the high-profile 1994 trial of Hollywood madam Heidi Fleiss, it was revealed that Sheen had a weakness for hookers. (Between 1991 to 1993, the actor paid over $53,000 for 27 get-togethers with Heidi's girls.)

In September 1995, after he and model Donna Peele had dated for a few weeks, they married. However, the union fell apart within six months (and the couple divorced in November 1996). Soon Sheen, now a born-again Christian, was said to be out of control again. Meanwhile, his career declined with roles in such minor movies as 1996's *Loose Women*.

In late 1996, a day after allegedly hammering a female friend's vehicle with a baseball bat, Charlie was arrested for supposedly assaulting his ex-girlfriend Brittany Ashland (aka porn actress Tanya Rivers) at his Malibu Lake home. She insisted she was shoved to the floor and knocked unconscious. The next February, he was charged with misdemeanor battery. He pleaded no contest and was sentenced to 300 hours of community service and placed on probation until June 1999.

During May 1998, Sheen was rushed to a hospital in Thousand Oaks, California, after a severe drug overdose. After being released, he checked into the Malibu-based Promises, a rehab center, but he decamped a day later. In an act of tough love, Martin Sheen signed a warrant for his son's arrest. Charlie was apprehended by the police and given the choice of substance abuse treatment or jail time. He reentered Promises in June. With the court's approval, he was released from the treatment facility in November 1998, but remained on probation until June 2000.

Later, in need of work, he accepted his brother's offer to costar in a 2000 made-for-cable picture, *Rated X*. At this critical juncture in his professional and private lives, Sheen, 34, caught a major career break. He was hired (under a $2.7 million pact) to replace the ailing Michael J. Fox in the TV sitcom *Spin City*. Sheen debuted in the show in fall 2000, playing the tailor-made role of a ladies man with a past. That show left the air in April 2002. Two months later, Sheen, seemingly reformed from his past unruly ways, wed actress Denise Richards, with whom he had worked in films and on TV.

In the fall of 2003, he starred in a new television comedy, *Two and a Half Men*, which proved to be a substantial hit. Sheen and Richards became the parents of a baby girl (Sam) in March 2004. Then, in March 2005, Richards filed for divorce. (At the time, she was pregnant with their second child, Lola, who was born that June.) The breakup had each party lambasting the other, with many media sources suggesting that Charlie had returned to his old bad ways. Their split led to a much publicized chronicle of the battling couple reuniting, then separating again. Later, she obtained a restraining order against him, and the bitter duo fought over custody of their children. By August 2006, however, they had resolved their issues and were ready to move on in life. In 2007, Sheen provided one of the voices for the animated feature *Foodfight!*

After years of an excessive lifestyle, Sheen admitted, "If I've learned anything at all, it's that I know nothing about women. They remain a mystery. But I've learned to stop trying to figure them out. There's no end to the journey, and that's what makes it so compelling."

Gale Storm

(April 5, 1922–)

Wholesome, vivacious, and pretty are apt descriptions of actress Gale Storm, who paraded pleasantly through largely innocuous budget movies (several of them musicals) in the 1940s. In the next decade, she gained far greater acclaim as the agile star of successful TV sitcom series (especially *My Little Margie*) and as a pop vocalist with hits like "I Hear You Knocking, but You Can't Come In." (She also had several profitable albums to her credit.) Married and the mother of four children, she was an ardent churchgoer. To keep professionally active in the 1960s and early 1970s, she traveled around the United States starring in summer theater productions. Then she largely disappeared from public view.

Suddenly, in 1980, Storm emerged anew on TV commercials. She was *not* a spokesperson for the typical consumer product. Rather, she was extolling the virtues of Raleigh Hills Hospitals, which utilized aversion therapy to help patients deal with their alcoholism. On air, she admitted candidly that she suffered from the disease and that it had once robbed her of her "self-respect, self-esteem, and sense of worth." In that more innocent era, the shock of a beloved TV/movie star—with such a sweet, upbeat image—making such a public confession was both astounding and controversial. How did our Little Margie become an alcoholic?

Gale Storm, the star of TV's Oh Susanna *(which ran from 1956 to 1960) arrives in New York in the late 1950s.*

• • •

Josephine Owaissa Cottle was born in 1922 in Bloomington, Texas, the fifth and last child of William and Minnie Cottle. When Josephine was 11 months old, her father, a potter, died. His widow supported the household—now based in Houston—by being a piecework seamstress. When Josephine was about 13, her mother remarried. The teenager had little love for her stepfather, who had come between her and her beloved mother.

When Josephine was 17 and a high school senior, she had appeared already in several drama club productions. Two of her teachers urged her to audition for an upcoming talent contest to be held in Houston. The competition was being sponsored by the radio program *Gateway to Hollywood*. The winner would be sent to Holly-

wood to appear on the CBS network radio show in the playoffs among regional champions from all over America. The prize for the two finalists (one male, one female) was a guaranteed screen appearance in a forthcoming RKO release and a possible term contract at the studio. Josephine won the local audition and was dispatched to Hollywood, where the judges at the finals voted her and Lee Bonnell, her male counterpart, the national winners.

She was christened with the screen name Gale Storm and made her movie debut in 1940's *Tom Brown's School Days*. After she made another picture for RKO, her studio option was dropped, and she freelanced. Meanwhile, she had fallen in love with Lee Bonnell, her fellow contest winner. They married in September 1941. Bonnell continued in minor roles at RKO until he enlisted in the Coast Guard in 1943. That same year the first of the couple's four children was born. By this point, Storm was under contract to Monogram Pictures, a low-caliber studio, where she performed brightly in such modest entries as 1945's *Sunbonnet Sue*. Her winning personality and her growing acting skills made her a great asset to Monogram's product line.

When Bonnell returned to civilian life after World War II, he attempted to reactivate his movie career. He suffered through several nondescript assignments and then quit the industry. His show business failure—in contrast to Gale's relative success—caused great tension in the Bonnell household. Finally, she offered to abandon her film career. This pushed Bonnell into finding a new profession—in the insurance field—and he became quite successful in his new endeavor.

Storm made her last feature in 1952. That same year she was offered the title role in a new TV series, *My Little Margie*. The show proved to be exceedingly popular and remained on the air through the summer of 1955. The next year she began a four-year run in another TV situation comedy, *The Gale Storm Show* (aka *Oh Susanna*). Meanwhile, the energetic leading lady began a recording career and taught Sunday school classes. At the peak of Storm's music career, her husband became extremely jealous about her supposed romantic relationship with a top executive at her label, Dot Records. She repeatedly insisted that her spouse's accusations were not true. However, to save her marriage, she reluctantly ended her recording contract.

Storm always said (including to this book's author) that she had *no* idea why she became an alcoholic. In her 1981 memoir, she claimed that she had never had an alcoholic drink until she was 21. She had gotten ill from the experiment and did not have another alcoholic beverage for nearly 10 years. As she remembered, "I started to drink in the early 1960s . . . and I started to drink too much in the early 1970s." According to the actress, by the late 1970s, her alcoholism had become so severe that her health was being seriously undermined. Her physician warned her that she was drinking herself to death. The badly bloated actress agreed to be hospitalized for treatment. However, in that era, alcoholism was regarded by many hospitals as a form of mental disease. After various failed "cures" and an unsuccessful attempt at relating to the regimen at Alcoholics Anonymous, she feared there was no hope for her. However, in early 1979, Storm admitted herself to Raleigh Hills Hospital in Oxnard, California. There she dealt successfully with her substance abuse problem. Doing volunteer work (including TV promotions and counseling) for that facility was her way of thanking Raleigh Hills for saving her life.

In May 1986, Lee Bonnell died. Two years later, in April 1988, Storm married Paul Masterson, a retired television network executive. The next year, Storm made a brief show business return with a guest-starring role on TV's *Murder, She Wrote*. In May 1996, Masterson died of cancer.

As for her long bout with alcoholism, Storm said in the new millennium: "Licking my addiction was one of the hardest things in my life. But it can be done."

PART 5

So Much Power

Johnny Carson

(October 23, 1925–January 23, 2005)

Actor Robert Blake once commented about the enormous pressure of being a guest on TV's *The Tonight Show Starring Johnny Carson*, "There's a certain enjoyment in facing death, periodically." He added, "There's no experience I can describe to you that would compare with doin' [it]. It is so wired, and so hyped, and so up. It's like Broadway on opening night. There's nothing casual about it. And it's not a talk show. It's some other kind of show. I mean he [Johnny Carson] has such energy, you got like six minutes to do your thing. . . . And you better be good. Or they'll go to the commercial after two minutes."

Entertainment critic Kenneth Tynan recalled visiting Carson's office suite at NBC-TV's Burbank, California, facility. "The studio is his native habitat . . . you have invaded his territory. Once you are on Carson's turf, the onus is on you to demonstrate your right to stay there. If you fail, you will decorously get the boot." Comedian David Brenner noted: "Nowhere is where I'd be without the *Tonight Show*. It's a necessary ingredient. . . . TV excels in two areas—sports and Carson. The show made my career."

Between 1962 and 1992, Johnny Carson was the monarch of late night television. At the peak of his popularity, he averaged a home audience of well over 17 million; when he retired from his program, 50 million viewers tuned in to bid farewell to an institution. Much of Carson's reign occurred in an era before cable/satellite channels became popular; it was a time when three networks (ABC, CBS, and NBC) ruled the medium. Most home audiences had limited program options, which made Carson's influential late evening offering all the more powerful. Appearing on Johnny's chat show was equivalent to being on Oprah Winfrey's syndicated TV series today. Carson's forum could dramatically boost a performer's career, make a book a best-seller, or give public credence to a point of view on a particular issue. On the other hand, if the mighty Carson took a dislike to a person, nothing would persuade him to book the individual on *his* show, no matter how advantageous it might be to the program's ratings. During his lengthy TV tenure, Johnny was one of the key ruling powers of show business, and a major influence on pop culture.

Carson's Midwestern background, bland good looks, and unflappable public demeanor belied the reality that he was an extremely sharp wit. Off camera, he could be opinionated, sometimes hot-tempered, and quite capable of negating a long-standing loyalty to a friend or a business associate in a flash. He remained a very self-contained, private individual, even to family and friends. (A *TV Guide* profile of Carson described him as "a wary, aloof human being who seems to be on guard against some invisible danger," adding, "Johnny Carson isn't holding the lid on himself to safeguard his private life. It's to safeguard his anger.") However, on the air he seemed accessible, affable, and down-to-earth. It made his large viewership extremely loyal for several decades—something few TV celebrities can count on today.

• • •

John William Carson was born in 1925 in Corning, Iowa, the middle of three children of Homer Lloyd and Ruth Hook Carson. His father was a utility company lineman. Later, he became a manager for the Nebraska Light and Power Company in Norfolk, Nebraska, and the family moved there. At age 12, Johnny became fascinated with magic, and within two years he put on his first professional magic show, at the local Rotary club for a $3 fee. The extremely shy teenager discovered that when he performed in front of an audience, he got "a high, a great feeling." After graduating high school, he went into the Navy, serving in the Pacific for much of World War II. Afterward, while attending college, he found his first professional job—writing for a local radio station. In October 1949, he married his college sweetheart, Joan "Jody" Wolcott. (The couple would have three children.)

By 1951, Carson had moved to Los Angeles. There he worked first as a TV announcer, then as the star of his own weekly afternoon series, *Carson's Cellar*. That led to his writing for Red Skelton's network TV show, and then to having his own nighttime program in 1955, which ran for a season. Its failure prompted Johnny to relocate to New York City, where, from 1957 to 1962, he hosted the television game show

Who Do You Trust?, which became a huge hit. While he was successful professionally, Carson and his wife grew apart, and they separated in September 1959. He had already begun drinking heavily, and would sometimes get into nasty snide sessions at parties. This behavior reached a peak when he was beaten up for being rude to a Las Vegas showgirl. Carson described this period before he finally divorced Joan in 1963 as "the worst personal experience" of his life. In August 1963, Carson wed Joanne Copeland, a former flight attendant turned actress whom he first started dating in 1960.

Meanwhile, on October 1, 1962, Carson began his impressive run on *The Tonight Show Starring Johnny Carson*, aided by his TV sidekick, Ed McMahon. *Time* magazine noted, "Johnny never goes beyond his intellectual depth. Neither does he use his terrible swift wit to cut down his guests." Watching this show—with its mix of Carson's opening monologue, the skits, and celebrity interviews—became a ritual for a good number of home viewers. Soon Carson was one of the most famous individuals in the United States, and his annual salary escalated from under $200,000 to a few million dollars. In June 1970, Carson and his second wife separated. When the divorce was finalized in the winter of 1972, Joanne received a very healthy settlement. In May 1972, *The Tonight Show* moved to Los Angeles. To house their moneymaking talk program (which at one point accounted for nearly 17 percent of NBC's profits), the network spent $1.5 million to construct an annex at its Burbank studio. That September, Carson wed Joanne Holland, who had already been twice married and had a son.

TV talk show host Johnny Carson chats on air in 1977 with singer Alice Cooper while dealing with a frisky reptile.

She was nearly 20 years younger than Johnny.

In 1976, NBC renewed Carson's contract at a $3 million fee. Meanwhile, his popularity had grown to such heights that he could earn as much as $200,000 to perform his club act in Las Vegas for one show a night for a week. By the late 1970s, Carson, who once had a restaurant franchise (which failed) and his own clothing line (which succeeded magnificently), branched out into other businesses—ranging from a California bank to a Nevada TV station. When Carson threatened to leave NBC in 1980, the network raised his yearly stipend to $5 million, plus made him producer/owner of his showcase. (His Carson Productions produced several programs besides *The Tonight Show*.)

In April 1982, Carson, who was still drinking too much, pleaded no contest to driving while intoxicated. By now, he and his third wife had separated, and Johnny used his mighty talk show forum to "joke" about the split and to make digs about Joanne's monetary demands. The couple finalized their divorce in August 1985 with her receiving a reported $7.7 million in cash, plus $12 million in other assets and $35,000 monthly alimony for the next 64 months. However, with an estimated net worth of $42 to $100 million, the rich and powerful Carson could well afford the payout. In June 1987, Carson married Alexis Maas, a stockbroker's secretary, who was 25 years his junior. (Reputedly, they met when he spotted her walking on the beach in front of his Malibu, California, home.)

Over the decades, many other personalities (including Merv Griffin, Joan Rivers, Joey Bishop, and Pat Sajak) hosted rival TV talk shows, but each was quickly vanquished in the home audience ratings. It was not until Arsenio Hall began his late night program in 1989—which catered to a younger, more ethnically diverse audience—that Carson met with serious on-air competition. On May 22, 2002, Johnny, 66, bade his TV audience a "a very heartfelt goodnight." (Three days later, Jay Leno took over as Johnny's late night show successor, but neither he nor David Letterman—his main challenger on a rival network—ever matched Carson in ratings.)

Once Carson retired from his nighttime showcase, he never found another TV project that interested him sufficiently to want to return to the public eye. When he was not at his Malibu compound, he sailed on his 130-foot yacht or played golf. He remained a great enthusiast of TV, and occasionally provided David Letterman with jokes for his opening monologue. In 1999, Carson suffered a heart attack and underwent quadruple bypass surgery. During his last 20 years, Johnny, long a chain-smoker, suffered from emphysema, the disease that caused his death in January 2005.

Back in 1991, Johnny Carson's announcement that he was again thinking of retiring from his TV chores prompted Bob Hope, another comedic icon, to say that losing Carson on air would be "sort of like a head falling off Mt. Rushmore."

Michael Eisner

(March 7, 1942–)

In the mid-1990s, Michael Eisner, the chairman and chief executive officer of the Walt Disney Company, seemed to be in an unshakable, golden entertainment industry position. The Disney Channel, Walt Disney Television, Touchstone Pictures, Miramax Films, Hyperion Books, and the Anaheim Mighty Ducks (the professional ice hockey team) were all components of the expansive Disney kingdom, which also included—besides its film and animation divisions—stores, theme parks, resort hotels, and cruise ships around the world. In February 1995, under Eisner's stewardship, Disney acquired the conglomerate Capital Cities/ABC. This $20 billion purchase gave Disney control of a major broadcast TV network (ABC), cable channels such as ESPN, 8 TV stations, 21 radio stations, 7 newspapers, assorted magazines . . . and much more.

Three years later, in 1998, Eisner wrote (with Tony Schwartz) *Work in Progress: Risking Failure, Surviving Success* in which he hoped "to rethink Disney's future, in part by re-examining its past." He professed in the preface to this often self-congratulatory memoir, "Whatever new directions we take, I see more clearly than ever that they are guided by an unchanging set of simple core values and beliefs . . . the commitment to excellence, the importance of teamwork, the discipline to behave gracefully under difficult circumstances." Many in Hollywood inner circles found such lofty statements far removed from the truth of how the success-obsessed Eisner truly operated in the corporate trenches. However, even Eisner's most ardent detractors could not have fully anticipated the swift fall that this high-achieving, hugely powerful industry figure would suffer within the next few years.

• • •

Michael Dammann Eisner was born in Mount Kisco, New York, in 1942, the second child (following older sister Margot) of Lester and Margaret Dammann Eisner. His father was an Ivy League–educated attorney and investor who served in the Air Force during World War II. His mother was the daughter of a self-made multimillionaire, Milton Dammann, a cofounder of the American Safety Razor Company. The Eisners resided on Manhattan's swanky Park Avenue, and their children attended the best schools and summer camps. Despite the family's affluence, Michael was brought up not to spend money frivolously.

Michael attended Denison University, a small liberal arts college in Granville, Ohio, where he majored in theater and English literature and hoped to become a playwright or an author. During the summer following his junior year, he worked as a page with the NBC network in New York City. After graduating in 1964, he moved to Paris to write a novel. Within 10 days, he returned to New York and found work as a logging clerk at NBC. Six weeks thereafter, he moved over to the programming department of the CBS network, where he supervised the insertion of commercials into children's TV fare.

Wanting a bigger challenge, Eisner mailed out over 100 résumés to industry sources. The only individual to answer him was Barry Diller, at the time a fledgling programmer at ABC. Diller convinced his network bosses to hire the applicant as the assistant to the national program director in New York. By 1968, Eisner had been promoted to director of specials and talent, and later he was placed in charge of the network's Saturday morning children's programming. As Eisner continued to climb the corporate ladder, he played a pivotal role in ABC's rise to ratings dominance. In 1976, Michael became the network's senior vice president for prime-time production and development. Meanwhile, in July 1967,

Eisner had married Jane Breckenridge. (The couple would have three children—all sons—born in 1970, 1973, and 1978.)

In late 1976, Eisner accepted an offer from Barry Diller (who had become board chairman of Paramount Pictures) to become president and chief operating officer of the floundering studio. Under his tough-as-nails supervision, the film lot went from being the least successful of the major studios to becoming the industry leader with such films as 1978's *Grease* and 1984's *Beverly Hills Cop*. By 1984, the demanding Eisner, known to be very difficult to work with, was ready to move on. His mentor, Barry Diller, had left the lot to become chairman at Twentieth Century-Fox. Increasingly, Eisner was unable to get along with Marvin Davis, the recently installed chairman of Paramount's parent company, Gulf & Western Industries. When Davis refused to appoint Eisner to the studio's number one post, Michael left the lot.

Eisner was approached by Roy E. Disney, the nephew of the late Walt Disney, to take over as chairman and chief executive officer at Walt Disney Productions (soon renamed the Walt Disney Company). Eisner accepted the impressive job offer, which included a $750,000 base annual salary, a $750,000 signing bonus, a yearly bonus based on studio profitability, and options to purchase 510,000 shares of Disney stock at $57 a share. Industry veteran Frank Wells became Eisner's second-in-command. Eisner brought over Jeffrey Katzenberg from Paramount (where he had been chief operating officer) and put him in charge of Disney's feature film divisions and its sagging animation division.

During the next years of growth, Disney regained its predominance in the animation field, had both box-office and TV series hits, successfully syndicated its product to television, and mined the growing home entertainment marketplace. (However, it endured some failures, including the money-draining Euro Disneyland project on the outskirts of Paris.) Eisner was not shy about becoming the new face of Disney: he took over hosting the *Disney Sunday Movie* TV program. In the process of running Disney, Eisner made several industry enemies, including his former boss, Barry Diller.

If any moment pinpointed Eisner's mighty fall from the pinnacle of success, it was the April 1994 death of Frank Wells in a helicopter accident. Jeffrey Katzenberg expected to be promoted to the sudden vacancy of the corporation's president/chief operating officer. When Eisner refused to make the appointment, Katzenberg left Disney and helped to found a new studio, Dreamworks SKG. (Later, Katzenberg sued Disney for money he alleged the studio still owed him. After a nasty public battle, which put Eisner in a bad light, the suit was resolved out of court. Katzenberg received a settlement estimated to be as high as $250 million.)

As Katzenberg's replacement at Disney, Eisner hired longtime friend Michael Ovitz, the high-voltage founder/head of the Creative Artists Agency. Within 14 months of Ovitz's taking office, he was let go by Disney's board of directors and received approximately $38 million in cash and $100 million in stock as a severance package. As with the Katzenberg departure, the costly, rancorous dismissal of Ovitz did much to dampen Eisner's industry reputation and his standing with Disney stockholders. (Eisner's reputation was further diluted by several hard-hitting new books that traced the vicious battle for power at Disney over recent decades.)

In November 2003, Roy E. Disney, whose power at Disney had waned, left the company's board of directors. In his resignation letter, he complained about Eisner's micromanagement, his failure to make the enormously expensive ABC television network really profitable, weak policies in the theme park sector and poor choices in film

Brian Henson (left), son of Muppets creator Jim Henson joins Walt Disney Company chairman/chief executive officer Michael Eisner to promote a new attraction at the Disney-MGM Studios Theme Park in Florida in 1991.

properties in recent years, and for converting the Walt Disney Company into a "rapacious, soulless" organization that lacked a firm succession plan. Thereafter, Roy E. Disney campaigned vigorously to dislodge Eisner.

In March 2004, at Disney's annual stockholders' meeting, 43 percent of the shareholders voted against Eisner's reelection to the corporate board of directors. This powerful mandate led the board to remove Eisner from his chairmanship and replace him with former U.S. senator George Mitchell. Stuck in a lame-duck position, Eisner finally resigned both as Disney's top executive and a board member in September 2005 and was replaced by his former subordinate Bob Iger. (Even in Eisner's trouble-plagued final year, he earned a giant $10.1 million in salary and bonuses, a mere pittance compared to the

$576 million he earned in 1998 when he exercised Disney stock options.)

After leaving the Mouse Kingdom, Eisner authored a 2005 book extolling the practical life lessons he learned in childhood while attending a Vermont summer camp, hosted a less-than-stellar 2006 cable TV interview show (*Conversations with Michael Eisner*), created his own investment vehicle (the Tornante Company), and bought into an Internet video distribution network (Veoh). In March 2007, he announced the formation of Vuguru, a Web-based studio geared to produce and distribute original content for the Internet.

The professional tumble of Michael Eisner was another example of how hubris and excessive self-reliance can help to tumble a corporate heavyweight.

Mel Gibson

(January 3, 1956–)

At 2:36 A.M. on July 28, 2006, sheriff's deputies stopped film superstar Mel Gibson—one of Hollywood's wealthiest and most powerful actors—as he drove his 2006 Lexus LS 430 along the Pacific Coast Highway in Malibu. He was detained on allegations of speeding, and, after tests were administered, for the additional count of driving under the influence of alcohol. Reportedly, while he was being taken to jail he acted belligerently, and made several obscenity-laced remarks. His cracks included slurs about a female law enforcer's anatomy and the Jewish heritage of another officer. Within a short time, the Internet

and the media were abuzz with reports of Gibson's reputed anti-Semitic comments. Many sources believed that Gibson's bad behavior could make even this towering industry personality an anathema within the business: not only limiting his future acting/directing assignments with major studios and networks but also adversely impacting the December 2006 release of his new movie, *Apocalypto*.

The next day, Gibson issued an apology through his publicist: "I acted like a person completely out of control when I was arrested. I disgraced myself and my family with my behavior and for that I am truly sorry. I have battled with the disease of alcoholism for all of my adult life and profoundly regret my horrific relapse."

• • •

Mel Columcille Gerard Gibson was born in 1956, the sixth of 10 children of Hutton and Anne Reilly Gibson (later, his parents also adopted a child). Mr. Gibson was a railroad brakeman, and the strongly Irish Catholic family lived in Peekskill, New York. When Mel was 12, his father became fed up with the political atmosphere in the United States and feared his elder sons would be drafted into military service. He used proceeds from his workman's compensation settlement from an on-the-job accident—plus winnings from being a contestant on the game show *Jeopardy!*—to move his family to Australia. They settled in Sydney, not far from several of his wife's relatives.

In high school, Mel considered a career as a journalist or a chef. However, he became intrigued with acting. He studied at the National Institute of Dramatic Arts in Sydney and then joined the State Theatre Company of South Australia. He made his film debut in the locally filmed *Summer City*, a 1977 release. This resulted in his being asked to audition for a sci-fi action picture, *Mad Max*. The night before his meeting with the director, the rambunctious Gibson engaged in one of his frequent drunken barroom brawls. Despite his battle scars, he kept his appointment. Ironically, his battered face helped him win the title role of the postapocalyptic law enforcer. The 1979 movie became a cult hit and led to two sequels. The next year, in June, Gib-

son wed nurse's aide Robyn Moore, who was an Anglican. (They had seven children, six sons and one daughter, born between 1980 and 1999.)

The rising star made his Hollywood movie debut in 1984's *The Bounty*. He already had a reputation for being a heavy drinker who became a rabble-rouser when inebriated. During the making of *The Bounty* he suffered facial lacerations during a saloon brawl and his recovery period held up production. His costar, Anthony Hopkins, was vastly annoyed by Gibson's bad behavior and warned, "He's in danger of blowing it unless he takes care of himself." While shooting 1984's *Mrs. Soffel* in Toronto, Canada, Mel was arrested for driving while intoxicated. (He said to the angered driver of the car he rear-ended, "Hey, I'm for love, not war. How about we have a beer?") Gibson paid a fine and was banned from driving in Canada for three months but served no jail time.

This latest escapade caused the willful actor to rethink his life and finally to accept responsibility for his self-destructive actions. He took two years off from moviemaking, retreating with his family to their 800-acre cattle farm in Australia. He returned to the screen in 1987's *Lethal Weapon*. By now he was back to downing several beers before the start of the workday. Once again, he promised to curb his alcohol abuse, but he continually broke his vow of sobriety. However, because his box-office clout was so strong he continued to get away with his errant behavior. Then, in 1991, he embarked on a particularly wild alcohol-fueled spree during which his longtime habits accelerated dramatically. At long last, Gibson's wife and his agent were able to push the wayward star into entering Alcoholics Anonymous.

In the 1990s, Gibson formed his own production company (Icon), continued to appear in the hugely successful *Lethal Weapon* film franchise, and produced/directed such other major movies as 1995's *Braveheart*, in which he starred. (The film won five Oscars, including those for Best Picture and Best Director.) By now, the hugely affluent Mel and his family had homes in Los Angeles, Montana, and Connecticut, besides their Australian farm. Thanks to Gibson's excessive nervous energy and his love of playing juvenile pranks on friends and castmates, he was known in the industry as "Manic Mel."

All conventional wisdom said that Mel's ambitious project *The Passion of the Christ*—with its dialogue all spoken in Latin and Aramaic—had little chance of commercial success. He self-financed the $30 million movie (which he produced, directed, and coscripted). When the Biblical drama debuted in 2004, it stirred up huge controversies, particularly about its alleged anti-Semitism. To the industry's amazement, the picture grossed $604 million worldwide. Its success inspired Gibson to fund and direct 2006's *Apocalypto*, a historical saga dealing with the Mayan civilization in which all the dialogue is spoken in the ancient Mayan language.

During the new century, Gibson suffered from repeated bouts of drinking, which he claimed filled him with dismay and guilt. He said, "I got to a very desperate place. . . . And I didn't want to hang around here [on Earth], but I didn't want to check out. The other side was kind of scary. . . .

But when you get to that point where you don't want to live, and you don't want to die, it's a desperate, horrible place to be. And I just hit my knees. And I had to use *The Passion of the Christ* to heal my wounds."

Following Gibson's gigantic misstep in late July 2006, he and his advisers did their best to repair his battered industry image and protect his previously potent box-office standing. This high-level damage control included making apologetic phone calls to several powerful Jewish industry leaders. Some observers felt the actor's "quick fix" did not resolve people's wondering about his overt bigotry. (In the past, the strongly Roman Catholic actor had sullied his public image with homophobic and Anglophobic remarks, as well as by his stubborn refusal to contest inflammatory comments made by his father, a Holocaust revisionist. However, because of his general popularity within the industry and with the public, none of these politically incorrect episodes had seriously damaged his career.)

In mid-August 2006, Gibson's attorney was in court in Malibu to finalize his client's no contest plea deal. The wealthy defendant was fined only $1,200, ordered to undergo a full year of rehab classes and make a public service announcement (regarding the hazards of driving while under the influence), and placed on probation for three years. (The required rehab, however, did not demand inpatient treatment.) Thereafter, the A-list actor largely kept a low profile, even when he supervised test screenings of *Apocalypto* in Oklahoma in late September 2006. However, a few days earlier, Gibson had been spotted in an Austin, Texas, bar, where he was playing pool but, according to sources, "was only drinking water" and not making any play for the women patrons, as had been the case just before his notorious Malibu arrest.

In an effort to clear the air and protect the financial investment of his soon-to-be-released *Apocalypto*, Gibson did a two-part (taped) interview for *Good Morning America*, which aired in mid-October 2006. In this carefully controlled Q & A session, he told interviewer Diane Sawyer regarding his ill-chosen words the night of his arrest on the Pacific Coast Highway, "I'm ashamed that they came out of my mouth. . . . That's not who I am." As to why he had such inappropriate thoughts to start with, Gibson claimed they were a residue of having been "subjected to a pretty brutal public beating" by Jewish leaders when *The Passion of the Christ* was released. The top-level movie star reasoned, "The human heart cannot bear the scars of resentment, and it will come out when you are overwrought and you take a few drinks."

When *Apocalypto* opened in the United States in December 2006, it received mixed reviews. Made on an estimated $40 million budget, it drew in a disappointing $51.9 million in domestic distribution. Industry observers were uncertain whether the film's tepid box-office returns were due largely to Gibson's recent bad press or because his new movie contained such excessive violence and gore. Mel seemed unbowed by the misfire of *Apocalypto* and began planning new film projects. Undoubtedly, a less powerful celebrity than Mel Gibson caught in such a high-visibility scrape would have endured far greater repercussions to his or her Tinseltown reputation and career.

Louis B. Mayer

(July 4, 1884–October 29, 1957)

N o one got to know [Louis B.] Mayer but Mayer," said Fredericka Sagor Maas, a screenwriter who worked at Metro-Goldwyn-Mayer in the 1920s. "He was a chameleon—strong and brutal. His people respected him highly, but he could destroy you with his pinkie and he damn well knew it. He brooked no contradiction or anything else that would diminish his power. And he was obsessed by his fear of Nicholas Schenck [chairman of MGM's parent company, Loew's, Inc.], who was more powerful than he was." Evie Johnson, the wife of MGM star Van Johnson, observed, "He was a bulldog; you had to believe what he believed. His opinion was the right one, and no debate was possible. Socially, as a dinner partner he was a lot of fun—ingratiating and kind. But you had to remember he was also a despot who used the carrot-and-stick approach." Esther Williams, once the studio's bathing beauty sensation, warned, "He was always acting. He was the best actor on the lot. . . . But you believed him at your peril." According to producer David Lewis, "A rattlesnake was tame compared to

Mayer. But all in all [he was] a man of genius."

During Hollywood's golden age, MGM was the Tiffany of all the Hollywood studios. From its founding in the mid-1920s until the end of the 1940s (with a few more years thereafter in a titular capacity), Mayer ruled the film lot (which he had helped to found) as a benevolent despot. He was not a creative craftsman (like Darryl F. Zanuck of Twentieth Century-Fox), but a highly intuitive businessman who knew how to sell films to the public. For decades, he stuck tenaciously to his optimistic vision that movies should be entertaining (not edifying) and have happy endings. He insisted that a movie's plot line was secondary to its stars and that MGM releases must always showcase the studio's array of talents as glamorously as possible. His rule of thumb was "Spare nothing, neither expense, time, nor effort. Results are what I am after."

For several years—beginning in the late 1930s—the hardworking Mayer was the highest-paid executive in the United States. His enviable salary (plus his many perks and powerful industry status) reflected his great worth in highly competitive Hollywood. For a long time, L. B. (as he was often called) had tremendous influence over the way the American film business operated and how its product was shaped for public consumption.

On the home lot, Mayer was the great arbiter who resolved problems among his huge staff and did his best—through wheedling, cajoling, and playacting—to keep his high-priced stars in line. He was an astute judge of new talent and also a great believer in nepotism (as when he brought his son-in-law, David O. Selznick, and his nephew, Jack Cummings, into the MGM fold as producers). Mayer could be extremely loyal to actors (such as Lewis Stone, Marie Dressler, and Jean Hersholt) who were terrific team players or he could carry a longtime grudge against a star (like John Gilbert or Francis X. Bushman) who had, somehow, offended him. Sometimes, the capricious Mayer could "forgive" luminaries (for instance, Buster Keaton and Ramon Novarro) whom he had dismissed from the studio roster by later allowing them to return to work at MGM—albeit in reduced capacities. The short, squat Mayer

Louis B. Mayer, the head of the Metro-Goldwyn-Mayer studio from the mid-1920s until his ouster in 1951.

could also be pugnacious, as demonstrated by his once getting into a fistfight with Charlie Chaplin when the latter made a statement that offended Louis B.

In his heyday, Louis B. Mayer was the king of Hollywood.

•   •   •

He was born Lazar Mayer in Dumier [Dymer] in Ukraine, the third of five surviving children of Jacob Mayer, a laborer, and Sarah Meltzer Mayer, who were from Austro-Hungary. (Sources varied as to whether the future film mogul was born in 1884 or 1882 and whether July 12 was his actual birthday, but when filling out paperwork in 1911 to become an American citizen, he chose the patriotic date of July 4 as his birthday and 1885 as his birth year.) A few years thereafter, the Jewish family emigrated to the United States, but by 1892, they had relocated to Saint John, New Brunswick, Canada, a seaport on the Bay of Fundy. Initially, Mr. Mayer was a peddler, but he later developed a small junk business, which included salvaging wreckage that drifted into the local bay. Louis (as he became known) and his brothers (who had been born when the Mayers lived in New York) learned to dive to gather scrap metal and other salable objects. In early 1904, Louis moved to Boston, intent on bettering himself. He soon met Margaret Shenberg, the daughter of a kosher butcher, and they wed in June 1904. (They had two daughters, Edith and Irene, both of whom would become influential members of the film colony through their father, their husbands, and their own ambitions.)

In 1907, Mayer purchased a rundown burlesque house in Haverhill, north of Boston, and turned it into a family-oriented theater that showed wholesome films and stage presentations. Within a few years Louis B. (for Burton) Mayer, as he was now known, had established the largest chain of cinemas in New England. He had great success in distributing 1915's *The Birth of a Nation*, which led him into film production. He moved his family to New York and then to Los Angeles to pursue filmmaking. By 1924, Loew's, which owned a large chain of movie theaters, had taken control of three film production companies (including Mayer's) and merged them into what became Metro-Goldwyn-Mayer. Louis B. Mayer was put in charge of the West Coast operation at the Culver City lot, with young Irving Thalberg as his supervisor of film production. While Thalberg focused on the studio's slate of pictures, Mayer concentrated on building an impressive stable of exciting stars (including John Gilbert, Greta Garbo, Lon Chaney, Norma Shearer, and Joan Crawford) while battling New York–based Nicholas Schenck, who was now president of Loew's.

With an array of hit pictures (such as 1932's *Grand Hotel* and *Tarzan, the Ape Man* and 1933's *Dinner at Eight*), MGM was the most profitable of Hollywood's film factories. A growing problem within Mayer's impressive fiefdom was the ambitious Thalberg. While the latter was away recuperating from a near fatal heart attack he suffered in late 1932, Mayer installed a coterie of producers and an executive committee to work with him, thus greatly diminishing his rival's power base. After Thalberg's death, in September 1936, Mayer was supreme on the studio lot—the fly in his ointment being the watchful eye of Schenck and his minions on the East Coast.

By 1937, Mayer was earning nearly $1.3 million in annual salary and bonuses, was the social leader of Hollywood (welcoming the crème de la crème of visiting dignitaries to town), and remained a stalwart of the Republican political party. Louis B. held court in his "throne room" on the third floor of the sprawling studio's executive building. In this inner sanctum, the walls were lined with white leather and the floors were covered in plush white carpet. At the rear of the large expanse sat the mogul's white, kidney-shaped desk with its special chair (built to make the five-foot-three-inch Mayer look taller). Adjacent to his deliberately intimidating headquarters was a private room (complete with a full bathroom, a daybed, and a refrigerator) that had a special elevator going to the first floor.

Over the Mayers' decades in Los Angeles, Louis B. and his socially retiring wife drifted into an uneasy marriage of convenience. The mogul was not above chasing after women (including actresses Esther Ralston and Jean Howard, and talent agent Adeline Schulberg), whom he sometimes wined and dined on the Hollywood club circuit, and with whom he demonstrated his prowess on the dance floor. However, most of his objects of affection found him too courtly in his pursuit of them, and went off to find more viable suitors. In the 1940s, Mayer pursued both singer/actress Ginny Simms and dancer/actress Ann Miller. In 1944, the executive separated from his wife, and they divorced in April 1947. (Margaret received a settlement of several million dollars plus the family home.) In December 1948, Mayer married the much-younger Lorena Jones Danker (a former showgirl/actress) and adopted her daughter from a prior marriage.

In the late 1940s, MGM, like the other Hollywood studios, experienced great financial difficulties. Nicholas Schenck used this opportunity to force Mayer—who had been spending an increasingly large amount of time on his personal life and his sizable stable of prizewinning racehorses—to hire Dore Schary. (The studio's new production chief was supposed to work under Mayer's direction.) Schary not only restructured the lot's administration but also pared down the staff roster and focused MGM's product line on message pictures. Louis B. fumed for three years as he witnessed his moviemaking power and his philosophy on how to run the studio being eroded. Then, Mayer exploded and forced the issue with Schenck. The latter sided with Schary and, by June 1951, Louis B. Mayer was out of MGM.

Mayer was far too energetic and humiliated to retire. He signed on for a time as an executive with the Cinerama Production Corporation, optioned film properties for his own production company, and participated in a failed dissenting stockholders' effort to oust the current MGM regime. Louis B. died of leukemia in October 1957, leaving an estate in excess of $12 million.

Louella Parsons

(August 6, 1881–December 9, 1972)

In the era before supermarket tabloids, television, and the Internet, news and gossip about Hollywood was filtered to the public largely through daily newspapers and fan magazines. In the 1920s and 1930s (until actress/columnist Hedda Hopper emerged as a major rival in the early 1940s), Louella Parsons was the most formidable of all Tinseltown gossip columnists. As one Hollywood power figure quipped, "Louella Parsons is stronger than Samson. He needed two columns to bring the house down; Louella can do it with one."

Left unsaid was that Parsons operated in close collaboration with the studios to promote their players and product, while tactfully overlooking many of the scandalous antics of certain film colony favorites. In return for her cooperation, the studios allowed Parsons special access to their talent roster for interviews, gave her "dirt" on particular Hollywood miscreants in exchange for not tattling on favored big-name personalities, and ensured that she received many special perks. Not only would Lolly (as she was known to friends) be wined and dined throughout the year and treated regally at premieres, but at Christmastime, she received enough thank-you gifts from film colony members—who either liked her or feared her—to fill a semitrailer truck. (Parsons cautioned everyone that these expected expensive tokens should not be monogrammed—this allowed her to return or recycle unwanted offerings.)

Throughout the decades, this pioneering journalist was a resolute reporter, even if her facts and grammar often left much to be desired. While Parsons often seemed—in print, in person, or on the radio (where she chatted about the latest Hollywood gossip in a high-pitched, whiny voice)—to be a gushing, naive chronicler, in actuality she was a shrewd and tough newshound. This hardnosed lady was not above using intimidation to get her story and beat out the competition. (One time, fearful that rivals might learn of a particularly juicy story she had uncovered, she "kidnapped" her celebrity subject and held the person as "ransom" until she knew the presses were running and her exclusive was safe.)

Parsons's most endearing quality was her tireless advocacy for the motion picture business. She said, "Reporting on Hollywood is my life. I've made a fortune and spent a fortune, and I've never been bored a moment. Someone once said of me 'The secret of Louella's success is that she never stopped being a movie fan herself. She really believes that what she is doing is important.'"

• • •

She was born Louella Rose Oettinger in 1881 in Freeport, Illinois, the first of five children—three of whom died in infancy—of Joshua Oettinger, a clothing store owner, and Helen Stine Oettinger. (For many years, Parsons disguised her true age, listing

1893 as her birth year. She also avoided mentioning that both her parents were Jewish. Later in life, Louella became a devout Catholic.) In 1890, Mr. Oettinger died. The next year, his widow married John H. Edwards, who operated a grocery store. When this enterprise failed, he relocated his family to Dixon, 30 miles south of Freeport, where he returned to being a traveling candy salesman. By now, young Louella had developed a love of the theater and opera. In 1902, while at Dixon College, she won her first newspaper post, a part-time job as drama editor of the *Dixon Morning Star*. When that position was eliminated, she became a schoolteacher. In October 1905, she wed John Parsons, then employed at his father's real estate company. The next August, the couple's only child, Harriet, was born. By now, the Parsonses were living in Burlington, Iowa, and Louella was becoming increasingly bored with small-town life and worn out from coping with her arrogant, womanizing spouse. In 1910, she took her daughter and moved to Chicago. (She and Parsons divorced in September 1911.)

She found work writing movie scripts for the local Essanay Studios, then got a job in late 1914 with the *Chicago Herald* doing a column on how to write screenplays. (She turned these articles into a book in 1915.) Next, go-getter Louella persuaded the *Chicago Tribune* to allow her to do something innovative: write feature articles on movies and do interviews with cinema personalities. When that job was phased out in 1918, she relocated to Manhattan, where she wrote a movie news (and gossip) column for the *New York Morning Telegraph*.

(While still in Chicago, in January 1915, Parsons had wed the good-natured John McCaffrey, a riverboat captain. By the time she settled in New York City, he had largely disappeared from her life. Later, they divorced.) In New York, Louella fell wildly in love with Peter Brady, a charismatic labor leader who was influential in city politics. He was Catholic, married, hot-tempered, and the great romance of Louella's life. (He died in a plane crash in 1931.)

The ambitious Parsons set her sights on working for newspaper magnate William Randolph Hearst. She cultivated a friendship with movie star Marion Davies, Hearst's mistress, and that led to the hoped-for introduction. Parsons was hired for Hearst's *New York American*. In 1925, Louella contracted tuberculosis. Hearst put her on paid leave for a year, and ordered her to move to southern California to recuperate. Once she was better, Hearst assigned her to the *Los Angeles Examiner* and to be the motion picture editor for his International News Syndicate. Parsons bubbled, "At last the Hollywood writer is going to Hollywood."

By 1926, Parsons had a readership of over 6 million people. In September 1929, she wed Dr. Henry Martin, a feisty, witty, alcoholic urologist who had ties to the film studios. Parsons nicknamed her third husband "Docky." Throughout the years, he provided his wife with a great many tips on Hollywood figures gleaned from his medical practice and many industry contacts.

Louella was at the height of her newspaper power in the 1930s, augmented by her weekly radio show and articles for various publications. For many, the workaholic

Parsons was Tinseltown's final authority on morality, as she took celebrities to public task for their (mis)behavior and urged the industry to make more wholesome pictures. She occasionally appeared on camera, as in 1937's *Hollywood Hotel*. Meanwhile, Hollywood forces promoted out-of-work actress Hedda Hopper as a gossip column rival to Parsons, figuring that the competition would loosen Louella's tight grip on the movie town. In actuality, it just created a second gossip queen and Hollywood found itself at the mercy of these two high-powered newswomen.

In 1944, Parsons authored a best-selling memoir, *The Gay Illiterate* (which led to 1961's *Tell It to Louella*). She also promoted the career of her daughter, who had become a film producer. Louella's biggest scoop of the post–World War II era was revealing to her readership that movie star Ingrid Bergman, a wife and mother, was expecting a baby fathered by her married lover, director Roberto Rossellini. By now, Parsons was earning over $600 a week from her syndicated newspaper column, plus all her other ancillary income. She had both a Beverly Hills home and a house in the San Fernando Valley.

Everything began to fall apart for Louella in the 1950s. The Hearst newspaper syndicate had been shrinking long before the 1951 death of Hearst. (That same year, in June, Parsons's husband died of leukemia. Thereafter, Jimmy McHugh became Parsons's favorite companion about town.) Already, the serious competition from television was destroying the old studio system. In this new age, the public had sources for Tinseltown news other than the items pro-

The usually hyperactive movie star Betty Hutton (left) joins Louella Parsons, Hollywood's top gossip columnist, to read snatches of Parsons's just-published memoir, The Gay Illiterate *(1944).*

vided by Parsons and her equally tenacious challenger, Hedda Hopper. However, the determined Louella hung in there, despite being well into her 70s, increasingly alcoholic, and frail.

During the early 1960s, Dorothy Manners wrote much of Parsons's news copy. Louella officially retired on December 1, 1965. (The next February, Hopper died of a heart attack.) The aged Parsons became a resident of a convalescent home in Brentwood. In her final years, she became increasingly mentally confused, often spending hours staring into space. She died in December 1972, at 91, of arteriosclerosis. Relatively few celebrities attended her funeral mass. Most of her contemporaries had long since passed away, and the new generation of show business notables were too young to have been active when Louella Parsons was the potent queen bee of Hollywood journalism.

With the death of the once so powerful Louella Parsons, an era of Hollywood had come to a close.

Martha Stewart

(August 3, 1941–)

On October 19, 1999, Martha Stewart took her company (Martha Stewart Living Omnimedia) public on the New York Stock Exchange. The initial offering of 7.2 million shares was a tremendous success and made the already very wealthy Stewart even richer. It seemed that the "driven diva of domesticity"—also known as the "guru of good taste in American entertaining" and "the woman who knows what women want"—could do no wrong.

This acclaimed caterer, noted home decorator, and fashionable gardener had successfully authored lifestyle books, published magazines, hosted a syndicated TV talk show, had her own department store product lines, and produced how-to videos and theme-based DVDs, and was deeply involved in many other consumer-oriented activities. She seemed to be at the top of her profession as she strove to provide the world with "a sense of the old-fashioned values of a well-ordered house and garden" and to "make homemaking glamorous again."

Nonetheless, some complained that this world-famous businesswoman made (relatively) simple domestic tasks so labor intensive that few modern women had the time or patience to accomplish them. Other critics pointed to Stewart's reputation for being

self-serving, condescending, short-tempered, and a control freak in her determination to achieve absolute perfection. There were also individuals who alleged that Martha's push to mega success led her to march over anyone who stood in her way, whether it be family, friends, business associates, or neighbors. (Regarding the gossip that she was a martinet, Stewart retorted, "I'm not a fanatic, but I am a hard taskmaster.")

However, no one could contest that Stewart had become a vital force as a promoter of domesticity and an upscale lifestyle. When she suggested techniques to provide the homemaker with a more gracious way of life, her vast public not only heeded her advice but usually purchased the products she recommended.

•   •   •

She was born Martha Helen Kostyra in 1941 in Jersey City, New Jersey, the second of six children of Edward Kostyra, a pharmaceutical salesman, and Martha Ruszkowski Kostyra, a schoolteacher. When Martha was 3, the family moved to a bigger house in suburban Nutley, New Jersey. Her demanding father, who favored high-achieving, attention-seeking Martha over her siblings, taught the girl much about the art of gardening. From her mother, grandmother, and neighbors, she learned to cook and bake. By the time Martha was in grammar school, she was already organizing neighborhood birthday parties. When she was at Nutley High, she catered a breakfast for the school's football squad. She also did some modeling. This straight-A student (whose motto was "I do what I please and do it with ease") turned down a full scholarship to New York University when she obtained a partial scholarship to the more prestigious Barnard College in Manhattan.

In college she dropped thoughts of becoming a chemist to focus on art, architecture, and European history. As she had in high school, she took on modeling jobs (including TV gigs) to generate income. During her sophomore year, in March 1961, she wed Andrew "Andy" Stewart, then a law school student. Her modeling work supported them both. She graduated college in 1963 and continued modeling until she became pregnant. Daughter Alexis was born in September 1965. By 1968, Martha had quit modeling and become a broker at a small Wall Street firm. It was still a male-dominated field, and the ambitious Stewart found her sales work tedious and frustrating, especially when she was ordered to push product she had little faith in. She left the field in early 1973.

Meanwhile, in the spring of 1971, the Stewarts had purchased a home in Westport, Connecticut. It was a spacious but run-down property—an early-19th-century Federal-style farmhouse—on Turkey Hill Road. The couple set about restoring the unsightly property into something beautiful. (Previously, they had renovated a one-room

schoolhouse in Massachusetts into a livable weekend cottage.) Martha and Andy not only methodically rebuilt their new home but also added a barn, planted elaborate gardens and orchards, and even had beehives and a smokehouse. The massive undertaking proved to be a springboard for Martha's future career.

Seeking yet a new creative outlet, Stewart started a catering business with a friend (who later dropped out), operating from the basement of her Turkey Hill farm. Within a decade, the business had expanded into a $1 million enterprise that boasted a high-status clientele. (Martha also experimented with opening a boutique food/accessories shop at a local mall.) During this period, she contributed food, decorating, and hostessing articles to such publications as the *New York Times* and *House Beautiful*, and was a freelance food stylist for photography shoots. During these busy years, her low-key husband had overcome cancer, become the publisher of coffee-table books, and discovered that he and the pushy Martha had started to agree on less and less.

In 1982, Martha, in collaboration with Elizabeth Hawes, wrote *Entertaining*, an elaborate, oversized tome that detailed an assortment of upscale, imaginative dinner menus that the reader could prepare to impress guests. The expensive book became a major bestseller, even with buyers who knew they could never fashion such upmarket lifestyles for themselves. It was the first of several popular volumes about gracious dining, living, and gardening that Stewart wrote over the years. In April 1987, Andy left Martha. It was not until the summer of 1990 that the acrimonious divorce was settled, but

Martha Stewart, the doyenne of gracious living.

it took even longer for Andy to receive all the agreed-upon items in the complex division of the couple's assets. Subsequently, Andy remarried, while, over the years, Martha was linked romantically with a variety of well-to-do men, including software developer/entrepreneur Charles Simonyi.

Also in 1987, Stewart became the spokesperson for housewares sold at Kmart, which soon prompted the department store chain to start Martha's own product line (Martha Stewart Everyday). Three years later, she signed with Time Publishing Ventures to create a magazine (*Martha Stewart Living*), which debuted in November that year and became a success. In September 1993, she became the hostess of *Martha Stewart Living*, a weekly half-hour syndicated TV show that lasted until 2004, by which time it was a daily, hour-long program. To further fill her crowded plate, she was a correspondent for television's *CBS News This Morn-*

ing and was featured on various prime-time TV holiday specials. Her many achievements led *New York* magazine in mid-1995 to rate Stewart "the definitive American woman of our time." (Those business executives, members of her staff, and personal associates of Martha's who had run afoul of the celebrity during her strongly self-focused climb to success might not have agreed with such a positive assessment.)

With the establishment in the late 1990s of Martha Stewart Living Omnimedia (of which Martha was the majority shareholder and held nearly all voting control), the multitasking Stewart was riding high. Then came her great misadventure in December 2001, when she sold shares of ImClone Systems stock in what the United States Securities and Exchange Commission came to allege was an act of insider trading. In mid-2004, Stewart was found guilty of conspiracy, obstruction of justice, making false statements, and perjury in the wake of unloading her ImClone shares. She spent five months at an Alderson, West Virginia, prison camp, then six months under house arrest at her huge spread in Katonah, New York. (In August 2006, Stewart settled a civil case with the Securities and Exchange Commission for $195,000, which included a fine of three times the losses—$45,673—she avoided by her questionable ImClone sale. Among other terms, she also agreed not to serve as a director of a public company for five years, and for the same period to have a limitation on her services as an officer or employee of a public company. Said Stewart, "My personal nightmare has come to an end.")

While such a major scandal might have finished the public career of a less resilient person, Martha rose from the ashes of public ridicule. Beginning on September 25, 2005, she hosted *The Apprentice: Martha Stewart*, a short-lived spin-off from Donald Trump's TV reality series. She had more success with her new syndicated television lifestyle program, *Martha*. She also expanded her product line sold through Kmart (and its new owner, Sears). Stewart continued to write books, including 2005's *The Martha Rules* (about starting up business enterprises), was a lifestyle/gardening/hobby correspondent for NBC-TV's *Today* show, and had her corporation launch a line of homes to be built in locales nationwide. She was also developing an upscale line of housewares for Federated Department Stores and a brand of paper-based crafts for EK Success. In addition, the inexhaustible Stewart hosted a weekly phone-in program on her radio network begun in conjunction with Sirius Satellite Radio. In early 2007, Martha paid a reported $16 million for a full-floor (4,800-square-foot) condominium in a high-rise building in Manhattan's West Village

Clearly, Martha Stewart had every intention of regaining her status as the doyenne of gracious living.

Lew Wasserman
(March 22, 1913–June 3, 2002)

When film industry leader Lew Wasserman died in 2002 at the age of 89, the *New York Times* described him as "arguably the most powerful and influential Hollywood titan in the four decades after World War II." The *Los Angeles Times* pointed out, "His death marks the symbolic passing of an era in Hollywood that is unlikely to be repeated. Both feared and respected, power player Wasserman singlehandedly wielded the kind of behind-the-scenes clout that could settle labor disputes, bring together studios with conflicting agendas and influence power brokers in Washington, D.C." Sidney Sheinberg, for many years Wasserman's second-in-command at Universal Studios, noted, "Lew's big claim to fame is that he began to embrace television [in the early 1950s] when others weren't. There is always the question, to what degree is a person capable of making a successful transition? You may catch one wave, as you hit a certain age, but to be able to catch wave after wave—that's the trick."

Unlike an earlier generation of film moguls (such as Samuel Goldwyn, Louis B. Mayer, Harry Cohn, Jack L. Warner, and Darryl F. Zanuck), Lew Wasserman did *not* have an overwhelming passion for moviemaking as both art and entertainment. (Also, unlike past industry giants, he had no interest in becoming a public figure, preferring to work his magic behind the scenes.) For Wasserman, the film business was just that—a business, with its bottom line rooted firmly in quantifiable profit and loss. That was both his great strength (which allowed him to focus intently on reshaping the economics of moviemaking) and his great weakness (he was not terribly astute in assessing the quality of film projects or talent).

The Godfather of Hollywood, as Lew Wasserman was known, had a nearly uncanny business sense regarding the film/TV products he shepherded over several decades. As filmmaker Steven Spielberg, one of Wasserman's protégés, noted back in 1995: "I never cease to be amazed at his instant analysis. He is so sharp that he would call me with matinee figures on opening day and then accurately project [without the use of computer software programs] the film's ultimate performance. . . . It's been said that Lew Wasserman can guess the gross on a picture just by looking at the first hour's receipts."

Austere, soft-spoken (except when he flew into one of his legendary tirades), and conservatively dressed in black suits, Wasserman—noted for wearing owlish, oversized spectacles—did not reach his pinnacle of Hollywood power entirely on his own. He owed a great deal to his mentor, Dr. Jules Stein, the cunning founder of the Music Corporation of America (MCA) talent agency. It was Stein who spotted the tremendous potential in Wasserman and promoted the ambitious young man within his organization to such a point that his favored "son" became a frequent thorn in the dictatorial Stein's side. There was also Edith, Lew's wife for over 60 years, who played queen to his king in their vast show business realm. She was tough as nails and adept at working the Hollywood crowd in social settings, always angling to draw out intelligence from the wives and girlfriends

of industry figures to help Wasserman better control and manipulate the mighty entertainment empire he was building. (She could also be very vengeful, as on the night she told a friend about suspected enemies: "You just watch. We're going to piss on all their graves.")

• • •

He was born Louis Robert Wasserman in 1913 in Cleveland, Ohio, the third son of Isaac and Minnie Chernick Weiserman, Russian Orthodox Jews who had emigrated to the United States in 1907. (Two years before Louis was born, his parents had Americanized their surname from Weiserman to Wasserman.) His dapper father, who had been a bookbinder in the old country, had difficulty keeping a job in his new home. It soon fell to the two surviving Wasserman boys to support the family.

While Louis was a high school student, he worked a full shift as a movie theater usher. After graduating, he was hired by a Cleveland nightclub to handle its promotion. In this capacity he came to the attention of Dr. Jules Stein, an ophthalmologist who had started the Chicago-based MCA talent agency in 1924. Lew (as he was now known) joined Stein's organization in late 1936. That same year, in July, he married Edith Beckerman, the daughter of a lawyer who was tight with the city's political crowd and dealt with various underworld figures. (The couple's only child, Lynne, would be born in 1940.) In 1938, the Wassermans relocated to Los Angeles, where MCA had recently opened a branch office.

In 1946, Stein named Lew president of MCA. Under Lew's ruthlessly tightfisted watch, all his agents had to dress conservatively, remain tight-lipped about office business, be always on call to handle clients' needs, and employ whatever means necessary to beat out rivals. As MCA's fortunes escalated, Edith Wasserman continued hosting social gatherings at the couple's Beverly Hills home. There, she fortified her husband's growing status as an industry power force.

Wasserman brokered a landmark deal for James Stewart by arranging for the star to receive a profit percentage (rather than a salary) for starring in 1950's *Winchester '73*. The deal's success led to a shift in the Hollywood power base from the studios to its talent. In 1952, Lew, the adroit backroom politician, convinced Ronald Reagan (an MCA client whom he had helped to become president of the Screen Actors Guild) to arrange a blanket waiver from the Guild that allowed MCA to both represent talent and to hire them for their Revue Productions (which made TV product). Another Wasserman coup was having MCA, in 1958, buy the pre-1948 film library of Paramount Pictures, which was then leased out to TV stations. The next year, Wasserman audaciously purchased the plant facility of run-down Universal Pictures, allowing the ailing studio to rent production facilities on the lot. It was also in 1959 that MCA went public, which made millionaires of Wasserman and other key MCA executives. In 1962, MCA acquired Decca Records, the parent company of Universal. MCA now owned and operated a major film studio.

Since the early 1950s, the Justice Department had been threatening an antitrust case against MCA (known as "the Octopus"). To avoid a government clampdown in 1962, Wasserman had to dissolve MCA's talent agency. This setback taught Wasserman the need to have influence with political bigwigs in Washington, D.C. Lew and Edie became prime forces in Hollywood fund-raising campaigns on behalf of the Democratic party. First with President John F. Kennedy, and then with his successors, Lyndon Johnson and Jimmy Carter, Wasserman's team maintained powerful contacts within the nation's capital that made Lew a must-see on entertainment industry issues. (Wasserman also quietly fostered relationships with Republican leaders, and, reputedly, through his and Edie's close friendship with attorney Sidney Korshak, had a pipeline to useful underworld connections to help on labor union matters.)

Under Wasserman, Universal became a true film factory, where the quantity of product was the key issue. The company expanded into the studio tour business, invested in new technologies (including video recorders and CDs), and acquired ancillary businesses to keep an industry dominance. While over the years Lew sometimes let talent and projects slip through his fingers and made some unwise business decisions, he smartly promoted the concept of the summer blockbuster picture (starting with 1975's *Jaws*). Although Jules Stein had thought of ousting Wasserman in the late 1960s when Universal's fortunes sagged, the MCA founder officially retired in 1973 and Wasserman became the corporation's chairman.

Now fully in charge of his multifaceted business domain, Lew focused on corporate acquisitions and short-circuiting takeover bids—all at the expense of improving the studio's product line. In 1990, Wasserman, sensing troubled times ahead for MCA, brokered the company's sale (for $6.6 billion) to Matsushita Electric Industrial, the Japanese conglomerate. As part of the deal, Lew now held stock shares worth $327 million (and which paid him $28.6 million in annual dividends). Moreover, Wasserman was to remain the studio's chairman for the next five years at a yearly salary of $3 million.

Because of many significant successes, the arrogant Wasserman had not anticipated that Matsushita executives would not kowtow to Lew and his underlings. This situation led Wasserman to threaten not to renew his deal as chairman. Wasserman seemed totally surprised when Matsushita quietly made a deal in 1995 with Seagram to buy 80 percent of MCA for $5.7 billion. Lew was given the empty title of chairman emeritus with a $1 million yearly stipend. He still came to the studio daily, but his role had shrunk to counseling newcomers on industry pitfalls.

Wasserman died in June 2002 at his Beverly Hills home from complications of a recent stroke. He left an estate estimated at over $500 million, a portion of it to be donated to charities.

It seemed unlikely in the climate of the New Hollywood that another titan could ever gain the same tremendous clout that Lew Wasserman forcefully wielded for so long.

PART 6

So Much Rich Living

Marion Davies

(January 3, 1897–September 22, 1961)

For decades, many moviegoers and some movie historians were convinced that the pathetic character of Susan Alexander Kane in Orson Welles's cinematic masterpiece, 1941's *Citizen Kane*, was a devastating caricature of actress Marion Davies, the longtime mistress of media mogul William Randolph Hearst (1861–1951). In 1975, Welles belatedly sought to address that "misconception" when he wrote the introduction to Davies's posthumously published memoir, *The Time We Had: Life with William Randolph Hearst*. In that book, the apologetic Welles insisted that the untalented Susan character "bears no resemblance at all" to Davies. Welles also noted, "Marion Davies was one of the most delightfully accomplished comediennes in the whole history of the screen. She would have been a star if Hearst had never happened. She was also a delightful and very considerable person."

On screen, Davies was perky, comedic, and prone to mugging with broad reactions. Off camera, she had a wide circle of friends who cherished the lively star for her unpretentious nature, her fun-loving ways, her deep loyalty to others, and her continuous generosity toward those in need. Davies was well aware that having Hearst as her sponsor over the decades had furthered her film career. However, she also knew that the relationship had limited her choice of roles (because of his interference in selecting her screen projects) and that his extravagant promotion of her in his chain of newspapers had caused some moviegoers to react negatively to her.

For many years, Marion was W. R.'s unofficial hostess at his 240,000-acre coastal estate, San Simeon, located about 230 miles north of Los Angeles. There the couple lavishly entertained the royalty of Hollywood and notables from around the globe. Many guests at the art-filled mansion were well aware of the tug-of-war between teetotaler Hearst and the liquor-loving Davies, but it only made visits to the castle more amusing as the chipper Marion outfoxed watchful W. R. by dipping into her secret stash of booze.

Davies was generally quite unassuming about her film career. Although she was disappointed and somewhat humiliated that Hearst never divorced his wife to marry her, she nevertheless thrived on reigning over her consort's social gatherings at San Simeon and at his various other retreats. She teased, "When I'm entertaining at home, no one can tell me to get out."

●　　●　　●

Marion Cecilia Douras was born in 1897 in Brooklyn, New York, the youngest child of Bernard J. Douras, an attorney involved in Manhattan politics, and Rose Reilly Douras. (Marion had three older sisters and one brother; he drowned in 1906.) The social-climbing, money-loving Mrs. Douras passed along her practical point of view to her four girls, all of whom entered show business and adopted the surname Davies. Their mother encouraged her daughters to seek the most from their suitors on the theory that it was just as easy to love a rich man as it was to love a poor one. The pretty strawberry-blond Marion, who had a convent education, made her Broadway bow as a chorus girl in the 1914 musical *Chin Chin*. She also posed for many of the famous artists of the period. In short order, the fun-loving, calculating Marion had a coterie of rich suitors. While she was appearing in 1915's *Stop! Look! Listen!* she met the much older William Randolph Hearst, who was married and had several children. The newspaper baron became infatuated with Davies and made her his mistress. (Her nickname for Hearst was "Poppy.") Her film debut was in 1917's *Runaway, Romany*. So Hearst could keep Davies closer at hand, as well as further her movie career, he made her the star of pictures he produced. (In 1920, reputedly, Marion gave birth to W. R.'s love child, Patricia, who was passed off as the daughter of Davies's sister Rose, and her husband, George Van Cleve. The "facts" were not made public until Patricia's death in 1993.)

By the mid-1920s, Hearst had arranged for MGM to release Marion's pictures, such as 1925's *Zander the Great*. She was living well in Beverly Hills (with her large family often on hand), had had an affair with comedy giant Charlie Chaplin, and was leading an active social life with Hearst as her unofficial consort. Davies was a shrewd

In the 1930s, one of the most famous and luxurious residences in Santa Monica, California, was movie star Marion Davies's famous Ocean House.

businesswoman and had already begun accumulating real estate holdings in Los Angeles and elsewhere, not to mention her growing fortune in jewelry and furs (many of the items gifts from Hearst).

In 1926, with W. R.'s blessing and backing, Davies began construction on a massive beach house in Santa Monica, along the strip where several top industry figures had their homes. Davies's imposing gleaming white Ocean House, done in the Georgian colonial style, had a palatial three-story main building and four substantial guest structures (where many of her family members resided). The extensive compound, with its furnishings imported from Europe, boasted a dining room that seated 25, a special gallery for the actress's expanding art collection, 37 fireplaces, chandeliers from Tiffany, balustrades that took 75 workmen a year to finish, a tavern that seated 50, a large ballroom, a movie theater, and a huge, 110-foot outdoor swimming pool with a Venetian bridge over it. There were 110 bedrooms and 55 bathrooms in the complex. (Davies and Hearst had separate bedroom suites in the main house, connected to each other by a hidden door.) When Marion's new residence was finally completed in 1928, the construction had cost $3 million, with another $4 million spent on the furnishings. In this relaxed setting, with its staff of 32 full-time servants, Marion was in charge—not like at the gloomy, formal San Simeon, where W. R. made all the rules. Davies entertained frequently at Ocean House, delighting in hosting elaborate costume parties, for which an orchestra played in the ballroom for the 150 or more guests. There were hundreds and hundreds of lockers available when she invited a crowd over for a beach party.

Davies, who had a slight stutter, continued her career into the sound era with such entries as 1930's *The Florodora Girl* and 1933's *Going Hollywood* (a wonderfully satirical musical that teamed Marion with one of her crushes, Bing Crosby). After the poorly received 1934 entry *Operator 13*, she moved over to Warner Bros., with Hearst having her massive studio star "cottage" carted across town to her new film lot. Among Marion's vehicles at Warner Bros. were two features with Dick Powell, with whom she had become smitten.

After 1937's *Ever Since Eve*, 40-year-old Davies called it quits in films. By then, Hearst's empire was crumbling, despite infusions of funds from the faithful Davies and others. In 1945, she sold the famous beach compound for a mere $600,000 to resolve a troublesome property tax dispute. (The joke about town was that its sale had left thousands of people homeless.) Marion devoted her time to seeing friends, funding charities, drinking a good deal, and caring for the aged Hearst. He died in August 1951. (The Hearst family refused to allow her to attend W. R.'s funeral.) Five weeks later, she wed Horace G. Brown, a part-time actor and sometime sea captain who looked like a younger version of Hearst. The marriage was unhappy and twice she filed for divorce, but she withdrew her petition each time.

Marion Davies died of cancer in September 1961, leaving an estate of over $8 million. She was buried at Hollywood Memorial Cemetery (aka Hollywood Forever Cemetery) in the family crypt where her "niece" Patricia and her actor husband, Arthur "Dagwood" Lake, were later interred.

Zsa Zsa Gabor

(February 6, 1917–)

In another era, the beautiful, effervescent, and shrewd Zsa Zsa Gabor might have easily rivaled the most successful courtesans of the French royal court. Instead, she became one of the most colorful personalities of the 20th century. Based for many decades in Hollywood, where she dabbled in films and TV, she became as well-known for her bon mots ("To a smart girl men are no problem, they're the answer") as for her collection of sparkling diamonds, expensive jewelry, and lush furs. En route to the lifestyle of the rich and famous, Gabor wed nine times (although one marriage was declared invalid). In between, she found time to dally with an impressive array of male friends, including John F. Kennedy, construction industry millionaire Hal Hayes, Prince Aly Khan, international playboy Porfirio Rubirosa, attorney to the stars Greg Bautzer, communications entrepreneur William S. Paley, Rafael Trujillo Jr. (son of the Dominican Republic dictator), Frank Sinatra, and Nicky Hilton (the stepson of Gabor's second husband, Conrad Hilton, and the great-uncle of today's jet-setter Paris Hilton).

On the path to fame, fortune, and flashy abodes, Gabor made full use of her glamour, publicity savvy, and willingness to turn her materialistic, manhunting persona into an amusing caricature. Zsa Zsa graciously shared tips with the rest of the world on how best to snare the opposite sex in 1969's *Zsa Zsa's Complete Guide to Men* and 1970's *How to Get a Man, How to Keep a Man, How to Get Rid of a Man*. She imparted such useful advice as "Getting divorced just because you don't love a man is almost as silly as getting married just because you do" and "A man in love is incomplete until he is married. Then he's finished."

• • •

Sári Gábor was born in Budapest, Hungary, in 1917 (although she later maintained her birth year to be as recent as 1930). She was the second of three daughters of Vilmos and Jolie Tilleman Gabor and was soon nicknamed Zsa Zsa by her parents. Her father ran a jewelry firm and her mother owned a porcelain and crystal store. Jolie, who had stifled her ambitions to be an actress when she wed, believed that her girls were destined for fame, riches, and regal weddings. To ensure such outcomes, she gave her daughters lessons to play the piano, fence, dance, and speak several languages (to be able to flirt with eligible foreigners). At age 13, Zsa Zsa—in the family tradition—attended a fancy finishing school in Lausanne, Switzerland. During one summer holiday, she participated in a Miss Hungary beauty contest. (She was disqualified from a top prize because she had fibbed about her age.) Later, she studied at Vienna's Academy of Music and Dramatic Arts, where she won the attention of famed tenor

Richard Tauber. She joined him in the cast of an operetta performed in Vienna in the summer of 1934. During this time, Gabor had her first affair. Her lover was Willi Schmidt-Kentner, the well-established German composer.

To get away from her parents' strict discipline, she wed the middle-aged Burhan Belge, the press director of the Turkish foreign ministry. Once Gabor was residing in Ankara as a diplomat's wife, she came into her own as a social hostess. (Later, she maintained that during this time she had become close with Mustafa Kemal Ataturk,

The vivacious Zsa Zsa Gabor made occasional movies, such as 1952's Moulin Rouge, but she gained much of her fame and fortune through her nine marriages.

Turkey's president). Zsa Zsa visited England in 1939 for her sister Eva's first marriage. By this juncture, wherever Gabor went, she was the center of media attention.

Gabor ended her first marriage in 1941 and went to Hollywood to visit Eva, who was then working in films. Zsa Zsa's next mate was the far older Conrad Hilton, a hotel tycoon. They wed in April 1942 and set up housekeeping in Bel Air, the tony Los Angeles suburb. The incompatible duo divorced in 1947, although Zsa Zsa was expecting Hilton's baby. Their child, Francesca, was born in March 1947.

While still Mrs. Conrad Hilton, the restless Gabor had developed a strong yen for film actor George Sanders—she was impressed by his screen presence. When she was introduced to the suave Continental actor, he was amused by her luscious looks and her endless chitchat. He and Cokiline (his nickname for her, which in Russian meant "little cookie") wed in April 1949. All too quickly she realized that there was a wide gulf between her high-spirited personality and his sarcastic, dour nature. He often was away for months at a time making movies, which left her with too many unfilled hours. In this restless mode, she found Sanders's actor brother, Tom Conway, a pleasant social escort. She also used her free time to cheer up Nicky Hilton (her ex-husband's son), who was having problems in his marriage to Elizabeth Taylor.

While in Manhattan in 1952, Zsa Zsa was charmed by and, in turn, captivated Dominican diplomat/playboy Porfirio Rubirosa. It was the start of a lengthy on-again/off-again romance that played out in America and abroad. (During this much-publicized courtship, she was still legally married to the undemonstrative Sanders.) The Rubirosa liaison ultimately sputtered out. In the meantime, Gabor and Sanders divorced in April 1954.

It was during her frustrating marriage to George Sanders that Zsa Zsa made a guest appearance on a TV quiz show. Because she proved to be both charming and catty on air, she was able to launch a career as a popular guest on television gab shows and variety programs. This led to a spotty movie career, with roles in such pictures as 1953's *Lili* and 1957's *The Girl in the Kremlin*. As a well-known personality, she was hired in 1970 to take over the lead in the Broadway hit *40 Carats*. However, the best venue for Gabor's cavorting was TV (as during her lengthy tenure on *Hollywood Squares*).

Zsa Zsa never had a hit TV series to her credit, but she remained in the public eye with her multiple marriages, endless romances, additional television guest shots, and her ability to come up with a clever line at the right public moment. In July 1986, she became real nobility when she wed Prince Frédéric von Anhalt, the Duke of Saxony. During this domestic merger, Gabor had a notorious encounter with the police. In June 1989, she was detained by a Beverly Hills cop for driving with expired registration tags on her Rolls-Royce. The duo got into a spat, with Gabor allegedly slapping him in the face. This led to her being handcuffed and escorted to jail. The incident prompted tremendous media coverage of her trial on two counts of driving violations (including one for reputedly changing vital statistics on her driver's license) and one count of battery. During the 15-day courtroom hearing, Zsa Zsa paraded an assortment of fashions, entertained herself by drawing sketches, and complained to reporters about the injustice of it all. Her husband, Prince Frédéric, did not help her cause when he sniffed, "The rich and famous should be judged differently. This city couldn't live with the little people's tax money." In the end, Gabor had to serve three days in jail, do 120 hours of community service, and pay a $12,350 fine.

In 1993, Zsa Zsa and her consort lost a $3.3 million suit filed against them for their having made negative remarks about movie actress/painter Elke Sommer that were published in a German publication. The costly judgment led Zsa Zsa to declare bankruptcy, but this technicality did not prevent her from continuing her upscale lifestyle.

In November 2002, by which time her two sisters and her mother had passed away, Gabor was seriously injured in a car accident but recovered. Two years later, she suffered a severe stroke and endured a long recuperation. Thereafter, she has lived in semireclusion. However, everyone's favorite "dah-link" has the satisfaction of knowing that she has enjoyed a zesty and fashionable life as one of the 20th century's most mesmerizing divas.

Sonja Henie

(April 8, 1912–October 12, 1969)

Throughout Sonja Henie's remarkable career as a world-class figure skater and then as a popular Hollywood movie star, much of the public viewed the dimpled blond darling through rose-tinted glasses. They regarded the cherubic Norwegian as a glamorous sports queen whose Pavlova-like skills on the ice were the result of athletic prowess and ample good fortune. In actuality, the astute, extraordinarily competitive Henie rarely left anything in her life to chance. She was a highly calculating individual whose hunger for fame and fortune was matched only by her strong sexual drive. She coldly manipulated anyone—including family and friends—to satisfy her insatiable appetites.

Money was always of paramount importance to Henie. She thrived on outsmarting business associates, overworking staff, and draining her ice show casts with her intense rehearsals and demands. Even after she had become exceedingly wealthy, Sonja considered it her duty (and right) to strip a hotel room bare (of soaps, towels, etc.) to compensate for the "outrageous" rates these establishments charged her. When not hoarding her piles of money in secret Swiss bank accounts or investing in real estate, La Henie had a keen eye for amassing high-quality jewelry, furs, and paintings. She always knew the full inventory of her items and could recite the current market value of each piece.

When Henie's Los Angeles home was burglarized, the thieves made off with 17 of her fur coats before the police arrived. Eventually, the stolen goods were traced to a Las Vegas warehouse that also contained a stash of other furs. The Ice Queen hastened to Nevada to identify her property. When a detective inquired how she could pick out her possessions so easily (many of them were now without their mono-grammed linings), Henie retorted, "How do you know which woman is your wife?"

• • •

She was born in 1912 in Oslo, Norway, the second child (following older brother Leif) of Wilhelm and Selma Nielsen Henie. Her father was a well-to-do fur merchant who had been a world champion bicyclist. Her mother had inherited a tidy sum from her family's fleet of ships that transported lumber abroad. The Henies lived exceeding well. Besides their upscale primary home, they owned a mountain hunting lodge as well as a 5,000-acre summer estate situated on Denmark's west coast.

Sonja received her first pair of ice skates when she was 6, and she quickly displayed a skill for figure skating. Later, her coddling father hired private coaches to instruct his agile daughter. Because of her intensive training schedule (in both skating and ballet) and frequent traveling with the family about Europe, the girl relied on private tutors to guide her through her academic studies.

By 1923, the 11-year-old was becoming a

seasoned figure skating competitor in her homeland. That year she was named senior national champion of Norway. Henie finished eighth in the 1924 Olympics. In 1927, she claimed the first of 10 consecutive world championships in her field. At the 1928, 1932, and 1936 Olympics, she won gold medals. Already, the internationally famous young woman was being credited with revolutionizing figure skating—making it an art by incorporating music and dance into the free-skating portion of her routine.

In 1936, the ambitious Henie abandoned her amateur status to go professional in the skating world. She explained in her seemingly guileless way: "If I have to practice two times every day, cannot smoke or drink, and have to put up with the stares of total strangers, then I might as well get something out of it besides silverware and entertainment." (Reputedly, Sonja and her father had long been negotiating enticing perks for her appearances at skating events, money that was rumored to be stashed away in Swiss bank accounts.)

Next, the skating star embarked on a splashy, lucrative United States tour that ended in Los Angeles. There her stellar performances prompted Twentieth Century-Fox studio mogul Darryl F. Zanuck to sign Henie to star in pictures. She engineered a $125,000 per film contract with cagey provisions for lucrative extra payment should filming go over its deadline. Her debut Hollywood vehicle was 1936's *One in a Million*, which was a whopping success. The next year, she teamed with Tyrone Power for *Thin Ice*, another large moneymaker. While there had already been other men in her

life, Henie set her sights on marrying Power. It was a major disappointment when the screen's latest Adonis instead married French actress Annabella.

Besides Henie's remunerative moviemaking, she headlined profitable ice revues and coproduced other such productions. Her tremendous acclaim made Sonja a natural for lucrative endorsement deals, and by 1940 she was a millionaire several times over. Befitting her status, she acquired a stately five-acre home in Holmby Hills (adjacent to Beverly Hills), ensuring that the costly real estate purchase was completed *before* her June 1940 wedding to Dan Topping, her

The dimpled ice-skating champion and Hollywood movie star Sonja Henie was a shrewd businesswoman who made a sizable fortune over the decades.

already twice-divorced socialite fiancé. The star explained to her intended, "I like to keep things straight. What's mine is mine." In February 1946, the couple finalized their divorce. Three years later, in September 1949, she married Winthrop Gardiner Jr., a twice-divorced aviation executive. By now, her movie career was over and she focused on her touring ice revues, which still packed in the crowds. Her second marriage ended in May 1956. (For a time, there were rumors that Henie and Liberace—who shared a love for diamonds and furs—might one day wed, but that improbable coupling never happened.) Less than a month after shedding Gardiner, she married wealthy ship owner Neils Onstad in Norway.

Henie had known Onstad since childhood, but that did not prevent the ultra-materialistic celebrity from negotiating a stringent prenuptial agreement with her new mate. By now, Henie, whose fondness for drinking had grown, had retired into private life. She devoted much energy to her regal lifestyle, socializing with her "gem-studded friends," supervising her many holdings, and expanding her art collection. Later, she and Onstad funded a building near Oslo to house their donated 250 paintings. The museum opened in the fall of 1968.

Nine months before she died, in October 1969, Henie was diagnosed with leukemia. She remained socially active almost to the end, succumbing to the disease as she was en route by ambulance plane from France to Norway. It was estimated that Sonja Henie's estate was worth 25 to 50 million dollars.

Paris Hilton

(February 17, 1981–)

In the years before World War II, several New York society debutantes became famous for being madcap, glamorous, and the center of press attention. These included Gloria Vanderbilt, Doris Duke, Barbara Hutton, and Brenda Frazier. Times changed, and in the late 1990s there emerged a new version of the social blue-blood striking out on her own. She was known as a "celebutante." One of the first of these was Paris Hilton, who was initially dubbed "Paris the Heiress." The savvy socialite quickly became a media darling. In the process, the princess of moneyed entitle-ment transformed herself into a new entity in the early 21st century—an entertainment brand who dabbled in acting, book writing, perfume manufacturing, club ownership, a party-hearty nightlife, and an assortment of tabloid-chronicled romances. And, oh yes, she was the star of a home-made, X-rated video (*1 Night in Paris*) that became an international bestseller.

•   •   •

Paris Hilton's great-grandfather Conrad Hilton bought his first hotel in 1919 and proceeded to build an international chain of hotels. When he died in 1979, he left the bulk of his huge fortune to charities and nothing to his heirs. Several of them contested his will, and one in particular—his second son, Barron—ended up with a large portion of the estate. Barron was himself industrious. Besides being chairman of the Hilton hotel chain, he controlled many other business enterprises. By 2005, he was worth over $1 billion and still adding to his wealth. Barron had eight children, one of whom was Richard (known as Rick). In addition to being an heir to the Hilton hotel chain, Rick became a tremendously successful real estate broker/developer who specialized in high-end properties. He married actress Kathy Richards in 1978, and they had four children: Paris (born in 1981), Nicholai ("Nicky"; born in 1983), Barron (born in 1989), and Conrad (born in 1994).

Paris Whitney Hilton grew up in the lap of luxury. The family divided their time between a 40-room Beverly Hills mansion, an expansive Hamptons estate on Long Island, and luxurious suites at Manhattan's Waldorf-Astoria (the flagship hotel in the Hilton chain). Called Star by her family when she was a child, Paris attended such exclusive, posh learning establishments as the Buckley School in Sherman Oaks, California, the Canterbury School in Connecticut, and the Dwight School in Manhattan. She dropped out of the latter, and later earned her GED. Like her siblings, Paris enjoyed every creature comfort that money, power, and family fame could provide, even if her peers at school were not always kindly disposed to their superrich classmate.

As an adolescent, Paris and her more conservative sister, Nicky, attended society fund-raisers, which often included chic fashion shows. Paris decided to become a model and ignored her parents' objections to such a mundane goal. The leggy blonde was soon lighting up runways and fashion magazines with her dazzling looks and defiant stance. Although still only in her teens, Paris attended trendy nightclubs geared for adults and dated older men. Wherever she went, she used her intuitive knack for generating attention from the paparazzi and getting her name and photo into print. She quickly became known as the wild Paris Hilton, a young woman who reveled in being in the limelight and who always seemed to be having fun. Regarding her detractors who insisted that she (and sister Nicky) lacked class and self-respect, Paris retorted, "People love to hate us. But when you know us, you love us."

Paris became ambitious to move beyond the fashion industry and the club scene into show business. (After all, her great-grandfather Conrad had once been wed to movie personality Zsa Zsa Gabor, and, decades ago, her great-uncle Nicky had been married briefly to film queen Elizabeth Taylor.) With Paris's pedigree, her modeling success, and her party girl notoriety (which included her trademark scanty outfits), she found it rather easy to break into film and TV. During her "struggle" to make it in Hollywood, she resided in an impressive Los Angeles home that she shared with Nicky, drove about town in her assortment of high-priced cars, and shopped at the best Beverly Hills boutiques.

Paris won small parts in 2000's *Sweetie Pie* and 2001's *Zoolander*, often playing (versions of) herself. Then the neophyte

Heiress Paris Hilton, part of the famous Hilton hotel/real estate dynasty, made her mark in the late 1990s as an international "celebutante." When not on the social scene, she made forays into films, such as 2005's House of Wax.

entertainer was asked to headline a new reality series, *The Simple Life*, in which she and Nicole Richie (the daughter of singer Lionel Richie) were cast as fish out of water trying to adapt to life on a Midwestern farm. Before the show debuted in late 2003, an X-rated home movie of Paris and her former boyfriend Rick Salomon circulated on the Internet and then debuted as a hot-selling DVD. Rather than damaging Paris's

career, it stimulated terrific interest in her TV series (which became a hit and went on for additional seasons). She was now a household name.

The self-assured, mercurial Paris had been linked with Salomon back in 2000 (when the naughty tape was made). The I'll-Do-What-I-Want Girl then went on to date, among many others, model Jason Shaw, actors Leonardo DiCaprio and Edward Furlong, playboy Brandon Davis, and Australian tennis player Mark Philippoussis, as well as having a several-months fling with boy-band musician Nick Carter that ended in mid-2004. Between roles in such films as 2005's *House of Wax* (for which she won a Razzie for her inept performance), Paris became engaged to Paris Latsis, the Greek shipping heir. She announced that she was abandoning her public life: "I thought it was cute to play a dumb blonde. On TV I do it because it's funny. I consider myself a business-woman and a brand. I don't enjoy going out anymore. It's such a pain. It's everyone saying, 'Let's do a deal! Can I have a picture?' I'm just like, These people are such losers. I can't believe I used to love doing this."

Meanwhile, Paris branched out into other creative arts. She coauthored a best-selling book, 2004's *Confessions of an Heiress*, formed her own music label (Heiress Records), and, in 2006, released an album (*Paris*) of pop songs, which drew some positive critical response. With her various projects, she was now generating over $6 million a year.

After her relationship with Paris Latsis fell apart (when his mother learned of Hilton's sex tape), the young heiress decreed she was giving up dating (and sex). However, she soon returned to the club/party scene and, later, began dating another shipping heir, Stavros Niarchos. She continued to maintain that her reality series showcase had not presented the real her, and that she was definitely *not* the dim bulb she pretended to be on her reality showcase. However, when she was questioned by the Los Angeles police in the fall of 2006 about information she might have regarding a potential suspect in a 2004 robbery at a Hollywood producer's home, she insisted to law enforcers, "Like I really . . . I don't remember. I'm not like that smart. I like forget stuff all the time." Also in September 2006, she garnered more headlines when she was arrested by the police in Los Angeles for allegedly driving under the influence after leaving a Hollywood party. (In

January 2007, she pleaded no contest to alcohol-related reckless driving. The court placed Hilton on 36 months probation and ordered her to pay fines. The next month, Paris was stopped by Los Angeles police for driving without her car's headlights turned on, and her vehicle was impounded when they realized she was driving with a suspended license. She received a 45-day jail sentence for her misdeeds.)

On another recent occasion, pampered Paris said of her life's accomplishments to date: "People are going to judge me, 'Paris Hilton, she uses money to get what she wants.' Whatever. I haven't accepted money from my parents since I was 18. I've worked my ass off. I have things no heiress has. I've done it all on my own, like a hustler."

Howard Hughes

(December 24, 1905–April 5, 1976)

There's an old saying that "money can't buy happiness," and that was certainly true in the case of Howard Hughes, a man strongly fixated on power and riches. As the eccentric entrepreneur—who gained his wealth and fame in the oil drilling, aircraft, and film industries—reached middle age, he became increasingly victimized by debilitating health and severe emotional issues. These included his obsessive-compulsive disorder, serious body damage suffered in several plane crashes, reputed syphilis, drug addiction, an extremely poor diet, and destructive antisocial behavior.

Even with all of his mounting physical and mental plights, Howard still knew his priorities. When someone accused him of exhibiting bizarre emotional conduct, he retorted, "I'm not a paranoid deranged millionaire. Goddamit, I'm a billionaire!"

• • •

Howard Robard Hughes Jr. was born in Humble, Texas, in 1905, the only child of Howard Robard Hughes Sr. and Allene Gano Hughes. His father had made a fortune with his profitable oil drilling equipment company and used his assets to pamper his family and himself. His well-bred mother was both excessively possessive and indulgent with her son, whom she kept on a very tight leash. As a result, young

Howard never learned to properly interact with his peers. In addition, the doting Allene was obsessed with avoiding germs of all sorts, and passed along this dread to her son. In the process, he became a hypochondriac. When Mrs. Hughes died in 1922, her 16-year-old son was devastated.

During his formative years, Howard demonstrated a great interest in the field of aviation and also revealed superior mechanical skills. Because of his obsessive-compulsive disorder—an ailment not known about in those times—he developed strange eating habits. (He fixated on the proper thickness of a tomato slice and the correct size and amount of green peas to be on his dinner plate.) He also had strange notions about hygiene that included his neurotic frequent hand-washing ritual and, later in life, his refusal to bathe, cut his hair, or trim his fingernails or toenails. Meanwhile, his father had begun dallying with Hollywood beauties. It taught the impressionable Howard a lesson: financial resources could buy a lonesome man the attention of exciting cinema lovelies.

Thanks to Mr. Hughes's contacts, Howard was admitted to the California Institute of Technology and then continued his sporadic academic studies at Rice Institute. In early 1924, Mr. Hughes died suddenly and Howard Jr. inherited enormous wealth. After the young man consolidated his control of the Hughes Tool Company, which provided him with a lavish income of over $5,000 a day, he entered into a loveless marriage in June 1925. His bride was Ella Rice, the daughter of a rich Houston businessman. The couple had little in common, especially once he began to indulge his

enthusiasm for moviemaking and the glittering nightlife that surrounded the film industry. (By December 1929, Howard and Ella had divorced.)

Dapper, lanky, and charming, Hughes might have easily become a movie leading man. However, he chose to become a producer, starting with such silent entries as 1926's *Swell Hogan*. Meanwhile, Hughes turned his attention to winning a movie star for himself. He fumbled in his efforts with film actress Eleanor Boardman. (She judged him to be too aloof and shy, not realizing that some of his odd behavior was the product of his growing deafness and his embarrassment at not hearing what she was saying to him.) Next, he turned his attention to Billie Dove, a beautiful movie leading lady. Although she was already wed (to film director Irvin Willat), Hughes extravagantly pursued Dove. He paid Willat $325,000 to divorce her (plus spent an additional $20,000 in fees to process the divorce), $500,000 to purchase Dove's contract from Warner Bros., $350,000 for a yacht to properly impress Billie, $185,000 to purchase and refurbish a new Los Angeles home in which to entertain his lady fair, and $20,000 for a European jaunt with Dove. In addition, he spent thousands of dollars more on the furs, jewelry, and other gifts he lavished on her. In typical Hughes fashion, he soon lost interest in her.

Between 1927 and 1930, Hughes spent $6 million on making films, including his aerial epic, 1930's *Hell's Angels*. After producing 1932's *Scarface: The Shame of a Nation*, Howard quit the industry until the early 1940s. His new priority became the world of aviation: shattering flight records, surviving plane (and car) crashes, and building a major airline (TWA). When Hughes was not flying about the world, the progressively more peculiar industrialist chased after a flock of Tinseltown lovelies, including Jean Harlow, Katharine Hepburn (whom he actually considered marrying), Joan Fontaine and her sister, Olivia de Havilland, Ginger Rogers, and Bette Davis. Besides having several personal aircraft, he now owned the *Southern Cross* (the world's fifth largest yacht) to use as an exciting backdrop when courting his celebrity girlfriends.

Hughes was in his late 30s when he turned the curvaceous Jane Russell into a movie sensation in 1943's *The Outlaw*. He was obsessed with women's chest size, and for Russell, he devoted much time and many dollars to designing an innovative bra to showcase her remarkable cleavage. However, the forthright Russell was not Hughes's big love. He far more fancied the exciting process of discovering young screen candidates (like Jane Greer and Faith Domergue) and luring them to Hollywood to be his private possession and, perhaps, a film actress. (When Domergue complained to Hughes that he was smothering her professional chances, he responded by featuring her in 1950's *Vendetta*, which resulted in a $1 million fiasco.) Other less lucky young women contracted by Hughes over the years never made it on camera. They remained secluded in Howard's many Los Angeles hideouts, unaware of their several rivals. Sooner or later, most of these cinema aspirants left town without ever having made a mark on show business, but usually better off financially.

The eccentric billionaire Howard Hughes spent a fortune producing his 1930's aerial epic, Hell's Angels.

One of the more celebrated of Hughes's costly love interests was the down-to-earth movie goddess Ava Gardner. They met in 1943 soon after she and movie star Mickey Rooney divorced. Their on-and-off-again relationship endured for a decade—during which she wed and divorced Frank Sinatra.

In the late 1940s, starlet Terry Moore supposedly secretly wed Hughes on the high seas, a union that allegedly survived until shortly before he married movie actress Jean Peters in January 1957. By then, Hughes had become disenchanted with moviemaking (and had profitably sold his RKO film lot).

In the mid-1960s, Hughes became increasingly reclusive and ill (both physically and mentally). More and more, the management of his business empire was left to others. But sometimes the ailing Howard had a brainstorm that he actually acted upon. He moved to Las Vegas and decided to take control of the gambling capital. Between 1966 and 1967, he purchased the Desert Inn for $13.25 million, the Sands for $23 million, the Castaways for $2.2 million, the Frontier for $23 million, and the Silver Slipper for $5.4 million. (He also acquired a Las Vegas TV station for $3.6 million so he could be assured of having his favorite films air at any hour of the day or night.)

Later, he expanded his holdings to Reno, where he bought the Landmark for $17.3 million and Harold's Club for $10.5 million. Despite such glittery acquisitions, Hughes spent most of his time isolated in a Las Vegas hotel suite, insulated by his staff of personal and business employees, and dining largely on TV dinners and ice cream.

In his final years, the onetime Hollywood playboy was plagued by drug addiction, phobias, machinations within his vast corporate realm, and his rapidly declining physical and mental health. The Old Man (as his retainers called him) lived variously on several continents sequestered in a darkened room where he sat naked, engrossed in minutia, unaware that unscrupulous underlings were robbing him blind. The pathetic recluse died in 1976, long since detached from a world he once sought to control. It was estimated that Howard Hughes's estate was worth nearly $2 billion (about $9.8 billion in today's terms).

Demi Moore

(November 11, 1962–)

Demi Moore once admitted, "I'm sure there are a lot of people who think I'm a bitch." It was probably a correct assessment. At the peak of her box-office power in the mid-1990s—and even thereafter—Moore was noted for making excessive demands for lavish perks above and beyond her premium filmmaking salary. It reached the point where she was known within the movie industry as "Gimme Moore." Seemingly, Moore didn't care. The ambitious actress reasoned, "I want it all."

On the sound stage, Moore had a reputation for being super controlling—no matter what her whim. Her rationale was, "I don't care because I know that what I fight for is something I feel strongly about."

• • •

The future screen star was born in 1962 in Roswell, New Mexico. Her mother, Virginia King, had been ditched by Charles Harmon after a two-month marriage. Three months after the birth of Demetria Gene, Virginia remarried. Her new husband was Daniel Guynes, a newspaper advertising salesperson. (Moore did not uncover these facts about her parentage for years to come.) The couple had a child, a boy named Morgan. Her teenaged parents nicknamed their scrawny daughter Demmie. Because of Daniel Guynes's drinking and gambling habits, the family moved over 30 times in the next years, usually existing in (near) poverty. As a youngster, Demmie suffered from kidney infections, and at 12, she underwent corrective surgery twice to repair a crossed right eye. In the mid-1970s, Virginia (who frequently drank to excess) and Daniel divorced, rewed, and then split again. (In 1980, Daniel committed suicide.) In the meantime, Virginia and her children relocated to West Hollywood, California. (By now, Demetria had shortened her name to Demi [French for "half"].)

She enrolled at Fairfax High but gave priority to smoking marijuana, drinking liquor, and consuming prescription drugs over studying. She dropped out of school at 16, lived with a boyfriend, and worked for a collection agency. Soon she was involved in a new relationship: with Freddy Moore, a married musician who was 12 years her senior. Already, Demi dreamed of becoming an actress and had begun taking acting classes. She also modeled, including in some revealing poses for *Oui* magazine. In February 1980, Demi and Freddy Moore wed. She was now Demi Moore.

One of Moore's first acting assignments was a role in a low-budget feature, 1981's *Choices*. Soon, Moore was hired for the daytime TV drama *General Hospital*, where she gained popularity. She left *General Hospital* in 1983 to make *Blame It on Rio*, a movie noted for her being topless in a beach scene. The actress broke up with her husband in 1984, and their divorce became final in August 1985.

Moore was signed for 1985's *St. Elmo's Fire* to play a character who was deep into drugs. At the time, Demi herself was still heavily drawn to illegal substances, and her erratic behavior led director Joel Schumacher to fire her from the film. She pleaded for a second chance, promising to enter rehab. The filmmaker agreed and she was rehired for the movie. *St. Elmo's Fire* was a major Hollywood Brat Pack showcase and Moore quickly joined the ranks of its high-profile members: Rob Lowe, Matt Dillon, Ally Sheedy, Andrew McCarthy, and others. Meanwhile, Moore began a three-year relationship with Emilio Estevez, another Brat Packer from the movie. The twosome became engaged, but their nuptials were put off time after time. They broke up in August 1987 after Emilio introduced Demi to actor Bruce Willis. Moore and Willis (seven years her senior and the colead of the TV series *Moonlighting*) became an item on the Hollywood scene.

Besides appearing in such films as 1986's *About Last Night*, the workaholic Moore made her stage debut that year in the off-Broadway production of *The Early Girl*. Demi and Bruce wed in Las Vegas in November 1987. Two weeks after their civil ceremony, they remarried on a sound stage at the Burbank Studio in southern California. The elaborate festivities cost an estimated $875,000.

The newlyweds moved into a $2 million, two-story house on Malibu's Carbon Beach. Their first child, Rumer Glenn, was born in August 1988. The next year, Moore and Willis (whose career was in overdrive) purchased an $8 million triplex penthouse

Demi Moore amassed a fortune in the 1990s, allowing her and then husband Bruce Willis to lead an extravagant lifestyle. Moore appeared with Gaby Hoffman (left) in 1995's Now and Then.

apartment in Manhattan. Within their 14-room dwelling, Moore showcased her $2 million collection of antique dolls. Adding to their real estate holdings, the duo acquired a homestead in the mountains near Hailey, Idaho. Also in 1990, Demi teamed with Patrick Swayze for *Ghost*. According to its director, she was "difficult and frustrating" during filming. Nevertheless, the tearjerker was a tremendous success, and her price per film leaped to $2.5 million. By the end of 1990, *People* magazine had named Moore (pregnant with her second child) and Willis "Hollywood's Hottest Couple."

Moore was also known in Tinseltown as a "tough broad" who was "gutsy enough to take on all comers." During the shoot of 1991's *Mortal Thoughts*, which she coproduced, Demi had the initial director let go, saying "What he's getting was not what I was wanting." On 1991's *The Butcher's Wife*, the film's coscripter noted of Moore, "She had a strong conception of her role that wasn't up for discussion." Her most noteworthy appearance that year was her audacious pose for the cover of the August issue of *Vanity Fair*. She was nude (except for an earring). The very pregnant star had one hand covering her breasts, and the other placed beneath her bulging tummy. The highly controversial shot made Demi the talk of America. Meanwhile, she gave birth in July 1991 to her second daughter, Scout LaRue.

By this juncture, Moore was labeled a prickly perfectionist who was totally goal-oriented. In February 1994, she and Willis became the parents of their third daughter, Tallulah Belle. While Demi was bounding up the Hollywood success ladder, her mother was plummeting down the social scale. Virginia was arrested several times on drunk driving charges, got embroiled in barroom arguments, and posed naked for a girlie publication. Demi stopped communicating with her mother, only reconciling with her soon before Virginia's death from lung cancer in July 1998.

The pampered Moore maintained a high profile in Idaho during 1995. She and Willis had a 25-acre estate on the outskirts of Hailey (population around 6,000). In this former mining town, the movie star couple owned and refurbished the only movie theater, built a retail shop/office building, and spent $1.5 million to renovate a honky-tonk bar into The Mint—an eatery/club where Bruce jammed with visiting musicians. Among other projects the Willises planned was an elaborate doll museum to feature Demi's prized collection. Meanwhile, to herald Bruce's 40th birthday in 1995, Demi decided money was no object. She flew in over 100 pals so the notables could tour the couple's estate and town and participate in Willis's big party.

While Demi industriously supervised her Idaho fiefdom, her film career sagged. Her edition of *The Scarlet Letter*, in 1995, was a bomb. She was cast as a stripper in 1996's *Striptease*, which displayed her extremely buff figure, but the one-dimensional movie still failed, as did the 1997 service drama *G.I. Jane*, for which Moore shaved her head. (While making this picture, Moore had such a large support staff that the studio had to hire a second jet plane to accommodate everyone on flights to the location sites.)

After several years of tabloid-chronicled breakups and reconciliations, the Willises separated in June 1998. They shelved their pending Hailey projects and closed down some of their active operations there. It took nearly two years before the couple reached an agreement on the division of their estimated $150 million holdings. By the time of their October 2000 divorce, each party was dating. Also by then, Demi's long-finished new film, *Passion of Mind*, had come and gone quickly from distribution.

By the new millennium, Moore's once impressive film career seemed largely over. But then she launched an *expensive* comeback. She purchased a $2.8 million Beverly Hills residence as her new Los Angeles headquarters. In addition, she spent a reported $380,000 on cosmetic surgery and dentistry and personal trainers before her guest-starring role in 2003's *Charlie's Angels: Full Throttle*. The industry grapevine claimed Moore was her old self on the set: demanding superstar treatment. Neither she nor the movie received positive reviews. Moore generated far more publicity by being seen about Tinseltown with her new boyfriend, TV/movie star (and producer) Ashton Kutcher, who was 14 years her junior. After a long, high-profile romance, the couple, both followers of Kabbalah, married in September 2005. Among those attending the lavish, exclusive reception was her ex-husband Bruce Willis.

Marriage seemed to agree with the high-maintenance Moore. She returned to an active filmmaking schedule, appearing in 2006's *Bobby* (with her former beau Emilio Estevez) and 2007's *Mr. Brooks* (with Kevin Costner).

Mary Pickford

(April 8, 1892–May 29, 1979)

Mary Pickford, known as "America's Sweetheart," was a major icon of the silent cinema. In her heyday (from the mid-1910s to the late 1920s) the "Girl with the Golden Curls" was one of the world's most famous and highest paid talents. It seemed only fitting that the Queen of Tinseltown—along with her husband, swashbuckling film king Douglas Fairbanks Sr.—should rule the movie industry's social scene during the Roaring Twenties. Their royal domain was Pickfair, the most famous film colony mansion of them all.

When they moved into their remodeled rustic hunting lodge in the late summer of 1920, Hollywood wondered why the regal couple had elected to reside in the "wilds" of Beverly Hills rather than the civilized sections of downtown Los Angeles or Hollywood. However, the remote hilly location on Summit Drive nearby to Benedict Canyon provided the aristocratic couple with all the privacy they desired as well as a splendid view of their expansive domain.

•   •   •

Gladys Marie Smith was born in 1892 (she favored using 1893) in Toronto, Ontario, Canada. She was the firstborn of John and Charlotte Hennessey Smith, who had two more children: Charlotte, called Lottie, and John Charles Jr., known as Jack. When Gladys was 5, her laborer father died.

Young Gladys not only had to supervise her younger siblings, but she also became the family's prime wage earner. Billed as "Baby Gladys," she performed with several touring stock companies. By 1907, she was being featured on Broadway in *The Warrens of Virginia*. (She was now using a new stage name: Mary Pickford.) Two years later, the petite, five-foot-tall performer began her film career, working for director D. W. Griffith at Biograph Films in New York. Before too long, "Little Mary" had won the adoration of audiences with her steady stream of short silent pictures.

Between 1909 and 1912, Mary acted for several studios. She and her mother proved to be shrewd businesswomen. Pickford's salary had risen to an impressive $500 a week when she signed with Famous Players Company and made such films as 1913's *In the Bishop's Carriage*. Within a few years, her income had zoomed to $10,000 weekly. Meanwhile, she created the Mary Pickford Company to produce her movies. In 1918, she was hired by First National Pictures at an enormous $350,000 fee per movie project.

When Pickford was first at the Biograph studio, she had encountered Irish performer Owen Moore, the younger brother of actors Tom and Matt Moore. A romance bloomed and, in January 1911, Mary and Owen wed. It was not long before she realized that her marriage had been a bad decision. Moore was a heavy-drinking, volatile individual who reacted poorly to his wife's growing success. In late 1915, Pickford (who already had had an affair with actor/director James Kirkwood), met Douglas Fairbanks Sr., a dashing actor who was making an indelible mark in motion pictures. At the time, he was unhappily married and was the father of a young son (future movie star Douglas Fairbanks Jr.).

By 1917, Pickford had moved from the East Coast to southern California to be with Fairbanks. Both Mary and Doug were still officially wed to their respective spouses, but they found ways to pursue a clandestine romance. In March 1919, Fairbanks Sr. gained his matrimonial freedom at the cost of $625,000 (over $7.3 million in today's terms). Meanwhile, in February 1919, Pickford, Fairbanks Sr., Charlie Chaplin, and D. W. Griffith formed their own studio, United Artists Corporation.

The next year Moore agreed to a divorce settlement from Pickford, and she and Doug married in late March 1920. The groom's wedding gift to his bride was their 22-room home in Beverly Hills. The elaborate Tudor-style abode, with its green-tiled roof, frescoed ceilings, adjacent oyster-shaped swimming pool, and large formal gardens, sat on a high point of their more-than-15-acre estate. Each area of the mansion—with its two massive wings—was impressive; there was an expansive living room with an enormous fireplace, a large formal dining room that could seat a large number of guests, and a huge, well-equipped kitchen. There was also an appropriate number of live-in uniformed staff to handle the day-to-day demands of the King and Queen—who both affected a pseudo-British accent and could be snobbish—and to ensure that the Fairbankses' pets and

guests were properly cared for. The media christened the fabulous fairy-tale estate Pickfair.

The couple continued to turn out screen successes in the 1920s (such as his *Robin Hood* and *The Black Pirate*, and her *Tess of the Storm Country* and *Sparrows*). They hosted frequent formal dinner parties (liquor was not served and the evenings usually included the screening of a new

Mary Pickford, queen of Hollywood in the 1920s, shared a regal estate (Pickfair) with her cinema swashbuckler husband, Douglas Fairbanks Sr. In 1923, Pickford was hostess to a royal visitor, Marie, duchess of Gramont (left).

picture). It became de rigueur for visiting notables (including stars, politicians, socialites, and writers) to be the guests of honor at Pickfair with the crème de la crème of the Hollywood smart set angling for invitations. At the world-famous estate (often called the second White House), one might run into George Bernard Shaw, Albert Einstein, Lord and Lady Mountbatten, or Babe Ruth.

With the coming of sound movies, Pickford shed her now passé image of Little Mary. There was a great fuss when she cropped her famous curls and transformed herself into a modern maiden for 1929's *Coquette*. (She won an Academy Award for her daring.) Also in 1929, the imperial duo costarred in *The Taming of the Shrew*, which was not a success.

Fairbanks Sr. had difficulty coping with advancing middle age and the changing tastes in pictures. He fled to Europe without Pickford in May 1930. Over the next few years, they drifted further apart. He had affairs, while she pondered her future once she retired from the screen in 1933. They finally divorced in January 1936. He was soon remarried (to Lady Sylvia Ashley) and died of a heart attack in late 1939. Meanwhile, in June 1937 Mary wed actor Charles "Buddy" Rogers, who was 12 years her junior. They lived at Pickfair, where Pickford was the queen bee. In the World War II years, Mary and Buddy adopted two children, whom she alienated over the years through her rigid, old-fashioned parenting methods.

Pickford often spoke of making a movie comeback, but she never did. She had substantial income from her United Artists stock, businesses, and real estate investments. By the 1960s, Mary had become extremely reclusive and alcoholic. Rogers still entertained guests, relatives, and the media at the big house, which was falling into disrepair. As for Mary, she had retired almost permanently to her bedroom, where she drank and reminisced about the golden years of her past. Her final public appearance was on the March 29, 1976, Academy Awards telecast. (She was filmed in her bedroom accepting an honorary Oscar, and it was sad to see how infirm and incoherent America's Sweetheart—with her wig askew—had become. She died of a stroke in May 1979, leaving an estate worth an estimated 25 to 50 million dollars. (Two years after her death, Rogers remarried—to a real estate agent. He died in 1999 at age 94.)

As for the once magnificent Pickfair, the estate of which had been subdivided over past decades, it was sold months after Pickford's death for the sum of $5.36 million. It was later purchased by entertainer Pia Zadora and her then husband, Meshulam Riklis, an Israeli millionaire. In the construction of their gauche new showcase residence, the main house was essentially demolished in 1990. Pickfair, and all that it had once been in the glory days of Hollywood, was no more. When the new Pickfair went onto the real estate market yet again in 2005, the asking price was $37 million. It sold in 2006 for less than half that sum.

Gloria Swanson

(March 27, 1897–April 4, 1983)

L ate in her life, veteran movie star Gloria Swanson still thrilled to recall the supremely lavish lifestyle that she and her peers thrived on in 1920s Hollywood. "We lived like kings and queens, and why not? We were in love with life. We were making more money than we ever dreamed existed, and there was no reason to believe that it would ever stop. We had just fought the war that was to end all wars, and everyone believed there was nothing but peace and pleasure ahead."

Swanson could well afford to live opulently in the Roaring Twenties, as she had agreed to a five-year pact with Paramount Pictures. For starring in four films per year for the studio, she would receive an annual fee of $130,000 ($1.32 million in today's terms) during 1921. That yearly salary would escalate to $364,000 ($3.69 million in today's terms) by 1926. In addition, the contract provided Swanson with a plush bungalow on the studio lot (created to the star's specifications), musicians on the set (to play inspiring mood music for La Gloria), studio-provided luxury cars when she requested them, and assorted helpers to be available for all her filmmaking needs.

With such money, power, and fame, Swanson could easily make her every whim come true. It was a fulfillment of her grandest ambition: "I have decided that when I am a star, I will be every inch and every moment the star! Everybody from the studio gateman to the highest executives will know it."

• • •

Gloria May Josephine Svensson was born in Chicago in 1897 (some sources list 1898 or 1899), the only child of Joseph Svensson, of Swedish descent, and Adelaide Klanowski, whose ancestors came from Alsace, Germany. Mr. Svensson was a military officer. As an army brat, Gloria was enrolled at various schools before her family returned to the Windy City when she was in her early teens. She abandoned thoughts of becoming an opera singer when she happened to tour the local Essanay movie studio in 1913. Thanks to her strong profile and distinctive bearing, she was hired to work in the film factory's silent short subjects. There she met the hefty actor Wallace Beery, who was more than a decade older than Gloria. When Beery relocated to southern California in 1915 to expand his career options, she joined him (accompanied by her mother, who was now separated from her husband). Berry joined Mack Sennett's Keystone studio and convinced the comedy filmmaker to sign Gloria (whose professional surname was now Swanson). She and Beery eloped in March 1916, but they were a bad match from the start,. He was rough, abusive, and totally self-focused. They separated after several months and filed for divorce in December 1918.

By then, Swanson had graduated to leads in maudlin dramas at Triangle Pictures. The following year she transferred to

During the Roaring Twenties, film luminary Gloria Swanson enjoyed a sumptuous standard of living at her extravagant Beverly Hills mansion. Here she performs a scene with Maude Eburne (left) in 1931's Indiscreet.

Paramount Pictures, where, under the guidance of prestigious moviemaker Cecil B. DeMille, she appeared in *Don't Change Your Husband*, the first of her several sophisticated bedroom tales. Although Gloria was only a petite four feet eleven and a half inches, she was soon standing tall as a major Hollywood movie queen.

Swanson purchased a 24-room home — done in the Italian Renaissance style — which sat on four acres of well-manicured grounds across the street from the Beverly Hills Hotel. It was one of the town's greatest showplaces and required a staff of 11 servants. Later, the movie monarch added to her holdings a country estate near Croton-on-Hudson, New York. As the decade progressed, Swanson was spending $10,000 a

month to maintain her residences. In addition, the renowned fashion queen had a staggering clothing bill. This included $50,000 a year for gowns, $35,000 for fur coats and wraps, $10,000 for lingerie, $9,000 for stockings, $6,000 for perfume, and $5,000 each for headdresses, purses, and footwear. Unquestionably, Gloria was living life to the hilt.

In December 1919, Swanson had wed Herbert K. Somborn, the former chief of Equity Pictures who owned the local Brown Derby restaurants. Their daughter, Gloria, was born in October 1920. Somborn was twice Swanson's age and she had married him for emotional and financial security. Instead, he concentrated on "managing" her business deals, and she was stuck with paying all their expenses. They separated in the spring of 1921; their divorce became final in September 1923. Soon after the breakup, Swanson adopted a baby boy, whom she named Joseph in honor of her father. (The movie idol denied rumors that the infant might be her illegitimate child.)

In the mid-1920s, Swanson's renegotiated Paramount deal allowed her to make most of her new pictures in New York so she could enjoy the city's exciting cultural and social events. Later, she sojourned in France to film the sumptuously mounted *Madame Sans-Gêne*. On location, she fell in love with dashing but financially strapped Henri, marquis de la Falaise de la Courdraye. They wed in Paris in January 1925. (The next day, the bride had an abortion, fearful that having a child so soon after her nuptials would offend her fans.) When she and her nobleman spouse arrived back in the United States that spring, the studio underwrote gala premieres of the picture in New York and Los Angeles. Swanson rightly sensed that she was at the pinnacle of her movie career.

In 1926, Swanson parted company with Paramount, despite the studio's offer of a new $1 million annual salary contract plus 50 percent of her films' profits. Instead, she established her own production company, urged on by her adviser (and lover), Joseph P. Kennedy. (Swanson's husband had been assigned an industry job that conveniently kept him largely abroad.) Her moviemaking firm failed on its third entry, 1929's *Queen Kelly*. The disastrous production was shut down and Swanson lost almost $1 million of her own money. Soon thereafter, Kennedy ended his liaison with Gloria to reunite with his wife and children.

Gloria made a strong comeback with her first sound film, 1929's *The Trespasser*, for which she was Oscar-nominated. She and Henri divorced in November 1930 and, the next year, in August, she wed Irish "sportsman" Michael Farmer. Their daughter was born in April 1932; two years later (in November 1934) the pair divorced. After starring in 1934's *Music in the Air* as a freelance artist, Swanson did not make another movie until 1941's unremarkable *Father Takes a Wife*. To fill the emptiness in her life, she became a dynamic businesswoman. She took on husband number five, retired businessman George W. Davey, in January 1945. About six weeks later, they separated, and their split was finalized in December 1948.

The enduring Swanson made a remarkable new screen return in 1950's *Sunset Boulevard*, which netted her her third and final Academy Award nomination. Her movie appearances thereafter were infrequent and led to her last picture, 1974's *Airport 1975*. She did stage work and made occasional guest appearances on TV talk shows. Her last marriage was in February 1976, to author William Duffy. (The union suffered when she became entranced with a young man who tried to control her life.) Swanson wrote a highly successful memoir in 1980 and pursued sculpting. She died from a heart ailment in New York in April 1983.

Above and beyond her exciting movie career and fruitful life, Swanson remains forever associated with her extravagant lifestyle in the 1920s, when she expended over $8 million in the pursuit of gracious living.

PART 7

So Much Romancing

Warren Beatty

(March 30, 1937–)

For much of his life, heartthrob Warren Beatty was obsessed with scoring sexually. Sometimes, the motion pictures he made reflected his all-consuming interest in sex. For example, when preparing 1975's *Shampoo*, for which he was a producer, writer, and star, he said, "I wanted to explore contemporary sexuality through the medium of a Don Juan . . . [who] just wants to fuck because he just likes to fuck."

Unlike such contemporaries as Jack Nicholson and Al Pacino, Beatty generally avoided public scandals concerning his womanizing, demonstrating both his discretion and a businesslike attitude toward his playboy behavior. In fact, before he wed actress Annette Bening late in life, Warren often seemed quite calculating in his romantic dealings with the opposite sex. To some observers, his longer-lasting relationships—including with such well-known actresses as Joan Collins, Natalie Wood, Leslie Caron, Julie Christie, Diane Keaton, and Madonna—often smacked of opportunism. In most instances, these liaisons ended with Beatty moving on to his next love, a woman of greater current fame than the previous one.

• • •

Henry Warren Beaty was born in 1937 in Richmond, Virginia, although the family soon thereafter moved to Arlington, Virginia. He was the second child (sister Shirley was born in 1934) of Ira Owens Beaty, a former real estate agent, and the Canadian-born Kathlyn MacLean Beaty, who had taught dramatics. In their Baptist household, Mr. Beaty, who unhappily substituted a career in education for a preferred one as a musician, found outlets for his disappointments in heavy drinking and dominating his family. Meanwhile, Mrs. Beaty was noted for her extreme emotional reticence. In their repressive home ambiance, Shirley became a brash tomboy, while "Little Henry" turned into a shy loner who loved to read and play the piano.

As the years passed, the future actor sprouted into a six-foot-one football champ and high school class president who had a flock of girlfriends. Although Henry had offers of college football scholarships, he feared the gridiron sport might damage his good looks and, in turn, spoil his chances of becoming an actor. (His sister—now billed as Shirley MacLaine—was already making Hollywood movies.) In the fall of 1955, he enrolled at Northwestern University School of Speech and Drama but dropped out at the end of his freshman year.

He moved to New York, where he took odd jobs and studied acting. He dated, among others, young actress Diane Ladd. Eventually, he found minor work on New York–based TV shows. This led to a recurring role on the sitcom *The Many Loves of Dobie Gillis*, which was shot in Los Angeles. By now, he was known as Warren Beatty. MGM signed him to a $400 weekly pact.

Beatty dated Jane Fonda (with whom he had made a screen test), but he soon became entranced with Joan Collins.

At the time, Collins, a Britisher, was 26 and under contract to Twentieth Century-Fox. She and Beatty soon became ardent bedmates. Associating with Joan gave Beatty status in the film colony, and she introduced him to her circle of industry friends. Soon, Warren bought his way out of his MGM contract and returned to New York. Collins pursued him there while he starred on Broadway in the short-running *A Loss of Roses*. That show's playwright, William Inge, arranged for Beatty to test for the writer's original film script, *Splendor in the Grass*. Beatty won the lead opposite Natalie Wood in this 1961 film. During this period, Collins aborted her and Beatty's baby.

After *Splendor in the Grass*, Beatty flew to Rome to make *The Roman Spring of Mrs. Stone*. While there, he became enamored of young actress Susan Strasberg—except when he was with the more mature film/TV talent Inger Stevens. Once Warren was back in Hollywood, he and Collins parted ways. Now, Beatty turned to Natalie Wood, who was splitting up with her husband, actor Robert Wagner. Soon, Beatty was sharing Wood's Brentwood digs. That situation fell apart when he ditched her one night at a restaurant to date a hatcheck girl. Later, he became friendly with Natalie's younger sister, actress Lana Wood.

In the early 1960s, Beatty suffered two screen flops and decided to focus on his social life. One of the women he turned to was Leslie Caron, the French dancer/actress. She was then wed to British director Peter Hall, with whom she had two chil-

Warren Beatty, Hollywood's favorite lothario in the 1970s.

dren. She and the six-years-younger Beatty became a steady couple. Later, Hall sued Caron for divorce. As Leslie grew more dependent on Warren, he grew more distant. While filming 1966's *Kaleidoscope*, Beatty pursued costar Susannah York.

When Beatty went into preproduction for 1967's *Bonnie and Clyde*, he vetoed casting Caron as his leading lady, although she had been instrumental in bringing the project to his attention. Eventually, the role of bank robber Bonnie Parker went to Faye Dunaway. Warren became totally absorbed in making his new feature and drifted further away from Leslie. To save face, she broke off their relationship.

Next, Warren found romance (and a new costar, for 1971's *McCabe & Mrs. Miller*) with Oscar-winning British actress Julie Christie, who was 10 years Caron's junior. Although Julie and Warren became an item, he still found time to court, among others, opera singer Maria Callas, Princess Elizabeth of Yugoslavia, and actresses Britt Ekland and Goldie Hawn. (Hawn was Beatty's costar in 1971's $ and one of his leading ladies in 1976's *Shampoo*.) Christie coped with Warren's multiple indiscretions. Later, when he rejected her suggestion that they make their domestic ties more permanent, the couple went their separate ways. Nevertheless, she appeared in two more of his films, including 1978's *Heaven Can Wait*.

In the mid-1970s, Beatty had a lengthy live-in romance with singer Michelle Phillips, with the two sharing a Beverly Hills home. By 1977, Beatty was socializing with model Barbara Minty, only to lose her to superstar Steve McQueen. Next, Beatty was drawn to Oscar-winning actress Diane Keaton. He invited her to team with him in 1981's *Reds* and to be his new offscreen lady. That movie earned Beatty his Best Director Oscar, but the difficult shoot cost him Keaton's romantic affection.

In the mid-1980s, Warren was involved with TV news anchor Jessica Savitch. When that relationship ended, he made *Ishtar*, a film flop released the year that Beatty turned 50. The bachelor was now showing his age but continued to play the field—usually with women decades younger than he.

Beatty's long-planned movie *Dick Tracy* came together in the late 1980s. Warren wanted a hot performer for the female lead and courted the music industry's Material Girl. Madonna was then 31 and was ending her marriage to actor Sean Penn. Her screen career had been iffy, and she was eager to be in a Hollywood hit. She and Beatty played the dating game and, not unexpectedly, she was cast as chanteuse Breathless Mahoney in his new picture.

As producer, director, and star of *Dick Tracy*, Beatty was ostensibly in charge of the colorful production, but Madonna led him on a wild chase during the filming. While *Dick Tracy* was in postproduction, she set out on a concert tour and expected Beatty to be her faithful attendant. Beatty was bemused by this demanding woman, and his relationship with her—which many observers thought had been a publicity stunt—fell apart.

At a glittery Hollywood party following the March 1991 Oscars, Beatty chatted with 32-year-old actress Annette Bening. She became his leading lady in that year's *Bugsy*. Their first child, Kathlyn, was born in early 1992, and the couple married that March. They teamed in the unsuccessful *Love Affair* (1994), and had three more children: Benjamin (in 1994), Isabel (in 1997), and Ella Corinne (in 2000).

Now a middle-aged patriarch of a sizable family, Beatty seemingly was nostalgic for his past glory days. When he starred in 2001's *Town & Country*, he cast two old flames (Diane Keaton and Goldie Hawn) in key roles. The trouble-plagued comedy was a flop. Warren Beatty had become that most unforgivable thing in Hollywood—old hat.

Clara Bow

(July 29, 1905–September 27, 1965)

In her 1920s' heyday, and forever after, Clara Bow was known as the "It" girl. She was Hollywood's first authentic sex symbol, and the "It" referred to her terrific sex appeal. Her screen persona of a fun-loving flapper was built on her uninhibited, friendly, and enthusiastic personality.

Few such major cinema talents have been so exploited and then so unceremoniously dumped by the Hollywood film factory as was Bow. Thanks to her emotional insecurities—and because she was so untutored academically and socially—she easily became fortune's fool in Tinseltown. Her studio bosses, as well as relatives, lovers, and so-called friends, took full advantage of her naïveté and generous nature. As a result, the high-strung, unsophisticated movie star was easily manipulated by others and then discarded. Her greatest release from the demands of nonstop filmmaking and the pressures of being a major movie star was to engage in often reckless romances. During these entanglements she gave little heed to the possible consequences.

•   •   •

Clara Gordon Bow was born in 1905 in Brooklyn, New York. She was the third (and only surviving) child of Robert and Sarah Gordon Bow. He was a disgruntled, ugly, short man who preferred carousing with pals in the local saloons to earning a tenuous living as a busboy. Mrs. Bow, whose mother had suffered from insanity, had a melancholic nature that was aggravated by epilepsy. Robert drifted in and out of his family's nomadic life as they moved from one depressing Brooklyn tenement building to another. When he was home, he battled with his moody, suicidal wife. When he vanished for long periods, Mrs. Bow supported the household through prostitution. Despite the squalid slum surroundings and oppressive home environment, the amber-haired little Clara was a feisty survivor. She masked the miseries of her young life by blanking out as much of the unpleasantness as possible. She remained fiercely loyal to her parents despite the fact that her father ignored or (sexually) abused her and that her tormented mother made it clear that she wished Clara had died at birth.

Tomboy Clara dropped out of school at age 7, devoting much of her childhood to caring for her life-weary mother. In 1921, the teenager entered a movie magazine contest and was astonished to be named a winner. The prize was a screen role. To her disappointment, her few scenes in her film debut (1922's *Beyond the Rainbow*) were cut from the release print. However, the plucky young woman gained other screen assignments. Meanwhile, when Mrs. Bow learned that her daughter had entered the supposedly morally corrupt world of film-making, she declared her nothing better than a whore. One night, Clara awakened to find her mother standing over her with a kitchen knife, intent on killing her. The shock of the event left the movie actress a lifelong insomniac.

In 1923, the year Mrs. Bow died, Clara went to Hollywood as a contract player for B. P. Schulberg's Preferred Pictures. Despite the fact that she already had a boyfriend (cinematographer Arthur Jacobson), Bow succumbed to the sexual advances of Schulberg's brother-in law

Clara Bow, Tinseltown's own "It" girl in the 1920s.

(Sam Jaffe), Preferred's production manager. (She may also have had an affair with her married boss.) Schulberg made a sizable profit loaning out Bow to other film companies. In the process, her cinema career accelerated. While shooting 1925's *The Plastic Age* she fell in love with one of her leading men, the handsome Gilbert Roland. Clara was thrilled by her attentive young lover, but she was uncertain if she wanted to marry him. This was especially true after she became entranced with the older Victor Fleming, who first directed her in 1926's *Mantrap*. By 1927, movie actor Gary Cooper had entered Bow's hectic romantic life and the jealous Roland stopped being one of her boyfriends. (Bow also had a partiality for muscular college football players, but the long-circulated myth that she indulged in orgies with the USC gridiron squad was just that—a tabloid fantasy.)

When Schulberg was hired by Paramount Pictures in 1925, he brought Bow along to the prestigious studio as a contract leading lady. However, he did little to look out for the guileless Bow's welfare. Nevertheless, thanks to her box-office hits, especially 1927's *It*, she became a major star. (However, the pert actress with the famous bob hairdo and cupid-bow lips was worth far more to the studio than the $5,000 a week fee she was earning by the end of the 1920s.)

In 1928, while Bow was recovering in the hospital from an appendectomy, she became infatuated with a good-looking intern, William Earl Pearson. Unfortunately, he was already married. It led to a messy situation, with the nervous studio paying off the irate wife—with Bow's own money! This latest cover-up did nothing to endear the crisis-a-day Bow to Paramount executives. That same year the star had a fling with the Hungarian actor Bela Lugosi, who was starring on the Los Angeles stage in *Dracula*. Then, in 1929, she fell in love with egotistical entertainer Harry Richman. This womanizer traded on her fame to gain publicity for himself. The couple had a much headlined on-again, off-again engagement before she finally realized his true nature and broke with him in 1930.

Bow had begun to lose enthusiasm for moviemaking in the late 1920s. She was tired of being showcased in thrown-together features that made Paramount a fortune but did nothing to help her grow as an actress. Then came talkies. She had a greater fear than most of the microphone. It was not just because it revealed her strong Brooklyn accent, but because the primitive sound equipment restricted her spontaneous, unbridled behavior in front of the camera. Her paranoia grew and it made moviemaking hellish for Clara.

In January 1931, Bow charged her former secretary (Daisy DeVoe) with 37 counts of grand theft. The high-profile trial ended with the plaintiff being the true victim: DeVoe revealed in court various gambling, romantic, and lifestyle indiscretions of her ex-employer. The scandal largely ruined Clara's reputation with moviegoers and caused her to have a nervous breakdown.

Paramount, meanwhile, wanted to end her expensive contract. Bow agreed, and the pact was terminated by "mutual" consent. At the time, she was only 25 years old.

Actor Rex Bell, who had been in the supporting cast of Bow's *True to the Navy* (1930), had already fallen in love with her. He stood by her through her courtroom turmoil and the aftermath and they wed in December 1931. They moved to his Nevada ranch. Later, Bow made two successful films at Fox Films. The second, 1933's *Hoopla*, was her last. She had had enough of being a movie star.

The Bells became the parents of two sons, and she doted on her children. Increasingly, she suffered from emotional and physical maladies, all of them accentuated when Bell decided to run for political office, ruining her desire for privacy. This led to the couple's separation, with her living modestly in seclusion in Los Angeles. Rex Bell, who became lieutenant governor of Nevada, died in 1962, and she made a rare public appearance to attend his funeral. The reclusive Clara Bow died of a heart attack in 1965.

Till the end of her life, Bow never appreciated how great a star she had been during her meteoric career. For Clara, stardom had been a tremendous ordeal: "Being a sex symbol is a heavy load to carry, especially when one is tired, hurt, and bewildered." As to entanglements with the opposite sex—which once had meant so much to her—she had concluded long ago: "The more I see of men, the more I like dogs."

Louise Brooks

(November 14, 1906–August 8, 1985)

French critic and filmmaker Adonis Kyrou wrote, "Louise [Brooks] is the perfect apparition, the dream woman, the being without whom the cinema would be a poor thing." Such fulsome praise was not uncommon for this unique actress, who started in American films in 1925 and made her last important feature in France in 1930. The impetuous, self-indulgent Brooks was only 23 when her career imploded. Her consolation later in life was becoming a cult figure in film circles.

Brooks was innovative in her jet-black bobbed hairstyle (likened by some, including critic Kenneth Tynan, to a black helmet). She was also ahead of her time in her subtle acting technique. Like several of her flapper screen characters, the vivacious Louise was very much a modern woman in her personal life: self-focused, daring, and outspoken. The forward-thinking Brooks once observed, "Love is a publicity stunt, and making love—after the first curious raptures—is only another petulant way to pass the time waiting for the studio to call." She also noted, "From the age of fifteen I was pursued by lesbians and I was attracted to them, but not sexually." Louise claimed that among her social set she was nicknamed "Hellcat" because she frequently told pals, "I like to drink and fuck."

• • •

Mary Louise Brooks was born in Cherryvale, Kansas, in 1906, the second of four children of Leonard Peter Brooks, a lawyer, and his young wife, Myra Rude. Early on, Mary Louise was attracted to dancing, and she made her artistic debut at 4 in a church-sponsored production. When she was 12, the family moved first to Independence, and then to Wichita, Kansas. In this more sophisticated setting, the girl enlarged her dance repertoire and performed professionally for local groups. At age 14, the sexually precocious Mary Louise became involved with a local businessman.

In November 1921, Brooks attended a performance of the touring Denishawn dance company. After the show she talked with its cofounder, Ted Shawn. He proposed that she enroll in the avant-garde troupe's training school in New York. With her parents' support, and accompanied by a chaperone (who was never able to control her reckless charge), the teenager moved to Manhattan in July 1922.

Louise Brooks—as she was now known—survived the Denishawn's grueling training regime. Next, she toured the United States with one of the school's performance groups. The willful Louise despised the troupe's regimentation, and she reacted by being ill-tempered and unruly. She also expended her frustration by having flings with members of the tour crew and men whom she encountered on the road. Eventually, at the end of the 1923–1924 season, Ruth St. Denis discharged Louise. The headstrong 17-year-old had no intention of returning home to the tame Midwest. She found work in the chorus line of *George White's Scandals* in mid-1924, where her insolent attitude caused difficulties with the producer. Meanwhile, the uninhibited showgirl was so unrestrained in her partying that she was asked to vacate her quarters at the Algonquin Hotel.

At the end of 1924, the spontaneous Brooks abandoned the *Scandals* and traveled to England. Within a few months, Louise returned to New York City and became a cast member of the musical *Louis the 14th*. Several weeks thereafter, the show's producer, Florenz Ziegfeld, reassigned the attention-grabbing iconoclast to the summer edition of his *Follies*. There she became pals with another chorine, Peggy Fears (who was supposedly bisexual).

In the summer of 1925, Louise had a glorious two-month tryst with screen comedy giant Charlie Chaplin who was in Manhattan on business and holiday. Later in the year, Brooks distracted herself from the tedium of *Follies* by making her movie debut. She was seen as a gun moll in the silent photoplay *The Streets of Forgotten Men*, shot at Paramount's Long Island facilities. (Her film entrée was engineered by producer Walter Wanger, with whom she had a brief affair.) Soon, she was offered a five-year studio deal, which a blasé Brooks accepted "just for the money." In the meantime, she generated a stir when she initiated legal action to stop a theatrical photographer from exhibiting draped nude shots for which she had posed. She claimed the photos might spoil her matrimonial opportunities.

During the filming of 1926's *It's the Old Army Game*, she was romanced by the movie's director, A. Edward Sutherland. The British-born filmmaker had divorced cinema actress Marjorie Daw in 1925. He and the 11-years-younger Brooksie (as pals called her) wed in July 1926. While she was quite fond of Sutherland, she was still in love with actor William (Buster) Collier Jr., with whom she had worked in *Just Another Blonde*. However, the handsome Buster was far too attached to his mother, and besides, he'd already returned to southern California. Brooks and Sutherland had only a few days for their honeymoon before he hurried back to Hollywood to direct a new movie. She remained in New York to make—on loan to Fox—1926's *Love 'Em and Leave 'Em*. Thereafter, she joined her husband in Los Angeles and began her tenure at Paramount's Hollywood film lot.

The adventurous, willful Louise Brooks displays her captivating, petulant look in the late 1920s.

Brooks made five features in 1927. Meanwhile, her marriage had become tenuous. Increasingly, each partner was relying on new companions for diversion. Buster Collier remained part of Louise's life, as did laundry entrepreneur George Preston Marshall, whom she had met a few years prior. In June 1928, Brooks and Sutherland ended their marital charade. After making 1929's *The Canary Murder Case*, the headstrong Brooks quit Paramount when they refused to raise her $750 salary as per her contract. Thereafter, accompanied by her possessive lover, George Marshall, Louise sailed for Europe. Her destination was Berlin, where she made the 1929 silent *Pandora's Box* for filmmaker G. W. Pabst. This was followed by another silent entry (*Diary of a Lost Girl*) that year, also with Pabst directing. When Brooks returned to the United States, she refused Paramount's offer of $10,000 to rush to Hollywood to film sound sequences for *The Canary Murder Case*. This imprudent act of defiance wrecked Louise's reputation with the major Hollywood studios. She went to France to make *Prix de Beauté*, directed by René Clair. Once back in the United States, she found occasional movie work, but her assignments were minimal and demeaning.

Having declared bankruptcy, Louise turned to a new marriage to solve her financial woes. She wed wealthy Chicago playboy Deering Davis in October 1933. They teamed briefly in a society dance act, but soon parted ways. (They finally divorced in February 1938.) Brooks created another dance act in New York City, and one of her lovers in this period was William Paley, the rising communications industry magnate. Later, she traveled to Hollywood, hoping for a comeback. However, after making 1938's *Overland Stage Raiders*, she quit films.

During the 1940s, Louise was based in Manhattan, where she had infrequent jobs on radio and was a salesclerk and a sometime escort for well-to-do men. By the end of the decade, she had become a recluse. In the 1950s, at the prompting of a curator (James Card) at the George Eastman House film collection, she moved to Rochester, New York. There she began studying movies and writing for film journals. In 1982 *Lulu in Hollywood*, her reminiscences of Golden Age Hollywood, was published. In August 1985, the once celebrated Louise Brooks died of a heart attack in Rochester, New York—alone and broke.

Charlie Chaplin
(April 16, 1889–December 25, 1977)

Charlie Chaplin was esteemed by film critics as the "King of Comedy." He was beloved by moviegoers for his baggy pants Little Tramp character, who wore oversized shoes and a too-small derby hat and twirled a cane. Off camera, the once impoverished Britisher who had become a worldwide success in Hollywood movies was far removed from his simplistic screen alter ego. He was erudite, aristocratic, and somewhat snobbish.

Chaplin, who had become a man of the world, once observed, "The most beautiful form of life is the very young girl just starting to bloom." To prove his point, he spent years pursuing nubile young women. Another time, he remarked, "Like everyone else's, my sex life went in cycles. Sometimes I was potent, other times disappointing." This seemed a modest comment from the star who claimed that he was exceptionally well-endowed and who was known for his remarkable sexual stamina. In the decades before he wed 17-year-old Oona O'Neill in 1943, Chaplin enjoyed many, many affairs. All of them contributed to his reputation as a great lover, and a few of them resulted in scandal.

• • •

Charles Spencer Chaplin was born in London, England, the only child of vaudevillian Charles Chaplin and his wife, Hannah Hill Chaplin, a music hall singer. (Hannah had another son, Sydney, from a previous relationship.) His father abandoned the family in 1890, later returned, and then died of alcoholism in 1901. His emotionally fragile mother was often confined to an insane asylum. Off and on, the two boys were dispatched to a workhouse or, sometimes, to an orphanage. Later on, Syd enlisted in the Royal Navy, while Charlie roamed the streets. The adolescent Chaplin made his acting debut in early 1900 on the London stage. By 1906, Chaplin had joined Fred Karno's music hall group, where Syd was already a troupe member. In Charlie's years with Karno, he not only refined his comedic

talents but also took note of his married boss's randy way with shapely chorus girls. This observation had a great impact on the impressionable young performer.

When Charlie was 19, he fell deeply in love with a 15-year-old chorine (Hetty Green). He soon proposed marriage, but she insisted she was too young to wed. They parted, but he never forgot Hetty. He was crushed to later learn that she had died in 1918. She remained his lifelong romantic ideal.

Chaplin traveled to the United States a few times with the Karno tour, and in 1913 agreed to make movies for Mack Sennett's Keystone Studio in Los Angeles. By 1915, Charlie had moved on from Sennett and was now a very well paid star of silent comedy shorts. That same year, he met Edna

Charlie Chaplin, one of the cinema's great clowns, found time to romance an assortment of young Tinseltown lovelies. He is shown here, in an advertisement for 1936's Modern Times, *with costar Paulette Goddard (Chaplin's third wife).*

Purviance, a blond onetime stenographer whom he chose to be his leading lady and his lover (despite the fact that she was an older woman of 20). However, the increasingly sophisticated Chaplin had no concept of faithfulness, and pursued liaisons with prostitutes and available young Hollywood beauties. Purviance hoped that Chaplin might eventually settle into domesticity, but he didn't. On impulse she embarked on an affair with screen notable Thomas Meighan. When Chaplin discovered this "betrayal," he ended their romance. However, he continued their working relationship. Even when Purviance left films, he continued to pay her a salary.

During 1916, Charlie met 14-year-old cinema performer Mildred Harris. Right away he was smitten by the very young beauty. Her shrewd mother, a wardrobe mistress, promoted the improbable relationship. In 1918, she advised Chaplin that Mildred was with child. He feared potential criminal prosecution and chose to wed her that October. It developed that her pregnancy was nonexistent. However, in 1919, she gave birth to a badly deformed baby boy, who died within three days. By now, Chaplin, who continued to play a humorous little bum on camera but enjoyed a life of refined elegance off camera, had fallen back on his habit of dallying with (would-be) young actresses in his studio dressing room suite. The death blow to his marriage was when Mildred returned to filmmaking and dared to bill herself as Mrs. Charlie Chaplin. The mismatched couple divorced in November 1920.

Having learned from the Harris debacle, Chaplin now directed his attention to more

seasoned women, including film actresses Pola Negri and Claire Windsor, playgirl beauty Peggy Hopkins Joyce, and sculptress Clare Sheridan. In the midst of Charlie's ardent relationship with Negri, a young Mexican lady named Marina Varga entered the comedian's life. Marina Varga had left her spouse in Vera Cruz to steal across the border. She was intent on meeting her film idol, Chaplin. One day, Charlie's servant found that Varga had snuck into Chaplin's house and was now encamped in the comedian's bed, garbed in a borrowed pair of the star's pajamas. The valet persuaded the interloper to get dressed and then Chaplin spoke a few pleasant words to the troubled soul as he coaxed her out of the house. The next day, the disturbed woman returned to Chaplin's home, lay down on the garden grass, and waited for the arsenic she had supposedly just consumed to take effect. A doctor was summoned and assessed that the woman was merely suffering from hysteria. Soon thereafter, Negri arrived at Chaplin's and discovered Marina there. The two women got into an intense squabble. Supposedly, the Little Tramp threw a bucket of water on the combatants to cool down their anger.

Chaplin hired adolescent Lita Grey for a small role in his 1921 feature film, *The Kid*. Three years later, he selected the fetching teenager to costar with him in his new project, *The Gold Rush*. It was not long before the filmmaker seduced her. She became pregnant and he proposed she have an abortion. When she refused, and her greedy relatives egged her on to threaten a paternity suit, a displeased Chaplin married her in November 1924. (They had two children: Charles Jr., born in 1925, and Sydney, born in 1926.) Meanwhile, Charlie replaced Grey in *The Gold Rush*. By early 1927, the constantly bickering Chaplins were on the verge of divorce. (During the marriage, he had continued his many dalliances, including with film stars Marion Davies and Louise Brooks.) To gain leverage, Lita's family arranged for publication of her divorce complaint. The lengthy document contained explicit, spicy details of the couple's love life, Chaplin's sexual preferences, and the comedian's extracurricular romps. A desperate Chaplin approved a $625,000 divorce settlement plus a $200,000 trust fund for their sons. By August 1928, he was a free man again.

In the 1930s, Chaplin made a successful transition to sound movies and even wed again (in June 1936), this time to the stunning, amusing, and highly ambitious screen actress Paulette Goddard, with whom he costarred in that year's *Modern Times*. His union to the 23-years-younger actress ended in a June 1942 divorce. While Chaplin's Goddard phase was ending, he met the Brooklyn-born Joan Barry in 1941. She was a wannabe actress who had a reputation for partying. Charlie put her under studio contract and took her to bed. She became pregnant at least twice, but agreed to abortions. Over time, she began drinking more heavily and behaving in an erratic manner. (On one occasion, to make her presence known, she pranced nude on his well-manicured front lawn.) He paid her to relocate to the East Coast, but, instead, she made a surprise visit to the star's mansion with gun in hand. (Later, she insisted that this deed had prompted a heated sexual reunion with Charlie.)

By this point, in 1942, Chaplin was courting playwright Eugene O'Neill's teenage daughter, Oona. Charlie intended to marry her and, once and for all, be through with Barry. The determined Joan struck back one day by sneaking into his house, disrobing, and jumping into his bed. This caper landed her in jail but she was soon released. Later, when she learned that she was pregnant and told Chaplin, he declared that the child was not his. Thereafter, the FBI had Chaplin arrested for, purportedly, violating the Mann Act (regarding interstate prostitution) in his affair with Barry. The movie star went through a hellish ordeal to prove that he was not guilty of the charges. Nevertheless, to quiet down the scandal, he agreed to pay Barry a weekly stipend until her child was born and blood tests could be taken to determine paternity. When the baby girl was born in October 1943, tests verified that Charlie was *not* the father. Nevertheless, the press and the public had already found Chaplin guilty. Because the medical testimony was not admissible in court at the time, Charlie lost the case and was ordered to support Joan's daughter.

In 1952, Charlie and Oona and their four children sailed for England. When Chaplin—who had never become an American citizen—was later barred from reentry to the United States because of alleged Communist sympathies and his past record of immorality, the Chaplins settled in Switzerland. There the couple had four more children. (The last one was born in 1963, when Charlie was 74.) Chaplin died in December 1977 at his 37-acre estate near Vevey, Switzerland.

Joan Collins

(May 23, 1933–)

Joan Collins has recalled of her mid-1950s arrival in Hollywood that her studio (Twentieth Century-Fox) saturated the media with stories—no matter how outrageous or untrue—about their latest contract leading lady. According to the plucky British actress: "I was maligned, scorned, criticized, lied about, and my fairly normal mode of living was considered scandalous and disgraceful. All of a sudden I found myself with a reputation as a raving sexpot, swinger and homewrecker whom Beverly Hills wives were supposed to live in fear of in case I cast my green 'orbs' in the direction of their men." Collins has maintained that "ninety-nine percent of this was total fabrication."

On the other hand, Joan's sister, Jackie Collins, the best-selling novelist, has observed of her famous sibling: "She always lived her life like a man. If she saw a guy she wanted to go to bed with, she went after him, and that was unacceptable behavior at the time." Over several decades of international fame, Joan married five times. In addition, over the years she enjoyed a large array of lovers. They included actors (Warren Beatty, Sydney Chaplin, Terence Stamp, and Ryan O'Neal), a playboy (Nicky Hilton), a film producer (George Englund), businessmen (Arthur Loew Jr. and Peter Thereodoracopolis), and an art dealer (Robin Hurlstone). Like her alter ego Alexis Carrington Colby on the 1980s nighttime TV soap opera *Dynasty*, Joan Collins unapologetically indulged her voracious appetite for the opposite sex.

• • •

Joan Henrietta Collins was born in London, England, in 1933, the oldest of three children (besides sister, Jacqueline, there would be a brother, William). Her parents were Joseph William Collins, a vaudeville booking agent, and Elsa Bessant Collins, a

The frisky Joan Collins with Paul Newman in 1958's Rally 'Round the Flag, Boys!

housewife (who was overprotective of her offspring). As a youngster Joan was introverted. She dreamed of one day breaking out of her shyness and becoming a movie star. During her school years in London, the aspiring actress made her professional stage bow in a West End presentation of *A Doll's House*. Within two years, she had quit conventional academics to enroll at the Royal Academy of Dramatic Art.

To supplement the allowance provided by her father, Collins modeled. She was spotted by casting executives at Rank Organization, a leading British film firm, and placed under studio contract. She made her movie debut in 1951's *Lady Godiva Rides Again*. During her starlet phase, Collins became entranced with actor Maxwell Reed, who was 14 years her senior. The couple wed in 1952, but it was an uneasy alliance. He was a heavy drinker, violently jealous concerning her, and physically abusive toward her. (Later, she asserted that he once attempted to trade her to an elderly, obese Arab sheik for £10,000.) The disastrous marriage ended when the couple filed for divorce in April 1956. By then, Hollywood movie studio chieftain Darryl F. Zanuck had become interested in her and signed the actress to a seven-year contract at Twentieth Century-Fox. Once in Los Angeles, the self-assured and high spirited Collins fought being typecast on screen as the sexpot (such as in 1956's *The Opposite Sex*). As a result, she often found herself on studio suspension.

With so much free time, the fiery British bachelorette was a frequent figure on the Tinseltown social scene. During this period, the media tagged the pleasure-seeking Joan with such labels as "the British bombshell" and "the streamlined vamp." One of Collins's liaisons—with Hollywood heartthrob Warren Beatty—led to an engagement and her aborting their baby. The end of the affair between the two hedonists was inevitable.

After concluding her Twentieth Century-Fox pact, Collins returned to England. There she fell in love with multitalented entertainer Anthony Newley. She claimed to be "obsessed with the bloody man," adding, "I thought he was a genius." They wed in May 1963. During their seven-year union, she gave birth to their two children (Tara and Alexander [known as Sacha]), had an affair with actor Ryan O'Neal, and, infrequently, accepted screen jobs. Collins finally acknowledged that Newley would never abandon his passion for very young women, and she was divorced from him in August 1971.

Subsequently, she met record industry executive Ron Kass. According to Collins: "He was the man I had been searching for all my life, and I didn't want to injure our blossoming friendship and love by jumping instantly into bed." The duo married in March 1972; their daughter, Katyana, was born that June. Later, the Kasses relocated from London to Los Angeles. Occasionally, Joan appeared in movies. By the late 1970s, Kass had become a film producer, and he collaborated with his wife to make such films as *The Stud* and its sequel, *The Bitch*, based on sister Jackie's best-selling novels. These pictures revived Collins's currency within show business circles.

In 1980, Collins's 8-year-old daughter Katyana suffered severe brain damage in a car accident. In order to pay the tremendous medical bills and to distract herself from her child's serious condition (which ultimately improved), Collins agreed to almost any employment offer. One of these was for the TV series *Dynasty*. Playing the stylish and calculating heavy in this prime-time offering quickly made her extremely popular. In 1983, she filed for divorce from Kass. Then, in October 1985, the sleek Collins married the much younger Peter Holm, a Swedish pop vocalist/businessman. Soon he became her financial adviser. Belatedly, she discovered that the arrangement was enormously to his advantage and hugely to her detriment. This unlikely match burned out in less than two years. After a nasty court battle in which he sought an enormous settlement and ongoing monthly alimony, Holm accepted a far more modest sum when the couple divorced in August 1987.

Over more recent decades, besides acting in films, writing novels and memoirs, and dating (including having a long-term relationship with art dealer Robin Hurlstone), Collins performed on stage. While touring the United States in *Love Letters*, she became friendly with Peruvian Percy Gibson, a theater manager, who was the same age (mid-30s) as her son, Sacha. Collins ignored the objections of pals and the amazement of the media, and she and the congenial Gibson wed in February 2002 at an elegant ceremony in London.

In the new millennium, Collins continued to guest star on TV series (such as *The Guiding Light* and *Footballers' Wives*). In 2006, she authored the upbeat *The Art of Living Well: Looking Good, Feeling Great*, which explained her lifestyle philosophy as a chic and privileged survivor. In 2007, the vivacious Collins joined with Linda Evans (another *Dynasty* veteran) in a stage tour revival of the comedy *Legends!*

Tony Curtis

(June 3, 1925–)

In the late 1950s, the charismatic Tony Curtis—he of the dark curly hair, flashing blue eyes, and lithe physique—was reaching the peak of his box-office popularity and had been Oscar-nominated for his dramatic performance in 1958's *The Defiant Ones*. During an interview that year he pondered his meteoric career rise. "You know where the real trouble lies with a guy like me? You go too far too fast. So—you begin to think about it. . . . You're on a quick ride and going great, but the question always is: Are you really talented or just dumb lucky?" The answer was a mixture of both. As for Curtis's acting career, it continued on for several more decades as he evolved from matinee idol to character lead.

Of equal and sometimes paramount interest to the impetuous Curtis throughout these years was his enormous sexual drive. His libido led him into encounters with many women. Some liaisons ended after a night, others led to a passionate fling or, in five instances, to marriage. Looking back, the woman-chasing star observed, "It was the lusty-looking ones, breasty and voluptuous in the hips, that I found most fascinating, maybe because my mother was built like that."

•   •   •

He was born Bernard Schwartz in 1925 in New York City, the first of three sons of Emanuel and Helen Klein Schwartz, both Jewish immigrants from Hungary. (The second child, Julius, died when he was 9— he had been run over by a truck. The last born, Robert, was a schizophrenic who died in 1992 after years of institutionalization.) Mr. Schwartz operated a tailor shop, while his volatile, sometimes brutal wife ran roughshod over the family. By age 14, the cocky Bernard dreamed only of becoming a movie star. When he was 18, he quit high school to enlist in the Navy for World War II service. After the armistice in 1945, he took acting classes in Manhattan and worked in low-rate stock companies. Later, while appearing in an off-Broadway show, he was noticed by a talent scout from Universal-International Pictures and signed to a studio pact. He made his screen debut in 1949's *Criss Cross*.

As a movie contract player he did yeoman service on camera in a wide variety of genres. The studio renamed the swarthy, Italian-looking young stud Anthony Curtis. (This was soon shortened to Tony Curtis.) Recalling his early filmmaking years, the actor noted, "I went around with a lump in my pants and chased all the girls. That is what I reflected on the screen." During this period, Curtis devoted tremendous energy

A young Tony Curtis sharing a romantic moment with Piper Laurie in 1952's The Son of Ali Baba.

and a great deal of time to pursuing liaisons with actresses on the lot and about town, including Suzan Ball, Ann Blyth, Susan Cabot, Peggy Dow, Anita Ekberg, Coleen Gray, Wanda Hendrix, Piper Laurie, and Mamie Van Doren, as well as movie newcomer Marilyn Monroe.

While Curtis was climbing up the Hollywood ladder, his parents and brother relocated to Los Angeles and made Tony their financial caretaker. He escaped some of these stressful emotional ties when, in June 1951, he wed pretty Janet Leigh, a twice-divorced MGM contract leading lady. At the time, Curtis was more entranced by his wife's impressive figure and industry status than by her acting expertise. The fan magazines hyped the nuptials and the newlyweds became Hollywood's most popular young couple. They teamed for 1953's *Houdini*, the first of five costarring vehicles. Over the next several years, they became the parents of two daughters, including future movie star Jamie Lee Curtis. By the late 1950s, Curtis was increasingly womanizing and drinking. The unhappy couple divorced in June 1962.

Curtis became entranced with the 19-years-younger Christine Kaufmann, a German actress with whom he made 1962's *Taras Bulba*. They wed in February 1963, had two children, and, by April 1968, were divorced. By then, his long-term Universal contract had ended and his film output was a mixed bag of efforts. While making 1968's *The Boston Strangler* in Massachusetts, the veteran leading man romanced a 23-year-old local model named Leslie Allen. They wed that April. The couple had two children. By 1974, around the time the hard-partying Curtis was introduced to cocaine, the union had become tenuous. According to the star, the estrangement "wasn't necessarily because of drugs, but the drug use contributed to it. . . . After two or three pipefuls, you say, What wife? What infidelity?" The pair finally divorced in 1982.

In 1971, Curtis had costarred with Roger Moore in *The Persuaders!*, an adventure TV series produced in England. It lasted but one season. In the coming years he headlined other teleseries without great success, and his feature film efforts (such as 1978's *The Manitou*) were decidedly unstellar. During the next decade, the high point of his picture-making was 1985's *Insignificance* (in which

he played Senator Joe McCarthy); the nadir was 1989's *Lobster Man from Mars*.

By the early 1990s, Curtis, now a feisty senior citizen, had lessened his substance abuse, reduced his once lavish lifestyle, continued with his avocation of painting, and remained his most charming self when a pretty *young* woman was nearby. A chance meeting with Lisa Deutch, a 30-year-old attorney, led to a courtship and a February 1993 marriage. Despite the couple's initial enthusiasm about their future together, they soon realized the nuptials had been a mistake. They divorced in 1994. Thereafter, in November 1998, Curtis, ever the game swinger, marched down the aisle anew. This time his bride was Jill Vandenberg, a horseback-riding instructor, who was three inches taller than he and 45 years his junior. The ceremony was held in a swank Las Vegas hotel suite and the groom sported a new face-lift. The ebullient Curtis boasted, "I may be 73, but Jill tells me I'm still the best guy she's ever had."

Moving into the new millennium, Curtis appeared in a 2002 stage tour of *Some Like It Hot*, a revival of the musical based on the 1959 hit movie he made with Marilyn Monroe and Jack Lemmon. The dapper veteran star remained energetic and enthusiastic about life. He noted "Since I'm [still] married to a young, gorgeous lady, that isn't difficult to accomplish." In late 2006, however, he suffered a siege of serious health problems, including colon surgery. Nevertheless, the buoyant Curtis remained optimistic about the quality of his future, insisting, "I'm no quitter."

Marlene Dietrich

(December 27, 1901–May 6, 1992)

Marlene Dietrich was perhaps the cinema's most exotic star. She noted, "Glamour is what I sell; it's my stock in trade." Hollywood may have (re)packaged Dietrich in the early 1930s to emphasize better her sensual allure for American moviegoers, but Dietrich was her own amazing creation. As a performer, the German actress provided an enticing mixture of fantasy and mystery that captivated her public for several decades. She thought of her celebrated persona in the third person, and devoted herself to perfecting the illusion on the screen. This dedicated, crafty professional left little to chance in showcasing herself, tirelessly intent on perpetuating her mythic stature as one of the 20th century's greatest femme fatales.

Off screen, the pragmatic, calculating celebrity envisioned herself as a hausfrau who happened to have a demanding career in the public eye. In her private life, the narcissist was often a nurturing soul—especially to her man of the moment, but rarely to her shunted-aside daughter, who grew up in her shadow. (By the early 1930s, the star's only marriage had evolved into a stagnant situation in which each partner led a largely separate life.)

Dietrich professed, "No man falls in love with me that I don't want to have fall in love with me." She might have added women to that statement. Just as Marlene popularized the fashion of women wearing slacks, so in her love life was she bisexual. Like other sophisticated screen leading ladies of Dietrich's era—including Greta Garbo, Katharine Hepburn, and Kay Francis—the cosmopolitan Marlene gravitated back and forth between male and female love partners. It was an avant-garde lifestyle at the time, but love goddess Dietrich felt she owed it to herself to sample whoever took her fancy.

• • •

Maria Magdalena Dietrich was born in 1901 in Schöneberg, Germany, a suburb of Berlin. She was the second daughter of Prussian police officer Louis Dietrich and Wilhelmina Felsing Dietrich. Her father died when she was 9, and her mother later married Edouard von Losch, a German army officer. Wilhelmina was a stringent disciplinarian, which strongly impacted her daughters, especially Maria.

As a youngster, Maria dreamed of becoming a performer. In her teens, she played the violin, but was forced to stop when she suffered a wrist injury. Meanwhile, she'd already experienced her first love affair (with her far older music instructor). By 1921, the ambitious Maria was taking acting classes in Berlin and winning small parts in stage dramas and revues. Now known as Marlene Dietrich, she auditioned at the film studios, eventually being hired for screen parts, as in 1923's *Die Tragödie der Liebe*.

The bisexual Marlene Dietrich wears an androgynous outfit in her first Hollywood-made feature, 1930's Morocco. *The nightclub owner is played by Paul Porcasi.*

Dietrich's entry into moviemaking had been eased by Rudolf Sieber, an assistant director who quickly became enamored of the spirited, plump young performer. The couple wed in May 1924. The next January, their only child, Maria, was born. Unconcerned with the responsibilities of marriage or motherhood, Marlene pursued a vigorous social life, which encompassed liaisons with both men and women. She mingled with Berlin's young intelligentsia, including future filmmaker Billy Wilder (who would direct her in 1948's *A Foreign Affair*) and writer Erich Maria Remarque (with whom she engaged in an off-and-on affair over the

decades, ultimately losing him to cinema star Paulette Goddard).

Hollywood's Paramount Pictures assigned movie director Josef von Sternberg to travel to Germany to shoot 1930's *Der Blaue Engel* (The Blue Angel). He hired Dietrich to play the lead role of the unprincipled cabaret singer. The studio was so pleased with its new release that they contracted Marlene to come to America to make a follow-up film with von Sternberg. She blithely left her husband and daughter behind in Germany as she smoldered through 1930's *Morocco* in Tinseltown and had an affair with her handsome leading man, Gary Cooper. She also continued her intense, complicated relationship with von Sternberg, which led his infuriated wife to sue Dietrich for alienation of affections. Meanwhile, the strikingly beautiful actress and von Sternberg collaborated on such other pictures as 1932's *Shanghai Express* and 1935's *The Devil Is a Woman*.

During this exciting period, Dietrich perfected being the grand star on the sound stage, becoming increasingly demanding about every aspect of her career. Between screen vehicles, she indulged in a wide assortment of overlapping romances (including with cinema stars Maurice Chevalier, John Gilbert, and Kay Francis, as well as author Mercedes de Acosta) that only a highly disciplined luminary of Marlene's level could have accomplished. By now, the star's daughter, Maria, was living with her mother in Los Angeles but rarely saw her self-absorbed parent. (Dietrich's spouse, Sieber, was then residing in Paris with Russian dancer Tamara Matul.

They remained together until her passing in 1968. He died in June 1976, at the southern California chicken farm that Dietrich had purchased for him.)

After 1936's *Desire* (which reteamed Marlene with Gary Cooper) and the anemic *Angel* in 1937, Paramount's new management felt it could survive without the costly, difficult Dietrich. Two years later, she made a stunning comeback in Universal's *Destry Rides Again*, in which she teased her past image as an aloof sex siren. (During the filming of this Western, she had an affair with her leading man, James Stewart.) A trio of her early 1940s features (such as 1942's *Pittsburgh*) teamed Marlene with her new lover, John Wayne. To pacify him, she devoted some of their time together to hunting and fishing trips, although such outdoor diversions were not to her liking.

In the 1930s, Dietrich had refused the "requests" of dictator Adolf Hitler that she return to Germany to star in movies exalting the Third Reich. To underscore her deep allegiance to the United States, she became an American citizen in 1938. During World War II, she was an indefatigable volunteer at the Hollywood Canteen, embarked on nationwide war bond–selling tours, and performed overseas (often in combat zones) for the troops. Less known at the time of her many USO tours was that she had sexual flings with Allied officers. When her schedule and wartime conditions allowed, she reunited with French movie star Jean Gabin, who was then serving with the Free French Army. (She and Gabin had had a passionate relationship in late 1930s France and, later, when he was

in Hollywood. After the armistice, they teamed for one film together—1946's *Martin Roumagnac*—but their romance burned out soon thereafter.)

Now in her mid-40s, Dietrich revamped her glamorous image to adjust to changing tastes. Among other new cinema vehicles, she paired with Ray Milland for 1947's *Golden Earrings*. By this time, Marlene's daughter had married for a second time, and the couple had their first child in 1948. Dietrich manipulated the situation to publicize herself as the "World's Most Glamorous Grandmother."

The 1950s found Marlene headlining a radio program (*Café Istanbul*), making records, and starring in occasional movies (such as 1952's *Rancho Notorious*). She continued to enjoy an assortment of romantic trysts, with actor Yul Brynner, singers Frank Sinatra and Eddie Fisher, composer Burt Bacharach, and politician John F. Kennedy, among others. She also had a close relationship with her protégée, vocalist Marti Stevens. Meanwhile, Marlene embarked on a new phase of her lengthy career: as an elegant cabaret chanteuse. Her live performances continued well into the 1970s. By then, advancing age and growing alcoholism had caught up with her. She retired her stage act and went into seclusion at her Paris apartment. She made a brief return to moviemaking—receiving $250,000 for two days' work—in 1979's *Just a Gigolo*. Dietrich devoted the remainder of her life to protecting her exalted legend. She died in May 1992 in Paris, and was buried next to her mother at the Friedenau cemetery in Schöneberg.

Errol Flynn

(June 20, 1909–October 14, 1959)

Devil-may-care Errol Flynn seemed to have it all. The six-foot-two-inch, 175-pound actor was handsome, charming, and literate. He led an amazingly raucous life both before and after he became a successful film actor in the mid-1930s. He quickly became Hollywood's leading swashbuckling star and had the thrill of playing out on camera all those adventurous fantasies of which boys' dreams are made. He was extremely well paid for his celluloid capering.

Off the sound stages, the suave Flynn had a reputation as a world-class carouser who—when not getting into drunken scuffles at nightclubs—bedded an impressive number of nubile young women. (The rumor mill alleged that he also acted upon his sexual attraction to men.) Flynn felt compelled to measure up to his reputation as a 20th-century Casanova, explaining, "The public has always expected me to be a playboy, and a decent chap never lets his public down." (Another time, he bemoaned, "I'm just a goddamned phallic symbol to the world.")

The dapper Errol noted, "I like my whisky old and my women young." He admitted, "I don't have to seduce girls. For Christ's sake, I come home and they're hiding under my bed." As for his attraction to prostitutes: "I enter a whorehouse with the same interest as I do the British Museum or the Metropolitan—in the same spirit of curiosity. Here are the works of man, here is

an art of man, here is his eternal pursuit of gold and pleasure."

Despite Flynn's wild playboy lifestyle, he wed three times: "Women won't let me stay single, and I won't let myself stay married."

• • •

Errol Leslie Thomson Flynn was born in 1909 in Hobart, the capital of Tasmania, an island south of Australia. His father, Theodore, was a marine biologist and his self-interested mother, Lily, was preoccupied entertaining her men friends. When Errol was 11, his sister, Rosemary, was born and the family moved to Sydney, Australia. (Eventually, Mrs. Flynn decamped for France, forcing her spouse to seek romance elsewhere.) By 17, the robust Errol had become a ladies' man with a penchant for being an exhibitionist. (The unruly teenager had also been dismissed from his school.) Errol tried being a civil servant in New Guinea but failed at the task. Later, Flynn managed a copra plantation and, thereafter, prospected for gold. He and a friend purchased a small schooner and took a passenger, Dr. Herman Erben, on an expedition through the waters of New Guinea so he could shoot a travelogue. (Supposedly, the trek turned out to be a covert intelligence operation on behalf of Germany. Later, Erben allegedly recruited Flynn to help the Nazi cause during World War II.)

The good-looking Flynn was filmed as part of the Erben expedition and this "screen test" led to his being cast in a 1933 movie, the Australian-made *In the Wake of the Bounty*. Errol followed his film debut with sojourns to Manila, Hong Kong, Ceylon, India, and Marseille. When he moved on to England, he gravitated toward stage repertory work in the provinces, then appeared on the London stage. He was in *Murder at Monte Carlo*, a 1934 film turned out by Warner Bros.' British facility. This prompted the American studio to bring him to southern California. During the transatlantic crossing, Flynn met Lili Damita, the fiery French actress, who was returning to California to make more movies. According to her, she and Errol experienced love at first sight. She was eight years his senior and proved quite cooperative about introducing him to the right film colony crowd. The duo wed in May 1935, but this did not prevent his ongoing womanizing, which encompassed a fling with Hollywood-based Mexican actress Lupe Velez. Flynn was handed the lead in 1935's *Captain Blood*, which was directed by Damita's ex-husband, Michael Curtiz. The picture's success led to Flynn's starring in other romantic, swashbuckling entries.

Thanks to such well-received features as 1938's *The Adventures of Robin Hood*, Flynn became a major success. Although still wed to the tempestuous Damita, he continued to seduce an impressive number of women. During one of the couple's many reconciliations, she became pregnant. Their son, Sean, was born in May 1941. The next year (in April), he and Lili divorced. Due to health problems, Flynn, a naturalized U.S. citizen, was classified 4-F during World War II. This allowed him to remain on the home front and headline such movies as 1942's *Gentleman Jim*.

One of the star's sexual conquests in the early 1940s was 15-year-old Peggy LaRue Saterlee, an aspiring actress. Another underage bed partner in this period was Betty Hansen. Such activity led the Los Angeles District Attorney to prosecute Flynn on charges of statutory rape. Rarely had a courtroom case garnered such global attention. The starstruck jury acquitted the movie star. (The scandal spawned a sexual catchphrase—in like Flynn—that was forever associated with the celebrity defendant.)

This notorious episode brought Flynn his next wife, Nora Eddington, the 18-year-old daughter of a Los Angeles sheriff. (During the courtroom hearings, she had been working at the cigar counter at the Los Angeles

The ever debonair Errol Flynn, with S. Z. Sakall (center) and Alexis Smith in 1950's Montana.

County Hall of Justice.) They wed in August 1943 and had two daughters: Deidre (in 1945) and Rory (in 1947). During the couple's extremely rocky relationship, he persisted in his philandering, including having a liaison with Argentina's Eva Peron and various trysts in Acapulco, Panama, and Jamaica (where he had acquired an estate). Eddington won her Nevada divorce in July 1949. (However, even years later, she still carried a torch for Flynn, saying, "I wish I could hate him. But I can't. No one can.")

By 1950, Errol's hectic lifestyle had prematurely aged him, but he continued to make films—albeit lesser vehicles. While shooting 1950's *Rocky Mountain* he fell head over heels in love with his 24-year-old blond leading lady, Patrice Wymore. They wed in October 1950, and their child, Arnella, was born in 1953. One of Flynn's last substantial movie roles was in 1958's *Too Much, Too Soon*, in which he portrayed his onetime drinking buddy, movie and stage star John Barrymore. While filming that picture, Flynn became involved with a 15-year-old would-be actress, Beverly Aadland. At the time, he was still married to Wymore.

Aadland became Flynn's constant companion and they appeared together in 1959's *Cuban Rebel Girls*, a truly shoddy yarn. A few weeks after Errol's 50th birthday, he suffered a heart attack and was informed that he had, perhaps, a year to live. He shrugged off the deadly news and continued to lead a dissipated lifestyle. Months thereafter, he and Beverly flew to Vancouver, British Columbia, to sell his $100,000 yacht (he was deeply in debt at the time). He died there in October 1959, of another heart attack. Later, Aadland's mother, a former chorine, sued Flynn's estate for $5 million, alleging he had debauched her daughter with his "perverted philosophy for wringing every pleasure out of life." The suit was dismissed.

Even at the end, the hard-living, self-indulgent, woman-chasing Flynn, who had "seen everything twice," got his way. He had said once: "I intend to live the first half of my life. I don't care about the rest." He got his wish.

Ava Gardner

(December 24, 1922–January 25, 1990)

Like such other noteworthy sex symbols of Hollywood's golden age as Jean Harlow, Rita Hayworth, Lana Turner, Elizabeth Taylor, and Marilyn Monroe, the tantalizingly beautiful Ava Gardner never achieved a satisfying marriage. Gardner claimed, "I found the love of my life three times. The pity is my husbands didn't also find it."

Gardner also pointed out, "All I ever got out of any of my marriages was the two years Artie Shaw [spouse number two] financed on an analyst's couch."

Eventually, Gardner became cynical and reckoned that pursuing blissful romance was not worth the bother (or as the bawdy lady phrased it, "Love is nothing but a pain [in the ass]).” Instead, she adopted the practice long favored by men: passionate flings that ended when the lust flickered out. On the other hand, the self-reliant Gardner, once a simple country girl, had an excessively sentimental streak. When her first husband (movie star Mickey Rooney) fell on financial hard times in later life, Ava mailed him a check with the amount left blank. Her third and final mate, crooner Frank Sinatra, was the consuming passion of her hectic life. Even though the two of them were too combustible and self-focused to live together, they remained extremely fond of each other.

• • •

Ava Lavinia Gardner was born in Grabtown, North Carolina, in 1922. She was the seventh and last child of Jonas Bailey Gardner, a tobacco sharecropper, and his wife, Mary Elizabeth “Molly” Baker. Ava’s impoverished childhood (during which she often went barefoot) grew worse in 1932 when, during the Great Depression, Mr. Gardner became unemployed. (He died two years later.) Her mother took Ava and her sister Myra to be with her in Smithfield, where she ran a boardinghouse. They moved often, depending upon where Mrs. Gardner found a boardinghouse to operate. After high school, Ava attended Atlantic Christian College, intending to become a secretary. However, at the time, she had little ambition in life.

In the summer of 1941, Ava visited her eldest sister, Beatrice (called Bappie), in New York City. Bappie’s husband was a photographer and he asked Ava to pose for a layout. The results were displayed in the Fifth Avenue store where he worked. An MGM employee noticed the photos in the shop window and was so captivated by the model’s looks that he circulated copies of them at the film company’s New York office. This led to Gardner’s being screen-tested. MGM signed the radiant young woman with a thick Southern accent and no acting experience to a $50-a-week contract.

Ava had been at the Culver City–based studio for just a week when she met Mickey Rooney on the lot. He was three inches shorter than she, but he was then the studio’s biggest star. Ava was not particularly impressed by his industry status, but Rooney was agog over her. Thanks to his dogged persistence, he and Gardner began to date. He even gave her acting tips for her first movie (a bit in 1942’s *We Were Dancing*). The couple married in January 1942. MGM demanded that a publicity department member “chaperone” them on their honeymoon in northern California. Gardner soon discovered that Rooney was more interested in gambling, playing golf, and carousing with his buddies than in establishing a workable marriage. With her strong ego, she rapidly grew annoyed at being known as Mrs. Mickey Rooney. The incompatible duo divorced in May 1943, on the same day her mother succumbed to breast cancer.

At MGM, the stunning Ava was tossed into several B pictures, in which she slowly learned her craft. Off the sound stages, she dated an assortment of bachelors and married men, including actors Peter Lawford, Turhan Bey, and Robert Walker. These episodes were a mere warm-up for her complicated relationship with billionaire industrialist/filmmaker Howard Hughes.

He was as weird and indecisive with her as he had been with countless other Hollywood actresses. Her veneer of indifference piqued Hughes's interest in her. Her refusal to be at his beck and call—not to mention her unfaithfulness—sparked his jealousy. The twosome got into heated arguments and even brawls. They parted repeatedly, but somehow he could not leave her alone.

During one of Gardner's several separations from Hughes, she met famed band-

Ava Gardner living up to her seductive screen image in 1946's The Killers, *with Burt Lancaster.*

leader Artie Shaw, who already had been married four times (including to MGM's Lana Turner). The mismatched pair wed in October 1945. The groom devoted much of their honeymoon to trying to improve her mind. In typical Shaw fashion, he was soon criticizing her in public regarding her unsophisticated background. (One time, he yelled at her in front of others: "For God's sake, what are you doing? Do you think you're still in a tobacco field?") The two put an end to their domestic misery in October 1946. By then, Gardner had visions of abandoning acting and pursuing a higher education. MGM promptly convinced her to discard that notion.

In the mid-1940s, Gardner received her best acting showcases on loan to other studios, as with 1946's *The Killers*. Both the film and Ava earned solid notices. At last, MGM decided to groom her as competition for the lot's resident movie sexpot, Lana Turner. Gardner again began dating Hughes, but she found she could not tolerate his demands (let alone his strong body odor). Meanwhile, the new person in Ava's increasingly reckless life was handsome actor Howard Duff. Like several others, he was overwhelmed by the combination of her beauty and the vulnerability beneath her shell of toughness. However, he was unsure how to deal with this complicated woman. They parted in 1949. By the end of the decade, Gardner had become increasingly jaded about her rags-to-riches life and bitter about her unchallenging movie career. These feelings led to her bouts of heavy drinking and carousing.

Because Gardner and Frank Sinatra both

worked for MGM in the 1940s, they sometimes encountered each other on the lot. Initially, they disliked each other, but by 1950, these feelings changed to passion. By then, Sinatra, married and the father of three, was in a career decline, which brought out the mothering/dominating aspects of Gardner's nature. Before long, she was as fixated on him as he was on her. MGM urged them to break up for the sake of their careers. This only encouraged the rebellious Ava to chase Frank all the more. The studio did not want to lose their rising box-office star, and kept Gardner working (such as on 1951's *Pandora and the Flying Dutchman*). However, the hard-to-manage Sinatra was considered dispensable, and his MGM contract was terminated.

While filming *Pandora* on location, Gardner came to adore Spain and found herself irresistibly attracted to bullfighters. This fueled spats between her and the highly jealous Sinatra (who would soon be a bachelor again). Finally, Ava and Frank patched up their differences and wed in November 1951.

When Gardner went to Africa to make 1953's *Mogambo*, Sinatra was slowly coming out of his professional freefall. She helped matters by arranging for him to screen-test at Columbia Pictures for *From Here to Eternity*, a film job he passionately wanted. He got the part and won a Best Supporting Actor Oscar for his efforts. Meanwhile, as he regained his show business standing, she progressively grew less interested in preserving their relationship. (This prompted her to have an abortion to spite him.) Each of them had been having flings on the side,

and they finally called it quits in 1954 (even though their divorce did not become official until 1957). Once their domestic battle scars healed, they became friends. In subsequent years, Sinatra often came to Gardner's financial and emotional rescue.

After shooting 1956's *Bhowani Junction*, Gardner made Madrid her new home base. There, her wild living included romances with assorted Spanish matadors as well as the Italian actor Walter Chiari. Of the latter, she assessed, "Walter was *nice*." However, she noted, "The distance that separates liking from love is as wide as the Pacific."

By 1959, her MGM contract had expired. Thereafter, she had an occasional solid film role (such as in 1964's *The Night of the Iguana*). Unfortunately, her years of reckless living had taken a toll on her beauty. When she played in 1966's *The Bible*, she had a scorching romance with abusive costar George C. Scott. In later years, she accepted acting gigs only for the "loot." (Long ago, she had concluded that being a movie star was "a big damn bore.") Her last performances were for television, including an appearance on the series *Knots Landing* in 1985.

By the mid-1970s, Ava had relocated to London. Her escorts included the Spanish financier Riccardo Sicre and the young singer Freddie Davies. By the latter 1980s, she was plagued by poor health, including strokes. The once-vivacious Gardner became a recluse. In her final years, she worked on her memoir (*Ava, My Story*). She died of bronchial pneumonia in January 1990, not living to see her book published. She was buried in Smithfield, North Carolina, in the family plot.

Lorenzo Lamas

(January 20, 1958–)

Considering his genes, it was almost inevitable that Lorenzo Lamas would grow up to be a handsome hunk. His father was Argentina-born Fernando Lamas, a handsome big-screen leading man in his homeland and in Hollywood, and his mother is Arlene Dahl, the ravishing red-headed leading lady of many 1940s and 1950s Tinseltown features. From his lothario dad, Lorenzo inherited a heavy dose of swaggering machismo; from his mom, who has been wed six times, he developed the itch to jump in and out of matrimony. To date, Lorenzo Lamas, a veteran TV soap opera and action movie/teleseries star, has been married four times, broken off several engagements, and has six children.

● ● ●

Lorenzo y de Santos Lamas was born in 1958 in Santa Monica, California, the only child of strikingly attractive movie stars Fernando Lamas and Arlene Dahl. When the boy was 2, his parents divorced. For the next several years, Lorenzo lived largely with his father, who, in 1969, wed his former costar Esther Williams. (She was the celebrated aquatic star who had splashed her way through many profitable MGM musicals during the 1940s and 1950s.) When Lorenzo was 13, he moved to New York with his mother. He spent the next four years on the East Coast at the Admiral Farragut Academy, from which he graduated in 1975.

Lorenzo had made his screen debut in a bit role in 1969's *100 Rifles*, a Hollywood action picture featuring his dad. After completing his military school education, the teenager returned to the West Coast. His actor/director father encouraged him to take acting classes, so he would be equipped for the show business career he now wanted. His preparations led to small guest roles on TV and then a tiny part in the screen musical *Grease*. By now, Lorenzo was six feet two inches and had a strapping build. His appealing physical presence was sufficient to make the newcomer professionally in demand. After being a regular on a short-lived TV drama series, he was hired to play the conniving playboy role on *Falcon Crest*, a prime-time TV soap opera that ran from 1981 to 1990.

With a steady income, a great smile, and a winning look, Lorenzo had his pick of appealing dates. However, his bachelor lifestyle ended in 1981 when he married model Victoria Hilbert, an aspiring actress whom he had asked to move in with him after their third date. That brief union came to an end in 1982, the same year Fernando Lamas died. In 1983, Lorenzo wed actress Michelle Smith, with whom he had two children. Their marriage ended in 1985. A few years later, Lamas was in a serious relationship with actress Daphne Ashbrook. Although they did not wed, they had a child in 1988. Thereafter, the couple split up. In January 1989, he tried marriage yet again:

this time with actress Kathleen Kinmont, the daughter of Abby Dalton, who had costarred with Lamas for several years on *Falcon Crest.*

With his expertise in karate and his love of racing fast cars and motorcycles (and piloting private planes), the handsome Lorenzo turned to making action features (such as 1989's *Snake Eater*). By the fall of 1992, he was starring in his own syndicated teleseries, *Renegade*, a fast-paced action entry. One of his costars was his wife, Kathleen. This could have presented a problem when the couple divorced in 1994. However, Kinmont remained friendly with her ex-husband and continued to appear in some episodes of the show through 1996, a year before the series went off the air.

Ever optimistic, Lorenzo wed for the fourth time in April 1996. His bride was Shauna Sand, a striking blonde who had been a *Playboy* Playmate. The couple's wedding date was chosen by the groom's mother—now a celebrity astrologer—who charted the day most favorable for the couple's harmonious domestic future together. The buoyant groom enthused, "I feel like I've won the lottery in my life." To support his new household (which, in coming years, included the three children he had with Shauna) and fulfill his financial obligations to his former wives and his other children, Lamas appeared in another syndicated TV series (the short-lived *The Immortal*). He continued to make B movies, some of which were released directly to DVD.

By 2002, Lorenzo's fourth marriage had soured, and the couple were accusing each other in their pending divorce suit. (Among other things, he claimed that she was a

The macho Lorenzo Lamas in 1984's Body Rock.

physical threat to him and that he required a restraining order to ensure his safety; she insisted that he had urged her to help bolster the family's finances by becoming a high-priced escort and an exotic dancer in Las Vegas.) By year's end, the fractious duo had resolved the custody of their children and had divvied up their joint property.

In 2003, Lamas was one of the judges on the reality show *Are You Hot? The Search for America's Sexiest People*. When asked what qualified him for the task, he replied, "Here's the thing. I've met and worked with some very beautiful women. I've even married a couple of them! Plus, my kids are gorgeous."

By early 2004, Lamas was in love again. This time his bride-to-be was Barbara Moore, another shapely blond *Playboy* Playmate. Thanks to his fresh love interest and a new steady job (as a regular on the daytime TV soap *The Bold and the Beautiful*), the 46-year-old actor felt he was again on top of the world. Then things began going wrong. He filed for bankruptcy in mid-2004. Lamas and Moore had been scheduled to wed on July 16, 2005, the one-year anniversary of their first date. However, a few days before the planned ceremony at the Beverly Hills Hotel, he broke off the engagement. (Tabloid accounts of the split suggested that Lamas had learned belatedly that Moore was not partial to the idea of having his six children from past relationships be frequent visitors to their new home and that he questioned her behavior at her bachelorette party. Other "insiders" insisted the real reason for the breakup was that the groom-to-be had gotten cold feet.)

Undaunted by his checkered romantic past, Lamas soon returned to the dating game. By mid-2006 he had found love with Hunter Tylo, one of his costars on *The Bold and the Beautiful*. By the fall of 2006 Lamas embarked on a new phase of his show business career: as a cabaret singer. The theme of his act—"Lorenzo Sings about Love"— reflected the actor's greatest passion in life.

Jude Law

(December 29, 1972–)

During his rapid rise to international film success in the early 2000s, the handsome British actor Jude Law complained of being pigeonholed professionally as a sex symbol: "Whenever there is a role for a pretty boy, people quickly say, 'Okay, let's take Jude Law.' I can really understand how women feel when they are reduced to their outward appearance." With Law's killer good looks, he had to battle constantly against such stereotyping. In the process, he proved to have sizable dramatic talents. (He turned in Oscar-nominated performances in 1999's *The Talented Mr. Ripley* and 2003's *Cold Mountain*.) In 2004, he was cast as the misogynistic Brit in the remake of *Alfie*. He played the cynical antihero who observes, "Whenever you meet a beautiful woman, just remember somewhere there's a man who's sick of shagging her." At the time, it seemed this screen part was far removed from Law's real-life role as a loyal husband and conscientious parent. However, time soon proved that, like his *Alfie* counterpart, Law had a roving eye for women.

• • •

He was born David Jude Law in 1972, the second child (following sister Natasha) of Peter and Maggie Law, both schoolteachers. Early on, the youngster decided that he wanted to become an actor. By age 6, he was performing in school plays and thrived on the activity. "It was like a language I immediately understood and enjoyed. Perhaps that's what made me seem cocky at school." By age 13, he was a member of Britain's National Youth and Music Theatre, a troupe that performed throughout the United Kingdom. Four years later, he quit school to accept a role in the British TV soap opera *Families*.

Law made his feature film debut in the 1994 British independent project *Shopping*. Already he had appeared in several noteworthy stage presentations both abroad and at home. He made a strong impression in the London production of Jean Cocteau's *Les Parents Terribles*, in which he played a scene nude in a bathtub. Under the title *Indiscretions*, the show was brought to Broadway with Law again receiving critical praise for his performance. By this time, the actor had fallen in love with the free-spirited Sadie Frost, one of his costars from *Shopping*. Soon he sported a tattoo on his left arm in honor of his love mate. (She was five years his senior and then still wed to rock musician Gary Kemp, with whom she had a son.) By 1996, Law and Frost were living together and she gave birth to their son. The next year, Frost divorced Kemp and she and Law married that September. (The couple became parents of a daughter in 2000 and of another son in 2002. They purchased a three-story home in London's popular Primrose Hill section.)

Meanwhile, Law had gained attention on screen playing the young gay lover in 1998's *Wilde*. The following year he made his American film debut in *eXistenZ*, coproduced by Natural Nylon Entertainment, of which Law and Frost were two of the cofounders. While his next film, 2001's

Enemy at the Gates, was not enthusiastically received, the actor's career nevertheless remained on a strong roll with 2001's *Artificial Intelligence* and 2002's *Road to Perdition*.

During the making of 2003's *Cold Mountain*, there was gossip that Law and his costar, the recently divorced Nicole Kidman, had embarked on an off-camera romance. (Kidman vehemently denied the claim and successfully sued British tabloids featuring this rumor.) When Frost gave birth to the Laws' third child in September 2002, Jude took a few days off from his hectic moviemaking schedule to be with his wife. Thereafter, she suffered from severe postpartum depression, a condition accentuated by her husband being away so often on filming locations. (It was during this stressful period that their toddler daughter accidentally swallowed half of a discarded Ecstasy pill during a private children's party at a London club and had to be rushed to the hospital for emergency medical treatment. The child fully recovered, but sources claimed that Law blamed his spouse for the situation.)

In the coming months, reports of explosive rifts in the Laws' domestic relationship accelerated. Then, while Jude was shooting *Alfie* in New York, he spent a good deal of time with Sienna Miller, one of his several leading ladies in the picture. By August 2003, the Laws had separated, and Sadie (who had become a successful fashion designer) filed for divorce in October. The couple agreed to joint custody of the children. When interviewed on British TV, Law said of his new single status: "I certainly feel stronger emotionally and happier in myself, if not a little battered and bruised." Meanwhile, Sienna Miller, nine years

The charming Jude Law, one of today's Hollywood most in-demand leading men.

younger than Jude, was telling the press about her lover: "I still pinch myself when I wake up with him. He's such a gorgeous man." Months later, on Christmas Day 2004, Law proposed marriage to Miller.

During early 2005, while Miller was busy with her own filmmaking projects, Law was in the New Orleans area, costarring with Sean Penn in a remake of *All the King's Men*. Then, midyear, a maelstrom hit the engaged couple. Daisy Wright, the 26-year-old nanny who had been caring for Law's three children when they visited him on the *All the King's Men* shoot, declared publicly that she and the movie star had embarked on an affair during those weeks. She acknowl-

edged that on one occasion, they had been caught in Law's bedroom by one of his children, who, in turn, had told Sadie Frost of the situation. A contrite Jude made a public apology to his fiancée. He told the British press: "I am deeply ashamed and upset that I've hurt Sienna and the people most close to us. . . . There is no defense for my actions." In the wake of this scandal, there was renewed interest in the claims made previously by an American mortgage broker who asserted that in 2001, while she was working as an exotic dancer in a Windy City nightclub and Law was shooting *Road to Perdition*, she and Jude had enjoyed a fling of several weeks. There were also allegations published in a British tabloid in 2005 that back in 2001 Law and his then wife, Sadie Frost, had engaged in a wife-swapping gambit while on holiday with singer Pearl Lowe and her musician boyfriend. Law vehemently denied this assertion.

As for the Law-Miller relationship, in the wake of the hubbub about Jude's indiscretions, the couple went through a rocky period. For a spell, their engagement was off, then they reconciled in October 2005. By January 2006, they had broken off again. Thereafter, each was linked with new romantic interests. However, by midyear the couple had reunited once again, with Miller reporting, "We're working things out." But their reconciliation did not stick, and by November 2006 the couple had split up yet again and gone their separate ways—this time seemingly permanently.

With such a complex private life, Jude Law might well be pondering the recurrent question of Alfie, his celluloid alter ego, who repeatedly asked, "What's it all about?"

Julia Roberts

(October 28, 1967–)

Julia Roberts seems to have it all. She is radiantly beautiful, earns $20 million or more per film assignment, has won an Academy Award, is married, and is the mother of two children and pregnant with another child. However, there was a time during Roberts's spectacular climb to fame and fortune in the 1990s when the actress was well known for her many romances that grew intense and then suddenly fell apart. (The situation prompted syndicated columnist Liz Smith to write about Roberts: "I think it would be great if she concentrated on her career and not on the men in her life.")

Over those years, Roberts experienced a string of broken love relationships and one divorce. Many onlookers wondered if she would ever settle down, and, even if she did, how long it would last. More cynical souls were amazed that Julia's long-standing playgirl reputation had not seriously impinged on her box-office standing. It suggested that the public would forgive a movie star her romantic fickleness (and commitment issues) *if* she was sufficiently pretty and charming and continued to turn out pleasing motion pictures.

• • •

She was born Julie Fiona Roberts in Smyrna, Georgia, in 1967, the youngest of three children of Walter Roberts and Betty Lou Brademus. Both parents aspired to be actors and, by the time of Julie's birth, were running the Actors and Writers Workshop in the Atlanta area. By 1972, exhausted by their career struggles and personal troubles, they had divorced. The two girls stayed with their mom (who became a secretary), while their brother lived with his dad (who, among other jobs, became a vacuum cleaner salesman at an Atlanta department store). Although both her siblings (Eric and Lisa) knew early on that they wanted to be actors, Julie thought initially of becoming a veterinarian. However, in high school, she discovered film as an art form and decided to join her siblings.

After graduation, Roberts relocated to Manhattan and roomed with her sister. To support herself, she modeled, and in her spare time, she took acting classes. In 1986, she won her first screen assignment (*Blood Red*), thanks to her brother, Eric, who had been working in films for seven years. Now billed as Julia Roberts, she had the small role of his sister in this modest entry. After a few TV jobs, she gained a part in 1988's *Satisfaction*. While making this featherweight movie, she and coplayer Liam Neeson fell in love. (The Irish actor was 15 years older than Roberts.) The relationship fell apart after several months, and remained a sore subject with Neeson, who would not discuss it publicly. (However, the two patched up their differences sufficiently to costar in 1996's *Michael Collins*.)

Also during 1988, Roberts made a vivid impression on screen in *Mystic Pizza*. This led to her being hired for 1989's *Steel*

Magnolias, in which she played the dying daughter of Sally Field's character. Julia received a Best Supporting Actress Oscar nomination for her touching performance. Moreover, she found a new boyfriend on the set: rising young actor Dylan McDermott, who played her husband in the movie. The couple became engaged, but then, just as suddenly, the romance evaporated.

For 1990's *Pretty Woman*, Roberts earned an Academy Award nomination—this time in the Best Actress category. While making *Flatliners*, her other release that year, she acquired a new beau, colead Kiefer Sutherland. (He had been married, had a child, and was in the process of divorcing.) After the shoot ended, each party went off to fulfill picture commitments, but found time to stay closely in touch. On her 23rd birthday that October she got a tattoo and proclaimed, "My love for Kiefer will last as long as this tattoo." (By then Sutherland had finalized his divorce.)

When Roberts starred in 1991's *Sleeping with the Enemy*, she was paid $1 million, demonstrating that she was climbing fast within the industry. She purchased a $1.5 million home in the Nichols Canyon area of Los Angeles, and Sutherland moved in with her. Julia publicly declared her love for Kiefer, but soon there was gossip of domestic problems. Nevertheless, the couple announced that they would marry that June 14. As the wedding date approached, tabloid stories alleged that Sutherland was having an affair with a stripper he'd met in Hollywood while his fiancée was away moviemaking. Days before the elaborate nuptials were to take place, the ceremony was called

off. Roberts said later that the split had been a mutual decision, but the film colony grapevine wondered which party had really instituted the breakup.

On the very day the nuptials had been scheduled, Roberts was seen dining at a hip West Hollywood restaurant with actor Jason Patric—Sutherland's pal. The following day, the new pair flew to Ireland. Their affair continued for several months, but now Roberts, becoming more cautious as she progressed up the career ladder, declined to comment on her current personal relationships to the press. By January 1993, the Roberts-Patric love connection was over. (This occurred after the couple engaged in a noisy dispute both inside and then outside his Hollywood digs.) Supposedly, the fight was prompted by his growing jealousy over gossip that Julia and actor Daniel Day-Lewis had become overly friendly in the autumn of 1992 when they were being considered as costars in *Shakespeare in Love*. (The picture was eventually made with other actors.)

Although Julia Roberts and country singer Lyle Lovett each had brief cameos in 1992's *The Player*, they became better acquainted while she was making 1993's *The Pelican Brief* in New Orleans. Because the low-keyed Lovett was so unusual looking, onlookers were amazed when he and gorgeous, high-powered Roberts married in late June 1993. Rather than embark on a honeymoon after the ceremony, she returned to the set of her current picture. Over the next months, the newlyweds spent little time together, each claiming that their career obligations kept them apart. It was little surprise when this mismatched couple announced in late March 1995 that they were divorcing. Thereafter, Roberts was linked romantically with actors Matthew Perry and Ross Partridge and health club owner Pat Manocchia.

By 1997, Julia's film salary had jumped to $12 million, a sum she claimed for each of her two new releases: *My Best Friend's Wedding* and *Conspiracy Theory*. Between pictures, she found time to start a romance with Benjamin Bratt, then costarring in the TV series *Law & Order*. Roberts said, "He's very good-looking, and his handsomeness pales in comparison to his kindness." In 1999, Julia guest-starred on an episode of Bratt's TV show. By 2000—the year she made *Erin Brockovich*, for which she won an Oscar— she was saying of her romance with Bratt, "I'm happier than I've ever been in my life." (However, there were rumors that the celebrity couple had serious relationship issues: he wanted to get married and have a family, but she was unwilling at the time.)

Then, while making 2001's *The Mexican*, Julia met handsome cameraman Danny Moder. Reportedly, there were almost immediate love sparks between the two, in spite of the fact that she was coping with her wavering liaison with Bratt and Moder was a married man. By June 2001, Roberts and Bratt had split. Afterward, Julia and the slightly younger Moder became an open item, enjoying time together at her New Mexico ranch and in Los Angeles. Eventually, in May 2002, he negotiated a divorce from his makeup artist wife. In July 2002, she and Moder wed at her New Mexico spread.

Roberts went on to make such movies as

The charismatic Julia Roberts in her 1993 hit, The Pelican Brief.

2003's *Mona Lisa Smile* (for which she was paid over $24 million) and 2004's *Closer* and *Ocean's Twelve*. That November, she gave birth to fraternal twins, Hazel Patricia and Phinnaeus Walter, after which she took time off from picturemaking to be a mother. She made her acting return in a limited run engagement in a 2006 Broadway drama, *Three Days of Rain*, and continued filmmaking with such projects as 2007's *Charlie Wilson's War* with Tom Hanks. Meanwhile, she and her husband were expecting the birth of their third child in the summer of 2007.

In Julia Roberts's case, all's well that ends well. However, along the thorny path to domestic satisfaction, she admitted, "I've made plenty of mistakes and everyone's [made] sure that I've known about them."

Mickey Rooney

(September 23, 1920–)

Still professionally active in his late 80s, veteran entertainer Mickey Rooney began performing decades earlier in vaudeville and then moved on to silent movies and talkies. Over the years, he was heard on radio and starred in four TV series. He conquered Broadway in 1979 when he headlined *Sugar Babies*, a long-running burlesque revue. Over the course of his extraordinarily long show business career, he directed features, composed movie music, and won many accolades (including an honorary and a special Oscar, an Emmy, and a Tony Award).

All that aside, the ebullient five-foot-three-inch Rooney is perhaps best known as a world-class groom, a man who has wed many, many times. He once quipped, "When I say I do, the Justice of the Peace replies, 'I know, I know.' I'm the only man in the world whose marriage license reads, 'To Whom It May Concern.' But to have been married eight time is not normal. That's only halfway intelligent."

• • •

He was born Joe Yule Jr. in 1920 in Brooklyn, the only child of Joe and Nell Carter Yule. His parents were vaudeville performers and the infant toured with them. Before he was 2 years old, the precocious tot had made his debut in the family's act. To avoid the scrutiny of the Children's Society—which protected the welfare of minors—the Yules presented their boy on stage as a dwarf: outfitted in a tuxedo and a derby hat with a fake cigar in his mouth.

During 1924, his parents separated (and divorced three years later). His mother took her boy—nicknamed Sonny—to Los Ange-

Movie star Mickey Rooney tallied up eight marriages over the years. Here he celebrates in Los Angeles in June 1949 with his third wife, actress Martha Vickers.

les. She was determined to maneuver a film career for her talented youngster. Eventually, he made his debut in the 1926 silent feature *Not to Be Trusted*. His big break came when he was cast in a comedy series based on the popular cartoon strip about Mickey McGuire. Between 1927 and 1932 the youngster made 78 of these short subjects. When that project wound down, the 12-year-old found himself suddenly having to rebuild his industry standing. He now used the professional name Mickey Rooney.

By 1934, he was signed to an MGM contract at $150 a week. The career maker for Rooney was being cast as Andy Hardy in *A Family Affair*. This 1937 film about a spirited teenager living in small-town America did so well at the box office that it led to many other entries in the enormously popular series. For his telling dramatic performance in 1938's *Boys Town*, he was a corecipient of a special Academy Award. Between his Andy Hardy installments, screen dramas, and highly popular film musicals with Judy Garland, Rooney became America's leading box-office attraction. He had a new studio contract that would pay him $3,000 a week in its seventh year, and he was given a $25,000 bonus for each film he completed.

Rooney was 21 and a brash, hard-living bachelor when he met Ava Gardner, a brand-new MGM contractee. She was 19 and naive about Hollywood ways when Mickey began courting her relentlessly. She finally said yes (in January 1942) to his oft-repeated marriage proposal, later saying, "He wanted to get in my britches, and I wasn't going to let him in there until we were married." As Gardner gained self-confidence in her career, she bridled at her immature spouse's playboy ways. They divorced in May 1943. She refused any alimony, and they remained friends for life.

Soon after completing 1944's *National Velvet*, Mickey was drafted into the army. He did his World War II duty as a member of the Special Services that entertained troops both in the United States and on battlefronts abroad. While stationed in Alabama, Private Rooney met 17-year-old Betty Jane Rase, a local beauty contest winner. In September 1944, a week after they began dating, they married. During their years together, the couple had two children (Mickey and Timothy). They divorced in May 1948, with Betty Jane winning a healthy divorce settlement (including $12,500 a year alimony for a decade).

After completing his military service, Rooney returned to MGM. He was now 26 and discovered that moviegoers' tastes had changed in recent years. In 1948, he recklessly ended his $5,000-a-week studio pact and found himself deeply in debt because of a movie production company he had set up with an unscrupulous partner. While struggling as a freelancer in the new Hollywood, Rooney wed sultry actress Martha Vickers in June 1949. During their more than two years together they became the parents of a son, Teddy. Mickey explained their September 1951 divorce with, "She drank too much, and we couldn't go on." (Vickers asserted that Rooney was often violent and was hardly ever at home.)

A year later, in November 1952, Rooney took wife number four, Elaine Mahnken. She was a statuesque beauty from Montana who, under her screen name Elaine Davis, would appear with Mickey in the 1954 film *The Atomic Kid*. Rooney's gambling addiction (especially at the horse races), his growing reliance on prescription drugs, and his passionate interest in 22-year-old model Barbara Ann Thomason (who had made a few films as Carolyn Mitchell) led to the end of the Rooney-Mahnken relationship. Thomason and Rooney were secretly wed in Mexico in December 1958 (after his Mexican divorce from Mahnken but *before* her California divorce from Rooney was official in May 1959). Thomason was pregnant at the time and threatened to kill herself if he did not marry her. Mickey and his fifth bride had four children together (Kelly Ann, Kerry Yule, Kimmy Sue, and Michael Joseph). By early 1966, Rooney was suing his wife for divorce, naming actor/chauffeur Milos Milosevic as corespondent. On January 31, 1966, Rooney—back early from a movie shoot in the Philippines—arrived at his Brentwood, California, home to discover two bodies in the bathroom. His wife's lover had killed her and then committed suicide because she and Mickey were considering a last-minute reconciliation.

Meanwhile, in 1963, the veteran entertainer had filed for bankruptcy, noting in his petition that he was $464,914 in debt (having earned and squandered an estimated $12 million in his career to that date). In September 1964, the resilient Rooney wed 45-year-old Margaret Lane, a close friend of the murdered Barbara Ann Thomason. Their union lasted but 100 days. Next, in May 1969, Mickey got hitched to Carolyn Hockett, a secretary he met in Florida (where he was now based, in Fort Lauderdale). The bride was 23 years younger than the groom. The couple had a child (Jonell), and he adopted Jimmy, her son from her prior marriage. In 1974, she filed for divorce, claiming his lack of financial responsibility was a chief cause of the breakup.

A few years later, Rooney met Janice Chamberlin, a Nashville country singer, at his agent's home. On July 18, 1978, they wed at the Conejo Valley Church of Religious Science, northwest of Los Angeles. Amazingly, considering the groom's poor domestic track record, they have been together ever since. He said that he found religion with her, adding, "God gave me my career. I was sent here to do my Father's work."

Over recent decades, Mickey kept busy with stage tours, films, TV appearances, writing his second memoir (1991's *Life Is Too Short*), and touring the United States with Jan in their joint club act. In the fall of 2000, he underwent successful double bypass heart surgery, and soon returned to doing what he did best: entertaining.

In a nine-decade career that has encompassed many dramatic ups and downs and comebacks, Rooney proved himself to be a durable show business trouper. In the wake of a colorful private life—punctuated with excesses and missteps—the serial honeymooner had practical advice for anyone considering matrimony: "Always get married early in the morning. That way, if it doesn't work out, you haven't wasted a whole day."

Frank Sinatra

(December 12, 1915–May 14, 1998)

Frank Sinatra once said, "I'm for anything that gets you through the night, be it prayers, tranquilizers, or a bottle of Jack Daniel's." He might also have added to his must-have list the company of women—or in hipster Sinatra's vernacular, "broads." Not only was the legendary singer reputedly very well endowed and attracted to a wide variety of women, but also—for decades—the opposite sex found him extremely appealing. Glamour queen Marlene Dietrich rated "Ol' Blue Eyes" "the Mercedes-Benz of men!" Cinema siren Ava Gardner, who was the crooner's second wife, noted of her ex-husband, "We were always great in bed." (On the other hand, Marilyn Monroe, in comparing Sinatra to her former husband, said of Frank's bedside manner: "He was no [Joe] DiMaggio.")

During Sinatra's extraordinary show business career, he established many entertainment industry records. He was equally proficient in setting standards in the boudoir. Besides his four marriages, the singing star enjoyed many liaisons, with vocalists Jill Corey and Peggy Connolly and actresses Marilyn Maxwell, Lauren Bacall, Juliet Prowse, Lana Turner, Zsa Zsa Gabor, Kim Novak, Natalie Wood, Angie Dickinson, Jill St. John, Grace Kelly, and Shirley MacLaine, among others. The randy Rat Pack chieftain also had a partiality for dating prostitutes because he felt he could be himself with them. One of Sinatra's more notorious party gal pals was

From 1939 to 1951, crooner/actor Frank Sinatra was wed to his first wife, Nancy Barbato, but during their union he frequently was out and about with other women.

Judith Campbell Exner, whom the obliging Sinatra introduced to both politician John F. Kennedy and mob titan Sam Giancana.

Frank's pal, singer/actor Dean Martin—no slouch himself when it came to the ladies—insisted, "When Sinatra dies, they're giving his zipper to the Smithsonian." However, the Chairman of the Board cautioned his public, "If I had as many love affairs as you've given me credit for, I'd now be speaking to you from a jar in the Harvard Medical School."

• • •

Francis Albert Sinatra was born in 1915 in Hoboken, New Jersey, the only child of his Italian immigrant parents, Anthony Martin and Natalie "Dolly" Garaventi Sinatra. His father—noted for his mild demeanor—was variously a boxer, a bartender, a boilermaker, and a fireman. His mother, who was hot-tempered and tough-edged, was both a saloon owner and a midwife (who performed abortions as a sideline). Street-ruffian Sinatra quit school when he was 15. By then, he wanted to be a singer—like his idol, Bing Crosby. Within a few years, Frank was performing with a local singing group, and then became a saloon singer in northern New Jersey. Bandleader Harry James heard Sinatra perform on the radio in 1939 and hired him. Several months later, Sinatra moved on to Tommy Dorsey's band, staying with that notable group until 1942. Thereafter, Frank became a solo artist and his singing career shifted into high gear. So did his fun times with a slew of women.

During Sinatra's longtime courtship of Nancy Barbato—whom he wed in February 1939—he told pals, "We're animals, fuckin' animals, each and every one of us . . . and we're damn proud of it too. . . . There's more to life than just Nancy, and I gotta have it." Frank's ambition to "make it with as many women as I can" did not lessen once he was a married man and father. (The Sinatras would have three children: Nancy, born in 1940, Frank Jr., born in 1944, and Tina, born in 1948.) Once Sinatra switched his base of operation to Hollywood, where he joined MGM (making such films as 1945's *Anchors Aweigh* and 1948's *The Kissing Bandit*), he was like a hungry boy in a candy factory full of delicious bonbons.

During the 1940s, Frank carried on with an impressive assortment of women, often staying out all night to party. His wife was not blind to his extracurricular social activities, but she reasoned, "When you have a successful man, certain women will try to snare him. And if you have a man with an inclination for that sort of thing, it's no surprise when he gives in to them." Sometimes, however, when Sinatra's philandering was too blatant for her to overlook, it led to gargantuan domestic squabbles. (On one occasion, when Nancy decided there was little hope for her wobbly marriage, she had an abortion. When Frank learned of this, he tamed his wild behavior for a while, and warned his wife, "Don't you *ever* do that again.")

In the late 1940s, Frank and Nancy split up officially for the first time. He rented a bachelor pad, where he and his buddies partied hard. He was seen frequently in the company of gorgeous Lana Turner and also with a lesser screen lovely, Marilyn Maxwell. Eventually, the celebrity moved back home—pressured by his mother, the Catholic church, and the studio.

In the late 1940s, the crooner tumbled for Ava Gardner, another MGM luminary. She already had been through two marriages and had developed a cynical approach to life. He became so beguiled by her that nothing else seemed to matter. He and Nancy finally divorced in late October 1951, and several days later, Frank wed Ava. At the time, Gardner was at the height of her beauty and her movie career was still climbing, while Sinatra was in a film career slump and had almost lost his golden voice.

While Sinatra was down and nearly out, the earthy Gardner thrived on mothering him. However, once he made a resounding comeback with his Oscar-winning role in 1953's *From Here to Eternity* and began to have hit recordings again, Ava lost interest in her newly self-confident spouse. Their boozing, brawling, and cheating escalated. The couple separated in 1954 and divorced in 1957, but remained close friends.

In the later 1950s, swingin' Sinatra was at the peak of his power and charisma. Among his passing romantic fancies was Natalie Wood, who was 23 years younger than he. Their dalliance was brief, but the two remained on good terms. (Often, as a parting gesture when ending a romance, Frank cast the lady in one of his films.) The famed singer was more serious about movie star Lauren Bacall, the widow of his good friend Humphrey Bogart. However, the thought of marrying again—especially a "pushy woman"—worried him. Rather than work through his concerns, he unceremoniously dumped Bacall. The humiliated actress termed her ex-beau "a complete shit."

During the mid-1960s, Sinatra was still on top professionally, with a flow of hit albums and popular movies. However, he was nearing 50 and was suffering a delayed midlife crisis. He became fascinated with 19-year-old actress Mia Farrow. The oddly matched couple wed in Las Vegas in July 1966. However, the tremendous age gap between the duo and their incompatible lifestyles were far too much for them to overcome. The two split in August 1968.

In 1975, the world-class playboy briefly courted Jacqueline Kennedy Onassis. (She rebuffed him, purportedly after discovering Sinatra's full role years earlier in setting up JFK on Hollywood dates.) By now, Frank was feeling his mortality, and told a reporter, "There's nothing worse than being an old swinger." Earlier in the decade, Frank had seriously dated actress Lois Nettleton, but their relationship soured after he threw one of his famous tirades. Then, in July 1976, 61-year-old Sinatra married Barbara Marx. The 46-year-old bride was the ex-wife of Zeppo Marx (of the Marx Brothers). There was little congeniality between the new Mrs. Sinatra and Frank's three children by his first wife, and Sinatra was caught in the middle. Now, in his senior years, Frank grew increasingly domesticated and spent far less time with his old cronies. In 1980, he made his last feature film (*The First Deadly Sin*), and in 1995, he gave his final live concert.

In May 1998, the 82-year-old icon died as a result of heart and kidney disease and cancer. He was buried in Desert Memorial Park in Cathedral City, California. The legend on his tombstone read: "The Best Is Yet to Come."

Elizabeth Taylor

(February 27, 1932–)

Elizabeth Taylor was first introduced to 23-year-old Conrad Nicholson "Nicky" Hilton in early 1950. Months later, in June, the 18-year-old MGM actress wed Nicky, the handsome son of hotel tycoon Conrad Hilton. At the time, multimillionaire Hilton bragged of his son's nuptials: "They've got everything, haven't they? Youth, looks, position, no need to worry about where their next meal is coming from." (Taylor gushed about the groom, "Your heart knows when you meet the right man. There is no doubt that Nicky is the one I want to spend my life with.") The high-profile couple honeymooned in England and on the Continent.

However, the dream marriage quickly fell apart while the pampered newlyweds were abroad. The groom complained later, "It was life in a goldfish bowl. One time a battery of reporters and photographers invaded our suite—it happened all the time—and one of the photographers said to me, 'Hey, Mac, get out of the way. I want to snap a picture!'" There were also rumors that hot-tempered Nicky was abusive toward his movie star bride. In February 1951, the two divorced. Taylor accepted no alimony, but she retained from the brief marriage her 100 shares of Hilton Hotel stock and a $50,000 diamond engagement ring.

In Alexander Walker's biography of Taylor, he noted that once Elizabeth broke with Nicky Hilton, "she faced the question that was a continuous source of harassment throughout the rest of her life: who would her next husband be? Marriage is the matrix of the myth that began surrounding Elizabeth Taylor from this early date. Whether it pleased her or not, she began to discover the public's craving to participate vicariously in her love life."

●   ●   ●

Elizabeth Rosemond Taylor was born in 1932, in London, England. She was the second child (brother Howard was born in 1929) of Francis and Sara Warmbrodt Taylor. Both parents were Americans residing in London. Her mother had been an actress, and her father, a supervisor of a London art gallery, was the nephew of a millionaire art dealer.

When World War II broke out in 1939, Mr. Taylor thought his family would be far safer if they left England, and he sent them to live in Pasadena, California, with his in-laws. Later, he joined them and opened a Los Angeles art shop. A few years thereafter, Elizabeth came to the attention of an executive at Universal Pictures and she was hired for her first film, 1942's *There's One Born Every Minute*.

Some months later, Elizabeth joined the prestigious MGM, where she performed in such pictures as 1944's *National Velvet*. By the time of 1949's *Little Women*, she had matured into a gorgeous young woman whose much-touted physical measurements were 37-19-36. She was also old enough to date 24-year-old athlete Glenn Davis, to whom she planned to be engaged before he left for military duty in Korea. Later, William Pawley Jr., scion of the former ambassador to Brazil, briefly became the new man in Taylor's hectic social life. Then came her fiasco with Nicky Hilton.

While Taylor was in the process of divorcing her first husband, she started a romance with Stanley Donen, the director of her current picture, *Love Is Better Than Ever*. He was a decade older than she, not yet a major name in the business, and Jewish. Both Taylor's studio and her dominating mother vetoed the relationship. Elizabeth was sent to England to film *Ivanhoe*. While there, she renewed her acquaintance with the debonair Michael Wilding. The 39-year-old British actor said of his romance with the American beauty: "I thought I'd guide this trembling little creature along life's stony path." She was not yet 20 when she married him, in February 1952, in London. (Taylor bubbled at the time, "I just want to be with Michael, to be his wife. This is for me, the beginning of a happy end.") The next January, she gave birth to their son Michael Howard. On her 23rd birthday, she gave birth to Christopher Edward.

The suave Wilding found life in Hollywood with the pampered Taylor to be extremely taxing. She was a major box-office success, while he had difficulty obtaining decent screen assignments. Elizabeth admitted later, "I gave him rather a rough time." By late 1956, she was already involved romantically with go-getter Michael Todd, the 47-year-old stage/film producer. The Wildings divorced at the end of January 1957, and a few days later

The screen beauty Elizabeth Taylor has wed eight times, twice to Richard Burton. One of their several joint acting ventures was 1967's The Taming of the Shrew.

she married Todd. Taylor said of these nuptials: "This marriage will last forever. For me it will be third time lucky."

In March 1958, during the making of *Cat on a Hot Tin Roof*, Taylor was stricken with the flu and was unable to join Todd on a flight to New York. His plane crashed, killing everyone aboard. Among those who consoled the brokenhearted widow was 29-year-old crooner Eddie Fisher. Months later, he left his wife, MGM movie star Debbie Reynolds. In May 1959, Fisher and Taylor (who had converted to Judaism) married at a Las Vegas temple. (When asked about her sudden remarriage, the widow snapped to the press, "What do you expect me to do? Sleep alone?")

Then came the movie *Cleopatra*, for which she was paid a $1 million salary plus many perks. During the initial shoot in England, she almost died from pneumonia.

(Her illness prompted the film colony and the public to forgive the star for breaking up the Fisher-Reynolds marriage. In a sign of Hollywood's support, Taylor won an Oscar for portraying a chic prostitute in 1960's *Butterfield 8.*)

Once Taylor recovered her health, the costume extravaganza resumed production in Rome in the fall of 1961. The largely recast movie now included Richard Burton as Mark Antony. By early the next year, she and Burton (who was then married and the father of two daughters) had fallen in love. The resultant scandal confirmed Taylor's reputation as the 20th century's most notorious siren. Eventually, Elizabeth and Richard won divorces from their mates, and they married in March 1964. Taylor enthused, "I'm so happy you can't believe. . . . I love him enough to stand by him, no matter what he might do, and I would wait."

The Burtons enjoyed a fabulously indulgent lifestyle, acted together in several films, and discovered that even the pleasures of regal jet-set living could not distract them from their growing domestic problems. They divorced in June 1974. Taylor amused herself with romantic flings, including with Los Angeles auto dealer Henry Wynberg. However, she was still drawn to the alcoholic Burton (whom she called the great love of her life), and the couple rewed in October 1975. The much-married Taylor announced, "There will be bloody no more marriages or divorces. We are stuck like chicken feathers to tar—for lovely always." Unfortunately, the remarriage was a disaster, and the couple divorced again in August 1976.

Months later, in December 1976, a lonely and restless Taylor marched down the aisle with 48-year-old John W. Warner, a past navy secretary and later a U.S. senator. (The bride declared, "John is the best lover I've ever had. . . . I want to spend the rest of my life with him and I want to be buried with him.") During their years together, her film career slowed down significantly, and she endured periods of being conspicuously overweight. Meanwhile, she grew bored with being a politician's wife and divorced Warner in November 1982. She diverted herself with acting assignments, including in such TV movies as 1987's *Poker Alice.*

Taylor was much in the news in her post–John Warner period, due to persistent health problems and for undergoing various detoxifying treatments. At one substance abuse center, she met Larry Fortensky, a former truck driver who had gone into the construction business. She was 59 and he was 39. When Taylor was questioned about the tremendous disparity between their financial situations, the movie legend chided, "No boy is poor if he's rich at heart." Their extravagant wedding in October 1991 was held at the California ranch of her then pal, singer Michael Jackson. She said of her latest groom, "Larry gives me a sense of security. I know I'm protected and he's there for me." But, as many in the film colony predicted, the marriage was doomed from the start. The unlikely couple divorced on October 31, 1996. Thereafter, Taylor continued to cope with grave health issues (including her fluctuating weight), pursued charity fund-raising (especially for AIDS causes), and focused on her highly lucrative perfume and jewelry businesses.

Taylor, often termed "the Last Movie Star," will perhaps always be best known for her colorful life and her many stabs at matrimony (and her extracurricular romances).

At one of her marriage ceremonies, the justice of the peace asked the bride for the names of her former spouses. Elizabeth joked, "What is this, a memory test?"

Lana Turner

(February 8, 1920–June 29, 1995)

Hollywood's Golden Age (from the 1930s to the 1950s) produced several memorable sex goddesses, including Jean Harlow, Rita Hayworth, Elizabeth Taylor, Ava Gardner, and Marilyn Monroe. One of the most stunning of this elite group was the 110-pound Lana Turner, a petite blonde with appealing blue eyes and a 35-23-35 figure. Few enjoyed their screen status as fully as did Lana Turner. Veteran journalist Adela Rogers St. John reported, "The real Lana Turner is the Lana Turner everyone knows about. She always wanted to be a Movie Star, and loved being one. Her personal life and her movie star life are one." In *Leading Ladies: The 50 Most Unforgettable Actresses of the Studio Era*, Andrea Sarvady described how Turner lived up to her enticing celebrity image: "Lana favored tight clothes in simple, strong colors. Diamonds were a staple, and a fur, preferably white, was often draped over one shoulder. Glamour was the key. Lana Turner was a movie star and dressed for the part nearly every day of her life."

As Turner's star ascended at MGM in the early 1940s, so did her salary, perks, and the degree of coddling she received from the studio. She thrived on being so indulged. She also adored captivating her leading men and flirting with the array of suitors who gravitated to her off the film lot. Turner said, "I find men terribly exciting, and any girl who says she doesn't is an anemic old maid, a streetwalker, or a saint." Or, as she phrased it another time: "I liked the boys and the boys liked me." In reviewing her hectic love life and many marriages over the decades, she pointed out, "I planned on having one husband and seven children, but it turned out the other way around."

• • •

She was born Julia Jean Turner in 1920 (although she later claimed 1921 as her birth year) in Wallace, Idaho, a small mining town. Her father, Virgil, an itinerant worker from Alabama, had met young Mildred Frances Cowan at a dance in Picher, Oklahoma. They soon eloped and later became parents to Julia (whom they nicknamed Judy). By the time the girl was 8, the Turners were based in San Francisco. In December 1930, Virgil Turner was a big winner in an all-night craps game. Hours later, he was found murdered. (His killer was never caught.) A few years thereafter, Mildred, now a beautician, and young Judy moved to Los Angeles, where the teenager

As in real life, the sex symbol Lana Turner was the center of attention with her screen leading men. She and Dean Martin paired for 1962's Who's Got the Action?

enrolled at Hollywood High School. Already the girl had a stunning adult figure.

One day while cutting classes, Judy met the publisher of the *Hollywood Reporter*. He, in turn, introduced her to a talent agent, who found the teenager work as an extra in 1937's *A Star Is Born*. That same year, filmmaker Mervyn LeRoy cast her in *They Won't Forget*. She made a strong impression in a scene where she paraded down a street wearing a tight skirt and sweater. LeRoy signed "The Sweater Girl" (as she was tagged by the media) to a personal contract at $50 a week. In 1938, he went over to MGM and took Judy with him. There, she adopted the screen name Lana Turner. Her first MGM picture was 1938's *Love Finds Andy Hardy*. She and the film's star (Mickey Rooney) had a romantic fling, which led to her having an abortion.

While acting in *Dancing Co-Ed*, in 1939, Turner was unenthusiastic about her egotistical, highly intellectual costar Artie Shaw. Months later, she changed her mind about the celebrated musician/bandleader. When her current boyfriend, playboy attorney Greg Bautzer, stood her up one evening, she accepted a last-minute date with Artie. During their night on the town, the pair impetuously flew to Nevada, where they married on February 13, 1940. Turner called her turbulent marriage to Shaw her "college education" as he was constantly berating her about and educating her on the many topics of which she was ignorant. After seven months, the incompatible couple divorced. By then, she had had a studio-arranged abortion. Single again, Turner accumulated a variety of new beaus: singer/actor Tony Martin, movie hunks Victor Mature and Robert Taylor (then still wed to movie queen Barbara Stanwyck), and bandleader Tommy Dorsey, as well as drummers Gene Krupa and Buddy Rich.

Turner ignited the screen with Clark Gable in 1941's *Honky Tonk* and became a full-fledged star. She reached a professional peak with her sensual performance in 1946's *The Postman Always Rings Twice*. Later, she was quite effective in 1952's *The Bad and the Beautiful*, proving that she deserved more than her usual fluff movie assignments.

There continued to be many men in Turner's life. She wed restaurant owner Stephen Crane in July 1942 after knowing him only a short time. Months later, the couple discovered that Crane's divorce from his prior wife had not been final when he married Lana (who was now pregnant).

The duo had their marriage annulled, then remarried in Tijuana, Mexico, in March 1943. Their daughter, Cheryl, was born in July that year, but the couple divorced in April 1944. Next, Turner had a romance with exotic actor Turhan Bey. However, the great love of Turner's life was bisexual movie star Tyrone Power. He was already married, played the field, and soon felt suffocated by Lana's all-consuming love for him. For distraction, Turner enjoyed romantic flings with a playboy bachelor (Howard Hughes) and two married men (fellow MGM star Frank Sinatra and the wealthy John Alden Talbot).

In April 1948, Lana tried matrimony yet again—this time with millionaire Henry J. (Bob) Topping, a Connecticut sportsman. In both 1949 and 1950, she suffered miscarriages. By now, the couple was living in a Beverly Hills mansion that Lana had paid for, as her hard-drinking spouse was suffering financial reverses. The Toppings divorced in 1952, not long after her suicide attempt, in which she cut her wrists. The following September, Turner wed hunky actor Les Barker, one of the screen's several Tarzans. The groom insisted later that their happiest times together were *before* they wed. The incompatible pair divorced in June 1957. (Thereafter, it came to light that Barker not only had a temper but had reputedly sexually abused Lana's daughter, Cheryl.)

Turner was cut loose from MGM after 1956's *Diane* and she felt vulnerable being on her own. However, she rebounded professionally the next year with her Oscar-nominated performance in *Peyton Place*. In the midst of that upswing came the scandal concerning her lover, gangland underling Johnny Stompanato, who was stabbed to death with a butcher knife by Lana's daughter at Turner's Beverly Hills home in April 1958. At the highly publicized coroner's inquest, the killing was ruled to be justifiable homicide.

Lana recharged her cinema popularity with 1959's *Imitation of Life* and made such later pictures as 1966's *Madame X*. She married department store millionaire Fred May in November 1960, but the couple filed for divorce less than a year later. Her next mate was author Robert Eaton. He was a decade younger than she. They remained together for four years. (Later, he wrote an exploitive novel, *The Body Brokers*, featuring a Lana Turner–like character.) In May 1969, the veteran star was married for the last time, to hypnotist/dietician Robert Dante. After they split in December 1969, Lana, nearing 50, decided to remain single. (She claimed that, thereafter, she was celibate.)

As A-list film roles dried up for the aging screen siren, she tried a TV series (1969's *The Survivors*), toured in plays, and made occasional lackluster movies, such as 1980's *Witches' Brew*. She had a recurring role on TV's *Falcon Crest* from 1982 to 1983. She died of throat cancer at her Century City, California, condo in June 1995.

In her 1982 autobiography, Lana Turner reflected, "The thing about happiness is that it doesn't help you to grow; only unhappiness does that. So I'm grateful that my bed of roses was made up equally of blossoms and thorns. I've had a privileged, creative, exciting life, and I think that the parts that were less joyous were preparing me, testing me, strengthening me."

Shelley Winters
(August 18, 1920–January 14, 2006)

Irrepressible, ambitious, unpredictable, brash, and hugely talented are a few of the adjectives that apply to the one-of-a-kind Shelley Winters, whose first film was released in 1943 and whose last screen appearance was in 1999. The forthright actress never learned to censor her actions or words but enjoyed an enormously long show business career with successes on the stage and in film and television. She was always her own best press agent, intuitively knowing how to grab the attention of gossip columnists and how best to make TV talk show hosts like Johnny Carson and Merv Griffin repeatedly invite her back to their forums.

In her two earthy memoirs (1980's *Shelley: Also Known as Shirley*, and 1989's *Shelley II: The Middle of My Century*) Winters exuberantly and uninhibitedly recounted the high and low points of her productive career and her many romances—which included lusty times with Marlon Brando, Burt Lancaster, William Holden, and Sean Connery.

Winters once said, "In Hollywood, all the marriages are happy. It's trying to live together afterwards that causes all the problems." That proved true with her first three unions, especially her tempestuous, relatively short relationships with Italian film star Vittorio Gassman and Hollywood leading man Anthony Franciosa. When these marriages fell apart, she felt that it was some lack within her that caused them to stray

with other women, and that if she had given matrimony greater priority over her career, these unions might have succeeded far better. What she did not acknowledge was that she was too much of a personality and talent for most any man to deal with successfully over the long run.

● ● ●

She was born Shirley Schrift in East St. Louis, Illinois, in 1920 (some sources list 1922 or 1923), the second daughter of Jonas Schrift, a cutter/designer for the men's clothing industry, and Rose Winter Schrift. Her mother, who adored music, had once won a singing competition at the St. Louis Municipal Opera. However, she abandoned her dream of studying in Europe to remain close to her parents until she married. When Shirley was only 3, she began her entertainment career by making her way onto the stage during an amateur talent contest and singing.

While Shirley was still an adolescent, the family moved to Brooklyn, New York. There, her father got into business difficulties and went to prison for a year (before new legal representation proved his innocence). During high school, the already ambitious teenager performed in class dramatics and worked after school to earn tuition for acting lessons. Some months before her graduation, shapely Shirley abandoned high school to become a model in the garment district. At night, she took acting classes at the New Theater School and chose her professional name, Shelley Winter (the "s" was added to her surname when she went to Hollywood). Determined to succeed, she made casting rounds, labored in a nightclub chorus line, and worked in summer stock.

In January 1942, she married Paul Mack Mayer, a Jewish textile salesman from Chicago whom she had met while on a play tour. Soon thereafter, he entered World War II military service; the relationship fell apart as her career took off, and they divorced in 1948. Also in 1942, Shelley won a supporting role in the Broadway operetta *Rosalinda*. This led to a low-paying term contract with Columbia Pictures, where she had bits in major films like 1944's *Cover Girl* and such B movies as 1945's *Dancing in Manhattan*. Because Winters did not fit into any established screen mold, the studio eventually dropped her contract.

But she refused to admit defeat. She took acting classes (including, later, with film star Charles Laughton), studied dance and speech, and had her pronounced overbite corrected. Shelley was tireless about industry networking, and finally her nerve and determination paid off. She was hired for the brief but flashy part of the waitress murdered by Ronald Colman in 1947's *A Double Life*. This prompted Universal-International Pictures to sign her to a long-term deal. The studio made her diet, and then promoted its svelte, brassy new contractee as a blond bombshell. In this career phase, she shrewdly planned her public life to gain maximum publicity. However, she claimed that her zesty private life just seemed to happen. (Her uninhibited

socializing included flings with an array of Hollywood notables, including Clark Gable, Errol Flynn, Burt Lancaster, Marlon Brando, William Holden, Howard Hughes, Lawrence Tierney, Sterling Hayden, and John Ireland.)

Between her many sexual encounters and film projects, Winters's career aspirations grew. She pushed hard to claim the part of the drab factory girl killed in 1951's *A Place in the Sun*. For her effective performance in this prestigious production, she won her first Academy Award nomination. By early 1951, Shelley was back in New York and was studying at the Actors Studio. She reluctantly returned to the sound stages to make such films as 1952's *Meet Danny Wilson* with Frank Sinatra.

The impetuous Shelley had a great weakness for sensual Italian men, which prompted her to wed actor Vittorio Gassman in April 1952. She gave birth to their daughter, Victoria, the following February. Vittorio was then making pictures in Hollywood, but frequently flew back to Italy, where he was better appreciated both on and off screen. Because Winters did not want to short-circuit her career trajectory, she remained mostly in California. Their stormy union ended in divorce in 1954, the same year they were seen on camera together in *Mambo*.

To prove her true acting range, Shelley quit filmmaking and tried Broadway again. In 1955's *A Hatful of Rain*, she teamed with Italian American actor Anthony Franciosa. (He was several years younger than she and was ending his first marriage.) Romantic sparks ignited between the two. Despite their conflicting egos and career rivalry, they wed in May 1957. By then, he had been grabbed up by Hollywood, where he soon was tempted into adulterous flings, including with movie star Lauren Bacall. By November 1960, the extremely emotional Winters and the similarly hot-blooded Franciosa had divorced. (Shelley said later, "All my men cheated on me and that's kinda sad. All I ever got out of marriage, except my daughter, was some jewelry and a recipe for ravioli.")

As in her personal life, Winters was a career survivor. She made a shift into character leads when, at age 37, she portrayed a plump, fiftysomething mother in 1959's *The Diary of Anne Frank*. Her performance won her a Best Supporting Actress Oscar and launched her into her new screen type. By 1972's *The Poseidon Adventure* (for which she won her fourth Oscar nomination), Shelley had become fat and truly matronly—she used these aspects as her new stock in trade. Unlike most of her contemporaries, she kept extremely active in movies, TV, and stage work during the 1970s, including playing Elvis Presley's mama in *Elvis*, the 1979 telefeature.

Thanks to the 1980 publication of her best-selling first autobiography—with all its spicy sexcapades—Winters enjoyed a burst of renewed popularity. She continued with screen roles (often as a yenta). In the 1990s,

Shelley won a new audience when she appeared in the recurring part of Nana Mary, the star's grandma on the TV sitcom *Roseanne*. A grandmother in real life, Winters also taught acting classes, did a few movie cameos (including in 1996's *The Portrait of a Lady*), and guested on TV documentaries about Hollywood's Golden Age. She coped with increasingly poor health and a reported addiction to pain pills (initially taken for a back problem).

In early 2006, Winters had a debilitating heart attack and stroke and became a patient at a Beverly Hills rehabilitation center. By then, her daughter, Victoria, had finally convinced Winters to create a trust fund of her approximately $15 million estate, on behalf of her two grandchildren. On the evening of January 13, Shelley exchanged wedding vows with 59-year-old Gerry DeFord, her companion of the past 18 years. The ceremony was conducted by Shelley's good friend/godchild, actress Sally Kirkland, a legally ordained minister. A nurse on duty served as witness. The next day, Shelley Winters died.

Looking back on her long, zesty, and remarkable existence, Winters said in September 2005, "It's been a wonderful adventure-filled life. I've achieved more than I ever could have expected—I have no regrets."

Bibliography

Alleman, Richard. *Hollywood: The Movie Lover's Guide*. New York: Broadway Books, 2005.

Alpert, Hollis. *Burton*. New York: G. P. Putnam's Sons, 1986.

Amburn, Ellis. *The Most Beautiful Woman in the World: The Obsessions, Passions, and Courage of Elizabeth Taylor*. New York: HarperCollins, 2000.

———. *The Sexiest Man Alive: A Biography of Warren Beatty*. New York: HarperCollins, 2002.

Amende, Coral. *Hollywood Confidential: An Inside Look at the Public Careers and Private Lives of Hollywood's Rich and Famous*. New York: Plume, 1997.

Ammons, Kevin, with Nancy Bacon. *Good Girl, Bad Girl: An Insider's Biography of Whitney Houston*. Secaucus, N.J.: Carol, 1996.

Andersen, Christopher. *Barbra: The Way She Is*. New York: HarperCollins, 2006.

Anderson, Loni, with Larkin Warren. *Loni Anderson: My Life in High Heels*. New York: Avon, 1997.

Artunian, Judy, and Mike Oldham. *Movie Star Homes: The Famous to the Forgotten*. Santa Monica, Calif.: Santa Monica Press, 2004.

Aylesworth, Thomas G. *Hollywood Kids: Child Stars of the Silver Screen from 1903 to the Present*. New York: E. P. Dutton, 1987.

Barbas, Samantha. *The First Lady of Hollywood: A Biography of Louella Parsons*. Berkeley: University of California Press, 2005.

Barrymore, Drew, with Todd Gold. *Little Girl Lost*. New York: Simon & Schuster, 1990.

Bart, Peter. *Boffo!: How I Learned to Love the Blockbuster and Fear the Bomb*. New York: Miramax, 2006.

Baxter, John. *Woody Allen: A Biography*. New York: Carroll & Graf, 1999.

Beard, Lanford (ed.). *E! True Hollywood Story: The Real Stories behind the Glitter*. New York: Chamberlain Bros., 2005.

Bego, Mark. *Julia Roberts: America's Sweetheart*. Boca Raton, Fla.: AMI, 2003.

Behlmer, Rudy (ed.). *Memo from David O. Selznick*. New York: Viking, 1972.

Bonaduce, Danny. *Random Acts of Badness: My Story*. New York: Hyperion, 2001.

Bosworth, Patricia. *Marlon Brando*. New York: Penguin, 2001.

———. *Montgomery Clift: A Biography* (reprint edition). New York: Limelight, 1990.

Bova, Joyce, as told to William Conrad Nowels. *Don't Ask Forever: My Love Affair with Elvis*. New York: Kensington, 1994.

Bragg, Melvyn. *Richard Burton: A Life*. New York: Warner, 1990.

Brando, Marlon, with Robert Lindsey. *Brando: Songs My Mother Taught Me*. New York: Random House, 1994.

Bret, David. *Errol Flynn: Satan's Angel*. London: Robson, 2000.

Britton, Ron. *Kim Basinger: Longer Than Forever—The True Story of Our Strange Marriage*. London: Blake, 1998.

Brooks, Louise. *Lulu in Hollywood* (reprint edition). Minneapolis: University of Minnesota Press, 2000.

Brooks, Tim, and Earle Marsh. *The Complete Directory to Prime Time Network and Cable TV Shows: 1946–Present* (8th edition). New York: Ballantine, 2003.

Brown, Peter H. *Such Devoted Sisters: Those Fabulous Gabors*. New York: St. Martin's, 1985.

Brown, Peter Harry, and Pat. H. Broeske. *Howard Hughes: The Untold Story*. New York: Dutton, 1996.

Bruck, Connie. *When Hollywood Had a King: The Reign of Lew Wasserman, Who Leveraged Talent into Power and Influence*. New York: Random House, 2003.

Byron, Christopher. *Martha Inc.: The Incredible Story of Martha Stewart Living Omnimedia Inc.* Hoboken, N.J.: John Wiley & Sons, 2003.

Callan, Michael Feeney. *Julie Christie*. New York: St. Martin's, 1985.

Callow, Simon. *Orson Welles: Hello Americans*. New York: Viking, 2006.

———. *Orson Welles: The Road to Xanadu*. New York: Penguin, 1997.

Cannon, Doris Rollins. *Grabtown Girl: Ava Gardner's North Carolina Childhood and Her Enduring Ties to Home*. Asheboro, N.C.: Down Home Press, 2001.

Carey, Gary. *All the Stars in Heaven: Louis B. Mayer's M-G-M*. New York: E. P. Dutton, 1981.

———. *Marlon Brando: The Only Contender*. New York: St. Martin's, 1985.

Carne, Judy. *Laughing on the Outside, Crying on the Inside: The Bittersweet Saga of the Sock-It-to-Me Girl*. New York: Rawson Associates, 1985.

Carrier, Jeffrey L. *Jennifer Jones: A Bio-Bibliography*. Westport, Conn.: Greenwood, 1990.

Carter, Graydon, and David Friend (eds.), with Christopher Hitchens (text). *Vanity Fair's Hollywood*. New York: Penguin, 2000.

Chandler, Charlotte. *The Girl Who Walked Home Alone—Bette Davis: A Personal Biography*. New York: Simon & Schuster, 2006.

Clarke, Gerald. *Get Happy: The Life of Judy Garland*. New York: Random House, 2000.

Collins, Joan. *Past Imperfect: An Autobiography*. New York: Simon & Schuster, 1984.

———. *Second Act*. London: Boxtree, 1996.

Considine, Shaun. *Bette & Joan: The Divine Feud*. New York: Dell, 1989.

Cottrell, John, and Fergus Cashin. *Richard Burton: Very Close Up*. Englewood Cliffs, N.J.: Prentice Hall, 1972.

Cox, Stephen. *Here's Johnny: Thirty Years of America's Favorite Late-Night Entertainer* (revised edition). Nashville: Cumberland House, 2002.

Crane, Cheryl, with Cliff Jahr. *Detour: A Hollywood Story*. New York: Avon, 1989.

Crawford, Christina. *Mommie Dearest* (20th anniversary edition). Moscow, Idaho: Seven Springs Press, 1997.

Crawford, Joan. *My Way of Life*. New York: Simon & Schuster, 1971.

Crawford, Joan, with Jane Kesner Ardmore. *A Portrait of Joan*. New York: Paperback Library, 1964.

Cunningham, Ernest. *The Ultimate Barbra: All the Facts, Rumors, and Controversies about the Legendary Superstar*. Los Angeles: Renaissance, 1998.

———. *The Ultimate Marilyn: All the Facts, Fantasies, and Scandals about the World's Best-Known Sex Symbol*. Los Angeles: Renaissance, 1998.

Curtis, Tony, and Barry Paris. *The Autobiography*. New York: William Morrow, 1993.

D'Agostino, Annette. *Soap Stars to Superstars: Celebrities Who Started Out in Daytime Drama*. Los Angeles: Renaissance, 1999.

Dardis, Tom. *Keaton: The Man Who Wouldn't Lie Down*. New York: Penguin, 1980.

Darin, Dodd. *Dream Lovers: The Magnificent Shattered Lives of Bobby Darin and Sandra Dee*. New York: Warner, 1994.

Daum, Raymond, with Vance Muse (ed.). *Walking with Garbo: Conversations and Recollections*. New York: HarperCollins, 1991.

David, Lester, and Jhan Robbins. *Richard & Elizabeth*. New York: Ballantine, 1978.

Davies, Marion, with Pamela Pfau and Kenneth S. Marx (eds.). *The Times We Had: Life with William Randolph Hearst*. New York: Ballantine, 1977.

Davis, Bette. *The Lonely Life* (updated edition). New York: Berkley, 1990.

Davis, Bette, with Michael Herskowitz. *This 'n That*. New York: G. P. Putnam's Sons, 1987.

Davis, Ronald L. *The Glamour Factory: Inside Hollywood's Big Studio System*. Dallas: Southern Methodist University Press, 1993.

———. *Zachary Scott: Hollywood's Sophisticated Cad*. Jackson: University Press of Mississippi, 2006.

De Cordova, Fred. *Johnny Came Lately*. New York: Pocket Books, 1989.

Dietrich, Marlene. *Marlene Dietrich's ABC*. Garden City, N.Y.: Doubleday, 1962.

Dietrich, Marlene, with translation by Salvator Attanasio. *Marlene*. New York: Grove Press, 1989.

Dramov, B. *The Life and Work of Errol Flynn: A Psychoanalytical Biography*. Bloomington, Ind.: Author House, 2005.

Duke, Patty, and Gloria Hochman. *A Brilliant Madness: Living with Manic-Depressive Illness*. New York: Bantam, 1993.

Duke, Patty, and Kenneth Turan. *Call Me Anna: The Autobiography of Patty Duke*. New York: Bantam, 1988.

Eberly, Stephen L. *Patty Duke: A Bio-Bibliography*. Westport, Conn.: Greenwood, 1988.

Eells, George. *Ginger, Loretta, and Irene Who?* New York: G. P. Putnam's Sons, 1976.

———. *Hedda and Louella: The Dual Biography of Hedda Hopper and Louella Parsons*. New York: Warner, 1973.

Eells, George, and Stanley Musgrove. *Mae West: A Biography*. New York: William Morrow, 1982.

Eisner, Michael D. *Camp*. New York: Warner, 2005.

Eisner, Michael, with Tony Schwartz. *Work in Progress: Risking Failure, Surviving Success*. New York: Hyperion, 1999.

Ekland, Britt. *True Britt*. New York: Berkley, 1982.

Eliot, Marc. *Burt! The Unauthorized Biography*. New York: Dell, 1982.

Elisofon, Eliot (photographer). *Hollywood Life: The Glamorous Homes of Vintage Hollywood*. Los Angeles: Greybull Press, 2004.

Ellis, Lucy, and Bryony Sutherland. *Drew Barrymore: The Biography*. London: Aurum, 2003.

Epstein, Edward Z. *Portrait of Jennifer: A Biography of Jennifer Jones*. New York: Simon & Schuster, 1995.

Epstein, Edward Z., and Joe Morella. *Mia: The Life of Mia Farrow*. New York: Dell, 1992.

Ewbank, Tim, and Stafford Hildred. *Julie Christie: The Biography*. London: André Deutsch, 2000.

Eyman, Scott. *Lion of Hollywood: The Life and Legend of Louis B. Mayer*. New York: Simon & Schuster, 2005.

———. *Mary Pickford: America's Sweetheart*. New York: Donald I. Fine, 1990.

Faris, Jocelyn. *Jayne Mansfield: A Bio-Bibliography*. Westport, Conn.: Greenwood, 1994.

Farrow, Mia. *What Falls Away: A Memoir*. New York: Bantam, 1997.

Ferris, Paul. *Richard Burton: The Actor. The Lover. The Star*. New York: Berkley, 1982.

Finch, Christopher. *Rainbow: The Stormy Life of Judy Garland*. New York: Grosset & Dunlap, 1975.

Fink, Mitchell. *The Last Days of Dead Celebrities*. New York: Miramax, 2006.

Finstad, Suzanne. *Warren Beatty: A Private Man*. New York: Crown, 2005.

Fiore, Carlo. *Bud: The Brando I Knew: The Untold Story of Brando's Private Life*. New York: Dell, 1975.

Fisher, James. *Al Jolson: A Bio-Bibliography*. Westport, Conn.: Greenwood, 1994.

Flamini, Roland. *Ava: A Biography*. New York: Coward, McCann & Geoghegan, 1983.

Flynn, Errol. *My Wicked, Wicked Ways* (reprint edition). New York: Berkley, 1979.

Fox, Julian. *Woody: Movies from Manhattan*. Woodstock, N.Y.: Overlook, 1996.

Fox, Patty. *Star Style: Hollywood Legends as Fashion Icons*. Santa Monica, Calif.: Angel City Press, 1995.

Frank, Gerold. *Judy* (reprint edition). New York: Da Capo, 1999.

———. *Zsa Zsa Gabor*. Cleveland, Ohio: World, 1960.

Fuller, Elizabeth. *Me and Jezebel: When Bette Davis Came for Dinner—and Stayed . . .* New York: Berkley, 1992.

Furman, Leah, and Elina Furman. *Happily Ever After: The Drew Barrymore Story*. New York: Ballantine, 2000.

Gabler, Neal. *An Empire of Their Own: How the Jews Invented Hollywood*. New York: Crown, 1988.

Gabor, Zsa Zsa. *How to Catch a Man, How to Keep a Man, How to Get Rid of a Man*. New York: Pocket Books, 1971.

Gabor, Zsa Zsa, with Wendy Leigh. *One Lifetime Is Not Enough*. New York: Delacorte, 1991.

Gallick, Sarah, with Nicholas Maier. *Divinely Decadent: Liza Minnelli—The Drugs, the Sex & the Truth Behind Her Bizarre Marriage.* Boca Raton, Fla.: AMI, 2003.

Gardner, Ava. *Ava: My Story.* New York: Bantam, 1990.

Garland, Patrick. *The Incomparable Rex: The Last of the High Comedians.* New York: Fromm International, 2000.

Glatt, John. *Lost in Hollywood: The Fast Times and Short Life of River Phoenix.* New York: Dutton, 1995.

Goldman, Herbert G. *Jolson: The Legend Comes to Life.* New York: Oxford University Press, 1988.

Gordon, William A. *The Ultimate Hollywood Tour Book* (2nd edition). El Toro, Calif.: North Ridge Books, 1997.

Grobel, Lawrence. *Conversations with Brando* (reprint edition). New York: Cooper Square, 1999.

Groteke, Kristine, with Marjorie Rosen. *Mia & Woody: Love and Betrayal.* New York: Carroll & Graf, 1994.

Guiles, Fred Lawrence. *Legend: The Life and Death of Marilyn Monroe.* New York: Stein and Day, 1984.

———. *Marion Davies.* New York: McGraw-Hill, 1972.

Guralnick, Peter. *Careless Love: The Unmaking of Elvis Presley.* Boston: Little, Brown, 1999.

———. *Last Train to Memphis: The Rise of Elvis Presley.* Boston: Little, Brown, 1994.

Hack, Richard. *Hughes: The Private Diaries, Memos and Letters—The Definitive Biography of the First American Billionaire.* Los Angeles: New Millennium, 2001.

Hadleigh, Boze. *Bette Davis Speaks.* New York: Barricade, 1996.

Hall, Elaine Blake. *Burt and Me: My Days and Nights with Burt Reynolds.* New York: Pinnacle, 1994.

Hammontree, Patsy Guy. *Elvis Presley: A Bio-Bibliography.* Westport, Conn.: Greenwood, 1985.

Hanut, Eryk. *I Wish You Love: Conversations with Marlene Dietrich.* Berkeley, Calif.: Frog Books, 1996.

Harrison, Rex. *A Damned Serious Business: My Life in Comedy.* New York: Bantam, 1991.

———. *Rex: An Autobiography.* New York: William Morrow, 1974.

Herndon, Booton. *Mary Pickford and Douglas Fairbanks: The Most Popular Couple the World Has Ever Known.* New York: W. W. Norton, 1977.

Heymann, C. David. *Liz: An Intimate Biography of Elizabeth Taylor.* Secaucus, N.J.: Carol, 1996.

Higham, Charles. *Ava: A Life Story.* New York: Delacorte, 1974.

———. *Brando: The Unauthorized Biography.* New York: New American Library, 1987.

———. *Errol Flynn: The Untold Story.* Garden City, N.Y.: Doubleday, 1980.

———. *The Life of Bette Davis.* New York: Macmillan, 1981.

———. *Merchant of Dreams: Louis B. Mayer, M.G.M., and the Secret Hollywood.* New York: Dell, 1994.

Hilton, Paris, with Merle Ginsberg. *Confessions of an Heiress: A Tongue-in-Chic Peek Behind the Pose.* New York: Simon & Schuster, 2004.

Houseman, Victoria. *Made in Heaven: The Marriages and Children of Hollywood Stars.* Chicago: Bonus Books, 1991.

Houston, Cissy, with Jonathan Singer. *How Sweet the Sound: My Life with God and Gospel.* New York: Doubleday, 1998.

Hyman, B. D. *My Mother's Keeper.* New York: Berkley, 1986.

Jacobs, George, and William Stadiem. *Mr. S: My Life with Frank Sinatra.* New York: HarperCollins, 2004.

Jenkins, Graham. *Richard Burton, My Brother.* New York: St. Martin's, 1990.

Johnes, Carl. *Crawford: The Last Years—An Intimate Memoir.* New York: Dell, 1979.

Johnstone, Nick. *Sean Penn: A Biography.* London: Omnibus, 2000.

Kalfatovic, Mary C. *Montgomery Clift: A Bio-Bibliography.* Westport, Conn.: Greenwood, 1994.

Kashner, Sam, and Nancy Schoenberger. *A Talent for Genius: The Life and Times of Oscar Levant.* Beverly Hills, Calif.: Silman-James, 1998.

Keats, John. *Howard Hughes.* New York: Pyramid, 1970.

Kelley, Kitty. *Elizabeth Taylor: The Last Star.* New York: Dell, 1982.

———. *His Way: The Unauthorized Biography of Frank Sinatra*. New York: Bantam, 1987.

Kelly, Richard T. *Sean Penn: His Life and Times*. New York: Canongate U.S., 2005.

Koszarski, Richard. *Von: The Life & Films of Erich von Stroheim* (reprint edition). New York: Limelight, 2001.

Krutnik, Frank. *Inventing Jerry Lewis*. Washington, D.C.: Smithsonian Institution, 2000.

Ladowsky, Ellen. *Julia Roberts: A Biography*. New York: Time, 1999.

LaGuardia, Robert. *Monty: A Biography of Montgomery Clift*. New York: Avon, 1978.

Lardine, Robert. *He-e-e-ere's . . . Johnny: The Real Johnny Carson Unmasked!* New York: Award, 1975.

Latham, Caroline, and Jeannie Sakol. *All About Elizabeth: Elizabeth Taylor Public and Private*. New York: Onyx, 1991.

Lax, Eric. *Woody Allen: A Biography* (reprint edition). New York: Da Capo, 2000.

Leamer, Laurence. *Fantastic: The Life of Arnold Schwarzenegger*. New York: St. Martin's, 2005.

———. *King of the Night: The Life of Johnny Carson*. New York: St. Martin's, 1992.

Leaming, Barbara. *Bette Davis: A Biography*. New York: Simon & Schuster, 1992.

———. *Marilyn Monroe*. New York: Crown, 2000.

———. *Orson Welles: A Biography* (reprint edition). New York: Limelight, 2004.

Leider, Emily Wortis. *Becoming Mae West*. New York: Da Capo, 2000.

Leigh, Wendy. *Arnold: An Unauthorized Biography*. Chicago: Congdon & Weed, 1990.

———. *Liza: Born a Star*. New York: Dutton, 1993.

Lenburg, Jeff. *Peekaboo: The Story of Veronica Lake* (reprint edition). Lincoln, Neb.: iUniverse, 2001.

Lennig, Arthur. *The Immortal Count: The Life and Films of Bela Lugosi*. Lexington: University Press of Kentucky, 2003.

Levant, Oscar. *The Memoirs of an Amnesiac* (reprint edition). Hollywood, Calif.: Samuel French, 1989.

Levy, Shawn. *King of Comedy: The Life and Art of Jerry Lewis*. New York: St. Martin's, 1996.

———. *The Last Playboy: The High Life of Porfirio Rubirosa*. New York: HarperCollins, 2005.

———. *Rat Pack Confidential: Frank, Dean, Sammy, Peter, Joey & the Last Great Showbiz Party*. New York: Doubleday, 1998.

Lewis, Jerry, with Herb Gluck. *Jerry Lewis in Person*. New York: Atheneum, 1982.

Lewis, Jerry, and James Kaplan. *Dean & Me (A Love Story)*. New York: Doubleday, 2005.

Lewis, Roger. *The Life and Death of Peter Sellers*. New York: Applause, 1997.

Linet, Beverly. *Star-Crossed: The Story of Robert Walker and Jennifer Jones*. New York: G. P. Putnam's Sons, 1986.

Louvish, Simon. *Man on the Flying Trapeze: The Life and Times of W. C. Fields*. New York: W. W. Norton, 1999.

Luft, Lorna. *Me and My Shadows: A Family Memoir*. New York: Pocket Books, 1999.

Lynn, Kenneth S. *Charlie Chaplin and His Times*. New York: Simon & Schuster, 1997.

Madsen, Axel. *Gloria and Joe: The Star-Crossed Love Affair of Gloria Swanson and Joe Kennedy*. New York: William Morrow, 1988.

Maguire, James. *Impresario: The Life and Times of Ed Sullivan*. New York: Billboard, 2006.

Mair, George. *Paris Hilton: The Naked Truth*. New York: Chamberlain Bros., 2004.

———. *Under the Rainbow: The Real Liza Minnelli*. Secaucus, N.J.: Carol, 1996.

Manso, Peter. *Brando: The Biography*. New York: Hyperion, 1994.

Marill, Alvin H. *Mickey Rooney*. Jefferson, N.C.: McFarland, 2005.

Martin, Mart. *Did He or Didn't He?: The Intimate Sex Lives of 201 Famous Men*. New York: Kensington, 2000.

———. *Did She or Didn't She?: Behind the Bedroom Doors of 201 Famous Women*. New York: Carol, 1996.

Marx, Arthur. *The Nine Lives of Mickey Rooney*. New York: Stein and Day, 1986.

Marx, Samuel. *Mayer and Thalberg: The Make-Believe Saints*. New York: Warner, 1980.

Masters, Kim. *The Keys to the Kingdom: The Rise of Michael Eisner and the Fall of Everybody Else*. New York: HarperCollins, 2001.

McBride, Joseph. *Orson Welles* (revised edition). New York: Da Capo, 1996.

McDougal, Dennis. *The Last Mogul: Lew Wasserman, MCA, and the Hidden History of Hollywood*. New York: Crown, 1998.

McPherson, Edward. *Buster Keaton: Tempest in a Flat Hat*. New York: Newmarket, 2005.

Meade, Marion. *Buster Keaton: Cut to the Chase*. New York: HarperCollins, 1995.

———. *The Unruly Life of Woody Allen*. London: Weidenfeld & Nicolson, 2000.

Metz, Allan, and Carol Benson (eds.). *The Madonna Companion: Two Decades of Commentary*. New York: Schirmer, 1999.

Metz, Robert. *The Tonight Show: The Surprising Inside Story of the Headliners, the Glamour, the Intrigue, and the Controversy*. Chicago: Playboy Press, 1980.

Meyers, Jeffrey. *Inherited Risk: Errol and Sean Flynn in Hollywood and Vietnam*. New York: Simon & Schuster, 2002.

Milton, Joyce. *Tramp: The Life of Charlie Chaplin*. New York: Da Capo, 1998.

Monti, Carlotta, with Cy Rice. *W. C. Fields & Me*. New York: Warner, 1973.

Morley, Sheridan. *The Brits in Hollywood: Tales from the Hollywood Raj*. London: Robson, 2006.

———. *Marlene Dietrich*. New York: McGraw-Hill, 1976.

Morton, Andrew. *Madonna*. New York: St. Martin's, 2001.

Moseley, Roy, with Philip Masheter and Martin Masheter. *Rex Harrison: A Biography*. New York: St. Martin's, 1987.

Moser, Margaret, Michael Bertin, and Bill Crawford. *Movie Stars Do the Dumbest Things*. Los Angeles: Renaissance, 1999.

Munn, Michael. *Hollywood Bad*. New York: St. Martin's, 1992.

Nasaw, David. *The Chief: The Life of William Randolph Hearst*. Boston: Houghton Mifflin, 2001.

Nash, Alanna. *The Colonel: The Extraordinary Story of Colonel Tom Parker and Elvis Presley*. New York: Simon & Schuster, 2003.

Nazel, Joseph. *Richard Pryor: The Man Behind the Laughter*. Los Angeles: Holloway House, 1981.

Norden, Martin F. *John Barrymore: A Bio-Bibliography*. Westport, Conn.: Greenwood, 1995.

Oller, John. *Jean Arthur: The Actress Nobody Knew*. New York: Limelight, 1999.

Oppenheimer, Jerry. *Martha Stewart: Just Desserts—The Unauthorized Biography*. Boca Raton, Fla.: AMI, 2003.

Paris, Barry. *Garbo* (reprint edition). Minneapolis: University of Minnesota Press, 2002.

———. *Louise Brooks: A Biography* (reprint edition). Minneapolis: University of Minnesota Press, 2000.

Parish, James Robert. *The Fox Girls*. New Rochelle, N.Y.: Arlington House, 1972.

———. *Great Child Stars*. New York: Ace, 1976.

———. *Hollywood Bad Boys: Loud, Fast, and Out of Control*. Chicago: Contemporary, 2002.

———. *The Hollywood Book of Breakups: The Outrageous, Often Vicious, and Sometimes Tragic Romantic Disasters of America's Film and TV Idols*. Hoboken, N.J.: John Wiley & Sons, 2006.

———. *The Hollywood Book of Death: The Bizarre, Often Sordid, Passings of More Than 125 American Movie and TV Idols*. Chicago: Contemporary, 2001.

———. *The Hollywood Book of Scandals: The Shocking, Often Disgraceful Deeds and Affairs of More Than 100 American Movie and TV Idols*. New York: McGraw-Hill, 2004.

———. *Hollywood Divas: The Good, the Bad, and the Fabulous*. Chicago: Contemporary, 2003.

———. *Let's Talk!: America's Favorite Talk Show Hosts*. Las Vegas: Pioneer, 1993.

———. *The Paramount Pretties*. New Rochelle, N.Y.: Arlington House, 1972.

———. *Today's Black Hollywood*. New York: Pinnacle, 1995.

———. *Whitney Houston: The Unauthorized Biography*. London: Aurum, 2003.

Parish, James Robert, and Don E. Stanke. *The Debonairs*. New Rochelle, N.Y.: Arlington House, 1975.

———. *The Glamour Girls*. New Rochelle, N.Y.: Arlington House, 1975.

———. *Hollywood Baby Boomers*. New York: Garland, 1992.

———. *The Leading Ladies*. New Rochelle, N.Y.: Arlington House, 1977.

Parish, James Robert, with Gregory W. Mank and

Don E. Stanke. *The Hollywood Beauties*. New Rochelle, N.Y.: Arlington House, 1978.

Parish, James Robert, with Jack Ano. *Liza! An Unauthorized Biography*. New York: Pocket Books, 1975.

Parish, James Robert, and Lennard DeCarl, with William T. Leonard and Gregory W. Mank. *Hollywood Players: The Forties*. New Rochelle, N.Y.: Arlington House, 1976.

Parish, James Robert, and Michael R. Pitts. *Hollywood Songsters* (updated edition). New York: Routledge, 2002.

Parish, James Robert, and Ronald L. Bowers. *The MGM Stock Company*. New Rochelle, N.Y.: Arlington House, 1973.

Parish, James Robert, and William T. Leonard. *Hollywood Players: The Thirties*. New Rochelle, N.Y.: Arlington House, 1976.

Parish, James Robert, and William T. Leonard, with Gregory W. Mank and Charles Hoyt. *The Funsters*. New Rochelle, N.Y.: Arlington House, 1979.

Parker, John. *Warren Beatty: The Last Great Lover of Hollywood*. New York: Carroll & Graf, 1993.

Pero, Taylor, and Jeff Rovin. *Always, Lana*. New York: Bantam, 1982.

Peters, Margot. *The House of Barrymore*. New York: Alfred A. Knopf, 1990.

Pierce, Arthur, and Douglas Swarthout. *Jean Arthur: A Bio-Bibliography*. Westport, Conn.: Greenwood, 1990.

Pizzitola, Louis. *Hearst over Hollywood: Power, Passion and Propaganda in the Movies*. New York: Columbia University Press, 2002.

Porter, Darwin. *Brando Unzipped: Bad Boy, Megastar, Sexual Outlaw*. New York: Blood Moon Productions, 2005.

———. *Howard Hughes: Hell's Angel—America's Notorious Bisexual Billionaire*. New York: Blood Moon Productions, 2005.

Presley, Priscilla Beaulieu, with Sandra Harmon. *Elvis and Me*. New York: G. P. Putnam's Sons, 1985.

Prigozy, Ruth. *The Life of Dick Haymes: No More Little White Lies*. Jackson: University Press of Mississippi, 2006.

Pryor, Richard, with Todd Gold. *Pryor Convictions and Other Life Sentences*. New York: Pantheon, 1997.

Quinlan, David. *Quinlan's Film Stars: The Ultimate Guide to the Stars of the Big Screen* (5th edition). Washington, D.C.: Brassey's, 2000.

Quirk, Lawrence J. *Fasten Your Seat Belts: The Passionate Life of Bette Davis*. New York: Signet, 1990.

Quirk, Lawrence J., and William Schoell. *Joan Crawford: The Essential Biography*. Lexington: University Press of Kentucky, 2002.

Ragan, David. *Movie Stars of the '40s: A Complete Reference Guide for the Film Historian or Trivia Buff*. Englewood Cliffs, N.J.: Prentice Hall, 1985.

———. *Movie Stars of the '30s: A Complete Reference Guide for the Film Historian or Trivia Buff*. Englewood Cliffs, N.J.: Prentice Hall, 1985.

Rapf, Joanna E., and Gary L. Green. *Buster Keaton: A Bio-Bibliography*. Westport, Conn.: Greenwood, 1995.

Rense, Paige (ed.). *Architectural Digest: Hollywood at Home*. New York: Harry N. Abrams, 2005.

Rettenmund, Matthew. *Encyclopedia Madonnica: The Woman and the Icon from A to Z*. New York: St. Martin's, 1995.

Reynolds, Burt. *My Life*. New York: Hyperion, 1994.

Ritz, David (ed.). *Elvis by the Presleys: Intimate Stories from Priscilla Presley, Lisa Marie Presley, and Other Family Members*. New York: Crown, 2005.

Riva, Maria. *Marlene Dietrich*. New York: Ballantine, 1994.

Robb, Brian J. *River Phoenix: A Short Life*. London: Plexus, 1995.

Robe, Lucy Barry. *Co-Starring Famous Women and Alcohol: The Dramatic Truth Behind the Tragedies and Triumphs of 200 Celebrities*. Minneapolis: CompCare, 1986.

Robinson, David. *Chaplin: His Life and Art*. New York: McGraw-Hill, 1985.

Rooney, Mickey. *I.E.* New York: G. P. Putnam's Sons, 1965.

———. *Life Is Too Short*. New York: Villard, 1991.

Rovin, Jeff. *Richard Pryor: Black and Blue—The Unauthorized Biography*. New York: Bantam, 1984.

Ryan, Joal. *Former Child Stars: The Stories of America's Least Wanted.* Toronto, Canada: ECW, 2000.

Sanders, Coyne Steven. *Rainbow's End: The Judy Garland Show: The Triumphs, the Controversy, and the Heartbreak Behind Judy Garland's Legendary TV Show.* New York: Kensington, 1992.

Sanello, Frank. *Julia Roberts.* Edinburgh: Mainstream, 2000.

Sarvady, Andrea. *Leading Ladies: The 50 Most Unforgettable Actresses of the Studio Era.* San Francisco: Chronicle, 2006.

Saxton, Martha. *Jayne Mansfield and the American Fifties.* Boston: Houghton Mifflin, 1975.

Schatz, Thomas. *The Genius of the System: Hollywood Filmmaking in the Studio Era.* New York: Pantheon, 1989.

Schechter, Scott. *Judy Garland: The Day-by-Day Chronicle of a Legend.* New York: Cooper Square, 2002.

———. *The Liza Minnelli Scrapbook.* New York: Kensington, 2004.

Schickel, Richard. *Brando: A Life in Our Times.* New York: St. Martin's, 1993.

Seal, Richard. *Whitney Houston: One Moment in Time.* London: Britannia Press, 1994.

Sealy, Shirley. *The Celebrity Sex Register.* New York: Simon & Schuster, 1982.

Server, Lee. *Ava Gardner: "Love Is Nothing."* New York: St. Martin's, 2006.

Shark, Kathleen. *Mr. & Mrs. Hollywood: Edie and Lew Wasserman and Their Entertainment Empire.* New York: Carroll & Graf, 2004.

Shipman, David. *The Great Movie Stars: The Golden Years* (revised edition). New York: Hill and Wang, 1979.

———. *The Great Movie Stars: The Independent Years.* Boston: Little, Brown, 1991.

———. *The Great Movie Stars: The International Years* (revised edition). New York: Hill and Wang, 1980.

———. *Judy Garland: The Secret Life of an American Legend.* New York: Hyperion, 1992.

Sikov, Ed. *Mr. Strangelove: A Biography of Peter Sellers.* New York: Hyperion, 2002.

Sinatra, Nancy. *Frank Sinatra: My Father.* New York: Pocket Books, 1986.

Sinatra, Tina, with Jeff Coplon. *My Father's Daughter.* New York: Simon & Schuster, 2000.

Singular, Stephen. *Power to Burn: Michael Ovitz and the New Business of Show Business.* Secaucus, N.J.: Carol, 1996.

Slater, Robert. *Martha: On Trial, in Jail, and on a Comeback.* Upper Saddle River, N.J.: Pearson/Prentice Hall, 2005.

———. *Ovitz: The Inside Story of Hollywood's Most Controversial Power Broker.* New York: McGraw-Hill, 1997.

Smith, Ronald. L. *Johnny Carson: An Unauthorized Biography.* New York: St. Martin's, 1987.

Souhami, Diana. *Greta & Cecil.* New York: HarperCollins, 1994.

Spada, James: *Judy & Liza.* New York: Doubleday, 1983.

———. *Julia: Her Life.* New York: St. Martin's, 2004.

———. *Streisand: Her Life.* New York: Crown, 1995.

Spignesi, Stephen J. *The Woody Allen Companion.* Kansas City, Mo.: Andrews McMeel, 1992.

Spoto, Donald. *Blue Angel: The Life of Marlene Dietrich.* New York, Doubleday, 1992.

———. *Marilyn Monroe: The Biography.* New York: HarperCollins, 1993.

———. *A Passion for Life: The Biography of Elizabeth Taylor.* New York: HarperCollins, 1995.

Staggs, Sam. *All About "All About Eve": The Complete Behind-the-Scenes Story of the Bitchiest Film Ever Made.* New York: St. Martin's, 2000.

———. *Close-Up on Sunset Boulevard: Billy Wilder, Norma Desmond, and the Dark Hollywood Dream.* New York: St. Martin's, 2002.

———. *When Blanche Met Brando: The Scandalous Story of "A Streetcar Named Desire."* New York: St. Martin's, 2005.

Stenn, David. *Clara Bow: Runnin' Wild* (reprint edition). New York: Cooper Square, 2000.

Stephens, Autumn. *Drama Queens: Wild Women of the Silver Screen.* Berkeley, Calif.: Conari Press, 1998.

Stevens Jr., George (ed.). *Conversations with the Great Moviemakers of Hollywood's Golden Age at the American Film Institute.* New York: Alfred A. Knopf, 2006.

Stewart, James B. *Disney War.* New York: Simon & Schuster, 2005.

Stine, Whitney. *Mother Goddam: The Story of the Career of Bette Davis with a Running Commentary by Bette Davis*. New York: Hawthorn, 1974.

Storm, Gale, with Bill Libby. *I Ain't Down Yet: The Autobiography of My Little Margie—Gale Storm*. New York: Bobbs-Merrill, 1981.

Strait, Raymond, and Leif Henie. *Queen of Ice, Queen of Shadows: The Unsuspected Life of Sonja Henie*. Lanham, Md.: Scarborough House, 1985.

Summers, Anthony. *Goddess: The Secret Life of Marilyn Monroe*. New York: New American Library, 1986.

Summers, Anthony, and Robbyn Swan. *Sinatra: The Life*. New York: Alfred A. Knopf, 2005.

Swanson, Gloria. *Swanson on Swanson: An Autobiography*. New York: Random House, 1980.

Swenson, Karen. *Greta Garbo: A Life Apart*. New York: Scribner, 1997.

Taraborrelli, J. Randy. *Sinatra: A Complete Life*. Secaucus, N.J.: Carol, 1997.

Taylor, Elizabeth. *Elizabeth Takes Off: On Weight Gain, Weight Loss, Self-Image, and Self-Esteem*. New York: G. P. Putnam's Sons, 1988.

———. *Elizabeth Taylor: My Love Affair with Jewelry*. New York: Simon & Schuster, 2002.

Taylor, Robert Lewis. *W. C. Fields: His Follies & Fortunes*. New York: Bantam, 1951.

Thomas, Bob. *Joan Crawford: A Biography*. New York: Bantam, 1974.

———. *King Cohn: The Life and Times of Hollywood Mogul Harry Cohn* (revised edition). Los Angeles: New Millennium, 2000.

Thomson, David. *Rosebud: The Story of Orson Welles*. New York: Alfred A. Knopf, 1996.

———. *Showman: The Life of David O. Selznick*. New York: Alfred A. Knopf, 1992.

———. *Warren Beatty and Desert Eyes: A Life and a Story*. New York: Doubleday, 1987.

Tormé, Mel. *The Other Side of the Rainbow with Judy Garland on the Dawn Patrol*. New York: William Morrow, 1970.

Tosches, Nick. *Dino: Living High in the Dirty Business of Dreams*. New York: Dell, 1993.

Turner, Lana. *Lana: The Lady, the Legend, the Truth*. New York: E. P. Dutton, 1982.

Turtu, Anthony, and Donald F. Reuter. *Gaborabilia: An Illustrated Celebration of the Fabulous, Legendary Gabor Sisters*. New York: Crown, 2001.

Tynan, Kenneth. *Show People: Profiles in Entertainment*. New York: Simon & Schuster, 1979.

Vickers, Hugo. *Loving Garbo: The Story of Greta Garbo, Cecil Beaton, and Mercedes de Acosta*. New York: Random House, 1994.

Victor, Barbara. *Goddess: Inside Madonna*. New York: HarperCollins, 2001.

Walker, Alexander. *Elizabeth: The Life of Elizabeth Taylor* (revised edition). New York: Grove Press, 1997.

———. *Garbo: A Portrait*. New York: Macmillan, 1980.

———. *Joan Crawford: The Ultimate Star*. New York: Harper & Row, 1983.

Wallace, David (text), and Juergen Nogai (photographs). *Dream Palaces of Hollywood's Golden Age*. New York: Harry N. Abrams, 2006.

Wanger, Walter, and Joe Hyams. *My Life with Cleopatra*. New York: Bantam, 1963.

Watts, Jill. *Mae West: An Icon in Black and White*. New York: Oxford University Press, 2001.

Wayne, Jane Ellen. *Ava's Men: The Private Life of Ava Gardner*. New York: St. Martin's, 1991.

———. *Crawford's Men*. New York: St. Martin's, 1990.

———. *The Golden Girls of MGM: Greta Garbo, Joan Crawford, Lana Turner, Judy Garland, Ava Gardner, Grace Kelly, and Others*. New York: Carroll & Graf, 2003.

———. *Lana: The Life and Loves of Lana Turner*. New York: St. Martin's, 1995.

———. *The Leading Men of MGM*. New York: Carroll & Graf, 2005.

———. *Marilyn's Men: The Private Life of Marilyn Monroe*. New York: St. Martin's, 1993.

Whitfield, Eileen. *Pickford: The Woman Who Made Hollywood*. New York: Faber & Faber, 2000.

Williams, John A., and Dennis A. Williams. *If I Stop I'll Die: The Comedy and Tragedy of Richard Pryor*. New York: Thunder's Mouth, 1993.

Winters, Shelley. *Shelley: Also Known as Shirley*. New York: William Morrow, 1980.

———. *Shelley II: The Middle of My Century*. New York: Pocket Books, 1990.

Wood, Bret. *Orson Welles: A Bio-Bibliography*. Westport, Conn.: Greenwood, 1990.

Woodward, Bob. *Wired: The Short Life & Fast Times of John Belushi*. New York: Pocket Books, 1986.

Yacowar, Maurice. *Loser Take All: The Comic Art of Woody Allen*. New York: Frederick Unger, 1979.

Zierold, Norman. *The Moguls: The Power Princes of Hollywood's Golden Age*. New York: Avon, 1972.

Publications

Among those utilized were *Architectural Digest, Backstage West, Biography, Boxoffice, Chicago Sun-Times, Chicago Tribune, Classic Film Collector, Classic Image, Current Biography, Daily Variety, Drama-Logue, Ebony, Empire, Entertainment Today, Entertainment Weekly, Esquire, Film Threat, Filmfax, Films in Review, Films of the Golden Age, Globe, Hollywood Reporter, In LA, InStyle, Interview, Jet, L.A. Weekly, London Daily Telegraph, London Guardian, London Sunday Telegraph, London Times, Los Angeles Daily News, Los Angeles Herald-Examiner, Los Angeles Times, Monthly Film Bulletin, Movie Collectors World, Movieline, National Enquirer, New York, New York Daily News, New York Observer, New York Post, New York Times, The New Yorker, Newsweek, Parade, People, Playboy, Premiere, Rolling Stone, St. Louis Post-Dispatch, San Francisco Chronicle, Saturday Review, Sight & Sound, Star, Time, Time Out London, Total Film, TV Guide, Us Weekly, USA Today, Valley Vantage, Vanity Fair, Variety, Village Voice, Virginian Pilot, Wall Street Journal,* and *Washington Post*.

Web Sites

Answers.com
www.answers.com

Box Office Mojo
www.boxofficemojo.com

Classic Images
www.classicimages.com

E! Online
www.eonline.com

Find a Death
www.findadeath.com

Find a Grave
www.findagrave.com

Former Child Star Central
http://members.tripod.com/~former_child_star

Internet Movie Database
www.imdb.com

Movieweb
www.movieweb.com

People Online
www.people.aol.com

Silents Are Golden
www.silentsaregolden.com/homes/homesofstars.htm

The Smoking Gun
www.thesmokinggun.com

StarPlus
www.starplus.com

Tiscali Film & TV
www.tiscali.co.uk/entertainment/film/biographies

Tmz.com
www.tmz.com

Who2
www.who2.com

Credits

Index

Page numbers in *italics* indicate illustrations

About the Author

JAMES ROBERT PARISH, a former entertainment reporter, publicist, and book series editor, is the author of many biographies and reference books about the entertainment industry, including *It's Good to Be the King: The Seriously Funny Life of Mel Brooks*; *The Hollywood Book of Breakups*; *Fiasco: A History of Hollywood's Iconic Flops*; *Katharine Hepburn: The Untold Story*; *The Hollywood Book of Scandals*; *Whitney Houston*; *The Hollywood Book of Love*; *Hollywood Divas*; *Hollywood Bad Boys*; *The Encyclopedia of Ethnic Groups in Hollywood*; *Jet Li*; *The Hollywood Book of Death*; *Gus Van Sant*; *Jason Biggs*; *Whoopi Goldberg*; *Rosie O'Donnell's Story*; *The Unofficial "Murder, She Wrote" Casebook*; *Let's Talk! America's Favorite TV Talk Show Hosts*; *Gays and Lesbians in Mainstream Cinema*; *The Great Cop Pictures*; *Ghosts and Angels in Hollywood Films*; *Prison Pictures from Hollywood*; *The Paramount Pretties*; *The RKO Gals*; and *Hollywood's Great Love Teams*.

Mr. Parish is a frequent interviewee on cable and network TV for documentaries on the performing arts both in the United States and in the United Kingdom. He resides in Studio City, California. His Web site is www.jamesrobertparish.com.